The Letters of Emily Lady Tennyson

Lady Tennyson,
from the portrait (1862) by G. F. Watts, R.A.
The original painting is in the Tennyson Collection at the
Usher Gallery, Lincoln, England. Reproduced by kind
permission of Lord Tennyson and the Director, City of
Lincoln Libraries, Museum and Art Gallery.

The Letters of Emily Lady Tennyson

Edited with an Introduction by

James O. Hoge

The Pennsylvania State University Press

University Park and London

Library of Congress Cataloging in Publication Data

Tennyson, Emily (Sellwood) Tennyson, Baroness,
    1813–1896.
    The letters of Emily Lady Tennyson.

    Bibliography: p. 377
    1.   Tennyson, Alfred Tennyson, Baron, 1809–1892.
2.   Tennyson, Emily (Sellwood) Tennyson, Baroness,
1813–1896.   I.   Title.
PR5581.A3   1974   821'.8 [B]   73-12629
ISBN 0-271-01123-8

Designed by Glenn Ruby

Printed in the United States of America

She with all the charm of woman, she with all the breadth of man,
Strong in will and rich in wisdom, . . .
Very woman of very woman, nurse of ailing body and mind,
She that linked again the broken chain that bound me to my kind.

To my Mother

No angel, but a dearer being, all dipt
In angel instincts, breathing Paradise.

and

To Carol

Contents

Alfred and Emily Tennyson with their sons Hallam (right) and
Lionel. This photograph was taken at Farringford by O. G.
Rejlander in the early 1860s.

Foreword

I am very glad that this extensive selection from my grandmother's letters is being published, for she meant a great deal to me in childhood and boyhood, and her memory still means much to me at ninety-four years old. My memories no doubt refer almost entirely to the last ten years of her life (1886-1896) when I was between seven and seventeen, and they include the year in which my grandfather died—1892.

This is a long time ago, but my recollections are very strong and vivid. I remember her as a frail, not very tall old lady, generally lying on her sofa in the drawing room at Farringford or Aldworth—for she had been an invalid since the autumn of 1874 when a severe illness struck her and she had had to give up being the poet's secretary and business manager, as she had been since very soon after their marriage in 1850. But she remained his intimate and entirely trusted comrade and adviser and the very competent director of all the domestic arrangements at both his homes. These included a considerable farm at Farringford and large areas of garden and woodland at both places. Not the least of her responsibilities was the poet himself, his wardrobe—to the state of which he was supremely indifferent, the supply of kitchen and cellar—to which he was very much the reverse, and the constant stream of visitors—mostly old and intimate; though very shy of strangers (a quality which imposed other very awkward obligations on his wife), he was extremely dependent on contact with congenial friends.

The quality which I remember most clearly in my grandmother was her wonderful serenity, which nothing seemed to disturb. Though she seldom left her sofa, except to walk slowly into the dining room on the arm of her husband or elder son, the house, with its large posse of servants, ran like clockwork. The upper servants—the Lady's Maid, "Smith," the Housekeeper, "Andrews," the Butler, "Godsall," and the Coachman "William Knight"—were all trusted friends. Each stayed with the family for forty or fifty years. Their peccadilloes were ignored and their dignity respected.

My grandmother herself had, in old age at least, great beauty of feature and expression. When I think of her, I picture her in a silk dress, black or lavender voluminous and trailing, her silvery grey hair very plainly done, drawn back from a central parting and covered by a white lace shawl.

A late watercolor drawing by Helen Allingham, now at the Tennyson Centre at Lincoln, comes as near to my memory as such a work can do. It shows a face with many traces of suffering. Perhaps it misses my grandmother's strong sense of humor. I don't remember ever hearing her laugh, but she had the most engaging smile.

But Mrs. Allingham surely caught the quality recorded by the great biologist Henry Tyndall, who dined with Alfred and Emily in 1858. The conversation turned to the influence of moral power on physical effort, and walking was taken as an example. "In the long run," said Tyndall, "one must fall back on muscular force." Emily turned towards him with that ethereal expression which G. F. Watts caught so marvelously in his portrait now at the Lincoln Centre, and remarked quietly, "You can at all events walk till you die."

Sir Charles Tennyson

Acknowledgments

The preparation of this book has been advanced in many ways by the influence, interest, and assistance of others, whom I wish to thank for their contributions. First of all, I want to express my gratitude to Sir Charles Tennyson, whose kind generosity and helpful criticism at various stages of my research and composition have been more valuable than I can easily say. More than that, it was Sir Charles who first roused my interest in his grandmother, and without his encouragement this edition would not have been undertaken.

Cecil Y. Lang, to whom I am particularly indebted for continuous instruction and reassurance, has helped me in ways too numerous to detail. Suffice it to say that from the beginning he has been my faithful, tireless, and sustaining guide. Also especially deserving of acknowledgment is George O. Marshall, Jr., whom I have consulted at every turn, and who has always been open-handed with expert substantive and editorial assistance. For a variety of reasons my appreciation is also due Christopher Ricks, James Martin Gray, James F. Loucks, Ralph Wilson Rader, J. Norman Clark, Lt. Colonel Sir Weston Cracroft-Amcotts, Charles S. Hutzler, Rowland Collins, W. D. Paden, George Hendrick, Morton N. Cohen, and June S. Hagen. And I must not forget to thank Charles I. Patterson, Jr., John Algeo, and my other colleagues at the University of Georgia for their advice and support.

I am profoundly grateful to the present Lord Tennyson for allowing me to publish these letters and to quote from Lady Tennyson's unpublished Journal and from Hallam Lord Tennyson's unpublished *Materials for a Life of A.T.* Although I must limit myself here to a general expression of appreciation, I am of course deeply indebted to all the libraries that have so kindly allowed me to publish their manuscript materials. To the City of Lincoln Libraries, Museum and Art Gallery I am especially grateful for permission to publish a vast number of letters here included which reside in the Tennyson Research Centre. Also, I want to acknowledge the extensive help given me by F. T. Baker, the Director of the Lincoln Libraries; by the late Raymond F. Smith and Laurence Elvin; and by others at the City Library during my prolonged visit in Lincoln.

I must also set down my appreciation to the staffs of the British Museum and the Boston Public Library, and my sincere gratitude to the librarians of both the Alderman Library at the University of Virginia and the Ilah Dunlap Little Memorial Library at the University of Georgia. And I should be remiss if I did not thank by name Leslie Bjorncrantz, Vivien Phillips, Donna Harman, and Kittsu Barks for the endless services they have accorded me. Finally, for her continual encouragement, I am most especially grateful to my wife.

Editorial Principles

Readability has been my first concern in transcribing and annotating these letters. At the same time, I have attempted to do justice to the individuality of Emily Tennyson by preserving the easy, unaffected flow, the tone, inflection, and style of her writing. Accordingly I have observed the following editorial principles:

Since the great majority of the letters that appear here are in the Tennyson Research Centre, Lincoln, I have not indicated the manuscript location for the Lincoln letters. If the holograph is extant, I have in every case transcribed it either from the original or from xerograph or microfilm, and the location is noted just above the text. If no holograph has been traced for a letter and my transcription has been taken from a secondary source, I have noted that fact.

Most of Lady Tennyson's letters are fully addressed and dated. I have normalized the date and address of any letter with an incomplete heading, adding brackets only when an essential part of the date is an editorial conjecture. I have lowered superior letters and expanded abbreviations in the names of months. Addresses and dates at the end have been moved to the heading. No distinction has been made between hand-written and printed, engraved, or embossed addresses. To save space, all valedictions have been omitted.

In all cases, even when the source of my text is a published letter, I have expanded the following: ampersands, abbreviated names of people, shortened titles of magazines and other publications, and all other abbreviations except for standard congealed forms which are obviously less obtrusive than whole words—for example, Mr., Mrs., Dr., and so on.

For the most part, long, run-on sentences have been preserved. I have broken down intolerably long paragraphs. Lady Tennyson often did not indent paragraph openings, and it is sometimes quite impossible to be certain of her intentions, as it is also in her punctuation and use of capitals. Commas have rarely been added, though sometimes deleted. Capitals have been normalized unless they seem to offer some insight into Emily Tennyson's attitudes—e.g., her capitalization of "Father" and "Husband," not to mention "She" and "Her," in reference to the one person in the realm whose claim to the upper-case was proprietary, if not actually prescriptive. Misspellings have been corrected. My general principle has been to emend silently, provided no substantive change is involved.

All ellipses are my own and, unless otherwise noted, indicate the editorial omission of unimportant material.

Frequently opening and closing remarks of indifferent substantive importance, in some cases as much as a paragraph, have been omitted without ellipses.

Much of what Lady Tennyson writes necessarily seems vague and allusive to any reader less than intimately acquainted with daily occurrences in the Tennyson household and in the social, political, and literary circles of nineteenth-century England. I have attempted to make the references as clear to the present reader as they would have been to her correspondents. I therefore have made all the annotations which seem necessary to the achievement of that goal, while trying to leave the main text as unimpeded as possible. Usually the persons, places, events, etc., mentioned in a letter are identified in the first reference, but not thereafter.

Abbreviations

AT   Charles Tennyson, *Alfred Tennyson* (London: Macmillan, 1949).

"For Her Sons"   James O. Hoge, "Emily Tennyson's Narrative for Her Sons," *Texas Studies in Literature and Language,* Spring 1972.

Journal   Emily Tennyson's Journal, unpublished, Tennyson Research Centre.

Memoir   Hallam Tennyson, *Alfred Lord Tennyson: A Memoir by His Son,* 2 vols. (London: Macmillan, 1897).

Rader   Ralph Wilson Rader, *Tennyson's Maud: The Biographical Genesis* (Berkeley and Los Angeles: The University of California Press, 1963).

"Recollections"   Emily Tennyson, "Recollections of My Early Life," *Tennyson and His Friends,* ed. Hallam Tennyson (London: Macmillan, 1911).

T.R.C.   Tennyson Research Centre, Lincoln, England.

Thomas Woolner   Amy Woolner, *Thomas Woolner: His Life in Letters* (New York: Chapman and Hall, 1917).

Emily Tennyson with Hallam (left) and Lionel.
This photograph (circa 1864) was taken by W. Jeffrey.

From the collection of the Tennyson Research Centre,
Lincoln, England. Reproduced by kind permission of the
Director, City of Lincoln Libraries, Museum and Art
Gallery.

Introduction

"The first time that I was at Somersby [the Tennyson home] as far as I remember, except for a morning visit, was one night and day in 1830 when Arthur Hallam was there. They were all fond of games such as capping verses. That night we played at 'The Emperor of Morocco Is Dead' and Arthur Hallam was pleased with me because I went through the trying story between my two big candles with so much gravity. Next morning we some of us went to Holywell [the forest just behind Somersby]. Arthur Hallam was walking with me when your Father made his appearance wrapt in a cloak, and sportively said, 'Are you a Dryad or a Naiad or what are you?' "[1] Thus Emily Tennyson recorded her initial meeting with her future husband in the 1869 "Narrative for Her Sons."[2]

Emily's account of her meeting with Tennyson in Holywell calls to mind all the traditional associations of elfin grots, wood nymphs, and sportive gods in pursuit which stem from sylvan encounters in works as far removed as Virgil's *Second Eclogue,* Horace's Ninth Ode, and Swinburne's "When the Hounds of Spring." Arthur Donnithorne and Hetty Sorrel meet in just such a wood charged with mythic, erotic suggestiveness, "the sort of wood most haunted by the nymphs," in Chapter 12 of *Adam Bede.*[3] And George Eliot's carefully contrived and highly artistic rendezvous of young lovers in the enchanted Fir-tree Grove is no more poetically ideal than the real-life meeting of Tennyson and the eldest daughter of Henry Sellwood, the "Naiad" or "Dryad" whom he greeted in Holywell Wood. "About six feet and strong in proportion, upright, broadchested with tapering waist,"[4] Tennyson must have seemed as godlike to the young girl of sixteen as she seemed nymphlike to him. In fact, Emily Tennyson ended her remarks on the initial overnight visit to Somersby Rectory with the comment that from the first Tennyson had seemed to her a mysterious creature somehow lifted above other mortals; and certainly it was as more a spiritual than a physical creature that Tennyson always regarded the "noblest woman" he ever met.

From all indications the Tennysons and the Sellwoods were on quite friendly terms before the visit to Somersby in the spring of 1830. The Sellwoods lived in Horncastle, just seven miles southwest of Somersby, and Emily's niece, Agnes Weld, has stated that there was "constant intercourse" between the two families.[5] Emily herself wrote that the Tennysons were among her family's closest friends, and she recalled that "Dear Aunt Cecilia and Aunt Matilda often came to my father's house and we lent each other books, and the brothers also came to us sometimes."[6]

It is rather odd then that she and Tennyson did not become acquainted sooner than they did, if the Sellwoods' visit early in 1830 actually occasioned their initial meeting. But it seems fitting that Arthur Hallam should have presented Emily Sellwood to Tennyson, and perhaps there would have been no other occasion for such a propitious introduction. As Oliver Huckel observes, Hallam that day in Holywell "by a strange premonition brought to Tennyson the one heart-friend to fill the vacant place in his life that his tragic death should shortly make."[7] The Hercules-Apollo, physically powerful Tennyson, who "could 'put a stone' against any of the strongest men in the village and hurl a crow-bar farther than the stalwart blacksmith,"[8] was immediately attracted by the willowy, fragile, auburn-haired beauty on Arthur Hallam's arm. Like Hallam, Emily Sellwood was as high-minded as Tennyson himself, yet less troubled, less given to doubts. Physically weak, but emotionally strong, she would be able to offer Tennyson just the sort of psychological support he needed, and one can scarcely refrain from realizing that the poet must have found in Emily Sellwood many of the qualities he had first responded to in Arthur Hallam.

Henry Sellwood had moved from Berkshire to Horncastle around 1810,[9] and there, on 15 September 1812, he married Sarah Franklin, daughter of William Franklin and Hannah Weekes, and sister of the Arctic navigator, Sir John Franklin. Sarah died of typhus almost exactly four years later (30 September 1816), leaving Sellwood with three young daughters, Emily (born 9 July 1813, as we know by the Horncastle Parish Register), Anne, and Louisa. At the age of eight Emily was sent with her sisters "to some ladies for daily lessons" (probably to one of the "Academies for the Education of Young Ladies," of which there were several in Horncastle), and later to "schools in Brighton and London, for my father disliked having a governess in the house." [10] When Emily was at home her contentment was threatened by her Aunt Betsy, who constantly warned against too much noise and gaiety. Aunt Betsy, from the little we know of her, seems more like a character (or caricature) in Dickens than a surrogate-mother of three young girls. To curb girlish exuberance she would beat stripes in their hands with a riding whip, for unfinished sewing prick their fingers with a needle, for lessons undone stand them in a corner with dunce caps on.

Away from home Emily was even more miserable, for she loathed school, and she remembered that at the Brighton seminary, "I appeared to be in a horrible dream, and the voices of the mistress and the girls around me seemed to be all thin, like voices from the grave." [11] Emily could not be happy away from her father, "who was my idol," [12] she said, and though surviving contemporary evidence is too meager for any suggestive psychological inferences, it is clear that there was always a particularly strong bond between Henry Sellwood and his eldest daughter. After his death she wrote that he "deserved, if ever Father deserved it, to be held in unapproachable sacredness by his children." [13]

Certainly Sellwood was devoted to all three of his motherless girls, and his loving attentions and the affection his daughters gave him in return were subjects of general remark among the residents of Horncastle. Shortly after Emily's death, Robert Roberts, a native of Horncastle, recalled how he had observed "Lawyer" Sellwood, "a tall, thin, gentlemanly man, with a pleasant expression and quiet manner, always dressed in a black frock coat," walking with his daughters. Like Tennyson, Emily's father was over six feet tall, as both Emily and Roberts tell us—the latter twice. It was Sellwood's daily custom about three o'clock in the afternoon, Roberts remembered,

> to walk past our house, which was in the outskirts of Horncastle, and he always had a daughter on each arm. The daughters were small, shy, sensitive-looking girls: and as their father was tall, and walked a long springy step, or, as our townspeople said, 'with a loup,' they had great difficulty keeping up with him. [14]

Emily had even more trouble keeping up with her father's horsemanship. Henry Sellwood was an expert rider, so good that he could ride horses no one else could manage. But Emily's dislike of riding was nearly as vehement as her aversion to boarding school, and, much as her father wished it, she never became a good horsewoman. To her father's delight in books, however, she responded with enthusiasm, and her favorite time of day was in the evening from half-past eight to ten, when he would read to Emily and her sisters from Gibbon, Macaulay's *Essays,* and the novels of Sir Walter Scott. In "For Her Sons" she wrote that in whatever respect she was fitted to be Tennyson's wife she owed it to her father, "who had so lovingly trained me by reading to me the best historians and poets and encouraging me to read them myself, and books of science and theology and all that could help life besides." [15] For Emily's private reading her father gave her Homer, Dante, Ariosto, Tasso, Molière, Racine, and Corneille; also in her youth she read Schiller, Goethe, Jean Paul Richter, Pearson, the seventeenth-century theologian, Paley's *Translation of the Early Fathers,* Coleridge, Wordsworth, Milton, and Shakespeare. [16]

Little else is known of Emily's youth before 1830, with the exception of a few incidents treated in her "Recollections" which I have not included in my glance at her early years. The Sellwood girls had walks and drives and music and needlework, and Emily painted as well. Although her special gift was no doubt music, a notebook of some dozen sketches of various churches and cottages in Kent and Sussex, all dated 1827, testify to no mean artistic ability. [17] Whenever the Sellwoods had guests, Emily helped her father entertain; once a year all the legal luminaries of Horncastle came to dine with them, and their neighbors and friends in the Horncastle area were of course more frequent visitors. Perhaps it was as her father's hostess that Emily first developed her gift for conversation and her talent for making all her guests feel the warmth of a special concern and attention.

The *Memoir* offers virtually no information about the progress of Tennyson's friendship with Emily from the time in 1830 when he was impressed by "the slender, beautiful girl of seventeen in her simple gray dress" [18] until the marriage of his brother Charles, on 24 May 1836, to Emily's youngest sister, Louisa. Clearly, by that time he was romantically involved. The tender emotion he declared in "The Bridesmaid," a charming sonnet he wrote soon after his brother's wedding, is the product of that strong fusion of respect and affection for Emily which enabled him to respond to her in a way he had been unable to respond to other women. During the five or six years between the meeting in the Fairy Wood and Charles's marriage, Tennyson was infatuated for a time with the captivating Rosa Baring, and he was also attached to Sophy Rawnsley for a brief period.[19] But the love for Emily that he expressed in "The Bridesmaid" argues for an intimacy prior to the wedding which provided the immediate inspiration for that poem.

Emily Tennyson's recollections of evenings spent at Somersby in "For Her Sons" indicate that she was frequently regaled with lively entertainments by the young Tennysons:

> Some evenings we had instrumental music and singing. Frederick accompanied on the flute, but your Father, though he amused himself with the flute, never, I think, tried to get so much mastery over it as to do this. . . . Some evenings at Somersby we had reading. Emily [Tennyson's sister, Arthur Hallam's fiancée] read Keats and Shelley beautifully and I was enchanted for then I had heard nothing of either. Well I remember too your Father's reading to me some of Campbell's ballads and among them the patriotic ones for he was patriotic then as ever.[20]

She also remembered the little dances, which were not uncommon at Somersby, as well as the balls given in the neighborhood where Tennyson "waltzed well and was a coveted partner."[21] Although she stated that she recalled no visit to Somersby, after the first, until after Arthur Hallam's death, it seems likely that some of these evenings at Somersby were scattered through the first three years of the decade, and that the visit following Hallam's death was simply one sharply particularized in her memory. In any case, John Randall's account of his June 1834 visit to Somersby,[22] where he found Alfred, Charles, John and Serjeant Heath, and the Sellwoods, indicates that Emily and her sisters were guests in the Tennyson home during the vacuous days that followed Hallam's death. Certainly Tennyson and Emily had ample opportunity to become well acquainted, especially after March 1831, when the death of Tennyson's father occasioned his return from Cambridge to resume continuous residence at Somersby.

It is impossible to determine just when Tennyson developed a serious romantic interest in Emily. During the dark and confused years following the deaths of his father and Hallam, he first looked to Rosa Baring, the beautiful stepdaughter of Arthur Eden, tenant of Harrington Hall, for the affection he craved and the stable direction he desperately needed. Rosa of course failed to satisfy Tennyson's needs. Her captivating graces were no more than the conventional charms of a sensually attractive but spiritually superficial young woman who proved to be "all unmeet for a wife," as was said of Maud, and she left the poet more disturbed and disillusioned than ever. Rosa was "A rosy-coloured jewel, fit to make / An emperor's signet-ring,"[23] but she was unfit to extricate Tennyson from his morbid self-centeredness, incapable of filling the void left by Arthur Hallam's death.

Even had Rosa Baring been more worthy of Tennyson's affection and less indifferent to his advances, and even had her wealth and social position not been insuperable barriers, there was that in Tennyson's own psyche which from the first had doomed the affair to failure. Tennyson associated feminine sensuality with moral temptation, and Rosa's very physical desirability must have alarmed the young poet's Calvinistic sensibility. The morbid despondency that haunted his early years was complicated by a guilt complex,[24] which undoubtedly fostered the sexual reticence we discover both in his verse and in his life. W.D. Paden has noted the peculiar absence in *Poems by Two Brothers* (1827) of women who are both attainable and physically desirable.[25] The women who appear in the 1830 and 1832 volumes are somewhat more numerous and more vividly drawn, but among the dramatic figures only the miller's daughter is beloved and blessed. Oriana is killed by her lover, the Lady of Shalott dies accursed, the May Queen dies repenting her flirtations, and Mariana and Oenone are forsaken and forlorn. In virtually every case love brings death or cruel madness. Among the nine lyrical descriptions of women—of Lilian, Isabel, Madeline, Juliet, Adaline, Eleanore, Rosalind, Margaret, and Kate—the only really successful characterization is that of Isabel. And Isabel, an exemplary heroine combining the virtues of chastity, female fortitude, prudence, and perfect wifehood, was modeled after Tennyson's mother, as we know from Hallam Tennyson's note in the Eversley edition of his father's works.[26] Elizabeth Tennyson was at this time the one woman for whom Tennyson could feel a love untainted by guilt and frustration; and Isabel was the one figure whose character the young poet could develop realistically and successfully.[27]

Tennyson's House at Blackdown, a photograph of the
engraving of Aldworth which first appeared in *The Leisure
Hour* in 1874.

From the collection of the Tennyson Research Centre,
Lincoln, England. Reproduced by kind permission of the
Director, City of Lincoln Libraries, Museum and Art
Gallery.

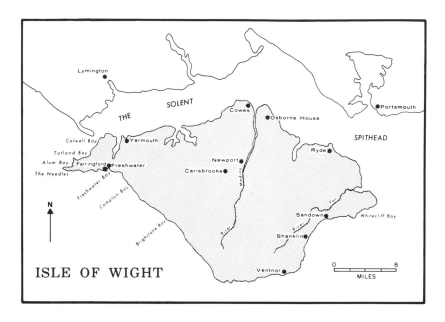

The Isle of Wight.

In Sophy Rawnsley, Tennyson for the first time found a compatible female contemporary.[28] His association with Sophy was free of the sensual dangers that had disturbed his relationship with Rosa Baring, and Sophy gave him some measure of the spiritual comfort he craved. Although there is a tradition that Tennyson proposed marriage to her, it seems unlikely that their relationship ever developed into an actual courtship. Nonetheless, Sophy's emotional stability and her unreserved intellectual receptiveness were certainly attractive to Tennyson, and she was far better suited to him than Rosa had been. But despite their apparently trouble-free relationship, Tennyson soon became more interested in Emily Sellwood, a woman in many ways like Sophy Rawnsley. Infinitely gentle and sympathetic, as well as deeply religious, Emily was destined to redeem Tennyson from a morbid religious skepticism which had been intensified by the death of Hallam. She would deliver him from a nearly fatal Slough of Despond, and she would give him many years free of the lonely anxiety that had long haunted him, years he would devote to the service of his muse and to the betterment of his age. "By her quiet sense of humour," Hallam Tennyson wrote, "by her selfless devotion, by her faith as clear as the heights of the June-blue heaven, she helped him to the utmost in the hours of his depression and of his sorrow."[29]

Emily's gentle nature was accentuated by a physical frailty which may have made her all the more attractive to a man of Tennyson's temperament. Certainly she was the very antithesis of the physically robust Rosa Baring. In a letter of 3 October 1850, written to his wife shortly after visiting the newly married Tennysons, Carlyle spoke of her as "a freckly *round*-faced woman . . . without shape" and "so very delicate in health, 'sick without a disorder.'"[30] And her pale, almost colorless face was as frequently remarked upon as her saintly expression. Nevertheless, even Carlyle, who found her "unpromising at the first glance," praised her "bright glittering blue eyes," and those sparkling, intelligent eyes, so often acclaimed, and her fine aquiline features gave Emily a real, though undoubtedly fragile, beauty. Carlyle's evaluation of her general physical debility is well substantiated. Emily was troubled throughout her life by a severe spinal disorder and by a general constitutional delicacy. John Tyndall remembered "her obviously frail physique,"[31] Mrs. James T. Fields, wife of the American editor and publisher, wrote of her "low faint voice" and her "slight and frail" figure,[32] and virtually every other acquaintance who found occasion to record his impressions of Emily Tennyson noted her physical weakness. Certainly it was fashionable for Victorian ladies to be delicate; and refinement seems often to have entailed sickliness as its accepted and expected corollary.[33] From all indications, however, Emily's weakness was physical, not psychic, or more anatomical than affected, though her specific ailments are rarely particularized, and her womanish infirmities may well have been expected and even encouraged by a husband predisposed to regard the highest type of woman as a rather unphysical being.

When he saw Emily at the wedding of his brother and her sister in May 1836, Tennyson was more strongly drawn to her than ever before; and he must indeed have reproached himself for lingering so long with Rosa Baring. Although he was in all likelihood already disenchanted with his first love, Emily's unrestrained joy in her sister's happiness impressed anew upon him the difference between a splendid but icy gem, like Rosa, and a truly "good woman," a woman lovely not only "in her youthful comeliness," but also "in comeliness of heart."[34] "The Bridesmaid" records Tennyson's realization of the "pleasant truth" of his singular rapport with that "wondrous creature," Emily Sellwood, the "woman kindred of his soul."[35]

> O Bridesmaid, ere the happy knot was tied,
> Thine eyes so wept that they could hardly see;
> Thy sister smiled and said, "No tears for me!
> A happy bridesmaid makes a happy bride."
> And then, the couple standing side by side,
> Love lighted down between them full of glee,
> And over his left shoulder laugh'd at thee,
> "O happy bridesmaid, make a happy bride."
> And all at once a pleasant truth I learn'd,
> For while the tender service made thee weep,
> I loved thee for the tear thou couldst not hide,
> And prest thy hand, and knew the press return'd,
> And thought, "My life is sick of single sleep,
> O happy bridesmaid, make a happy bride!"

Tennyson withstood the shock of Hallam's death remarkably well during the year immediately following that untimely tragedy. He struggled ahead, and despite his sorrow and despite John Wilson Croker's notorious, crushing review, his poetic achievement during 1834 was extraordinary. But he soon experienced other disappointments and anxieties which underlined the great loss of October 1833, and made his courageous, vigorously assertive response to Hallam's death seem pointless and futile. The mid-1830s were difficult years for all the Somersby Tennysons. Edward was by then permanently deranged, Septimus's mental state was rapidly deteriorating, and, with Frederick and Charles away from home, Alfred inherited primary responsibility for a family plagued by soul-sickness and instability. Furthermore, the publication of his grandfather's will in the summer of 1835 ended Tennyson's hopes for an independent establishment which would enable him to pursue his poetic career. The loss of Rosa Baring left him all the more lonely and life-weary, all the more aware of his continued need for the loving acceptance and the spiritual and psychological reinforcement he had found in Arthur Hallam.

For a time then Tennyson's determination to fight life through to the end as an active poet faltered, and he nearly surrendered to the temptation to quietude and retreat from a life where all things indeed seemed to be taken from him. Averse to exposing any more of his verse to the incivility of critics and editors, he very reluctantly complied with Monckton Milnes's request for a contribution to a volume called *The Tribute*.[36] And in January 1837, he described himself as "a nervous morbidly-irritable man, down in the world, stark-spoiled with the staggers of a mismanaged imagination and quite opprest by fortune and by the reviews."[37] Tennyson's low spiritual state suggests that his relationship with Emily had not advanced rapidly since the preceding spring. Much of the summer of 1837 was occupied with the move to High Beech and the responsibilities that devolved upon Tennyson as head of the house.[38] But by the first of the new year Emily was at least an occasional guest in the Tennysons' new home,[39] and in Hallam Tennyson's opinion it was the increased association with her and the subsequent engagement to her that "again braced [his] father for the struggle of life."[40]

During the next three years Tennyson was again vigorously at work. When he could put aside his writing for a day or two, he resorted to London to see his friends, Spedding, FitzGerald, Thackeray, J. M. Heath, John Kemble, R. J. Tennant, and others, or he visited Lincolnshire at Charles's vicarage or with the Sellwoods. Tennyson was now greatly encouraged about his

ultimate possibilities as a poet, and he was "on the whole happy
in his life, and looked forward to still better days."[41] Those
days of engagement to Emily were themselves better than anything Tennyson had known for at least four years,[42] and probably
since before the death of Hallam. Surely Emily must receive
credit for delivering a morbid, despondent Tennyson from a
spiritually desiccating cynicism and from "the sense of loss and
that all had gone by."[43] At a time of moral crisis, when Tennyson
had to choose between an active life of poetry and a withdrawal
into self-centered seclusion, Emily gave him her understanding
and her love. To some degree Tennyson would always remain
detached and dissociated from other men, but Emily enabled
him to extricate himself from a poisonous isolation and self-pity.
She brought to Tennyson, along with her love, a confident faith
in the ultimate spirituality of mankind and the universe, a faith
which would enable him to accept and to transcend a world
of immediate imperfection, failure, and pain.

Emily and Tennyson evidently corresponded all during the
1838–40 period of engagement, but Hallam Tennyson burned
most of the letters, according to his father's direction. Not a
word of Emily's correspondence from the early courtship survives; her letters may have been destroyed by Tennyson himself
long before Hallam burned the poet's own letters to her. Hallam
did preserve a few fragments of Tennyson's letters, which he
included in the *Memoir* (I, 167–76), but he was particularly
careful, he said, to obliterate "the many passages which would
show the intensity of feeling expressed in these letters." Sir
Charles Tennyson printed a few other fragments that survived
the purge,[44] and most of the scraps, printed by either the son
or the grandson, still survive in manuscript in the Tennyson
Research Centre. There is only one fragment from these bits
and pieces of manuscript which has escaped publication, and
that is the final portion of the 24 October 1839 letter, most
of which Hallam printed.[45] He omitted the last few sentences,[46]
however, obviously because in them Tennyson writes of Emily's
"feeling moments of jealousy," and Emily had been so adored,
so hallowed by her son, and indeed by all who knew her, that
it was unthinkable to document any momentary lapse in her
saintly unselfishness. However, the passage in question casts
no shadow on Emily's "huge brightness"; rather, it underlines
the intensity of her love for Tennyson and the fervent gratitude
of his equally loving response:

Knowest thou that I am pleased with thee for feeling moments of jealousy about Glenthorne.[47] I can't very well say why I am pleased. I suppose because it is a proof of thy love dearest; yet I have proof enough; it may be,
> That truth can never be confirmed enough
> Tho' doubt should ever sleep.[48]

but certain it is that I am gratified by thy jealousy. I hope to have a nice summary letter from thee enclosing full forgiveness for all my bantering and grumbling. Farewell, dearest-dearest, trust in me always and trust me always thine.

A.T.

Agnes Weld has indicated that Tennyson's letters to Emily during their period of engagement provide a "deep insight into his own inmost soul,"[49] and the portions of those letters which survive reveal something of how Emily's comfort and support enabled him to move through the "old hysterical mock-disease" of the mid-1830s into "the larger, saner existence." But early in 1840 their engagement was broken, and for nearly ten years Tennyson and Emily Sellwood were almost totally separated. Jerome Buckley overemphasizes the importance of the opposition of Emily's father to a suitor "far too bohemian in his manners, too slovenly in his dress, and too liberal in his religious views,"[50] and he consequently underestimates Tennyson's primary role in terminating the engagement. Although Henry Sellwood undoubtedly questioned the prudence of Emily's choice, in light of Louisa's unhappy experience with Charles,[51] the initial decision to part was Tennyson's, and Mr. Sellwood only forbade a continued correspondence after the engagement had already ended. The account of the matter given by a Mr. Symington, which Hallam included in his privately printed *Materials for a Life of A.T.*, takes much of the responsibility away from Henry Sellwood. According to Symington, who had his facts from Tennyson's brother Charles, when Alfred found that his monetary position was not improving as he had expected, he

> came to think that under the circumstances it was unjust and unfair in him to hold [Emily] bound. His own mother had such a high opinion of his choice that she offered to share her jointure with him to enable him to marry. This, however, Alfred Tennyson and Emily Sellwood

refused as being unjust to his brothers and sisters. So the engagement was broken off.[52]

Emily Tennyson's own account supports Symington's implication that the decision to part was the inevitable result of their refusal to accept Elizabeth Tennyson's offer of financial assistance:

> Previously your grandmother [Elizabeth Tennyson] had generously offered to allow us what would have enabled us to marry, but considering her large family it did not seem right to accept the offer. All this may have been a mistake. It was done from good motives but caused many miseries.[53]

Her suggestion in later life that the ten-year parting "may have been a mistake" perhaps indicates that Emily did not wholly understand or agree with Tennyson's decision that they stop seeing each other. The letter he wrote to her in December 1839[54] testifies to what Symington termed an "overstrained scrupulousness." And the tone of the poem "Love and Duty," addressed not to Emily's "alien ears," for which his renunciation has been "hard," "No, not to thee, but to thyself in me," leads me to believe that Emily's acquiescence in Tennyson's decision was less than wholehearted.

According to "Love and Duty," Tennyson and Emily now had one last meeting, lasting the whole of a summer night, when they "sat together and alone," overwhelmed by their mutual love and despair. The stars "hung/Love-charm'd to listen" to their passionate declarations; but "the end had come," and they wept "such tears/As flow but once a life." Nevertheless, Tennyson would not make his sundered love an excuse for surrendering to his old spiritual malaise. He felt himself a nobler and a stronger man for his relationship with Emily, and he believed that she too was "more thro' Love, and greater than [her] years." Emily would have to move forward, trusting in "some perfect end," and Tennyson would attempt to "earn a livelihood on which to marry,"[55] though he felt it unfair to tell Emily of his hope that they had not in fact "bade adieu for ever."[56]

There is little record of Emily during the 1840s. A cousin, Catherine Franklin, daughter of Sir Willingham Franklin, lived with the Sellwoods for two years after the death of her father in 1840. She left the Sellwood home in 1842 to marry Drummond Rawnsley; and later that same year Emily's sister Anne married Charles Weld. Emily and her father then lived alone together in Horncastle until 1848, when Sellwood sold his law practice to Samuel Sketchley and they moved to Hale, near Farnham, in West Surrey.[57] Emily stated that the reason for their departure from Horncastle was her own poor health: "During my ten years' separation from [Tennyson] the doctors believed I was going into a consumption, and the Lincolnshire climate was pronounced to be too cold for me; and we moved to London, to look for a home in the south of England."[58] Whether her separation from Tennyson in any way either induced or affected Emily's physical decline is impossible to say. She was not subject to the extreme depression and self-pity which complicated and perhaps even caused much of *his* illness during the 1830s, and again during the ten years apart from her.[59] Still she cannot have been content, and her mention of the "many miseries" caused by the decision to reject Mrs. Tennyson's financial offer suggests that the long period of detachment may have been as unpleasant for the lady as it was for her lover. In any case, Emily never blamed her father for forbidding correspondence with Tennyson; and she says in "For Her Sons" that they were "happy as father and daughter could be in each other,"[60] however much she may have longed for another kind of love and happiness.

Hallam Tennyson's record of his father's sending Emily Sellwood a copy of a laudatory letter from Carlyle in a letter to the poet's sister, Emily, indicates that the lovers, though separated, were still in indirect communication as late as 1842.[61] Furthermore, they seem actually to have met at least twice, probably between 1840 and 1843. Sir Charles reports a single accidental encounter at Maidstone where Emily had gone to visit Tennyson's sister, Cecilia Lushington.[62] Emily mentioned the initial chance meeting at Park House, but she also described a second meeting in more detail:

> Again afterwards we met there and again Edmund [Lushington, Tennyson's brother-in-law] came forward with his accustomed generosity and offered to give up his carriage horses that he might help us. But this, of course, could not be allowed.[63]

Evidently Emily was a frequent guest of the Lushingtons', and

without doubt both of the recorded meetings with Tennyson
were unintentional. Even when Edmund Lushington offered
them the means of being alone together, they were obedient
to Mr. Sellwood's mandate and true to their own resolve.

For a time after the 1840 parting Tennyson carefully pursued
his plan for gaining economic security and literary success, and
he found, as he had hoped he would, that his work could occupy
his mind and sustain his faith in the future. But the 1842 volume
sold fewer copies than expected, and Dr. Matthew Allen's
"Pyroglyphs" project, to which Tennyson had given both his
money and his enthusiasm, proved a ruinous failure which cost
him his whole patrimony, as well as the five-hundred-pound
legacy left him by an aunt of Arthur Hallam's.[64] Grievous domestic
problems continued to weigh upon him, and they added to the
anguish of seeing his hopes for financial security and reunion
with Emily suddenly destroyed. Edward's mental condition
remained unchanged; both Septimus and Horatio were suffering
from nervous instability and illness; and Arthur's alcoholism
had become so severe that it was necessary for him to go into
a home for treatment. Tennyson himself grew increasingly dis-
traught, his health suffered from his mental turmoil, and, by
the end of 1843, he had entered a hydropathic hospital to undergo
what he considered "of all the uncomfortable ways of living
. . . the worst."[65]

Tennyson emerged from the hospital in the spring of 1844
in a more peaceful state of mind; and, Lushington having insured
Dr. Allen's life in Tennyson's behalf, Allen's convenient death
in January 1845 restored much of the lost investment. As yet,
however, reunion with Emily seemed out of the question, despite
his confession to Aubrey DeVere "that he must marry and find
love and peace or die."[66] Tennyson's was always a dependent
personality. Lonely, alienated, self-consciously unhappy, he
needed someone basically independent and untroubled to divert
him from himself, and he had of course found and subsequently
lost such an individual, first in Arthur Hallam and then in Emily
Sellwood. Tennyson lacked the power to compensate for his
emotional deficiencies. Like the protagonist of "Maud," he
wanted a savior to rescue him from "the madhouse of self"
and to reconcile him to a world ill-suited to his delicate sensibility.

Despite his fear of the destructive possibilities of feminine
sensuality, Tennyson had always looked upon the "good" woman
as the primary source of man's salvation. Only through the vital

force of her chastening love could a man be redeemed from his own less spiritual nature.[67] For Tennyson, as for Spenser, the "good" or "beautiful" woman is a celestial creature who purifies her true suitor; she is a ministering angel who rescues man from his own incompleteness. Emily Sellwood was eminently qualified for the large work of Tennyson's ideal woman. She was the very embodiment of spirituality, and no one could have cultivated a finer "sympathy with all that is pure, and noble, and beautiful" in life.[68]

Tennyson gave full expression to his conception of the ideal relation of the sexes in *The Princess* (1847), a poem he had talked over with Emily in 1839 (the sentiments of which, as these letters show, she was still reflecting in the '80s and '90s). The prince, like Tennyson, needs "a strengthening influence," and the princess rescues him from his "weird seizures"[69] and nurses him back to health, even as Emily had once helped the poet recover from his own nervous illness. Now the success of *The Princess* bolstered Tennyson's income considerably and, more importantly, its popularity restored to him confidence in his own poetic prospects. He felt that the time had come at last to obey the dictates of love and approach Emily again. Accordingly, he proposed marriage in late 1847 or early 1848 and "was refused on the highest and noblest principles of self-abnegation by the woman who loved him."[70]

Emily's exact reasons for declining Tennyson's offer remain unknown. She probably wrote to her cousin, Catherine Rawnsley, about the proposal and her refusal, but none of her letters of this period have been preserved.[71] Emily continued to love Tennyson as fervently as ever, even though she considered their union impossible. Catherine's son, H. D. Rawnsley, wrote that "the lovers ate out their hearts of love in secret"[72] all during their separation, and his brother, Willingham Rawnsley, affirmed that Emily "always thought of him, and they each kept the sacred fire alight in their hearts."[73] Tennyson himself seems always to have been convinced of Emily's affection; on 10 July 1850, he wrote to a Scottish friend, Ludovic Colquhoun, that he had married a lady "who has loved me for fourteen years without variableness (or any shadow of turning)."[74]

Apparently Emily distrusted Tennyson's unorthodox religious speculations, so far removed from her own steady faith, and a feeling of spiritual incompatibility must have influenced her decision to refuse him. Writing in 1850 about Tennyson's long engagement, Thomas Wentworth Higginson posited that Tennyson had long since won Emily's heart, "but not her head or conscience, for she was very strait in her theology and he very lax in comparison."[75] Emily's moral fervor may not always strike us as entirely appealing, but there can be no doubt of its strength. Aubrey DeVere wrote of Emily in a letter, 24 September 1854, to Isabella Fenwick (Wordsworth's neighbor and dear friend): "She would, I have no doubt, make any imaginable sacrifice of her happiness to promote the real and interior good of her husband, and not of her happiness only, but of his also."[76] Perhaps her refusal of Tennyson's proposal was just such a sacrifice of happiness for what she considered to be his own best interest. Emily would have considered it wrong—spiritually damaging to both Tennyson and herself—to marry if there were serious differences in their religious convictions. Furthermore, according to her 1869 reminiscences, Emily "had lost courage" during the years of separation, and she feared her own inadequacy for "the great responsibility" of becoming Tennyson's wife.

The unexpected refusal plunged Tennyson back into his habitual melancholy and what Edward FitzGerald termed his "wrath against the world."[77] When he visited Ireland in the spring of 1848, Aubrey DeVere, his host, avowed that Tennyson would "not be right" until he found "someone to love him exclusively."[78] By late 1849 he was again in communication with Emily, and he sent her two versions of the song "Sweet and Low," evidently on 24 November, so that she might decide which he should use in the third edition of *The Princess*. By this time Tennyson had determined to try once again to renew the engagement. Probably encouraged by the recent reunion of Charles and Louisa Turner,[79] he went to see Charles to discuss the matter, and in January 1850, he paid a visit to Drummond and Catherine Rawnsley at Shiplake and almost certainly asked their advice and perhaps their aid as well.

In December Tennyson decided to reveal to other readers *The Elegies* (as he invariably referred to *In Memoriam*—the title Emily selected later on), which he had written "for his own relief and private satisfaction."[80] Whether or not he had any idea of the effect *The Elegies* would have upon Emily, Catherine Rawnsley obtained his permission to send her a copy. Responding just as Catherine must have expected, Emily felt "admiration and delight, not unmixed with awe"[81] upon reading Tennyson's powerful testimony to his own victory over spiritual despair.

Catherine continued to use her influence to further the reunion, and Charles Kingsley, then curate at nearby Eversley, met Emily at the Rawnsley rectory soon afterwards and added the pressure of his conviction that she should accept Tennyson. The major role Kingsley played in Emily's decision to marry Tennyson is apparent in her statement in "For Her Sons": ". . . I do not know whether I should ever, feeling the great responsibility, have ventured to become your Father's wife had not Kingsley . . . not only encouraged but urged me to do so."[82] Like Tennyson, Kingsley was one of the chief exponents of the idea that it is the role of the good woman to guide, to inspire, and, ultimately, to save, and his support of his friend's choice testifies both to his high opinion of Emily and to his belief in the likelihood of Tennyson's redemption from spiritual anxiety. Perhaps he expressed to Emily his conviction that Tennyson was winning his battle with doubt and that his faith would be especially sincere for being born of his long struggle with disbelief. According to C. F. G. Masterman, Kingsley in later years called Tennyson "the deliberate champion of vital Christianity and of an orthodoxy the more sincere because it has worked upwards through the abyss of doubt. . . ."[83] On the front leaf of volume four of his "Draft for Materials for a Life of A.T." (unprinted and unpublished, Tennyson Research Centre), Hallam has written this simple comment on the insistence of Emily's advisers: "Charles Turner urged that [there] should be no delay of the marriage and his advice was strenuously backed up by Charles Kingsley and consequently it took place forthwith." Kingsley, Turner, and the Rawnsleys all helped clear the way for the marriage, but they could never have been successful had not Emily herself come to appreciate Tennyson's faith that God is love. Emily could never have abided a real skeptic, and after she accepted Tennyson it was her constant desire "to make her husband more religious, or at least to conduce . . . to his growth in the spiritual life."[84]

Tennyson himself grew hesitant during the final months before the marriage when the happy resolution of his long quest was almost at hand.[85] There was little support for the marriage from either the Sellwoods or the Tennysons, excepting the Charles Turners. The Sellwoods remained aloof and disapproving, and there were those in the poet's own family who had strong misgivings. After the wedding Tennyson's sister Mary expressed her less than sanguine expectations for the couple's future:

> Well, all is over. Alfred was married to Emily Sellwood
> last Friday . . . *Friday, and raining,* about which I feel
> very superstitious . . . I hope they will be happy, but
> I feel very doubtful about it.[86]

Tennyson's uncertainty was probably in part the result of family
opinion on both sides, though he could not have encountered
much overt opposition since neither family was fully informed
of the couple's intentions.[87] His heart's true wisdom prevailed,
however, and he finally settled on a definite date. Alfred and
Emily were wed at Shiplake Church on 13 June 1850. Drummond
Rawnsley performed the service, which was attended by his wife
and Emily's cousin, Kate; his two small daughters, Mary and
Margaret, who served as bridesmaids; Emily's father; Charles
Weld; Edmund and Cecilia Lushington; and Greville Phillimore
of Shiplake House. The description in "For Her Sons" indicates
the informality of the hastily planned ceremony: "The cake had
not arrived in time nor the dress[88] and the white gloves had
disappeared in the depths of a carpet-bag. However things were
managed and at all events I had real orange flowers." All doubts
on either side were dissolved, and the "perfectly ideal marriage"
of Alfred and Emily Tennyson began auspiciously enough with
what Tennyson called "the nicest wedding he had ever been
at."[89]

Six months later Tennyson completed a poem he had begun
on his wedding day, which is addressed "To The Vicar of
Shiplake" and which evidences his heartfelt satisfaction with
his marriage and his bride:

> Have I seen in one so near
>   Aught but sweetness aye prevailing?
> Or thro' more than half a year,
>   Half the fraction of a failing,
> Therefore bless you, Drummond dear.
>
> Good she is, and pure and just.
>   Being conquer'd by her sweetness
> I shall come thro' her, I trust,
>   Into fuller-orb'd completeness;
> Tho' but made of erring dust.

(ll. 11–20)

Although every marriage is a private relationship which cannot be fully evaluated from outside, it is fair to say that Emily Tennyson truly fulfilled her husband. She brought him a happiness and a completeness unknown during two decades of rarely relieved despondency. With her comfort and guidance he would indeed "gain in sweetness and moral height";[90] he would be spiritually healed and uplifted, and he would come to know "the peace of God," which, as he remarked many years later, "came into my life before the altar when I wedded her."[91] Emily shielded and supported Tennyson, and she lessened the vexations he had formerly suffered. But more importantly, she freed him from the prison of selfhood and enabled him to bear the responsibilities of a less alienated existence than that in which he had long indulged. She helped him to survive the pressures and conflicts of a materialistic age which challenged his most cherished beliefs and to attain a position of comparative confidence and tranquility.

There is no dearth of testimony about the effect Emily Tennyson's understanding, her protection, and her wise and loving attention had upon her husband's troubled spirit. After visiting the newly married couple, DeVere observed that the new Mrs. Tennyson was "kindly, affectionate . . . and above all, deeply and simply religious." And DeVere felt that she would succeed in making Tennyson more devout,

> for piety like hers is infectious, especially where there is an atmosphere of affection to serve as a conducting medium. Indeed I already observe a great improvement in Alfred. His nature is a religious one, and he is remarkably free from vanity and sciolism. Such a nature gravitates toward Christianity, especially when it is in harmony with itself . . . .[92]

Although Tennyson never mastered his doubts, and likely never had a conventional belief in a personal God, DeVere was correct in predicting that he would become more religious. At times his faith may have dimmed, and certainly it remained cautious and tentative; but it never languished as it had during the lonely years of separation from Emily. DeVere also noted a vast improvement in Tennyson's disposition:

I have never before had half so much pleasure in Alfred's

society. He is far happier than I ever saw him before; and his "wrath against the world" is proportionately mitigated. He has an unbounded respect for his wife, as well as a strong affection, which has been growing stronger ever since his marriage. That marriage was obviously, equally creditable to his judgment and his heart, and it will, I doubt not, be attended by a blessing.[93]

Mrs. Monckton Milnes thought Emily "a wise and tender woman, such as ought to be entrusted with such a fragile affair as Tennyson's comfort and happiness."[94] And Coventry Patmore found that "she seems to understand [Tennyson] thoroughly, and, without the least ostentation or officiousness of affection, waits upon and attends to him as she ought to."[95] Carlyle, too, considered Tennyson "really improved" by his matrimonial adventure, "cheerful in what he talks and looking forward to a future less 'detached' than the past has been."[96]

No one has ever disputed the tenderness, the grace, the almost indescribable ethereality of Emily Tennyson's character, nor has there been any denial of her central role in Tennyson's victory over the worst excesses of his self-indulgent brooding. But there have been those who would take exception to Joanna Richardson's claim that "Tennyson's marriage to Emily Sellwood was, quite simply, the most fortunate action of his life."[97] Harold Nicolson characterizes Tennyson's wife as a "wistful lady" who bound "what was most wild in him and most original" and passed "timid but appropriate criticisms" upon the "tender little things" she encouraged the Laureate to write.[98] Very little of the available evidence supports Nicolson's assumptions. Unfortunately he seems to have been familiar only with those descriptions of Emily which emphasize her sweet wistfulness, her delicate beauty and spirituality, and her constant concern for the Laureate's well-being; consequently, he has pieced together an overly protective, poet-stifling Emily Tennyson, endowed with little intelligence and less personality.[99] In fact, Emily may not have infused a new glow into Tennyson's genius, but she did preserve that genius and prevent it from becoming lost in hopeless morbidity and isolation.

Nicolson implies that Tennyson's poetry lost its excellence when "the sense of unrest left him." And he finds Emily guilty of removing her husband from "the thorns of life,"[100] and thus of silencing those cries of discontent which had given birth to his best verse and which, but for her intervention, would have produced an endless stream of Tennyson seasoned to Edward FitzGerald's taste. Alfred's own statement to Patmore that "vexations are . . . destructive of the 'gay science' "[101] supports a less naive hypothesis that without Emily he would have been a less active poet, and quite possibly another brooding victim of the Tennyson "black blood." The "sense of unrest" never left Tennyson; after all it was during his married years that he wrote the *Idylls,* as well as "Maud," "Lucretius," "Vastness," and "Locksley Hall Sixty Years After." The themes and the tone of his poetry did not change substantially after 1850. Right until the end he continued periodically to recapitulate his old doubts and torments in verse. And it was Emily, tirelessly comforting and reassuring, who all the while tempered his unrest and prevented it from reverting to the "old hysterical mock-disease"[102] of his youth. It was she who kept him relatively content in body and soul and largely absorbed in his work.

Certainly Tennyson's psychological recovery from the loss of Hallam is a tribute both to his courage and to his faith in a beneficent, if inscrutable, God; but it is unlikely that either his courage or his faith would have endured had he failed to find someone to love. For Tennyson no man could be complete without a helpmate, and Tennyson himself particularly needed the steady serenity of a domestic establishment to temper the shrill emotionalism of his own unsteady heart. Without the aid, the encouragement, the stabilizing influence, and the uplifting support of his wife, Tennyson's life and his poetic achievement would indeed have been different. As James Knowles declared soon after the poet's death, "To his wife's perpetual and brooding care and love of him . . . the world owes, under Providence, many years of Tennyson's prolonged life and many of his immortal Poems."[103]

Of the many comments about Emily preserved in the writings of the Tennysons' contemporaries, only the observations of FitzGerald and Elizabeth Barrett Browning in any way support the idea that she bridled her husband's original genius. FitzGerald felt that Emily spoiled Tennyson's lyrical impetus, and he blamed the poet's "most lady-like, gentle wife" for encouraging the "coterie worship" and "London adulation" in which he found Tennyson lost after his marriage.[104] He thought her too delicate, too refined; he once remarked that Tennyson would have been better off with "an old Housekeeper like Molière's."[105] Mrs.

Browning also felt that Tennyson was "too much indulged. His wife is too much his second self; she does not criticize enough."[106] There is no question about the amount of patient indulgence the poet received. Everyone who knew the Tennysons was impressed by Emily's deft and tender handling of an often difficult husband. But it is her strength and independence, and her tactful, yet explicit, critical advice to Tennyson, not a servile obedience or an undiscriminating approval, which are usually remembered. After her first visit to Farringford, Annie Fields noted that Emily was "intellectually and morally strong, and with a direct personal influence about her such as Shakespeare has in some ways contrived to express most remarkably in his female delineations."[107] Elsewhere Mrs. Fields wrote that Emily told her of how her husband once took the sheets of a new poem to London "and showed them to Mr. Monckton Milnes, who persuaded him to leave out one of the best lines; but I persuaded him to replace it when he came home. It is a mistake in general for him to listen to the suggestions of others about his poems."[108] And Benjamin Jowett, the translator and theologian who in 1870 became the Master of Balliol, considered Emily "her husband's best critic, and certainly the one whose authority he would most willingly have recognized."[109]

Tennyson welcomed his wife's criticism, and he seems to have regarded her discernment as virtually infallible. Particularly when he had written several versions of a poem, Emily would assist in selecting and even revising the final rendition. It was she who chose the final versions of both "Sweet and Low" and "Helen's Tower," the latter from four slightly varied possibilities which Tennyson sent to Lord Dufferin in October 1861.[110] Tennyson was proud of Emily's intellect; she more than anyone else was his adviser in all literary matters, and, according to Willingham Rawnsley, he "always took his wife's opinion as final."[111] In his little volume entitled *Tennyson and the Isle of Wight*, A. Patchett Martin compares Emily Tennyson to Dorothy Wordsworth:

> As Wordsworth's gifted sister Dorothy was content to inspire the poet by her thoughts, so the personal literary gifts of Lady Tennyson are merged in her husband's . . . poems. But that judgment must have been indeed sound, to which Tennyson would finally submit his verse.[112]

Without doubt Tennyson's poetry was influenced by his wife's presence and by his knowledge that she would read everything he wrote, as well as by her critical readings. Very rarely, however, did Emily actually disapprove of what her husband wrote. Willingham Rawnsley recalled that when Tennyson read him some of the poems which he intended to include in the *Demeter* volume (1889), he said after a few stanzas of "The Leper's Bride" (unpublished): "My wife and son won't let me put those in; I don't know why: I see no harm in them."[113] In no other instance have I found Emily Tennyson disapproving of her husband's taste or exercising anything like the censorship or the excision often spoken of in nineteenth-century American studies in connection with the wives of Mark Twain and Nathaniel Hawthorne. In the books written after Twain's marriage, sex has almost entirely disappeared, and Alexander Jones posits that Olivia Clemens actually fanned the flames of her spouse's unnatural sexual guilt and either directly or indirectly imposed upon his work an almost absolute exclusion of sexuality.[114] Emily had just the reverse effect upon Tennyson's sexual fears. It was only after the poet married that he was able to accept his own physical nature and to escape from the excessive prudery which had previously permitted him little realism in the treatment of human love.

Certainly Emily Tennyson was a strict moralist, and she shared Tennyson's horror of "unbridled sensuality" and his belief in purity as the highest and most essential social ideal. But she was no prude by traditionalist Victorian standards. She vigorously defended "Maud," and she did not think "Lucretius" improper or shocking, though *Macmillan's* censored the "rosy knees and supple roundedness/And budded bosom-peaks" (ll.190-91) of the Roman naturalist's tormenting Oread for the sake of a squeamish reading public.[115] Nor did she fail to visit George Eliot and G. H. Lewes during the summer of 1871 when they were living at Shottermill, near Haslemere and the Tennysons. Emily recorded the visit in her Journal, and she wrote about it in a letter to Hallam (Letter 261), who eventually canceled from the *Memoir* his mother's Journal entry, with its reference to visiting Lewes and his famous mistress.

In no sense was Emily Tennyson the "new woman" demanding feminine equality in place of the feminine birthright to counsel, to chasten, and, above all, to serve. Her ideals were all of the older time, and no more than Tennyson could she abide any fracture in the social organization or any threat to long-cherished proprieties. But for all her traditionalism and for all her sweet humility, Emily was never mindlessly submissive, to her husband or to anyone else. She lacked Tennyson's perception of intellectual perplexities, and the single-minded strength of her convictions reflects a somewhat rigid attachment to familiar ideas. But although her set of principles was absolute, she never hesitated to reexamine her own beliefs or to challenge those of others. She even encouraged Tennyson to widen his own range of inquiry, and she read with him the classical philosophers and the higher critics, as well as the Bible. Yet despite her husband's reliance upon her insight into poetical effects, despite numerous tributes to her wide interests and her striking individuality, despite the real strength to which G. F. Watts testifies,[116] and which no reader of her correspondence can fail to detect, Emily Tennyson remains in the minds of too many a wistful saint with no mind of her own, no well-defined personality, and neither a full nor a proper appreciation of her husband's talent.

This edition of her letters makes possible a better understanding of Lady Tennyson. Her common sense and her erudition, her gentle, but real, sense of humor, her spirituality, her boundless kindness, her social and political awareness, her appreciation and her command of the arts, and her shaping influence on the lives of the people who knew her—all these aspects of Emily Tennyson are revealed in her correspondence. These letters come from the pen of a ready writer; most are written hurriedly, and in their spontaneity they give a fine impression of the sort of woman Emily really was. Candid and sincere, though incapable of an indiscretion, she gave her correspondents her initial, impulsive reaction to each new event which caught her interest, whether at home or in the world at large. Whether her attention focused on land tenure, the Irish Church Bill, or Tennyson's plans for a new poem, she was never in any doubt where she stood; remarkably enough, however, her inflexibility rarely dictated an inaptitude for being fully aware of both sides of an issue. Her tolerance, forgiveness, and overwhelming capacity to love are evident throughout these letters. And her ability to say the right thing at the right time to comfort and to reassure is as apparent in her correspondence as it was to her guests at Farringford and Aldworth. In his eulogy of Lady Tennyson Theodore Watts-Dunton stated that "she was born to hold a high place as a conversationalist, brilliant and stimulating."[117]

Her conversation has not been preserved, but these letters have the paramount value of letting Emily speak, and they greatly strengthen our impression of a rather shy-seeming woman who continually amazed people with the strength and resolution of what she said.

The letters in this volume, most of them personal letters to close friends and relatives, cover nearly fifty years of Emily Tennyson's life, from shortly before her marriage right up to the week of her death. Many of the innumerable letters of an official nature which she wrote for the poet have also come to light, but all of these, though in Emily's hand, have Tennyson's signature and must therefore be considered *his* letters.[118] I have tried to bring together all of Emily's letters that comment in any significant way on either the Tennysons or their friends and guests, many of them among the most illustrious people of the period,[119] or which have an importance as social report or literary commentary. I have omitted trivial notes and letters and unhelpful fragments, but these, in any case, form a small proportion of the whole of Emily Tennyson's correspondence. Lady Tennyson's Journal[120] has proved to be a valuable source of additional information, and I have made liberal use of it, particularly in a number of narrative links which frequently include extensive elaborations on occurrences only mentioned in the letters. Although the Journal is actually a redaction which Emily made for Hallam from a number of earlier journals, and from which she undoubtedly deleted much personal information, it nonetheless offers an abundance of previously unpublished material which lends this volume of letters an invaluable density of specification.

Nearly a hundred letters to Hallam and Lionel at school have been preserved, and most of those letters are included here. Oddly enough, there are long alternating periods when virtually all of the extant letters to her sons are addressed to either one brother or the other, though she must have written to both regularly. It may be that Lady Tennyson destroyed duplicating letters, preserving only the most informative, after her husband's death. As a group, the letters to Hallam and Lionel especially bear strong witness to their mother's sound and vigorous religious faith. She urged her boys to "shelve all in Christ," as she had ever done, to be active in His good work, and to avoid a fruitless search for "proof" of spiritual truth. "If more labour were spent in trying to teach people to follow in the steps of Christ," she wrote to Hallam at Marlborough in March 1871 (Letter 255), "and less in . . . straining after definitions of subjects beyond our grasp it would be better for us." "I quite agree with thee that death perfects the individuality, not destroys it," she affirmed in another letter to Hallam that May (Letter 256), and she wrote to Lionel at Hastings in August 1866 (Letter 168) her perception of "How sad life would be if one might not look to spending an eternity with those dearest to us and meanwhile what a help it is to one to bear absence that one may from the distance encourage each other in the work that God has given us to do." Equally apparent in the letters to her sons are Emily's deep interest in and shrewd judgment of literature. Repeatedly she advised Hallam and Lionel of her own opinions about the poets they were studying, from Homer to Milton to Matthew Arnold, and in the boys' essays she encouraged them to have as their motto "language undefiled."

Emily's sister, Anne Weld, and her daughter Agnes, who are often addressed jointly, trail only Hallam and Lionel in the total number of letters received which appear in this volume. The correspondence to Anne and Agnes is especially valuable for the last ten years of Emily's life, when she had resumed regular letter writing after nearly ten years of silence dictated by a complete physical breakdown in September 1874. After 1885 it was primarily her sister and her niece that Emily made privy to her observations on Tennyson's declining health and to periodic admissions of her own exhaustion, resulting, as it had before, from the endless public letters she had to consider and to which she resolutely replied. Many of her letters to the Welds are obviously the efforts of a tired woman, but they reflect a cheerful emotional serenity and a mental alacrity which suggest that Emily Tennyson changed remarkably little over the years, that she never really grew old.

Emily was both hostess and friend to many distinguished Victorians, and she became a regular correspondent of two of her most frequent guests, Edward Lear and Thomas Woolner. The long series of letters addressed to Lear show us a side of Emily Tennyson that is disclosed nowhere else. They are often written in a facetious, playful style, and they reveal her high spirits and her sense of humor as well as her kindliness and her genius for friendship. During thirty-six years of fairly regular correspondence, it was always her aim to rouse the chronically despondent nonsense poet from his sadness with a compliment, a sprightly reproof, or an amusing story, and to assure him of both her affection and her high regard. It was to Woolner that Emily herself most often turned when she needed help in coping with Tennyson or when she wished to confide her irritation with his naivete in practical matters. When the poet could find no subject to hold his interest in the early 1860s, Emily solicited from her sculptor friend the stories for "Enoch Arden" and "Aylmer's Field." She longed, however, for Tennyson to be about some greater work more suited to his talent, and she asked Woolner to support her efforts to persuade him to return to the Arthuriad. In March 1868, she told Woolner of her "exceeding annoyance" with the Moxon firm for their insistence on elaborate advertisements for a proposed Tennyson edition, and she expressed impatience with her husband's inability to "see the consequences as clearly as I do" (Letter 188).

Another of the largest surviving groups of letters was addressed to Margaret Gatty, author of *Aunt Judy's Tales* (1859) and the five series of *Parables from Nature* (1855-72), and wife of the Rev. Alfred Gatty, vicar of Ecclesfield, Yorkshire. When Mrs. Gatty first visited Farringford in November 1858, she and Emily formed an attachment which initiated a regular correspondence, and though some of these letters are unyieldingly commonplace, a few are particularly significant for their references to the Laureate's ordeal of writing and publishing in the face of constant demands for new poems from every quarter. Many of the letters to Margaret Gatty were written when Emily was overly tired, and they contain an unusual number of references to her ill health. But her attitude here, as always, is one of patient endurance, supported by the belief that, like personal loss, physical suffering is a burden necessary for all God's children.

The last correspondence that demands a brief comment is a group of some forty letters to Tennyson, virtually all of which appear in this edition. These letters testify to a love which grew and developed through the years. On their eighth anniversary Emily wrote with her usual tact and tenderness,

> I know thou dost not think of days so perhaps thou wilt not remember this. Nevertheless, I kiss thee on our wedding-day and I say God ever bless thee and us and a great deal more I say that I will not and cannot write and a great deal more I feel than I could say if I would. (Letter 73)

But for all her adoration of her husband, Emily did not hesitate either to counsel or to correct him. She rather often prodded him to remember his social obligations. And though she could pardon an overlooked anniversary, she reminded him on another occasion that the Sabbath is no time for writing letters and declared herself "puritan enough to be sorry thou shouldst have spent Sunday morning so" (Letter 55). Nor did she demur when an opportunity arose for offering Tennyson professional advice, and the instances in which she objects to one publishing plan or another are too numerous to mention.

Emily Tennyson's letters disclose how, by a happy inconsistency, she was able to defend the poet's solitude, to minister to his sensitivity, and to encourage his sociability at the same time. The Christian aura of the "school for husbands"[121] she conducted for forty-two years suffuses her writing. So does the chivalrous and medieval atmosphere of both Farringford and Aldworth, as apparent in her correspondence as in the words of Richard Jebb, who found in Emily "something of the sweet queenliness of a French mistress of the manor of the old régime."[122] Written with no thought of posterity, Emily's letters enable us to see the domestic Tennyson, just as he was, for the first time. Hitherto we have seen him steadily, but never before have we seen him *whole*. Her letters also tell much about Tennyson's reading and his intellectual and spiritual preoccupations, and, in time, they will help us to a better understanding of the complexities and subtleties of a body of poetry that is not always credited with these qualities. And, of course, most importantly, these letters provide a running account of the life of an individual as great in her own way as the poet himself.

Tennyson might be regarded as an "introvert" and Emily as an "extrovert," in the Jungian sense of those terms, though one must be cautious not to bestow such labels too readily. According to Jung, "there is a marked tendency for either type to marry its opposite. Each secretly hopes that the other will take care of the side of life they find uncongenial; the quiet, thoughtful man finds a lively, practical wife, who arranges the social activities that further his . . . career."[123] Emily was more a creature of action than Tennyson, and she was more unequivocal. She made decisions and stuck to them. He was moody and changeable, and his postponing of the wedding, like his long postponing of publication, is indicative of a lack of self-confidence. After his marriage Tennyson grew more sure of his own abilities. But for all his improvement, he remained that "singular compound of manliness and helplessness" that Henry Taylor described in 1851.[124] After Tennyson's death, Bram Stoker still had good cause to wonder at "the strange contradictions of human nature, when such feminine sensitiveness was incased in a frame of such splendid masculinity and virility."[125]

Emily Tennyson was the practical, stable partner who handled most of their often-trying social obligations, managed their financial accounts, and rescued Tennyson whenever he reverted to his old melancholy self-absorption. She was attracted by Tennyson's physical vigor and by other facets of his individuality that were most unlike herself. His unworldliness fascinated her, as did his broad, speculative mind. Perhaps she needed his uncertainty to complement her own assurance, and the confirmation of her husband's faith and the vitalization of his best self were tasks just suited to her taste as well as her ability.

Distinct in individuality, Emily nonetheless set herself to Tennyson "like perfect music unto noble words." Through the years they fulfilled each other, and, as Emily often remarked, their love waxed even larger than it was at first. "Purpose in purpose, will in will" they grew in single-minded dedication to Tennyson's work and to the destiny of England and the British Crown. "For me I cannot separate her from him," Henry Graham Dakyns wrote to Hallam Tennyson on 13 August 1896, "and perhaps in some mysterious manner beyond our intelligence they are, in the eternal of Eternity now, more than ever, One."[126]

Notes

1. Or, "Are you a Dryad or an Oread wandering here?" Hallam Tennyson's version of the initial greeting. See *Alfred Lord Tennyson: A Memoir by His Son* (London: Macmillan, 1897), I, 148. Hereafter cited as *Memoir*.

2. "Emily Tennyson's Narrative for Her Sons," James O. Hoge, *Texas Studies in Literature and Language*, 14 (Spring, 1972), 96. Hereafter cited as "For Her Sons." Lady Tennyson's account of her early acquaintance with the poet, their courtship, their honeymoon, and the first three years of their marriage, which she wrote for Hallam and Lionel Tennyson in 1869, is preserved in the Tennyson Research Centre, Lincoln, England (hereafter cited as T.R.C.). Emily Tennyson again mentioned the poet's sportive manner in her "Recollections of My Early Life" (hereafter cited as "Recollections"), where she described him as "kind, simple,

and dignified, with plenty of sportiveness flashing out from time to time." See *Tennyson and His Friends,* ed. Hallam Tennyson (London: Macmillan, 1911), p. 7.

Lady Tennyson did not explicitly say that the encounter with Tennyson in Holywell, or the Fairy Wood, was their first meeting. She merely indicated that the meeting occurred during her first visit to Somersby Rectory; but Hallam Tennyson has assumed that his mother and father were previously unacquainted (see *Memoir,* I, 148).

3. George Eliot, *Adam Bede,* edited with an introduction by John Paterson (Boston: Houghton Mifflin, 1968), p. iii.

4. "For Her Sons," p. 97.

5. Agnes Grace Weld, "Tennyson," *The Contemporary Review* 71 (November 1897), 691.

6. "For Her Sons," p. 97.

7. Oliver Huckel, *Through England With Tennyson* (New York: Crowell, 1913), p. 80.

8. "For Her Sons," p. 97.

9. See Appendix A for Sellwood family background.

10. "Recollections," p. 5.

11. "Recollections," p. 5.

12. "Recollections," p. 5.

13. From an unpublished early version of "Emily Tennyson's Narrative for Her Sons," T.R.C.

14. Robert Roberts, "Tennysoniana," *Literary Anecdotes of the Nineteenth Century,* ed. W. Robertson Nicoll and Thomas J. Wise (London: Hodder and Stoughton, 1896), II, 423-24.

15. "For Her Sons," pp. 99-100.

16. "Recollections," p. 6.

17. This notebook is preserved in the Tennyson Research Centre. Emily injured her right hand in her youth, and it is likely that the stiffening wrist which resulted in later life prevented her from sketching or painting more than she did. See Anne Thackeray Ritchie, *From Friend to Friend* (London: John Murray, 1919), p.7.

18. *Memoir,* I, 148. Hallam Tennyson either erred in calculating his mother's age, or he meant that she was almost seventeen. In the spring of 1830, Emily would still have been sixteen.

19. For an exhaustive analysis of Tennyson's relationships with Rosa Baring and Sophy Rawnsley, see Ralph Wilson Rader, *Tennyson's Maud: The Biographical Genesis* (Berkeley and Los Angeles: University of California Press, 1963), pp. 22-67.

20. "For Her Sons," pp. 96-97.

21. "For Her Sons," p. 96.

22. See Rader, *Tennyson's Maud,* p. 18.

23. "I lingered yet awhile to bend my way" (ll. 5-6), written c. 1835 and published in the *Nineteenth Century* by Sir Charles Tennyson in 1931. Rader shows that the "jewel" was Rosa Baring (pp. 34-35), and Christopher Ricks notes the reappearance of similar "jewel" imagery at least four times in "Maud," in *The Poems of Tennyson* (London and Harlow: Longmans, 1969), p. 647. All subsequent references to Tennyson's poetry are to the Ricks edition.

24. See Charles Tennyson, *Six Tennyson Essays* (London: Cassell, 1954), p. 75. Tennyson's guilt-laden psyche was unable to cope with the animal basis of life, and he must have been frustrated and tormented by the passion for Rosa Baring which argued against his attempt to repress his own sexuality. It was a similar inability to regard his own sexual impulses in a normal manner that tormented the young protagonist of "Maud." Roy Basler has noted that "sex and all physical aspects of human life are identified with nature and rapine in the mind of the agonized young man whose dark emotional conflicts bear a striking resemblance to Tennyson's own disturbances," in *Sex, Symbolism, and Psychology in Literature* (New Brunswick, N.J.: Rutgers University Press, 1948), p. 76.

25. W. D. Paden, *Tennyson in Egypt* (Lawrence: University of Kansas Press, 1971), pp. 17-23.

26. *The Works of Alfred Lord Tennyson*, ed. Hallam Tennyson, 6 vols. (New York: Macmillan, 1908), I, 655.

27. Isabel also closely resembles the poet's wife, in whom he discovered the same innocent, saintly femininity he yearned for. Physically both Emily Tennyson and Elizabeth Tennyson were small, delicate women, and both were remarkable for their gentle charity and simple piety. The fact that they were complementary models for Ida in *The Princess* again underlines their obvious resemblance. Surely there is much of Tennyson in the Prince who feels he first loved his lady through loving his mother.

Also interesting is the fact that Tennyson and Emily's father seem to have had much in common. Both were strong and vigorous men of six feet, three inches, and, according to Agnes Weld, Tennyson found much in Mr. Sellwood's personality that was congenial to his own nature. The two men were especially alike in "the determination to undergo any self-sacrifice rather than swerve one iota from the strictest truth and honour, and also the intense patriotism which, as it stirred my uncle to sing of his country's noble deeds, had made my grandfather long in his youth to emulate those deeds by serving in the campaigns then going on against Napoleon. I have often heard them talking of such deeds of valor as that Charge of the Light Brigade . . ." (Weld, "Tennyson," p. 3).

For a further treatment of Tennyson's inability to create a believable female character, see Gerhard Joseph, *Tennysonian Love: The Strange Diagonal* (Minneapolis: University of Minnesota Press, 1969), pp. 72-73. For a discussion of the destructive potential in many of his women, see Clyde de L. Ryals, "The Fatal Woman Symbol in Tennyson," *PMLA*, 74 (1959), 438-43.

28. See Rader, *Tennyson's Maud*, pp. 60-66.

29. *Memoir*, I, 331-32.

30. *Thomas Carlyle: Letters to His Wife*, ed. Trudy Bliss (London: Victor Gollancz, 1953), pp. 271-72.

31. *Memoir*, II, 472.

32. Quoted by M. A. DeWolfe Howe, "The Tennysons at Farringford: A Victorian Vista," *Cornhill Magazine* (October 1927), p. 450.

33. See William Empson, *The Structure of Complex Words* (London:

Chatto and Windus, 1951), pp. 44-46, 61-63. Thomas Woolner once wrote to Emily Tennyson (17 December 1856):

> All the best ladies I know are delicate. Mrs. Carlyle has been ill a long time; she scarcely sees any one and cannot get out and she looks dreadfully weak, it grieves me to look at her. Sir Walter and Lady Trevelyan are in town, but my pleasure has been shadowed in consequence of the same thing; she is so very weak and delicate. . . .

See Amy Woolner, *Thomas Woolner: His Life in Letters* (New York: Chapman and Hall, 1917), pp. 125-26. Hereafter cited as *Thomas Woolner.*

Elizabeth Barrett Browning was extraordinarily frail, and she never seemed to be really well. When Nathaniel Hawthorne visited the Brownings at Florence, he described his hostess as "a pale small person scarcely embodied at all," or at any rate only substantial enough to put forth her "slender fingers to be grasped, and to speak with a shrill yet sweet tenuity of voice." See "An Evening at the Brownings," *The Portable Hawthorne,* ed. Malcolm Cowley (New York: The Viking Press, 1969), p. 664.

34. Tennyson's own words from a letter to Emily. See *Memoir,* I, 169.

35. Rader, *Tennyson's Maud,* p. 69. Arthur Tennyson remembered meeting Emily at the time of his brother's wedding: "She read to me Milton's 'Comus,' which I had not known before and which I have loved ever since" (*Memoir,* I, 150). Although it seems that Tennyson was in love by May 1836, there is little indication of Emily's feeling for him before the quasi-engagement of 1838. In "For Her Sons" Emily merely noted that she once went with Alfred to see Charles and Louisa Turner at their vicarage in Tealby and that after that visit she remembered "nothing until the dreadful departure of the Tennysons from Somersby" in 1837. Certainly Emily would have considered the removal to High Beech "dreadful" because it was painful for the Tennysons themselves, but I think we may assume from Emily's statement that she also found it "dreadful" to be separated from Tennyson.

36. Tennyson sent the Marquis of Northampton, who was editing *The Tribute* (1837), the poignant lines beginning "Oh! that 'twere possible," which he had written two or three years before, after the death of Arthur Hallam. Tennyson later took these lines, which were published in *The Tribute* as "Stanzas," as the "germ" for "Maud."

37. From a letter to Richard Monckton Milnes, 10 January 1837, quoted by Sir Charles Tennyson, *Alfred Tennyson* (London: Macmillan, 1949), p. 167. Hereafter cited as *AT.*

38. About Tennyson's management of the settlement in High Beech, Emily Tennyson wrote in "For Her Sons": "People are apt to glance at poets as unpractical; all I can say is that your Father furnished the Tennysons' house at Beech Hill . . . throughout, not forgetting the kitchen. Pretty and inexpensive all I saw of the furniture was." She also remarked on the difficulty of managing a home "where all had sensitive nerves and none of the sons any work in life" (p. 98).

39. In "For Her Sons" she described in some detail one particular visit at High Beech during which she and Tennyson star-gazed together: ". . . a night of meteors came. He stayed up several hours and saw none. I stayed a little longer and saw no meteors but a magnificent Aurora" (p. 99).

40. *Memoir*, I, 165.

41. *Memoir*, I, 166.

42. Sir Charles has observed that the last date in the time sequence of *In Memoriam* is April 1838, the April immediately following the move to High Beech and Tennyson's engagement to Emily (*AT*, p. 177).

43. *The Complete Poetical Works of Tennyson*, ed. W. J. Rolfe, Cambridge Edition (Boston: Houghton Mifflin, 1898), p. 808 (note on Tennyson's comment to James Knowles about "Ulysses").

44. See *AT*, pp. 180–82.

45. See *Memoir*, I, 170–71. Hallam did not include the date, but in manuscript the letter is clearly dated, "October 24, 1839."

46. Earlier in this same letter there are three other sentences, just preceding the portion printed in the *Memoir*, which Hallam has excluded. They follow: "Thou hast proved time and space very prettily. So mayst thou and I and all of us ascend stepwise to Perfection. I chiefly meant by what I said to thee that where there is a mighty future before thee, thou shoulds't make it present by the hope that conquers all things."

Judging from these few sentences, one might surmise that Tennyson had written to Emily grumbling about his dissatisfaction with the immediate world of everyday experience and describing his perception of a truer, more real world beyond the physical. Just such a grumbling and just such a description are contained in a fragment that Hallam printed in the *Memoir*, I, 171–72: "Annihilate within yourself these two dreams of Space and Time. To me often the far-off world seems nearer than the present, for in the present is always something unreal and indistinct, but the other seems a good solid planet, rolling round its green hills and paradises to the harmony of more steadfast laws. Here steam up from about me mists of weakness, or sin, or despondency, and roll between me and the far planet, but it is there still."

The letter containing this passage must have been answered by a letter in which Emily "proved time and space very prettily." Quite characteristically she has attempted to show her unworldly fiance the opportunities for approaching blessedness and perfection in a God-given present. Although the "Annihilate within yourself these two dreams of Space and Time" fragment follows the 24 October 1829 fragment in the *Memoir*, the scraps are not all presented in chronological order, despite Hallam's contention to the contrary; e.g., the scrap dated "July 10" [1839] on page 171 immediately follows the fragment from the 24 October letter.

47. Situated on the Exmoor coast and facing a sheer drop of a hundred and fifty feet to the Severn Sea, Glenthorne House was built some time in the early nineteenth century by the Reverend W. S. Halliday, vicar of the church of St. John the Evangelist at nearby Countisbury. Whatever may be thought of its architecture, the house enjoys a singularly commanding view of the Welsh mountains, as well as the sea; and

it lies on the popular coastal route from Lynmouth to Minehead, which also passes Ashley Combe, the seat of Lord Lovelace, whose first wife was Byron's daughter Ada. Although there is no definite indication that Tennyson was acquainted with Halliday or his family, the poet must have visited the Glenthorne estate en route along the Exmoor coast, following the same path traced by Coleridge on his famous jaunt from the Quantocks in the company of Hazlitt and hero-worshipping John Chester.

Apparently Emily Sellwood regretted that she had not had the opportunity of accompanying her fiance to see Glenthorne. Or perhaps Tennyson had actually visited at the estate, in which case his absence from home and from Emily may have prompted her "moments of jealousy." In any case, there is no evidence suggesting that Emily resented Tennyson's relationship with any specific *person* at Glenthorne.

48. A misquoting of *Pericles,* V. i. 203–204:

> For truth can never be confirmed enough,
> Though doubts did ever sleep.

49. Weld, "Tennyson," p. 5.

50. Jerome Buckley, *Tennyson: The Growth of a Poet* (Boston: Houghton Mifflin, 1960), p. 75.

51. See *AT,* p. 179.

52. Hallam Tennyson, *Materials for a Life of A. T.,* II, 38. Ralph Rader also cites Symington's account to evidence that Tennyson and Emily themselves made the decision to separate (see pp. 69–70).

53. "For Her Sons," p. 100.

54. See *AT,* p. 181.

55. *Memoir,* I, 166.

56. Arthur Sidgwick described "Love and Duty" as "a passionate tragedy, the parting of two lovers at the call of duty. . . . The vision of dawn (11.92–98) is a *hope* for *her,* now that the new life, apart from each other, has to begin for both of them. . . . The passion barred from its issue rushes into new channels, and the exalted mood finds its only adequate vent in the rapturous vision of a future dawn, the symbol of his hopes for her, those hopes into which his sacrificed love is translated" (H. Tennyson, *Tennyson and His Friends,* pp. 330–31).

57. From 1842 to 1846 Henry Sellwood was in partnership with another solicitor, J. W. Covington, himself from an old Lincolnshire family. He sold his share to Covington in 1846, then bought it back again almost immediately, but in 1848 sold out to a Samuel Sketchley and left the town. (My informant is Mr. J. Norman Clarke, Woodhall Spa, Lincolnshire.)

58. "Recollections," p. 7.

59. In 1844, after the collapse of Dr. Matthew Allen's woodcarving project, "so severe a hypochondria set in upon [Tennyson] that his friends despaired of his life" (*Memoir,* I, 221).

60. "For Her Sons," p. 99.

61. *Memoir,* I, 214.

62. *AT,* p. 240.

63. "For Her Sons," p. 101.

64. See *Memoir*, I, 220-21; *AT*, pp. 186-88.

65. *AT*, p. 210.

66. Wilfrid Ward, *Aubrey DeVere: A Memoir* (London: Longmans, 1904), p. 72.

67. For Tennyson in *The Princess,*

> either sex alone
> Is half itself, and in true marriage lies
> Nor equal, nor unequal. Each fulfils
> Defect in each, and always thought in thought,
> Purpose in purpose, will in will, they grow,
> The single pure and perfect animal,
> The two-cell'd heart beating, with one full stroke,
> Life. (VI, 283-89)

68. See *Memoir*, I, 250.

69. The Prince's "weird seizures" first appeared in the fourth edition of *The Princess* (1851).

70. H. Drummond Rawnsley, *Memories of the Tennysons* (Glasgow: J. MacLehose and Sons, 1900), p. 71.

71. H. D. Rawnsley commented on Emily Tennyson's letters to his mother: "It has been one of my life's privileges to see the letters that passed in those days, before the marriage was arranged, letters in which she always used the thou and thee in addressing my mother, after the quaint fashion of the time—letters which she usually signed 'thy affectionate sister' " (*Memories of the Tennysons*, p. 71).

72. H. D. Rawnsley, *Memories of the Tennysons*, p. 71.

73. Willingham F. Rawnsley, *Tennyson, 1809-1909: A Lecture* (Ambleside: George Middleton, 1909), p. 19.

74. Unpublished letter, TRC. Apparently Tennyson and Colquhoun took the water cure together at Umberslade Hall in the spring of 1847.

75. John Olin Eidson, *Tennyson in America* (Athens, Ga.: University of Georgia Press, 1943), p. 74. Eidson quotes from Higginson's 1850 letter to his mother in which he recounted the story of Tennyson's courtship related to him by his Harvard friend, William Henry Hurlbut, who had just returned from a visit to England.

76. Ward, *Aubrey DeVere*, p. 67.

77. W. Aldis Wright, ed., *More Letters of Edward FitzGerald* (London: Macmillan, 1902), p. 22.

78. Ward, *Aubrey DeVere*, p. 146.

79. After an eleven-year separation, Emily's sister and Tennyson's brother were reunited, and he held the Grasby living until their deaths in the spring of 1879. Charles had changed his name to Turner when he inherited the Grasby estates of his uncle, Sam Turner, in March 1835.

80. Rader, *Tennyson's Maud*, p. 79 (quoted from Mr. Symington's narrative in *Materials for a Life of A. T.*).

81. *AT*, p. 242.

82. "For Her Sons," p. 101.

83. C. F. G. Masterman, *Tennyson As a Religious Teacher*, p. 191.

84. Ward, *Aubrey DeVere*, p. 158.

85. W. F. Rawnsley, *Lecture,* pp. 20-21.

86. Quoted in W. F. Rawnsley, *Lecture,* pp. 20-21.

87. In July Tennyson wrote to John Forster, who had expressed indignation at not being informed of his friend's intention to marry: "Come, Forster don't be angry with me. . . . I told nobody not even her who had most right to be told my own mother. She was not angry, why should you be? It is nothing but the shyness of my nature in everything that regards myself . . ." (*AT,* p. 244).

88. See Appendix B for speculations on the importance of Emily Tennyson's wedding dress.

89. "For Her Sons," p. 102. The "perfectly ideal marriage" is Charles Turner's phrase, according to Symington's account in H. Tennyson, *Materials for a Life of A. T.,* II, 39.

90. *The Princess,* VII, 265.

91. *Memoir,* I, 329.

92. Ward, *Aubrey DeVere,* pp. 158-59. In the previously cited 24 September 1854 letter to Miss Fenwick, DeVere wrote a good deal more about his high opinion of Emily Tennyson: "I can hardly say how deeply interesting she is to me. She is a woman full of soul as well as mind, and in all her affections, it seems to me that it is in the soul, and for the soul, that she loves those dear to her. . . . I regard her as one of the 'few noble' whom it has been my lot to meet in life; and with a nature so generous, and so religious a use of the high qualities God has given her, I cannot but hope that the happiness accorded to her after so many years of trial, may be more and more blessed to her as the days go by. She is a person to whom you will be greatly drawn whenever you are near her . . . (pp. 227-28).

In a letter of 10 November 1854, to Emily herself (unpublished, T.R.C.), DeVere expressed, briefly, something of his satisfaction in the conditions he had found during his stay at Farringford earlier that autumn: "I must not try to tell you what a delight it was to me as one of Alfred's old friends, to sit by his hearth, and see what manner of hearth it is. I shall not soon forget it, nor the kindness that made it a domestic hearth to me also." After Tennyson's death, DeVere again recalled the 1854 visit: "Dear Lady Tennyson, I need not tell you how much you and he whose happiness on earth came chiefly from you . . . have been in my thoughts and my poor prayers. I find my thoughts also constantly reverting to that happy fortnight which I passed with you both at Farringford, I believe in 1854 or thereabouts, when all things went well with you and those two beautiful children were always near you. Surely all good things in the past are a pledge of better still in the world that lies before us" (unpublished letter, T.R.C.).

93. Ward, *Aubrey DeVere,* p. 159.

94. Joanna Richardson, *The Pre-Eminent Victorian* (London: Jonathan Cape, 1962), p. 66.

95. Basil Champneys, *Memoirs and Correspondence of Coventry Patmore* (London: G. Bell and Sons, 1900), I, 197.

96. *Thomas Carlyle: Letters to His Wife,* ed. Trudy Bliss (London: Victor Gollancz, 1953), p. 271.

97. Richardson, *The Pre-Eminent Victorian,* p. 63.

98. Harold Nicolson, *Tennyson* (Boston and New York: Constable 1923), pp. 156-57.

99. Nicolson's view recalls John Addington Symonds's impression of Emily and may even reflect an acquaintance with his description. Symonds was struck by her "monastic" appearance, her "calm expression" and "white features." She is "too shy to be known at once," he declared, though she leaves "an impression of an indefinite charm and sweetness." See *The Letters of John Addington Symonds,* ed. Herbert M. Schueller and Robert L. Peters (Detroit: Wayne State University Press, 1967), I, 512. In fairness to Nicolson it must be noted that he does sense something of the incompleteness of his description. He wonders "whether the accepted picture of the sweet, spiritual, self-effacing lady in the shawl and the grey dress," a picture he has perpetuated, "is wholly fair. There was something more positive in Mrs. Tennyson than the evanescent, wistful charm which is generally attributed to her" (Nicolson, *Tennyson,* p. 157).

100. Nicolson, *Tennyson,* p. 157.

101. Champneys, *Coventry Patmore,* II, 305.

102. "Maud," III, vi, 33.

103. James Knowles, "Aspects of Tennyson," *Nineteenth Century* 33 (January 1893), 188.

104. Alfred McKinley Terhune, *The Life of Edward FitzGerald* (London: Oxford University Press, 1947), p. 127.

105. Quoted by James Pope-Hennessy from a letter of April 1872, to Richard Monckton Milnes, *Monckton Milnes: The Flight of Youth* (London: Constable, 1951), p. 58.

106. Quoted by Annie Fields, *Authors and Friends* (Boston and New York: Houghton Mifflin, 1924), p. 352.

107. Quoted by Howe, "The Tennysons at Farringford," p. 450.

108. Fields, *Authors and Friends,* pp. 352-53.

109. *Memoir,* II, 467. Before Jowett's first visit to Farringford in 1853, Tennyson was somewhat uncomfortable about inviting a cleric and a don to the intimacy of his home, but both he and Emily were delighted with their guest, and Jowett became an intimate friend and a regular Christmas visitor for nearly forty years (*AT,* p. 279). When Jowett's essay on atonement in his book *The Epistles of St. Paul* (1855) was attacked as unorthodox, and again when his contribution to *Essays and Reviews* (1860) prompted his opponents at Oxford to accuse him of heresy before the vice-chancellor's court, the Tennysons gave him their loyal encouragement and support.

Jowett corresponded primarily with Mrs. Tennyson, confiding to her the ups and downs of his Oxford affairs. In a 22 March 1861 letter, he wrote, "I cannot but express to you what I feel, especially in all this tumult, that it is the greatest blessing and good to me to have friends like you and Mr. Tennyson, who are so true and affectionate to me" (Evelyn Abbott, ed., *The Life and Letters of Benjamin Jowett* [London: John Murray, 1897], I, 356). Years later when he heard that the Laureate was dying, he attempted to comfort Emily Tennyson: "I am grieved to hear that life is slowly passing away. No one at this hour has a greater sorrow than yours—to lose the partner of your life, who was also the most distinguished man of his age. And no one has a greater consolation in the remembrance of the happy unclouded past, and in the unshaken faith that you are rendering him up to God. . . . There is a friend to whom you have been wonderfully kind for thirty-five years, and have shown him never-failing sympathy and not grown tired of him during all this long time—he too hopes that he may be able to say or do something which will soothe your life by reminding you of days gone past." Again on 4 October 1892, Jowett wrote to the woman to whom he felt he and his entire age owed an incalculable debt: "You have the satisfaction of knowing that you have contributed to that great life in a manner that no one else could . . . and that he has the most simple and absolute love of you; and that you have never been for an hour parted in sorrow or in joy" (Abbott, *Benjamin Jowett*, II, 419, 457).

110. All four versions of "Helen's Tower" are preserved in the Tennyson Research Centre. At the bottom of the last version, the one he later printed, Tennyson wrote to Dufferin: "This my wife likes best: she is most likely right." Emily's discernment in the selection of her husband's "best" poetry was in fact remarkably acute. However, her judgment in the selection of titles for his poems was perhaps less infallible. The title *In Memoriam,* her choice, is probably inferior to his original *The Way of the Soul.* At least it says much less about the poem and really misrepresents it and subtly deflects its meaning. Also there is much to be said for Tennyson's idea of following *Idylls of the King* with *Idylls of the Hearth,* the original title for the *Enoch Arden* volume which Emily persuaded the Laureate to change.

111. Willingham F. Rawnsley, "Personal Recollections of Tennyson," *Nineteenth Century,* 47 (February 1925), 195.

112. A. Patchett Martin, *Tennyson and the Isle of Wight* (London, 1898), p. 7.

113. W. F. Rawnsley, "Personal Recollections of Tennyson," p. 195.

114. Alexander Jones, "Mark Twain and Sexuality," *PMLA,* 71 (September 1956), 616.

115. See Ricks, *The Poems of Tennyson,* p. 1214n.

116. Arthur Paterson said of the picture of Emily Tennyson that George Frederick Watts completed in 1863, "It is a wonderful piece of characterization; . . . the great artist has caught the prevailing quality of the face—the tenderness and spirituality—a face not wanting either in its lines of strength." See Helen Allingham and Arthur Paterson, *The Homes and Haunts of Tennyson* (London: Adam and Charles Black, 1905), p. 80. The portrait is now located in the Tennyson Room in the Usher Art Gallery at Lincoln.

117. Theodore Watts-Dunton, *The Athenaeum,* 15 August 1896, p. 227.

118. Professors Edgar F. Shannon and Cecil Y. Lang of the University of Virginia are presently preparing a complete edition of Tennyson's letters.

119. Anne Thackeray Ritchie has catalogued some of the Tennysons' most prominent visitors: "The very names of the people who have stood upon the lawn at Farringford would be an interesting study for

some future biographer—Longfellow, Maurice, Kingsley, the Duke of Argyll, Locker, Dean Stanley, The Prince Consort. . . . Here came Clough in the last year of his life. Here Mrs. Cameron fixed her lens marking the well-known faces as they passed—Darwin, Browning, and Henry Taylor, Watts and Aubrey DeVere, Lecky and Jowett, and a score of others." See *Records of Tennyson, Ruskin, and Browning* (London: Macmillan, 1892), p. 44.

120. The manuscript Journal, an epitome made for Hallam Tennyson while he was working on his *Materials for a Life of A. T.*, is in the Tennyson Research Centre. The Journal is in very poor condition, owing largely to Hallam's practice of hacking it up to paste portions into his drafts for the *Memoir*. The quotations from the Journal included in this volume are designated by date of entry. When the text surrounding the quotation makes the date of entry obvious, no citation is given.

121. F. T. Palgrave's phrase. See *Memoir*, II, 512.

122. Quoted by Richardson, *The Pre-Eminent Victorian*, p. 67.

123. Quoted by Frieda Fordham, *An Introduction to Jung's Psychology* (London: Penguin, 1953), p. 33.

124. Quoted by Richardson, *The Pre-Eminent Victorian*, p. 76.

125. Bram Stoker, *Week Ending*, 21 October 1899.

126. Unpublished letter, T.R.C.

4 Seamore Place
Park Lane
Dec 6th 1873

My dear Mr Browning,

Having seen you
once we are all the
more greedy of seeing
you again during
our short stay here.
May we hope that you
will give us this pleasure
by dining with us
on Tuesday Dec 16th.
at seven o'clock?

affectionately yours
Emily Tennyson

A facsimile of Lady Tennyson's handwriting.

The Letters

1   To Emily Jesse[1]
Wellesley

[Horncastle, July 1844]

Dearest dear Emmie,

I fear I have been very selfish. I have pressed thee too much to
write. I have not enough remembered that One alone can
measure the capabilities of any living creature and woe be to
the man who dares pronounce his fellow can do this or that if
he would. Forgive me, dearest Emmie, it has been . . . a
selfish fear lest thy love for me had departed; a selfish desire to
have those anxieties relieved which sprang from my interest in
another. And yet strange that it should have been thus! I so
often thought of thee much as thou really wert. Oh well do I
feel from this, and numberless things, that there are thoughts
opposed to the ruined nature of man which he may constantly
entertain in his mind and still they will have no effect because
He the Life Giver is not invoked to give them a quickening
power.

Dearest Emmie, I know that to none canst thou describe
those things which are now passing within thee. I hope I shall
not teaze thee again. Only promise me that if any day thou
shouldst feel it would be a comfort to open thy heart to me
thou wilt speak; indeed, indeed I shall not be wearied or at
least I would fain flatter myself I shall not be such a wretch.

Wilt thou not go with Alfred into Wales?[2] Thou knowest I
am very jealous that he is thine brother and thou mayst go. And
would he not cheer thee and would not mountains and free air
cheer you both. And what shouldst say [illegible] to meet thy
old torment t'other Emmie in a Welsh vale? We have
speculated on a tour in North Wales. Somewhat wildly, it may
be though, but perhaps the autumn may tell me.

And wilt thou say whether it bores thee to read my scrawls.
Tell truly whether I shall write—ay or no. I will do either and
ask no reply. For fear however the no's should have it, I had
better not prolong this. Indeed I began it on this small sheet
thinking thou art probably rather I should say possibly on thy
way to Paris. . . .

Fare thee well. From my heart I thank thee for having made
that painful effort to write to me. I hope I shall not drive thee
to it again.

1. Tennyson's sister Emily, who had been Arthur Hallam's fiancee, married Richard Jesse early in 1842.
2. During the summer of 1844 Tennyson journeyed into Wales, where he climbed Mount Snowdon three times.

2   To Catherine Rawnsley
Harvard

1 April 1850

. . . Do you really think I should write a line with the "Elegies,"[1] that is a separate note, to say I have returned them? I am almost afraid, but since you say I am to do so I will, only I cannot say what I feel. . . . You and Drummond are among the best and kindest friends I have in the world, and let me not be ungrateful, I have some very good and very kind. The longer I live the more I feel how blessed I am in this way. Now I must say goodbye.

I thought I would write my note[2] before the others came. Here it is, no beginning nor end, not a note at all, a sort of label only:

Katie told me the poems might be kept until Saturday. I hope I shall not have occasioned any inconvenience by keeping them to the limit of the time; and if I have I must be forgiven, for I cannot willingly part from what is so precious. The thanks I would say for them and for the faith in me which has trusted them to me must be thought for me, I cannot write them. I have read the poems through and through and through and to me they were and they are ever more and more a spirit monument grand and beautiful, in whose presence I feel admiration and delight, not unmixed with awe. The happiest possible end to this labour of love! But think not its fruits shall so soon perish, for they are life in life,[3] and they shall live, and as years go on be only the more fully known and loved and reverenced for what they are.

So says a true seer. Can anyone guess the name of this seer?[4] After such big words shall I put anything about my own little I?—that I am the happier for having seen these poems and that I hope I shall be the better too.

I cannot enter things more particularly with him. I only hope he will not be vexed by this apology of a note.

1. Tennyson's original title for *In Memoriam* was simply *The Elegies*. Emily chose the final title in May 1850.

2. This note to Tennyson which Emily "was almost afraid to send" (W. F. Rawnsley, *Lecture*, p. 19), offers her heartfelt praise of *The Elegies* and indicates something of their effect on her opinion of the poet. However, the tone of the entire letter, including the note to Tennyson she reproduces, indicates that she "was still far from a definite understanding with him" (*AT*, p. 242). Her diffidence and her reluctance to address Tennyson may perhaps be explained by her earlier refusal of his proposal. Ralph Rader thinks that the circumstances of the refusal were explained to Mrs. Rawnsley in a missing portion of this letter (Rader, p. 82).

3. Both Alfred and Emily Tennyson were fond of such expressions. In a letter of 14 June 1865 (unpublished, T.R.C.) to Mrs. Thomas Woolner, Mrs. Tennyson wrote of her regret that Mrs. Woolner had not been able to accompany her husband on a recent trip to Oxford: "When one has once been blessed with the double solitude the single solitude except for some rare hours of life has lost its charm, has it not? The life in life so doubles life." Also see Tennyson's early poem "Life of the Life within my blood" (Ricks, *The Poems of Tennyson*, pp. 504–05).

4. Apparently Charles Kingsley. (See *Introduction*, p. 17 above for Emily's remarks on Kingsley's role in her decision to marry Tennyson.)

3   To Catherine Rawnsley
Harvard

14 June 1850

My dearest Katie,

I know you and Drummond will rejoice to hear I am as happy and comfortable as ever you could wish me. I must write again to tell you where to direct to us, probably somewhere near Weston-super-Mare, if not there.[1] I owe you a great deal. Please tell my Daddy all except the *In Memoriam*.[2] I am going directly. My best love and all thanks for kindnesses innumerable.

1. After spending the wedding night in Pangbourne, the Tennysons traveled to Weston-super-Mare on their way to Clevedon where they visited Arthur Hallam's grave.

2. Emily Tennyson's instruction to Kate Rawnsley not to tell Henry Sellwood about the part *In Memoriam* played in her decision to marry indicates that she had not fully informed her family of the reasons for her acceptance of Tennyson.

4   To Charles and Louisa Turner

Weston-super-Mare, 17 June [1850]

My dearest Louisa and Charley,
I am ashamed to write to you. We have every day after the very first talked of writing, both of us. Yours is the only note[1] I have yet seen with my new name. I cannot tell you how good Alfred is to me. Poor thing! he has got such a bad cold; he will take all the care of me and none of himself. We have stopped here because we both needed rest not because it is beautiful. We have only taken the lodgings till Saturday but I hope we may hear from you before we go. I hope you have had a note from Kate telling you all about us. She promised to write you one. I hope also you have got cake, gloves, favour. I wish you could both have been there. The smell and sight of real orange flowers was almost the only sign of a wedding. I am baby enough to be sorry I did not wear my white dress. Ally would have liked it but I took him literally about travelling dress. It was very pleasant to have Cissy and her husband[2] there. They were good to me more than I can say. . . . I bought a real ring brooch, the vest, and nearly a shawl with your five pounds! I fully meant to have written to you the last day before our wedding day but both Alfred and Mr. Lushington were in town from Monday[3] so even the most necessary shoppings had to be done as they could. . . .

You will wonder perhaps what brought us hither. It was my wish to see Clevedon and Arthur Henry Hallam's tomb.[4] I think we shall soon take a house and probably near town. I write lying down so forgive the scrawl. Write to me and then I hope I shall so be able to send you a better note.[5]

1. Charles Turner wrote a letter to the Tennysons postmarked 13 June 1850, but obviously written a day or so before (unpublished, T.R.C., the final paragraph was printed by Hallam Tennyson in the *Memoir*, I, 330). Charles's expectations for the marriage are free of any hint

of Mary Tennyson's superstitious forebodings. He believes that the newlyweds will "pass along most sweetly and happily together to a good old age full of all the blessings pronounced over you by God's messenger. . . . Good wishes in crowds from me I dispatch on doves' wings to you!" Charles Tennyson's appreciation of the wisdom of Tennyson's choice is worthy of the brother who was ever the poet's favorite. According to Mr. Symington's account to Hallam Tennyson of negotiations for the marriage, Charles believed all during the ten-year separation that his brother and Emily Sellwood "were mutually made for each other. He always regarded your father's and mother's union as a perfectly ideal marriage" (Rader, p. 80).

Emily's apology for having written no sooner refers to a comment in Charles Tennyson's letter: "I hope Emmy dear you will not follow your good man's example about letter writing; for I really shall be grieved if you do not let me hear how you both fare from time to time." Tennyson was a notoriously unreliable and erratic correspondent, as he freely admitted. He wrote to Emily from London in 1839: "My friends have long since ceased to write knowing me to be so irregular a correspondent. A brief and terse style suits the man, but the woman is well when she deals in words" (*Memoir*, I, 174). So far as letter-writing was concerned, it was primarily Emily Tennyson, rather than her husband, who "dealt in words" during their forty-two years of marriage. Evidently Tennyson's reluctance to write letters was somewhat characteristic of the Victorian male. Discussing the correspondence between the Tennysons and the Granville Bradleys, penned almost entirely by the wives, Margaret Woods (née Bradley) explained that "Men had already for the most part abandoned the practice of letter-writing outside their business and families, but Victorian women fed the flame of friendship with a constant flow of ink" (H. Tennyson, *Tennyson and His Friends*, p. 176).

2. Tennyson's sister, Cecilia, and her husband, Edmund Lushington, whose marriage (1842) Tennyson celebrates in the epilogue to *In Memoriam*.

3. The marriage was on Wednesday, 13 June.

4. Emily Tennyson wrote of their trip to Clevedon (the first for both) in "For Her Sons": "It seemed a kind of consecretion for us to go there where Arthur Hallam was buried." Hallam Tennyson included her comment in the *Memoir* (I, 332) with no indication that these are Emily's words. The newlyweds spent the night in Clevedon Court, home of Sir Charles Abraham Elton (1778–1853), Sixth Baronet, whose daughter Julia was the wife of Henry Hallam, the historian, and the mother of Arthur Hallam.

5. A variety of physical handicaps made writing difficult for Emily Tennyson. Because of her chronic spinal trouble she usually wrote from a reclining position, and a wrist injury she suffered in early youth made writing all the more difficult. Her wrist stiffened as she grew older, and her sight was very poor during the last fifteen years of her life.

On 20 June 1850 the Turners replied in a joint letter (unpublished, T.R.C.) which underlines their confident approval of the marriage of their "dear double sister and long-single brother": "We were both of us delighted to see your note. The happy strain thereof did only answer my expectations. I thought Alfred would pet and nurse and take care of his wife. . . . Kate told me you had a merry wedding. . . . I am glad you talk of taking a house; it sounds more cozy than roaming about. More as if you expected to find that in one another which would take away the necessity for running about for amusement."

5   To Ludovic Colquhoun[1]
Brotherton Library, University of Leeds

Park House, Maidstone, 26 December [1850]

Dear Mr. Colquhoun,
I am very sorry your kind notes should have remained so long without answer. You will, I am sure, forgive Alfred when I tell you how he has been employed, but first let me say how much we thank you for all your kind wishes. . . . When we have a house will you not come and let us try to cheer you a little and nurse you into better health.

Would I could tell you we have already a home of our own. We never had any intention of living permanently at Tent Lodge though most kindly pressed to do so by our Coniston friends,[2] but the damp climate did not suit either of us very well although Alfred appeared before we left to have got over its effects to a great degree. We have been here more than two months with most affectionate and agreeable relations and friends but our longing for a house has kept us from enjoying their society as much as we should otherwise have done.

Poor Alfred has been house-hunting in various directions and is sadly tired of the work. He has also been correcting his three books for new editions. *In Memoriam* is done, the others not.[3] Therefore I hope you will as I said before excuse his silence and I will now add accept this note of mine instead of one from him until he has a little more leisure for writing.

It was with great difficulty his friends here prevailed on him to accept the Laureateship.[4] Indeed a note of acceptance and one of refusal were actually put into the same envelope that at the very moment only of sending one to the post it should be determined which. His dread of levees and court balls and increased publicity caused this unwillingness originally and has since made him regret that it was overcome so far as it was.

I fear I shall be wearying you by all this chatter so I will only add my husband's kindest regards.

1. (1807–54), a Scottish friend with whom Tennyson had become acquainted while the two men were taking the water cure together at Dr. C. M. Gulley's establishment at Umberslade Hall in the spring of 1847. Colquhoun was a great admirer of Tennyson's poetry, and he wrote some poems himself. In a letter of 10 July 1850 (unpublished, T.R.C.), Tennyson thanked Colquhoun for his approval of *In Memoriam* and commented that since his friend had already obtained a copy of the paper, he would not send him another: "I do not think you want a presentation copy from me as a *proof* of my regard for you. Ovid says I think that women's vows are writ in water. Our friendship commenced under hydropathic auspices. May it last when douches and sitzbaths redden the spines and posteriors of unhappy patients no more." Colquhoun sent a sonnet to the Tennysons in 1852 celebrating the birth of their son Hallam.

2. The Tennysons stayed at Tent Lodge, Coniston, the home of James Marshall and his wife Mary, the sister of Tennyson's old Cambridge friend Stephen Spring-Rice, from the end of July until mid-October when they set about looking for a permanent home.

3. There were three editions of *In Memoriam* in 1850, a year in which Tennyson also published the third edition of *The Princess* and the sixth edition of his 1842 *Poems.*

4. On 5 November 1850 Tennyson received a letter from Windsor Castle offering him the Laureateship. He had heard little of the controversy which had been going on since Samuel Rogers's refusal in the spring, and the offer came as a complete surprise.

The Tennysons soon found their first home, a very old house at Warninglid, near Horsham, in Sussex, which they occupied on 20 January 1851. Initially they were impressed by the comfort of the house and by what Emily Tennyson termed a "beautiful Copley Fielding view" of the South Downs. The morning after their arrival Tennyson went for a long walk, and it seemed that the birds were singing as he had not heard them since leaving Somersby. Emily brought an excellent cook and housemaid with her; and Richard Monckton Milnes (1809–85, afterwards Lord Houghton), who had previously offered them a wing of his own home, Fryston, and Tennyson's sister Matilda also helped the couple unpack and "made matters much easier than they otherwise might have been" (Journal, 21 January 1850).

Their pleasure was short-lived, however, for a great storm blew down the bedroom wall the second night of their residence. The noise and wet of the storm made sleep impossible, and Tennyson and Emily passed the remainder of the night reading some of the books they had unpacked only the evening before. Not long thereafter they discovered that part of the house had once been a Roman Catholic chapel and that a baby was buried in the garden. More recently a notorious band of cutthroats, known as the Cuckfield gang, had actually lived in and operated from the lodge. These revelations, along with the realization that no postman came within reach of the house and that the nearest doctor was five miles away, dictated the decision to look immediately for another home.

Tennyson and Milnes investigated other houses in the neighborhood, and when they found nothing appropriate, Warninglid was abandoned. Tennyson drew his bride all the way to Cuckfield in a wheeled chair lest she should be too much jolted traveling the rough road by carriage. From Cuckfield they returned to Shiplake, arriving on 3 January at the home of the Drummond Rawnsleys, where they found Charles Kingsley and Drummond's father, the Rev. Thomas Hardwicke Rawnsley. After two weeks of unsuccessful house-hunting, they set off for a visit with the Lushingtons at Park House. En route they spent the night of the eighteenth at the Clarendon Hotel, where Emily fell down some steps, "though warned by him a minute or two before," sprained her foot, and made herself very ill for several days thereafter. Two days later the Tennysons arrived at Park House, where Emily was for some time ministered to both by a physician and by the poet, who doctored the sprained foot "water-cure fashion" (Journal, February 1851).

Tennyson went to London on the twenty-third to make arrangements for attending the Queen's levee in his honor as the new Laureate and to look for a suitable residence. While staying in Frank Lushington's rooms he met Henry Taylor, who took him to see Chapel House, Twickenham, the Early Georgian house which was soon to become the Tennysons' home. Returning to town on 3 March, after a single day back at Maidstone, Tennyson attended a party at Lord John Russell's, dined with the James Marshalls on the fifth, and next day signed the lease for Chapel House. On the eighth Emily sent servants ahead to Twickenham, and two days later she and Tennyson left Park House, slept at Rochester, and next morning were agreeably surprised by the arrival of Grigsby, the Park House coachman, sent to look after their baggage. At London Bridge Station they found waiting for them the Marshalls' "delightfully luxurious carriage with butler and coachman and groom," and, "thanks to all this care and kindness," they took possession of Chapel House under most promising circumstances.

Following visits from James Spedding, Coventry Patmore, James Marshall, Henry Taylor, Charles and Louisa Turner, and Emily's father, the Tennysons enjoyed a month of quiet and relaxation waiting for the birth of their first child. After breakfast Tennyson took short walks about Twickenham and Richmond, but they were "duty walks and alas! without pleasure," quite unlike the long walks in the open country which he had found so pleasant during their short stay at Warninglid. On 20 April their baby son was born dead, "an alabaster bust of his father," as Emily described him in the Journal. Very likely the fall on the journey from Shiplake to Maidstone had proved fatal for the unborn child. Again the Tennysons gladly received guests, and during the next month or so they entertained the Carlyles, the William Brookfields, Henry and Julia Hallam, William Allingham, and John Everett Millais, who was struck by Emily's beauty and expressed a desire to paint her. As time passed, however, the Tennysons were troubled by an increasing number of unannounced visits from strangers, and they grew less satisfied with Chapel House because of its public accessibility. In her next letter, addressed from Mrs. Elizabeth Tennyson's home at Cheltenham, Emily indicated that Chapel House was not what they had expected, but that they might be compelled to settle permanently in some such residence, although far removed from what they desired. By late June, Tennyson had determined to take his wife on an anniversary trip through Italy, for a time at least leaving unwanted guests and imperfect houses behind them.

6   To James Spedding[1]

10 St. James's Sq., Cheltenham, 7 June [1851]

My dear Mr. Spedding,

It was very good in you to send us that pleasant letter full of news of our friends but I did not mean to have said thank you for it until I could also say we hope to be at Twickenham on such a day, pray come and see us. However, I write now, though I can tell you nothing of our return except that we mean to go back as soon as some of the family come back from Brancepeth[2] where all now are with the exception of our mother, whom we cannot leave alone, but I write at Alfred's bidding. . . . He will not, I fear, be at Twickenham so soon as the 17th or he might offer you a seat in the Queen's box which is promised him on the occasion.[3]

We have most moving tales to tell of bad houses, and bad titles but no hint of some perfect home. I am only afraid of our taking up in despair with an exceedingly imperfect one. We have a great deal to say to you of other things, naughty sceptic that you are, when we meet—which we hope will be so soon that we will not write a word of it. We are very sorry about Mr. Forster.[4] How is he now? Our kind remembrance to him.

1. (1808-81), author and essayist, editor of *The Works of Francis Bacon* (1857), a former Cambridge Apostle, and Tennyson's lifelong friend. Spedding first met Tennyson's bride at the Speddings' home, Mirehouse, in Keswick, in July 1850, when the newly married couple were on their way to visit James and Mary Marshall. He subsequently gave Aubrey DeVere "an excellent account of Mrs. Tennyson, saying that she is very good, sensible, and anxious to make her husband write poetry. She is thirty-seven years old, and has much beauty, and they are happy together" (Ward, *Aubrey DeVere,* p. 158). Again Spedding was "deeply impressed with Alfred's happiness and serenity" when he dined with the Tennysons at Chapel House on 11 March 1851 (*AT*, p. 261).

2. Brancepeth Castle, the ancient home of the Neville family, in Durham. In 1797 Dr. George Tennyson's elder sister Elizabeth married Major Matthew Russell, the son of William Russell, a wealthy industrialist who had purchased Brancepeth. When his parents died, Major Russell moved his family to Brancepeth and began an extensive restoration of the castle, upon which he reportedly spent £80,000 a year for several years. Russell died in 1822, but his widow lived on for nearly fifty years. Although there was considerable animosity between Elizabeth Russell and Dr. Tennyson, Mrs. Russell often assisted her Somersby nieces and nephews during the hard years that followed Dr. Tennyson's death. Sir Charles notes that "she was always ready to help with money and was regarded with great affection by her nephews and nieces" (*AT*, p. 30). In 1828 Gustavus Frederick Hamilton (1797-1872), Seventh Viscount Boyne, married Emma Maria (d. 1870), daughter of Major and Mrs. Russell, who succeeded to Brancepeth Castle in 1850, on the death of her brother. At the time of this letter, then, the Boynes were master and mistress of Brancepeth.

3. The Queen had offered the Laureate her box in the Crystal Palace for the Great Exhibition of 1851, which she opened on 25 February. Instigated largely by the Prince Consort, the Exhibition was intended to promote industry and commerce and to inaugurate an era of peace.

4. John Forster (1812–76), Dickens's friend and biographer and, from 1847 through 1856, editor of *The Examiner,* in which Tennyson first published "Britons, Guard Your Own," "The Third of February, 1852," and "Hands All Round" (all three in 1852), and "The Charge of the Light Brigade" (1854). Forster always shared and supported Emily Tennyson's high opinion of the *Idylls of the King.* "Enid" was his favorite, and in a letter to Emily on 9 May 1857 he wrote: "It is a great word to say that Alfred himself never wrote anything more exquisite than this poem, but it has so strongly affected me, that I dare confidently to say as much. I cannot detect a flaw. It goes to the very bottom of the depths of truth and tenderness" (H. Tennyson, *Materials for a Life of A.T.,* II, 181).

7   To Henry Sellwood

Paris, 20 July [1851]

My dearest Daddy,

I have been longing to write to you. We are here with Cissy and Edmund[1] and we waited for them at Landgate till Tuesday last. Had I known we should have had to wait I should have written to ask you to let me hear again from you before we left England. . . .

We have had time for little else but [sightseeing] and unpacking and entertaining or being entertained by Mr. and Mrs. Browning. Whether she thinks being a poet's wife entitles me to rank with poetesses I know not but she has been extremely kind and even kissed me on parting. They are just come from Florence where they have been living four or five years. We have got valuable hints and promises of assistance from them particularly in the way. . . .[2]

1. Edmund and Cecilia Lushington.

2. The remainder of the letter is missing. On the way to Florence the Tennysons stopped in Paris, where they visited with the Brownings, who were en route home from Italy. Emily Tennyson and Elizabeth Barrett Browning were immediately drawn to each other, and Emily recorded that Mrs. Browning, "very fragile looking . . . with great spirit eyes," greeted her "more as a sister than a stranger." Tennyson offered the Brownings Chapel House for as long as they should care to reside

there, and Browning was deeply touched by the kindness. Emily Tennyson was always impressed with Browning's loyalty to Tennyson despite the Laureate's far greater public acclaim. "Having the greatest gifts he never got his due need of praise from the world," she wrote of him in her Journal entry on the Italian journey. Hallam Tennyson also touched on the Tennyson-Browning friendship: "These two brother-poets were two of the most widely read men of their times, absolutely without a touch of jealousy and revelling as it were in each other's power" (*Memoir*, II, 229-30).

8   To Elizabeth Tennyson

Bagni di Lucca, 13 August [1851]

Dearest Mother,

. . . We arrived here last evening, and to our great surprise saw Richard Jesse walk in just as we had finished tea. He had heard of our arrival from Mr. Garden at whose house Ally had called;[1] he is very kind in helping us. Emily[2] we have not yet seen. . . .

There seemed to be something very touching when on two occasions the priests bowed as they passed us, a sort of acknowledgement of universal brotherhood. Do not think from this I am likely to turn Romanist.[3] On the contrary from what Mr. Garden says there is great probability many Romanists may turn Protestants for there is a feeling both amongst priests and people that the people should read the Bible not that either one or the other have said this openly nor even distinctly whispered it to themselves. It seems at present to be little more than a dim feeling of want, of something wrong in their religion. . . . We are both pretty well. This valley though reputed the finest in Tuscany will not detain us very long unless we find on mounting the hills that the views are as enchanting as they are reported to be.[4] Here below where we are we see nothing but very steep wooded heights and a few houses, and the trees of Italy are saplings compared to our forest trees, those at least that we have seen. Still though Ally does describe these lands in the words "flies, fleas, filth, flame," and "fraud" perhaps he might say, you must not think there has not been much to delight us. I am decidedly stronger for my journey.

1. The Tennysons stayed for three weeks at the Baths of Lucca in the house of a Giorgio Basantino. While there, Tennyson visited with the Rev. Francis Garden, an old friend from the Arthur Hallam circle at Cambridge, who was assistant minister of the English Chapel at Rome from 1851 to 1852. In 1859 Garden succeeded Dr. Charles Wesley as sub-dean of the Chapel Royal, a position he held until his death in 1884.

2. Emily Jesse.

3. Emily Tennyson was always strongly distrustful of Roman Catholicism. Aubrey DeVere, himself a Catholic, wrote to Isabella Fenwick on 14 October 1850 that Tennyson's wife had "a great horror of Rome" and that at Coniston he had refrained from discussing theology with her for that reason (Ward, *Aubrey DeVere*, pp. 159-60). Less judicious was Baron Th[eodore?] H. de Schroeter, a friend of Sir John Simeon, Roman Catholic squire of Swainston Hall, near Newport, eight miles east of Farringford. Baron de Schroeter was a frequent guest of the Tennysons during an August 1854 visit at Swainston, and he devoted all of his apparently enormous Catholic zeal to the conversion of the Laureate's family. The Tennysons were "much impressed by the deeply felt religious enthusiasm of the Baron, who was like an old ascetic monk" (*Memoir*, I, 377), but Emily thought his arguments unduly coercive, and she wrote him a letter to that effect. (The letter has not survived, but its purport is obvious from the Baron's reply of 23 September 1854, unpublished, T.R.C.) De Schroeter expressed to Emily his gratitude for her letter, "which was such a pure expression of that extraordinary gentleness with which God has adorned your soul," but he assured her that she had misunderstood him if she thought it his intention to force upon her his religious persuasion. "My wish can only be to impress you with the necessity to take the religious question into a mature consideration," he wrote, "nay to make it the principle and only object of your inquiries and studies, till you have arrived at a clear and decided conclusion of the question. . . ." The religious question had always been and would remain the principal object of Emily Tennyson's scrutiny, but she never came to view that question through the Baron's eyes.

4. The Tennysons were well satisfied with the views, both natural and domestic. They rejoiced in "The glorious violet colouring of the mountains" and were equally pleased by "the sight of the peasants . . . , beating out the flax with their distaffs or spinning, and the children playing at ball" ("For Her Sons," p. 105). Late in the summer of 1853 Tennyson recalled to his wife the pleasing enchantment of their Italian tour in "The Daisy," which he wrote in Edinburgh, upon finding in one of her books a flower he had picked for her on that holiday. "The Daisy" is a charming verse epistle notable for its evocation of remembered Italian landscapes and for its testimony to the love which makes those scenes dearer in remembrance, even as it had made them more vital when first they were shared. Evidently time had worked its ministry of forgetfulness upon Tennyson's memory of Italy's less alluring views, for only the most splendid are preserved in the poem:

O Love, what hours were thine and mine,
In lands of palm and southern pine;
    In lands of palm, or orange-blossom,
Of olive, aloe, and maize and vine!
What Roman strength Turbia show'd
In ruin, by the mountain road;
    How like a gem, beneath, the city
Of little Monaco, basking, glow'd!

(ll. 1–8)

9   To Edward Lear

Chapel House, 4 December [1851]

What a choice "wedding present" and how very gratifying the
words that accompany your kind gift! Accept, my dear Sir,[1] our
best thanks. Very often shall we delight ourselves by looking
upon those beautiful drawings, which give one, as Alfred said
of one in particular, something of the glory of nature herself
looking upon them and now that we have seen views in a
measure similar they have the additional charm of reminding
us of these.[2]

When you can and will take the trouble of coming to us, let
it not be for a call but from Saturday to Monday and we will
try to get Frank Lushington[3] to come too that you may have
the more agreeable recollections of Twickenham and be
tempted to come again and again. Alfred begs to join me in
hearty thanks and best remembrances.

1. Though Emily's first letter to Lear is somewhat formal, her subsequent letters to him are infused with a touchingly sincere tenderness
and a real affection. It was Lear who in 1859 decided, "computing
moderately, that 15 angels, several hundreds of ordinary women, many
philosophers, a heap of truly wise and kind mothers, 3 or 4 minor
prophets, and a lot of doctors and schoolmistresses fall far short of
what Emily Tennyson really is" (*AT*, p. 317).
2. Lear was in Italy from 1837 until 1845, and the drawings he gave
the Tennysons were undoubtedly Italian landscapes from that period.
3. (1823–1901), brother of Henry and Edmund Lushington; Judge
to the Supreme Court of the Ionian Islands, 1855–58. In September
1855, the Tennysons selected Franklin Lushington to be official guardian
of their sons, Hallam and Lionel, in the event of their own demise.
Lear first met Lushington in Malta in 1849, and he developed for him

an intense affection which ultimately brought him great unhappiness. Although he probably did not realize it, Lear's attraction to Lushington was almost certainly homosexual, and Lushington's failure to return his love intensified Lear's chronic despondency. Vivien Noakes posits that "if Lushington had loved and encouraged him, theirs might have developed into a full homosexual relationship." Though Emily Tennyson may have been unaware of the sexual subtleties of Lear's love for Lushington, she understood the tortured extremity of his feelings, and in her letters to Lear "she comforted him as she might have done a young boy in love for the first time. More than anyone she realized the depth of his craving for affection, and Lear come to adore her." See Vivien Noakes, *Edward Lear: The Life of a Wanderer* (Boston: Houghton Mifflin, 1969), pp. 134, 128.

10   *To Coventry Patmore*
Boston College

Chapel House, 28 January [1852]

Dear Mr. Patmore,
We have distributed all the notices except two. It is really refreshing to see such earnestness of energy as yours. Who knows but when the secrets of all things are known you may in this instance be proved to have mainly contributed to the safety of your country.[1]

Will you not come on Saturday, Mrs. Patmore and yourself, and then you and Alfred can talk things over together. It seems to me he can be no more than an honorary member of your club (and an honorary member of such a club seems an absurdity), as you know we are trying to get a house in the country as soon as we can. . . . At all events do not speak of him as an "agitator" for any cause whatsoever. Neither him nor yourself if I might be so bold as to say so. The word has come to have so evil a meaning, a sort of hysterical lady meaning if nothing worse. I know you will be disappointed at not getting an answer from Alfred but I thought these hasty lines would be better than nothing.

1. The Tennysons had circulated notices for the organization of the volunteer rifle corps which Patmore was initiating. With this letter Lady Tennyson sent Patmore her husband's "Rifle Clubs!!!," one of a number of political poems of early 1852, after Louis Napoleon's December coup d'état had made war imminent (see Ricks, p. 996). Tennyson did not

join a rifle corps, but the publication of his "Riflemen Form!" in *The Times* on 9 May 1859, promoted the foundation of the Volunteer Force at a time when the outbreak of the Franco-Austrian War had again impressed Tennyson with the necessity for emergency national-defense measures.

11   *To Julia Margaret Cameron*[1]

Ritchie, From Friend to Friend, *p. 8*

Chapel House, 25 June 1852

My dear Mrs. Cameron,
We are by every post expecting a letter about a house which may send us in another direction, but I am not going to drag you house-hunting even on paper. My husband would, I am sure, listen with the most hearty interest to you. The East[2] is a great inspiring theme. Would that his brother Horatio were doing something there . . . he could have made a grand soldier of the old school.[3] You would like him if he were not too shy to show himself as he is. He is living with his mother, but we will with all pleasure bring him. I am going to let Mrs. Henry Taylor know when we can say with any certainty when we shall be at home. Hoping that you and they will be able to come to us.

1. (1815-79), wife of Charles Hay Cameron, the former president of the Indian Law Commission; famous for her portrait photography, as well as for her volcanic energy and her extragavant generosity. Introduced in the summer of 1852 by the Henry Taylors, the Tennysons and the Camerons, who were then living near Twickenham at Sheen, began a friendship which was to mature nearly a decade later after the Camerons settled permanently on the Isle of Wight.
    Tennyson was particularly fond of Mrs. Cameron, though she was forever pestering him and inveigling him to submit to a variety of eccentric demands. The poet often complained that Mrs. Cameron's portraits gave him much unwanted publicity, but he would endure for her sake what he would tolerate from virtually no one else. Perhaps the most successful and memorable of all the pictures she took of Tennyson is the 1865 "Dirty Monk" photograph, which Mrs. Cameron described as "A column of immortal grandeur—done by my will against his will" (quoted by Brian Hill, *Julia Margaret Cameron: A Victorian Family Portrait* [London: Peter Owen, 1973], p. 111).
    Mrs. Cameron was as attached to Emily Tennyson as she was to the poet, and she actually preferred to visit with her alone: "When

he is with her, I do not often go up. They are so complete in themselves"
(*AT*, pp. 324, 236). Mrs. Cameron had no sense of ever having done
enough for either Tennyson or his wife. She may have planned her
long, intimate visits with Emily for times when Tennyson would be
away from home, but she might arrive at any time, "entering by the
door, by the drawing-room windows, always bringing goodwill and
life in her train. She would walk in at night followed by friends, by
sons carrying lanterns, by nieces, by maids bearing parcels and photographs" (Ritchie, *From Friend to Friend*, p. 24). No votary, no friend
ever came to Farringford more warmly received or more lovingly
responsive than Julia Margaret Cameron.

   2. That is, India, where Cameron served from 1835 until 1848.

   3. Horatio Tennyson (1819–1899), youngest brother of the poet,
wanted to enlist in the army, but the suggestion so grieved his mother
that he went instead to try his fortune in Tasmania.

By the end of June the search for another house had to be given
up temporarily, as Emily was expecting her second child in
August. During the final week of the month Tennyson became
reacquainted with Archibald Peel, son of General Jonathan Peel
of Marble Hill, whom he had first met in 1851; and he accompanied Peel to Marble Hill, where his host pointed out the Richmond
Park Avenue where Scott placed the interview between Jeanie
Deans and Queen Caroline in *The Heart of Midlothian*.

   The Tennysons spent much of the first week of July alone
reading and talking in their little garden. Franklin Lushington,
the Coventry Patmores, and Thomas Woolner came to dinner,
and Tennyson occasionally strolled through the grounds at Marble
Hill. On the seventh Tennyson left for London and James
Spedding's rooms, on his way to Whitby and the sea, where
he hoped to rid himself of a prolonged attack of hay fever. While
he was away, the Charles Welds and Henry Sellwood came to
visit, as did George Stovin Venables, the barrister, *Saturday
Review* critic, and former Cambridge Apostle. Emily's father
remained until Tennyson returned, evidently before the beginning of August. Emily wrote the following letters of invitation
to the Brownings only two days before she gave birth to Hallam,
who arrived at least a week sooner than expected.

12   *To Elizabeth Barrett Browning*
Charles S. Hutzler

Chapel House, 9 August [1852]

My dear Mrs. Browning,
Right welcome will you be. I wish we could put off the time to a day more convenient to you than Friday but my doctor names the 15th as the latest day on which I may move to town. If it were not so I would say pray come here for several days and see all that is pleasant around us. As it is I am obliged to talk about dinner. Half past 5 is the hour our friends generally choose because of the quicker train which brings them down for that hour. Will this suit you?

I will not give you the trouble of writing again if it do, but if it do not, if you fear the night air or if any other cause make you wish to fix another hour, do so, we beg.[1]

1. London engagements and Hallam's premature birth prevented the Brownings from coming to Chapel House at this time; however, they wrote a joint congratulatory letter to the new parents (see *Memoir*, I, 357-58), which so moved Tennyson that he was unable to read it aloud to his wife, but put it by her bedside that she might read it herself as soon as she could read anything (*AT*, p. 269). The very day of the birth Tennyson wrote of Emily to Mrs. Browning: "I never saw any face so radiant with all high and sweet expression as hers when I saw her some time after." And in writing the news to John Forster, he declared he "never saw anything more beautiful than the mother's face as she lay by the young child an hour or two after . . ." (*Memoir*, I, 356-57).

13   *To James Spedding*

Twickenham, 30 September 1852

Dear Mr. Spedding,
You have been very badly treated as one's best friends are apt to be. The fact is, Alfred has out of pity for me written more letters these last few weeks than ever he wrote in his whole life before I do think and then he has been every day, even from the very first, so weary of them, he was secretly glad to avail himself of the excuse of not knowing where you were not to write this one more letter to you.

Since I have been able to write I have meant it daily but since I have been able baby has had a cold and I know you will not laugh very much at me if I say he has taken almost all my time and strength. I wish there were any chance of your being at his christening next Tuesday though in order to protect against all you naughty infidels we have been constrained to get Maurice to be one of the sponsors,[1] Mr. Hallam is another, Mrs. Marshall the third, or the first if I shock your courtesy by saying third. His name is Hallam. They will not let me call him Alfred.

The Henry Taylors have a splendid boy, as I dare say you know. Alfred is to be one of his godfathers. You must forgive me if I can write of nothing but babies. I really would not talk much about them though if you would come.

Charles and Louisa gave us the last news of you. They are here. How thin they both look! They recall vividly the pleasant days we spent with you and yours by telling of their wandering in your country.

1. Hallam Tennyson was christened at Twickenham on 5 October. The Christian Socialist F. D. Maurice (1805–72) had been a leading Cambridge Apostle prior to Tennyson's election to the society, and he was always a dear friend of the Tennysons, who again evidenced their regard for him after his forced resignation from his professorship at King's College, London, in October 1853. In his lines "To the Rev. F. D. Maurice," written in January 1854, Tennyson voiced his protest against the persecution of theologians who refuse to cower before bigoted authorities in the universities and the Church. He assured Maurice that "one lay-hearth" would always welcome him, even if "all our churchmen foam in spite" at his refusal to accept every orthodox interpretation of Scripture. When Maurice finally did visit Farringford in the autumn of 1858, Emily wrote of him, "I never saw anyone, except perhaps one, who seemed so to commune with the Most High" (*AT*, p. 314).

14 To James Spedding

Twickenham, 21 October [1852]

Dear Mr. Spedding,

I am sorry we are going away just when you are about to return but I believe we must go for baby's cold continues and mine too that I got at the christening and here we live in such gloom and mists when all the world talks of bright sunshine that we cannot reasonably expect to get well, but I have been so happy here I do not want to go and I hope we shall come back for the winter. . . .[1]

All kind things to all yours. Alfred is gone for a day to Park House. I have taken the opportunity of doing all sorts of bills and such disagreeable things[2] so I am very stupid. Charles has been several days at Park House. They will both come back for baby this evening.

1. Heavy floods in the Thames meadows increased Tennyson's dissatisfaction with Twickenham, and, leaving Chapel House in late October, he took his family first to Park House and then to Seaford, Brighton, and Farnham. The Tennysons were particularly hopeful of finding a new home in Farnham, but they failed to locate anything appropriate and returned to Twickenham before Christmas.
2. All of the household account books preserved in the Tennyson family papers are in Emily Tennyson's hand.

15   *To Frederick Tennyson*
Hugh J. Schonfield
Letters to Frederick Tennyson, *pp. 107–8*

Seaford, 9 December 1852

[1]. . . was lowered into the vault. After the funeral[2] Ally went to Shiplake to stand for Drummond Rawnsley's last child, Alfred Edward.

We have been here, that is at Seaford, a lovely seaplace between Beachy Head and Brighton, as I dare say you know, these six or seven weeks. We have a comfortable house, one that belongs to Lord Howard,[3] far from Skeggie [Skegness, Lincolnshire] bareness and desolation. It has a garden moreover with a high ivy-coloured arched wall dividing it and with urns and vases and balustrades besides. . . . It looks pleasant on sea and down, which has been fortunate for us since I, at least, have scarcely left the garden, the weather has been so stormy. The sea therefore of course fine. Great white-headed waves leaping up every moment from behind the shingle-banks and looking at us. Twickenham is still our home though, for we were disappointed in our hope to get a house which we should like to buy at Malvern, and we have not been able to find one yet elsewhere.

But two or three days ago Dunbar Heath's book[4] was sent to me by Mr. Peel of Bonchurch. . . . Of a book which we have purchased and which arrived at the same time Ally has read me a little. It is Hangstenberg's *Christology of the Old Testament;* we like much that we have seen of it. We have also got his *Psalms.*[5]

A little pamphlet, a collection of letters on mesmerism from Edinburgh papers, by Dr. Gregory,[6] would interest you, I think. Strange stories too we have heard lately of a house in London said to be haunted and now deserted by all except an old porter who does not fear the spirits, and who is paid to live there because the spirits have twice foretold it is to be burned down, and there is a fear some not altogether spirits may take the realisation of the prophecy into their own hands if the house is left unguarded. This is a huge volume; I will add no more except kind love from us both to you all.

1. The first page of the letter is missing. Schonfield also prints a postscript from Tennyson, p. 108.
2. The Duke of Wellington was buried in St. Paul's on 18 November.
3. Charles Augustus Ellis, Sixth Baron Howard De-Walden (1799-1868). Lord Howard succeeded as Second Baron Seaford, 1 July 1845.
4. *The Future Kingdom of Christ,* 2 vols. (1852-53).
5. Ernst Wilhelm Hangstenberg, *Christology of the Old Testament, and a Commentary on the Predictions of the Messiah by the Prophets,* translated by R. Keith, 3 vols. (1836-39); *The Psalms,* translated and explained by J. A. Alexander (1850), founded upon Hangstenberg's translation and commentaries.
6. Dr. William Gregory (1803-58), author of *Letters to a Candid Enquirer on Animal Magnetism* (1851), and numerous other works.

16   *To Ludovic Colquhoun*

Brotherton Library, University of Leeds

Seaford, December [1852]

Dear Mr. Colquhoun,
Many thanks for the sonnet. We both of us like it very much. Baby seemed charmed with it and will I am sure do more than seem some day. I really think he had an inkling it was

something for him. Did Ally tell you the good story about his name which is making the round of certain London circles? Mr. Hallam telling it with as much glee as anyone. He says, "Alfred Tennyson said to me, 'My friends will not let me call him Alfred but he should be a fool'; and so he called him Hallam." I need not tell you like many other good stories this is too good to be exactly true.[1]

I think we shall return home for Christmas so that if you are coming south we shall be more easily reached than here. I could live very contentedly here all my life looking on the sea and the headland and the bit of down. I might sometimes give a passing sigh for large trees to be sure, but only a passing one.

Do you know touching "Brother Jonathan"[2] I have not been fairly dealt with as I expressly stated I thought the petition might possibly exasperate the evils rather than diminish them and I have not signed and will not sign it. They should not have taken such unfair advantage of my saying I felt much interested in the subject. They ought only to have put my name to some general expression of such interest. However, it is best to let such things pass quietly for with my whole heart I hate the idea of women obtruding themselves into public affairs,[3] and I do not wish to call anyone's attention to the fact of my name appearing as if I had been meddling with them. The only women who have anything to do with them further than thinking and feeling about them at home are heiresses who represent families there. I think they should, when they have large estates, be allowed to have proxies in the House of Lords if noble and proxies for votes if commoners or the interests of many may suffer.

I am tired and stupid but I could not let a post go without thanks for the sonnet, without telling you how much we admire and value it and that we shall keep it very safely for our boy.

1. According to Sir Charles, it was Henry Hallam who first said, "I suppose they wouldn't call him Alfred for fear he might turn out a fool" (*AT*, p. 270).

2. The nickname of the American nation, as "John Bull" is of the English.

3. Emily Tennyson subscribed to her husband's opinion that woman, though man's equal, must never be his rival or his antagonist. Also see below, Letter 354. The first serious demand for women's suffrage in the United States was made at a meeting in Seneca Falls, New York,

in July 1848. Evidently some American suffragettes had sought Mrs. Tennyson's support, and she felt they had taken improper advantage of her interest in their cause.

Although only one letter written during 1853, a rather uninformative note to James Spedding, has turned up, the Journal provides helpful supplements to Sir Charles's account of the Tennysons during that year. In May they visited the Charles Kingsleys at Eversley. Mrs. Kingsley was immediately taken with Emily, and the day after their departure she wrote to her: "Your face is continually before me and so is the thought of your child. I cannot believe that I saw you yesterday for the first time,—it seems so very natural to me to know and love you" (*AT*, p. 273). Late in July Tennyson left his wife and son with the Turners at Grasby and journeyed into Scotland with Francis Turner Palgrave, the poet and critic who later was Tennyson's companion on trips to Portugal in 1859 and to Cornwall in 1860.

Tennyson and Palgrave parted at Glasgow, where Tennyson visited an old Cambridge friend named Menteith at his home on the Clyde. He then rejoined Palgrave, and the two spent several days with William Seller, the Virgil scholar, after which they traveled to Loch Fyne, Inverary, Carstairs, Staffa, and Iona, and finally to Edinburgh, where Tennyson fell ill and was cared for by Ludovic Colquhoun. As soon as he was able, the poet journeyed to Grasby and thence, with Emily and Hallam, to Twickenham.

Early in the autumn, while visiting at Bonchurch on the Isle of Wight, Tennyson heard of Farringford, at that time owned by a family named Seymour, from friends who thought it might make him a suitable home. Before he returned to Chapel House, Tennyson went to the east end of the island to see Farringford, but he arrived in the midst of a rainstorm and thought the house looked wet and wretched. Nevertheless, he soon brought Emily to Farringford, and she at once decided in favor of the isolated Late Georgian house. Looking eastward from the drawing room windows across the High Down and across Freshwater Bay to St. Catherine's Down in the distance, Emily decided that she would have to have that view, and her wishes determined Tennyson's decision to lease Farringford furnished for a year, with the option of purchasing.

A quaint, picturesque country house, Farringford stands about a mile from the southern shore of the Isle of Wight on a little eminence just north of the high chalk cliffs which rise five hundred feet above the sea. Although the land attached to the house became the property of one Walter de Ferringford in the fourteenth century, Farringford itself was not built until around 1800. Some time before the Tennysons acquired the house, the windows, shutters, and interior paneling had been redone in the Gothic motif, and the large drawing room had been added on the east side, making Farringford a fifteen-room house.

Despite its spacious views, Farringford was as secluded as Tennyson could have wished. Dense pine, elm, holly, and laurel sequestered it on the north and south sides; a thick belt of elms stretched behind the house; and to the east lay the great cliffs and the sea. Arthur Paterson has observed that "no wild bird's nest was ever better hidden" than was Tennyson's house in 1853 (Allingham and Paterson, *Homes and Haunts,* p. 18), and certainly that solitude must have been impressive which made two of Emily's maids "burst into tears saying they could never live in such a lonely place" when the Tennysons occupied Farringford on the morning of 25 November. Nonetheless, though unwanted intruders were discouraged for some time, the Tennysons were soon entertaining friends, who found the distance from London no great obstacle. Edmund and Franklin Lushington, Edward FitzGerald, Spedding, Lear, Arthur Hugh Clough, and Tom Taylor, the art critic and playwright, were among their first guests. Matilda Tennyson also came, and Emily's next letter to Tennyson relates to Matilda's proposal to return to Farringford with her mother to make a permanent settlement.

17   To Alfred Tennyson

Farringford, 30 January [1854]

Dearest,
I fear Tilly has shown sad want of tact in what she has said to Mother. I said what I did to Tilly when Mother had hurt me by speaking as if we were striving with the Jesses to get her to live with us as matter of gain. Do not think however I said anything in the very least unkind even then. It sounds harshly

put as Mother has put it but these were not my words.

I have written and said to her, "It would be a source of unhappiness and reproach to me all the days of my life if I kept you out of our house when you wished to come and live with us. What I meant to express to Tilly was, that it rather hurt me you should have spoken as if you thought we wanted you to live with us as a matter of help in a money point of view when your comfort and happiness alone made us think of the plan. Dearest Mother and Tilly, I entreat you as far as I am concerned to do exactly what you like best." Then I have added I was sure I spoke thy feelings too and I have said again that I had that perfect trust in herself and Tilly and that affection for them that I felt sure we should get on most lovingly together and that it would be a happiness to us to do anything we could to make them happy. . . .

I have told them as we should have to build and alter if they lived in the house with us I thought it best they should come first and try how they liked it, and I have added Mother must not think of that long journey to Twickenham for that I will look to the packing. Of course she is wholly unequal to it. I hope thou wilt approve of what I have done.[1]

1. Mrs. Elizabeth Tennyson never resided at Farringford for any length of time. She lived at Chapel House and then at Rosemount, Hampstead, until her death in February 1865. Matilda Tennyson was virtually a permanent "guest" from 1865 until Tennyson's death.

18   To Drummond Rawnsley
Harvard

Farringford, 3 May [1854]

My dear Drummond,

We want you to be one of baby Lionel's[1] godfathers. Will you kindly consent notwithstanding your strong suspicions of our want of orthodoxy? Mrs. Russell is the godmother-elect and I believe we shall ask Frank Lushington to share the sponsorship. Could you manage to be here on Ascension Day if this be one of the days on which Mr. Isaacson will baptize? We have only the choice of the last Sunday in every month and

Saint's days. I do not know whether Ascension Day would, for this purpose, be held on one of these.[2]

Dearest Katie, we hope you will come too. I trust I shall be pretty strong by that time. I have improved very much within the last week. Monday alas! was a rainy day so did not get to church. There is a beautiful rain again today which will do the country great good.

1. Lionel Tennyson was born on 16 March 1854. When Tennyson heard of the birth, he was in his little study under the bedroom, star-gazing. He had just been watching Mars culminating in the Lion, and that sight afterwards determined the baby's name. Emily Tennyson had a difficult time after Lionel's delivery. She was particularly troubled by insomnia which, after nine sleepless days, Tennyson cured by hypnosis.

2. Lionel Tennyson was christened on 6 June, with Franklin Lushington as one godfather and Edward FitzGerald, who had been at Farringford since 25 May, standing proxy for Drummond Rawnsley. Emma Maria Russell Hamilton (Lady Boyne), rather than her mother, Elizabeth Russell, was the designated godmother; but Emily herself stood for Lady Boyne, who had been thrown from a carriage and was confined to Brancepeth during early June.

19   *To Alfred Tennyson*

Farringford, 19 August [1854]

Own dearest,

I feel sick at heart thinking of thy disappointment when there was no letter yesterday and of all thy anxiety the livelong day afterwards. I can only hope thou hast returned to Wells and hast found the two letters which wilt set thy mind at ease.[1] Since I must love thee better than myself I cannot help hoping thou hast gone into South Wales or wherever thy fancy leads thee because thou oughtest to reap more than such a little from a journey of so many miles. Well, dearest, I went agadding yesterday in the donkey-chaise and I took Gandy[2] and baby and Hallam with me and first we called at Mrs. Cotton's. . . . Even we could not but have been satisfied with all that was made of our tinies. Then we went just to look at the sea and there were carriages and staring men and women galore and besides Captain Crozier and Miss Crozier who of course made

many inquiries about thee.[3] Miss Crozier seemed in high glee
at having got close to the Queen the other day at the Cowes
Regatta[4] and seen her run from one end of the ferry to the
other with all her children after her.

I showed Hallam thy dear letter this morning and
immediately he said, "Papa," and examined every part of the
picture with great interest. . . . At night I read Ruskin and
played some Mozart.[5] I will not agree with Ruskin's definition
of architecture.[6] He ought rather to have said it is "the art of
expressive form or fitting ornament in building," I think, and I
think it the more that part of this definition hints all the
so-called fine arts and only requires a distinctive addition or
omission to make it define every one of them. What beautiful
anecdotes he tells of poor Turner and how one wishes one
might have done something to soothe his spirit and make his
life happy. What he says too of the happy and independent life
of the workman I like much.

1. Tennyson left Farringford for Christchurch on 12 August in the
company of Alexander Grant (1826–84), later tenth baronet of Dalvey,
vice-chancellor of the University of Bombay (1863), and principal of
the University of Edinburgh (1868). After parting from Grant at Glastonbury, Tennyson went on to Yeovil and Wells, where he received this
letter, and thence to Cheddar, and he subsequently returned home on
the twenty-first.

2. A Farringford maid.

3. Among the Tennysons' few near neighbors, the Cottons and the
Croziers appear numerous times in both the letters and the Journal.
Benjamin T. Cotton, the Conservative candidate for Parliament from
the Isle of Wight in 1879, married a sister of Lady Grant (née Susan
Ferrier), and their daughter Tiny was one of Emily Tennyson's most
intimate young friends. The reference here is to William Pearson Crozier,
Captain, R.N., West Hill, Freshwater. Colonel Richard Pearson Crozier
(1842–1906) lent Tennyson his yacht, the *Assegai,* for trips to Exmouth
and Jersey in the summers of 1891 and 1892.

4. An annual celebration on the Isle of Wight.

5. Emily Tennyson was a fine pianist, and she composed as well,
setting many of her husband's poems to music. On 13 March 1891,
seven of her songs were sung at a concert at St. James's Hall, produced
by Mlle. Janotha, the famous Polish pianist; and Janotha subsequently
often included one or more of Emily Tennyson's songs in her concerts.
Hallam Tennyson's note in a book of his mother's settings preserved
in the Usher Gallery, Lincoln, indicates that she composed her songs
after hearing Tennyson read the verse she was to set, and that her
settings were intended to give an impression of the poet's readings.

6. In his addenda to a lecture on architecture delivered 1 November
1853, Ruskin spoke of the necessity of turning "dead walls and dead

roofs . . . into living ones . . . and that is to be done by painting and sculpture, that is to say, by ornamentation. Ornamentation is therefore the principal part of architecture, considered as a subject of fine art." See *The Complete Works of John Ruskin,* ed. E. T. Cook and Alexander Wedderburn (London: Macmillan, 1904), XII, 84.

20   *To Edward Lear*

Farringford, 12 October [1854]

My dear Mr. Lear,
I asked Mr. Millais[1] for your address and then stupidly forgot it and wrote to Frank Lushington and begged him to say to you, "Will you come to us at Christmas?" You know you will be right welcome only I am afraid you have already a hundred invitations and so we have no chance of seeing you. . . .

I wish we could ask [Frank] to meet you but we have not the heart to try to steal him from Park House then; nor should we, I suppose, succeed if we did try. However, if you do anything wicked of this kind whether you succeed or fail we will not betray you. Alfred's love.

1. John Everett Millais (1829-96), the Pre-Raphaelite painter, was a close friend of Lear's. From 22 to 25 October, Millais visited at Farringford, where he made sketches of Emily, Hallam, and Tennyson.

21   *To John Forster*
Usher Art Gallery

Farringford, 6 December [1854]

Dear Mr. Forster,
Will you kindly put this into *The Examiner* for Alfred? It was written yesterday[1] as a recollection of the first report of the *Times* which gave the number as 605. He prefers "six hundred" on account of the metre but if you think it should be altered to 700 which from later accounts seems to have been the number he says you are to alter it.

What dreary news! How one wishes to be some kind bird of fabulous size and power to carry warm clothing and nourishing

food to the poor soldiers and death and destruction to the
enemy.

We hope you are well. . . . We know you are to do that part
of the fighting that has to be done at home, and how much this
is!

1. "The Charge of the Light Brigade" first appeared in *The Examiner*
on 9 December 1854. The specification of 5 December as the date
of composition contradicts Hallam Tennyson's statement that the poem
was written on 2 December (see *Memoir*, I, 381).

22   To Edward Lear

Farringford, 16 December [1854]

Dear Mr. Lear,

Thank you for your kind letter but indeed there was no need
for it. I have so strong a feeling of the uncertainty of all human
things that I mean to burn it at once. I see clearly that whether
you wish or not you positively must come here that little
Hallam may make you laugh when he takes up his drum as he
did the other evening and when I asked him where he was
going, "To battle," he said. The good time will come, only be
of good cheer, hard indeed it is when you have so many causes
for sadness[1] but I remember when I first met you the tone with
which you said one Sunday evening, "I can only sing Sunday
songs today," and I feel sure you must understand what those
words mean, "Sorrowful but always rejoicing."[2] We cannot
dispute the first sight of your old friends to you and we will
yield it with a good grace if only you promise as far as we
mortals may promise to come.[3]

1. The winter of 1854 was perhaps the worst Lear had known. His
asthma was unusually troublesome and his throat constantly sore, and
he suffered epileptic attacks as often as twenty times a month. Also
Franklin Lushington's affection for him had cooled noticeably since
the days of their carefree spring together in Greece in 1849, and Lear
was saddened by Lushington's indifference.
2. 2 Corinthians 6: 10.
3. Lear had returned at the beginning of October from Switzerland,
where he had gone to escape the "gloom and cloud and mud and
beastliness" of England (Noakes, *Edward Lear*, p. 125).

23   *To Edward Lear*

Farringford, 21 December [1854]

My dear Mr. Lear,
I want you to see the bairnies. I am so afraid Hallam should
lose some of his old-picture beauty before you see him. Alfred
is not well. Some London doctor who was here in the summer
said this was too completely a sea-place to be good as a
constant residence though very good if change were had. Ally
has only been a fortnight out of the island for more than a year,
and I not a moment. We find it too expensive living here to
allow ourselves much change.

24   *To Frederick Goddard Tuckerman*[1]

Farringford, 8 February [1855]

My dear Sir,
My husband bids me write without delay to tell you he has
received the volumes of Poe you so kindly promised him and
strange to say from the last guest who preceded yourself in our
house, Mr. Palgrave. We hope this may be in time to spare you
the trouble of looking after the books. Perhaps his letter and
mine will reach you by the same packet for he wrote to you
two days ago and I cannot refrain from adding my assurance to
his of the great pleasure your letter and your gifts have
afforded him. The bright iris berries you put up in the card
racks are there still, so you see you have a kind of visible
presence by our hearth still, a pledge, I hope, that you will be
there yourself in your actual presence before very long.
    If you at all feel as we do, and I cannot but think you do so
feel, of the brotherhood of America and England as of the
bond never to be broken, you will grieve for us in our present
state.[2] The one comfort we have is in the heroic endurance of
our soldiers and I cannot rate this low, but how sad it is words
cannot tell. Sometimes, however, I dare to hope when I think
of "the cloudy porch"[3]—yes hope even for our officials.
    My husband joins me in all kind remembrances. We see
ships did not leave port that stormy day so we hope you have

escaped the worst of what we feared you had had to encounter
and that you will very soon be safe and happy with your little
ones.

1. Tuckerman (1821-73), the Massachusetts sonneteer, and his brother
visited with the Tennysons, 12-15 January 1855.
2. During January and February 1855, conditions among the British
troops in the Crimea were particularly bad, and public opinion began
to turn against the war and against the politicians responsible for its
mismanagement. The privations and extreme cold, coupled with epi-
demics of cholera, dysentery, and malaria, placed 14,000 men in camp
hospitals, and had there not soon been reinforcements from home, the
British force would have ceased to exist.
3. In "Love and Duty" the poet suggests that good may come out
of evil and "Sin itself be found/ The cloudy porch oft opening on
the sun" (ll. 9-10).

25   To Thomas Woolner[1]

Farringford, 29 March [1855]

Dear Mr. Woolner,
Many thanks for your kind letter. We cannot quarrel with you
if you borrow a little sunshine from imagination to throw over
your visit to Farringford, however puritanical we may be in our
worship of truth.

If you think the tone of the enclosed letter sufficiently
encouraging, Alfred hopes you will go and look at the statue by
Roubillac in Cambridge and then if you would like to see the
mask taken after death which is at the Royal Society, Somerset
House, I will send a letter to our brother-in-law, Charles Weld,
the acting secretary.[2]

Thanks to you, Alfred has had a very kind letter from Mr.
Ruskin offering to show him the Turners.[3] You will be glad to
hear his face has been tolerably easy. . . .[4]

Hallam is obliged now to make the best he can of his
mother. His chief delight is Mr. Burchell[5] and he exclaims,
"Fudge," with roars of laughter a hundred times together. He
insists on having this book and no other after dinner. Alfred
laughs at me because I maintain it is on account of the superior
grace of the designs.

Little Lionel lifts his hands in a very pretty way to the
Madonna and child when he comes into the drawing room and

says, "Lady," "pretty," "baby." If you could not admire his taste you would at least like to see him clap his little hands as he does sometimes at this picture. . . . I have another letter to write so farewell. There are three more tiny poems added to "Maud."[6]

1. Amy Woolner has printed portions of this letter and many other Emily Tennyson letters to her father, Thomas Woolner (1825-92), in her *Thomas Woolner: His Life in Letters.* I have examined in manuscript the large collection of Emily Tennyson letters to Woolner in the Tennyson Research Centre, as well as nine letters in the Bodleian Library, Oxford, and I include many letters which Amy Woolner omitted. *Thomas Woolner* has a few letters of which I have been unable to locate holographs, two of which I have included in this collection.

In 1851 Woolner did a plaster medallion of Tennyson, and he did another in 1855, when he became dissatisfied with the first. He completed his marble bust of Tennyson (now in the Library, Trinity College, Cambridge), in 1857, and, in 1859, his bronze medallion of Emily Tennyson, which he exhibited at the Royal Academy. In 1867 Woolner showed a three-quarter medallion of Tennyson at the Royal Academy; he finished a draped bust in plaster in 1874; and his final Tennyson study, the bearded bust (now in the National Gallery, Adelaide), he completed in 1876. Woolner was also the source for two of the Laureate's major poems. He provided the subject for "Enoch Arden" in 1859, and in 1862 he wrote out for Tennyson a story entitled "The Sermon," which the poet used to write "Aylmer's Field."

Frequently a guest of the Tennysons, Woolner was at Farringford from 1 to 15 February 1855, working on the second plaster medallion, which Emily thought "very beautiful, very fine, and shiny, the best likeness that has been made."

2. Apparently Woolner considered doing a statue of Sir Isaac Newton. The Tennysons advised him to see Roubillac's bust owned by the Royal Society, as well as the famous statue of Newton, "with his prism and silent face," that so moved the young Wordsworth when he entered Cambridge in 1787. See below, Letters 62 and 63.

Charles Richard Weld was assistant secretary and historian of the Royal Society from 1845 until 1861.

3. Woolner had served as intercessor between Tennyson and Ruskin, expressing the Laureate's desire to see the Turner collection in the National Gallery. Ruskin wrote to Tennyson, stating his pleasure in the poet's interest and his desire to show him the Turners (see *Memoir,* I, 383).

4. Tennyson was troubled by neuralgia.

5. In reality, Sir William Thornhill, a character in Goldsmith's *The Vicar of Wakefield,* who at the conclusion of every sentence would cry out, "Fudge!" to express indignant disgust.

6. Tennyson completed "Maud" on 7 July 1855.

26   *To Edward Lear*

Farringford, 7 April [1855]

Dear Mr. Lear,

. . . How I wish you could have been here while the snowdrops filled the plantations but daffodils and primroses are coming in their places and the cliffs will still be beautiful while the spring lights last, so you have time yet. I congratulate you on the pictures and I wish I could see them before they go where we never can see pictures.[1]

As to the judgeship my feeling is that if the nation were not so ridden by those same ugly genii you name, some few sensible and just men might be found even in our England of today who would make good judges, but I doubt whether one other could be found with all the gifts so much needed at home if Frank were sent away. Nevertheless if people cannot have the sense to see this I hope with all my heart they may at least see he is the fittest man for the judgeship though he will for many at home leave a void not to be filled, and you are going to run away too;[2] well, in self-defense we shall have to go also, I think. Hallam has looked a sturdy rosy little fellow all the winter but I dare say he will grow pale again when summer comes; he is already paler and baby too but I believe we all want change. It is too powerful a sea air to remain in it nearly a year and a half without going away for a day, but we admire the place quite as much as we did at first and if we were a little richer we should not hesitate about buying it.[3]

1. In a recent letter to Emily Tennyson (undated, T.R.C.), Lear had described in detail his "Quarries of Syracuse" (1852), evidently one of the pictures she wished to see before it was sold.

2. Franklin Lushington accepted the post of Judge to the Supreme Court of Justice in the Ionian Islands late in 1855, and he lived in Corfu until he resigned the judgeship and returned to England in August 1858. Lear sailed with Lushington for Corfu on 21 November 1855.

3. The Tennysons purchased Farringford in April 1856, and the surrounding farm in October 1861.

27   *To Thomas Woolner*

Park House,[1] *9 June [1855]*

Dear Mr. Woolner,
Many thanks for your kindness in wishing me to see the
medallion. I do not write now because I can answer your
question but just to say I cannot at present but I will do so as
soon as I am able. The length of the upper lip varies so much
according to the state of health that I fancy both yourself and
my sister may be right.[2] In which case I throw my weight into
your scale. Alfred is with us; he came last night. He seems very
much fagged by London hours. It is a disappointment to find
"Maud" yet where she was.

1. During the months of April–July 1855, the Tennysons had Farringford redecorated and refurnished, and they spent much of that time
with friends. They were at Park House with the Lushingtons from
31 May until mid-June.
2. Anne Weld apparently had criticized the upper lip of the second
Tennyson medallion.

28   *To Gerald Massey*[1]
National Library of Scotland

Farringford [c. 11 July 1855][2]

My dear Sir,
Thank you very much for having sent us your review. Our
mother and aunt[3] were so charmed with it that I ordered a
copy for each, and may I add, I also like it extremely. I only
remember one thing with which I cannot quite agree, for I
cannot quite help looking upon my husband as among the
universal poets. He is too human to be merely a subjective
poet, and I can't help thinking if you read his poems now as I
hope you will one day read them, in the light of himself, if I
may so speak, you will agree with me.[4] Is not his genius both
idyllic and lyrical, the first quite as much as the last, and is not
an idyll a kind of concrete drama, at least in its highest form is
it not so, and does not this imply universality? Where the
mortal meets with the immortal must be common ground,
though seldom reached.

Will you forgive me for writing this? Did you not see his poems so much as I see them, I should not be so anxious that you should see them still more as I do.

1. (1828–1907), poet, essayist, spiritualist, Chartist, and, with John Bedford Leno, editor of a paper for working men called "The Spirit of Freedom" (1849). When Massey sent Tennyson a copy of one of his volumes of verse in 1854, the Laureate wrote a letter stating his pleasure in coming upon "a poet of such fine lyrical impulse, and so rich half-oriental an imagination" (*Memoir,* I, 405). The Massey review mentioned by Emily Tennyson, entitled "The Poetry of Alfred Tennyson," appeared in *Hogg's Instructor,* later called *Titan,* in July 1855 (15, 1-14).

2. The letter is undated; Tennyson wrote a letter to Massey on 11 July informing him that he had asked his publisher, Edward Moxon, to forward to Massey "a little volume from me of my own poems" to express his gratitude for Massey's review (H. Tennyson, *Materials for a Life of A.T.,* II, 135).

3. Elizabeth Tennyson and her sister, Mary Anne Fytche, lived together at Rosemount, Hampstead, from 1856 until their deaths in February 1861.

4. Massey contended that any serious poet in a skeptical, materialistic age will necessarily write subjective verse, protesting those social tendencies most adverse to human freedom. In Tennyson, he wrote, poetic subjectivity has its culminating point. The review must have been particularly pleasing to Emily Tennyson, for Massey viewed the Laureate's marriage as an event likely to have the most salutary effect on his poetic achievement: "The interesting event of marriage has taken place since he gave us *In Memoriam,* consequently we may look for a growth of poetry gathered from a novel world opened up in his nature. There is nothing like the sweet influence of a noble woman for quickening and enriching a poet's genius" ("The Poetry of Alfred Tennyson," p. 8).

29   To Edward Lear

Farringford, 27 July [1855]

Dear Mr. Lear,

Our best thanks to you for your notes. It is hard to hope still in spite of Mr. Venables' words.[1] One scarcely can. When we look with a sickening anxiety for the post what must their feelings be! I do hope Frank knows nothing of this. To have to wait a whole week would be so terrible but then if it were to come to the worst the suddenness of the blow would be still worse. One knows not what to say. Only, will you not admit now I was right in being glad you were there? As Frank's friend you could not, I am sure, be in any place where you would so much wish to be. . . . I do not write to them. I could wish to be with them, but perhaps even if I could be spared here I should do no good. God grant he may even yet be restored to them.

  1. George Venables went to Malta to bring home the seriously ill Henry Lushington (1812–55), who had served as chief secretary of the Maltese government since 1847. Venables was with Lushington in Paris on 11 August when he died. Lushington's loss weighed heavily upon Tennyson, to whom no friend had been closer since the death of Arthur Hallam. He is one of the three immortalized in the poignant lines of "In the Garden at Swainston."

30   To Edward Moxon[1]
Harvard

Farringford [August 1855]

Many thanks, dear Mr. Moxon, for your kind note. We did not know Mr. Browning was in England. We want him to come here. Is Mrs. Browning with him?[2]

  Mr. Henry Taylor has also written very kindly about the poem but I am prepared for a different tone of criticism from the many. It will take, I think, some time before they understand either the metres or the thoughts but in the end I shall not wonder at its being popular. So much for my prophecy!

  Are you likely to be coming within reach of us this autumn? You know how glad we shall be to see you if it be so. Will you be so kind as to send us four more *Mauds*?

  1. (1801–58), Tennyson's publisher since 1832. It was largely because of Moxon's insistent persuasion that Tennyson published the 1842 volume, ending his decade of silence and establishing himself as a major poet. Moxon published the *Maud* volume in July 1855. For a discussion of Moxon's relationship with Tennyson, see Harold G. Merriman, *Edward Moxon: Publisher of Poets* (New York: Columbia University Press, 1939), pp. 169–187.
  2. The Brownings had returned from Rome in mid-July.

31   To John Forster
Usher Art Gallery

Farringford, 9 August [1855]

Dear Mr. Forster,
Thank you very heartily for your kindness in looking after
Alfred's affairs when you have scarcely time enough for your
own. He wrote yesterday to Moxon saying that another 1,000
copies might be printed if they were wanted or more even.[1] I
am glad you have not sent the letter.

September will, as far as we foresee, be perfectly convenient
to us and we hope nothing will rob us of the pleasure of seeing
you then. I know how precious your time is so I will only add
Alfred's love and our best thanks.

1. The original version of "The Charge of the Light Brigade" published
in John Forster's *Examiner* differed from the version published in the
Maud volume, which Tennyson altered at the advice of Frederick
Goddard Tuckerman, omitting the key line "someone had blunder'd."
A chaplain in the military hospital at Scutari wrote to Tennyson in
July 1855, telling how the poem had comforted and emboldened his
soldiers and requesting copies for distribution in the field. The reception
of the "soldier's copy" convinced Tennyson that it was finer than the
altered version and that he had erred in following Tuckerman's recommendation.

32   To Edward Lear

Farringford, 17 August [1855]

My dear Mr. Lear,
Thank you for staying—you know I feel you ought. Frank will
make it all easy for you and you will find you are a comfort
and blessing. . . .[1] To me it seems by no means certain Frank
will return now, not that I have heard anything to this effect.
Be this as it may, you must be good and not morbid and be
with him as much as you can. I feel one, or at least I myself,
often errs grievously through what in worldly parlance one
calls shyness, what in higher and sterner language is want of
faith in God and man, and now you are giving me a good
lesson, which late events have made me more apt to learn. For

how much is lost that can never be recovered now? My heart is stupid. I cannot write only I have a dim sad feeling we must help each other, those who at all understand each other and love each other; and to be sure, those who do not too or who do so only imaginatively.

Thanks, thanks for having thought of houses for us and looked at them besides. Alfred is continually saying we must buy this one if we can, but I fear we cannot and that you name at Ovingdean seems a better exchange than one could well hope for considering how bad a one one is generally forced to expect. Perhaps it may be just as beautiful a place as this even.

1. Lear felt that the Lushingtons had come to consider him a nuisance, and, despite Emily Tennyson's effort to reassure him, he left Park House deeply offended.

33   To Edward Lear

Farringford, 30 August [1855]

My dear Mr. Lear,
I am sick at heart today not having heard from Ally though very likely I could not have heard and I had said so to myself beforehand telling myself it was then probably a two days' post; but then when the letter did not come it seemed as if it might surely only be a one day's post just to please me.[1] What right have I to feel sad who have so unspeakably much to make me cheerful even when he is away; a love tried by all the changes and chances of a more than five years' marriage and tried only to prove its unimagined worth more and more. What of sorrow can this world hold which should not weigh light in the balance with this? But let me not talk of weighing and balancing, it is not good. I would rather feel that the God who has made me so rich in blessings will make me richer still. "Open thy mouth wide and I will fill it."[2] None of the niggard measure of man this.

Dear Mr. Lear, why do I say all this to you but from a feeling you are not to be always "alone" and you must now sympathize prophetically with me. I do not think you have been morbid but very good, far better than I should have been, and I think moreover it was quite right you should come away. If you were not often with them, the seeing you must often have been a reproach to them, for they must have felt a wish they could break through their reserve for the sake of one who had shared so much with them. I know you do not blame them.

The last I heard of Ally was at Lymington. When I hear more about him I will tell you. You may be sure I will write to you directly I know Frank is coming. Perhaps they will not spare him even to come here. It is strange Ally had written the saddest possible little poem before we heard the bad news,[3] and it was "alone" that was its burthen as far as feeling goes, though not as a refrain, for it is not a song but a poem for "Maud." I dare say he will let me copy it for you when he comes home. . . . Our tinies are well. Hallam's great delight is to ride on my back and then Lionel must ride too, so with her two romping boys Mother has a chance of being well tired.[4]

1. Tennyson was taking a walking tour through the New Forest, Hampshire.
2. Psalms 81:10.
3. "Courage, poor heart of stone," "Maud" (II, iii), which Tennyson wrote in mid-August, just prior to learning of Henry Lushington's death.
4. In light of her spinal disorder and general fragility, it seems strange that Emily Tennyson permitted her sons such exuberant freedom.

34   To Franklin Lushington

Farringford, 2 September 1855

Dear Frank,
We ask of you the greatest favour we can ask of any one, that you will undertake the guardianship of our children. We are sure you will do your utmost to have them brought up as Christian gentlemen, to give them the best education that can be given them in the highest sense of the words, and in your mind as in ours this we know implies a full persuasion of the sacredness of labour. You will see our children are brought up to work. We wish them to share equally in all we leave and to be separated as little as possible at school or college, to be brothers indeed all their lives.[1]

1. In "For Her Sons" Emily Tennyson wrote that Frank Lushington was to the end among her husband's "ablest and truest and most trusted friends" (p. 100). Lushington acclaimed his own regard for Emily Tennyson in a letter to Hallam Tennyson written after her death: "Your dear and sainted mother has been one of the stars of my life for more than fifty years. I have never known and cannot imagine a more noble and sweet and beautiful woman" (11 August 1896, unpublished, T.R.C.).

Hallam and Lionel Tennyson went to a school operated by C. Kegan Paul, the publisher, at Baillie, Dorsetshire, in May 1864. The next May Hallam enrolled at Marlborough, and in 1868 Lionel left Mr. Paul's and was entered at Eton. They were together at Trinity College, Cambridge, from the spring of 1873 until the autumn of 1874, when Hallam gave up his academic career to assist his father after his mother suffered a nearly fatal collapse.

35　　To Alfred Tennyson

Farringford, 25 September [1855]

Dearest,

Do not forget to bring thyself some tobacco and to get Moxon to send Burns' illustrated edition of *Nursery Rhymes and Jingles* unless indeed he know of a better. Hallam expressed great sorrow at thy departure and poor little baby sighed over it. Thy wifie, thou knowest, wishes thee back with all her heart but then with half of it she would have thee stay if there be good or pleasure in staying. 13 Dorset Sq., Baker St. is the Brownings' address. I would not willingly have thee miss seeing such good and great people. You ought to help each other.[1] God bless thee. All good things to Mr. Spedding.

1. In London from 25 September until 2 October, Tennyson spent the twenty-seventh and twenty-eighth with the Brownings, where D. G. Rossetti sketched him reading "Maud."

36　　To Edward Lear

Farringford [late September 1855]

Dear Mr. Lear,

You are not by any means going to be let off so easily as you think. In the first place . . . I must tell you what hard work is in store for you at Farringford. Not only are you to be sofa [*sic*] to my shyness and Frank's silence but you are to be yourself wellest and freshest and happiest. So, if you please, begin at once to cure that cough for I am afraid that is of itself such a hard task it will last you all the while from now till then.

I did not think of your being in London or I should have told you Ally was in his old quarters with Mr. Spedding, 60 Lincoln's Inn Fields.[1] Edmund [Lushington] was to go up yesterday to try to get him down. Ally said he could not go. Perhaps I shall hear tomorrow which has prevailed. Ally meant to come home on Monday. He had been dining with the Brownings and had had a very pleasant evening. Do you know them[2] and those wonderful spirit eyes of hers? I have asked Ally to go to the Brookfields'[3] also. She is very dear to us both, little as I know of her in reality. When we met circumstances at once put us upon an intimate footing. She received me more as a relative than a stranger, for feeling herself one of the Hallams she thinks of Alfred as a brother, she told me. I think we must found a Frank Lushington Brotherhood, and she is one of course; but we will be very stingy of our honors. What shall be our badge? I think we will not have any. How I wish we could all meet here, when we had had Frank and you to ourselves for a time. . . .

I must not write any more except heartiest congratulations about "Philae."[4] How I wish we could see it. Please tell us what Sir John Potter[5] says of it.

1. Tennyson often stayed with Spedding at his bachelor lodgings in Lincoln's Inn until Spedding moved to Westbourne Terrace in the late 1860s.
2. Lear met the Brownings in 1859.
3. W. H. Brookfield (1809–74), rector, school inspector, and later chaplain in ordinary to Queen Victoria, and his wife Jane (1821-96), the intimate friend of William Makepeace Thackeray, youngest daughter of Sir Charles Elton of Clevedon Court, and first cousin of Arthur Hallam. For many years a fashionable morning preacher at Berkeley Chapel in Mayfair, Brookfield is thought to be the original for the Rev. Charles Honeyman in Thackeray's *The Newcomes*.
4. Lear had just sold a picture of the island of Philae painted during his 1853 journey down the Nile.
5. (1815-58), mayor of Manchester, 1848-51, and M.P. for Manchester, 1857 till death. Possibly Potter was the buyer of Lear's picture of Philae.

37   To Edward Lear

Farringford [early October 1855]

Dear Mr. Lear,
The seven-inch hailstones of our Isle of Wight thunderstorm a
few days ago are dwarfs compared to those with which one is
mercilessly pelted in the matter of "Maud."[1] I come forth a
few seconds from the stir of the storm to write in peace to you.

How very good of you and Frank to have gone to Ovingdean
for us and to have made such arrangements . . . as will secure
us a chance of the house there if it be to be sold. When your
letter came into my hands yesterday the Frederick Pollocks[2]
were here. Your news of Frank had a painful interest for them.
It made me very sad but I am thankful to have it for if I do not
hear I only fancy worse things. Though I said to you, perhaps
he might not come, as a kind of break to any possible
disappointment, I found I had almost quite expected him
notwithstanding when I read what you said about his probably
not being able to visit us. Well, I am afraid he is too sad to
find much pleasure or comfort in it so regret is purely selfish.

You asked me about Alfred's tour. Poor Ally, he got no
further than Salisbury and Winchester and the New Forest was
his chief resting-place. It is a pity we are not rich enough to go
about all together without scruple for he has not much pleasure
in being long alone. However I am thankful to say he had
pleasure in this little tour. He bids me tell you nothing can be
more charming than New Forest.[3]

1. Sir Charles Tennyson has preserved two of the most vicious attacks
following the publication of "Maud." An anonymous correspondent
wrote:"Sir, once I worshipped you—now I loathe you: So you've taken
to imitating Longfellow, you B E A S T!" Another said: "If an author
pipe of adultery, fornication, murder and suicide, set him down as
the practiser of those crimes"(*AT*, pp. 289, 286).

2. William Frederick Pollock (later Sir, 1815-88), of the illustrious
family descended from David Pollock, saddler to George III. Pollock
was appointed a master of the Court of Exchequer in 1846, Queen's
Remembrancer in 1874, and, in 1876, senior master of the Supreme
Court of Judicature; in 1854 he published a blank-verse translation
of Dante. His wife Juliet was the daughter of the Rev. Henry Creed
of Corse, Gloucestershire.

3. When Tennyson and Palgrave returned to England from their trip
to Portugal in the late summer of 1859, they visited the New Forest,
and both agreed it was finer than anything seen on their travels.

38   *To Edward Lear*

Farringford, 12 October 1855

Dear Mr. Lear,

For decorum's sake it will be as well if Ally and I are not found following the example of our bairns and tossing up all attainable hats and bonnets with loud hurrahs supposing you and Frank do really get here on Wednesday. . . . You will laugh at me if I tell you to make them[1] spread a plaster of honey (let it be tolerably thick on the cloth) and flour and put it on your chest but it really does both Ally and me good, and then I would further prescribe a mixture of tincture of myrrh (2 spoonsfull), lemon juice (1 spoonfull) and honey, two spoonsfull about the portion to be taken, a teaspoonfull two or three times a day, only you will say I am a perfect quack. Nevertheless I will add this mess has done me more good than the whole range of poisons by whatever orthodox doctors administered.

Will you do me the favor to bring me down an "Edward Gray"[2] when you come? I am just giving mine away and I cannot do without one. Alfred's kind love.

1. Lear was visiting the Lushingtons at Park House.
2. A copy of Lear's musical setting of Tennyson's poem. In 1853 Lear published four of his Tennyson settings, including "Edward Gray," in a volume inscribed to Emily Tennyson. According to Sir Charles, Lear's settings "were always sincere and permeated with the spirit of the words," and they were among the few settings approved by the Laureate himself, who found that they cast "a diaphanous veil over the words—nothing more" (*AT*, p. 441). Emily Tennyson was no doubt especially fond of "Edward Gray" because the poet had included it in a letter to her in 1840, calling it, at that time, "Sweet Emma Morland."

39   *To Frederick Goddard Tuckerman*
Harvard

Farringford, 17 October 1855[1]

My dear Sir,

I cannot refrain from telling you how your poet's review of my husband has rejoiced my heart. The freshness of nature breathed into your souls from your virgin forests and

untrodden savannahs fit you better for hearing the . . . voice of
truth in "Maud," gives you more vigor to wrestle with her
quaint, if morbid, lover, than can be gathered from our ordered
parks and cultivated fields or our crowded cities and dingy
factories, save by the very few who "wax in every limb"[2]
under all circumstances. But are even all these poets? I think
not, but Christians they must be if not. Well, after all, you
know I do not wish to disparage England; you know I am
English and very English. I have not the remotest sympathy
with those who talk of the decrepitude of age, of dotage, when
they speak of England. The worst I say of her is that she has
lost her Arab[3] sensitiveness for the purest spring.

I enclose you the soldier's copy of "The Charge." I think you
will like to hear two thousand of them have been printed for
my husband and sent out by him to the army in the East
because the senior chaplain wrote that half the men were
singing it and all wished to possess what they so much
admired. We often think and speak of you and we hope the
time is not far distant when we may also speak to you.

Hallam is grown a big brown boy. Lionel runs alone and
some people admire him more than Hallam.[4] I hope you and
yours are well and happy. You have from time to time given us
such kind proof of your remembrance that I need not also add
I hope you sometimes think of us.

1. Emily's letter is a reply to a letter from Tuckerman to Tennyson,
which Samuel Golden in his *Frederick Goddard Tuckerman* has mistakenly dated 22 October 1855. Perhaps Tuckerman's letter was written
on 22 September; in any case Emily's reply is clearly dated 17 October.
Tuckerman's letter contains an elaborate rebuttal of *Blackwood's* censure
of "Maud": "Only poets can fully appreciate and enjoy the singular
beauty of 'Maud.' . . . The newspapers are loud, but the poet holds
it to his heart in silence. I have seen the attack in *Blackwood's,* and
gather from it that the reviewer, whoever he may be, accords you the
highest poetical rank, and his other propositions refute themselves,
strange that people because they cannot appreciate or rightly understand
a subject, abuse the treatment of it, which may be (and in this case
is) wholly in keeping." "As for affecting your fame however or influenc-
ing the notions of the masses by a magazine article, a man might as
well stand upon a sea-shore in a flood-tide and attempt to put the
waves back with a pitchfork." See Samuel A. Golden, *Frederick Goddard
Tuckerman* (New York: Twayne, 1966), pp. 39–40. A brief excerpt from
the *Blackwood's* review denotes its tenor: "We have at last received
'Maud' and we have arisen from its perusal dispirited and sorrowful.
It is not a light thing nor a trivial annoyance to a sincere lover of
literature to have it forced upon his conviction that the man, who has

unquestionably occupied for years the first place among the living British poets, is losing ground with each successive effort" (*Blackwood's Edinburgh Magazine*, September 1855, p. 313).

2. *In Memoriam*, ciii, 30.

3. She has in mind "Maud," I, 551: "From the delicate Arab arch of her feet."

4. Following a visit to Farringford John Addington Symonds included his impressions of the two boys in a letter to Charlotte Symonds on 24 November 1864. He found Lionel "a splendid creature, tall and lithe, with long curls and a pear shaped face extremely beautiful," who, like his mother, seemed "to have come out of a chapter of past history." "The other boy, Hallam, came in, also medieval, but not so handsome as his brother." See *The Letters of John Addington Symonds,* ed. Herbert M. Schueller and Robert L. Peters (Detroit: Wayne State University Press, 1967), I, 512. Edith Nicholl Ellison, daughter of George Granville Bradley, long-time headmaster of Marlborough and Dean of Westminster, remembered that the boys were "straight and tall dressed always in tunics and kneepants of the same shade of gray as their mother's gown—belted on week-days, crimson sashed and crimson stockinged on Sundays, holidays, and everyday evenings; low, strapped slippers always worn in the house; and on their broad, lace collars their long golden hair falling, Lionel's forever in his eyes." Both Hallam and Lionel were "fine boys, but the younger's beauty was so great that even we children were concious of it. He looked like his mother, whereas the elder had his father's deep-set eyes and high forehead." See Edith Nicholl Ellison, *A Child's Recollections of Tennyson* (New York: J. M. Dent, 1906), p. 33. Lionel's boyish beauty departed, however, with his boyhood, if we may rely on Swinburne's opinion. In a letter to George Powell, 2 November 1872, Swinburne recounted Lionel's description, to Jowett and himself, of swishings at Eton, and he fancied "what a delightful prey for the stinging and burning birch-twigs must my informant's young flesh and blood have been a very few years since, in the May of his beauty, ere he shot up into a tall loutish common-featured youth!" See *The Swinburne Letters,* ed. Cecil Y. Lang (New Haven: Yale University Press, 1959), II, 191.

40   To Edward Lear

Farringford, 27 October [1855]

Dear Mr. Lear,

It is a week today since you left us.[1] I am afraid you are in some mischief as we do not hear from you, gnawing your own heart or doing some other cannibal thing of the kind. If you were here the great round bright moon that looks tonight so

ineffably peaceful would give you something better to do. As
you are not I must try if I can not find a sugar plum or two or
at least a peppermint drop for you. Only I am afraid you will
not believe me when I tell you what a hero of romance you are
at Afton. How Miss Cotton[2] was found all pale after a sleepless
night, how her companion came and poured into my ear a
mighty river of thanks and praises and admiration of all sorts,
even the very manner not forgotten. Why do I say "even" when
I think so much of manner myself?

1. Lear and Franklin Lushington arrived at Farringford on the seventeenth, and they spent most of that day strolling about the estate with
Tennyson and Sir John Simeon. That night Emily Tennyson felt that
dinner was spoiled because she "forgot Friday and fish"; but after
dinner her disappointment was assuaged by Lear's singing of his settings
of "Mariana," "The Lotos-Eaters," "Tears, idle tears," and the lyric
"Oh! that 'twere possible" from "Maud." The Tennysons invited the
Simeons and the Cottons to hear Lear play and sing; the entire company
was in high spirits, and Lear performed his Tennyson songs "with
all his usual *verve,* so that his hearers were delighted and deeply moved."
See Angus Davidson, *Edward Lear: Landscape Painter and Nonsense
Poet* (London: John Murray, 1938), p. 92.
2. Daughter of Benjamin T. Cotton, Tiny Cotton's elder sister.

41   To Edward Lear

Farringford [mid-November, 1855]

Dear Mr. Lear,
This is not goodby from us but I write to thank you for that
one of your ever welcome letters which has come to us this
morning. I must say I am rather envious of the happy people
who possess "Morn broadens"[1] in the family. That picture has
always haunted me. But sooth to say were I rich not one of all
the set should belong to any one but myself. As it is, despite
my envy, I am glad that favorite picture of mine is in the hands
of those who will enjoy it. Both Ally and I exclaimed at the
charm of those two tiny pictures in your letter.[2] So did Hallam
too but I am bound to confess he turned them wrong side
upwards. I shall think of you on Thursday. Such pleasure as
such a visit can have will, I hope, come unalloyed to you now,
for you see they do understand you and are at heart grateful

and sympathizing though the gift of utterance is except on rare occasions denied them.[3] Then you know how much more a few words from them is worth than from almost anyone else.

I need not repeat what I have said more than once before how entirely I agree with you in what you say about Frank. For his health's sake I believe a winter or two in Corfu makes his present appointment more desirable than the most suitable post in England. . . . It seems so strange that anyone who knows Frank can think about his position as if he had not that which would make any position great, but those who speak so do not know him.

1. That is, "Morn broadened," from "A Dream of Fair Women," l. 265: "Morn broadened on the borders of the dark." Lear conceived the idea of illustrating the Laureate's poems in 1852, and he worked on his Tennyson illustrations periodically during the remaining thirty-five years of his life. In a letter of 11 November 1855 to Emily Tennyson (unpublished, T.R.C.), Lear wrote of the sale of his "Morn broadened" illustration, the first of his Tennyson landscapes to be sold. Beneath a miniature of the picture drawn in his letter, the artist described his inspiration for the work: "When I first read the words, 'Morn broadened on the borders of the dark,' they seemed to me to describe exactly what I had so often watched in other days,—that Darkness,—edged with broadening light, which I had seen through so many summer and autumn months during years of Italian wanderings, and most of all from the neighborhood of Civitella, a village near Subiaco, about 40 or 50 miles from Rome." Evidently there is no record of the picture from the time it left Lear's hands.

2. Lear also drew his "Philae," another product of his Italian rambles, in the 11 November letter.

3. Lear returned to Park House before leaving England. Though the Lushingtons were always sparing in the affection they showed Lear, he was, nonetheless, irresistably attracted to them. On 28 October 1855 he wrote to Emily Tennyson: "I wish sometimes I could settle near Park House. Then I might . . . moon cripply, cripply about those hills, and sometimes see by turns Hallam's and Lionel's children, and Frank's grandchildren, and so slide peacefully out of life" (Noakes, *Edward Lear*, p. 130).

42   *To Edward Lear*

Farringford, 17 November [1855]

Dear Mr. Lear,

You are not alone, Mr. Lear, you cannot be while you can be so much to those so very dear to you, to those to whom so few are anything but the mere outside world. But one would be all and in that one cannot be, here is the loneliness. Is there a single soul on earth entirely exempt from this? The greater the heart with which one loves, the greater the heart one loves, the more does one long to bless with those infinite blessings which belong to God alone. I cannot tell if this must be always so, if it is not possible to attain to such a perfect oneness in and with God that one knows all the fulness of infinite and eternal blessing in ours and his and hers whom we love. I think it is possible to attain to this, I am sure it is the one thing worth striving for in life. . . . God bless you, dear Mr. Lear, and prosper you in your labour of love.[1] Alfred's love.

1. As Franklin Lushington's unsolicited steward and companion.

43   *To Thomas Woolner*

Farringford, 21 November [1855]

Dear Mr. Woolner,
Many thanks for your kind letter. I am sure you will know I did not for one moment mean to ask you to give up more time to us than you have already done. I only felt I must tell you how it was that another was going to do a bust of Alfred, because it seemed to me after all your labour you would have a right to be hurt, if you did not know how it came to pass, and I cannot help wishing it were you who had to do it and to say also, that if you still wished it you should have an opportunity of fulfilling your wish. . . .[1] If you wished to do the bust it could be done I suppose any time you are here and finished when you had not other work in hand. Perhaps it is presumptuous to talk thus considering the uncertainties of life. What you say of my medallion is most kind, but some way I cannot feel it right to let you waste your time on my lean face which should have been drawn ten years ago at least, if at all.[2] But, if you think I say this with the slightest feeling you would not make a medallion we should both like, you are very much mistaken. Do you not remember how much we admired your ladies?[3] Perhaps you do not but I do!

1. The Scottish sculptor William Brodie (1815–81) began a bust of Tennyson before the end of the year. In a letter of 18 November 1855 to Emily Tennyson (*Thomas Woolner,* p. 106), Woolner wrote: "As regards doing a bust, it is what I have wished many years, to do one of him, and I know nothing that would please me so much. . . . If he will let me, will you at the same time allow me to make a medallion of you, for I feel certain I should be able to do one both he and you would be pleased with."

2. Woolner replied to Emily Tennyson's objection to a medallion of herself in his 23 December letter (*Thomas Woolner,* p. 108): "What you say of your medallion, that it should have been done 10 years ago, I can scarcely agree with, for tho' probably your face may have been rounder then, I know the expression was no better and I think not so good: the expression of persons whose minds are fixed upon high and holy things grows better every instant of their lives, thru' growing in fact nearer to that perfection they contemplate. I feel confident your face is admirably suited for sculpture, therefore, I hope you will be resigned to your fate. . . ."

3. Woolner had done plaster medallions of Mrs. Coventry Patmore, 1850, and of Rosaline Orme and Mrs. Orme, 1851, and bronze medallions of Mary and Edith Howitt, a Mrs. Bean, and a Mrs. Fanning, 1853–54.

44   To Julia Margaret Cameron

Ritchie,[1] From Friend to Friend, *pp. 8–9*

Farringford [c. Christmas 1855?]

Thanks, thanks, thanks. And for my frill, as Alfred calls it, and for the beautiful big ball which charms Hallam beyond measure and delights baby too, only with so much fear in the delight that he dare not approach the giant without Mother's hand in his. I do hope that I shall hear that you are all well and that things grow brighter and brighter as Christmas comes on, for I cannot accept old Herbert's gloomy version of things.[2] I will admit most thankfully that griefs are joys in disguise, but not the converse except as a half-truth, and half-truths are the most dangerous of all. God wills us to be happy even here . . . only let us give happiness its most exalted sense. I often think one is not told of joy as a Christian virtue as one ought to be.[3] This, however, is rather by the way, for joy can subsist with sorrow, but happiness cannot be without happy circumstances.

1. *From Friend to Friend* includes several other Emily Tennyson fragments (pp. 7–12), impossible to date, one of which acknowledges

Mrs. Cameron's gifts for another Christmas and reproaches her for her extravagant generosity: "The only drawback is the old complaint that you *will* rain down precious things upon us, not drop by drop, but in whole Golconda mines at once."

2. Perhaps Emily Tennyson shared Christina Rossetti's view of George Herbert as an ascetic whose verse reveals a profound dissatisfaction with mortal life.

3. Emily Tennyson's observations on happiness call to mind C. S. Lewis's discussion of Christian joy in his autobiography *Surprised by Joy: The Shape of My Early Life* (London: Geoffrey Bles, 1955): Life is a scene of altruistic toil, a pilgrimage of service, and only the unselfish find true contentment. In an October 1868 letter (unpublished, T.R.C.), Emily wrote to Hallam at Marlborough: "I remember how my wrath was raised as a girl by Paley's utilitarian greatest happiness morality, though I had, as I suppose most young creatures have, a thorough belief in happiness and a real longing for its topmost heights in this world. Yet I never dreamt of pursuing it for myself, though, strange contradiction, it seemed then and it seems still lawful to seek to give it to others if it be but of the right kind." Agnes Weld has written that despite disappointment, tragedy, and personal pain, her aunt remained all her life a remarkably happy woman, and that it was her "capacity for loving which, by making her a blessing to all around her, blessed her in return. . . ." Several years before her death Emily told her sister, Anne Weld, "I have had so wonderfully much in life of happiness, that I feel somewhat overwhelmed by the thought." See Agnes Grace Weld, *Glimpses of Tennyson and Some of His Relations and Friends* (Oxford: Williams and Norgate, 1903), pp. 107-08.

45   To Thomas Woolner

Farringford, 1 January 1856

A happy New Year to you, dear Mr. Woolner, lovely visions fixed forever in marble to astonish and delight the world, and whatever else your heart most longs for, and whatever there is good for you, whether you long for it or not! Many thanks for your kind letter. The time you mention will, I think, be quite convenient. If any unexpected hindrance should arise I will tell you. At present Alfred is at the Grange,[1] but he had no intention of staying more than three or four days. We must catch him as we can for the few sittings you will want. I hope it may be warm enough for us to be in the drawing room for I fear the study would not be so good a light for you. . . .

The clouds are threatening. I must get a little walk before

they do more than threaten. The children are well. They have been charmed today by a kite which Uncle Weld has made for them. Hallam wanted to know "if Hallam would go up in the sky with a string?" and Baby began flying a letter of mine for his kite.

1. Near Alresford, Hampshire, the home of Lady Ashburton, the renowned lion-huntress who entertained Tennyson at her celebrated Christmas literary party of 1855. The poet enjoyed the experience despite the presence among the guests of a Mr. Goldwin Smith who had written a scathing review of "Maud" for the *Saturday Review.* He spent much of the evening smoking and talking in the conservatory with Carlyle, who found the Laureate as gruff and as entertaining as ever.

46   *To Thomas Woolner*

Farringford, 1 February 1856

My dear Mr. Woolner,
We shall rejoice to see you here, the sooner the better, for I believe in a very little time I must go to Twickenham to pack up our furniture there.[1] May I be allowed to have a little case with fork and spoon sent to you for Lionel? and Tyler's *The Life of Henry V*[2] from the London library for Alfred?
    If I hear from you in time I will write both to the library and the goldsmith. I wish you could induce Mr. Hunt to accompany you hither.[3] Tell him how much pleasure it would give us to see him. Is it not fortunate I have been able to burn some insulting lies apparently from a newspaper sent anonymously to Alfred and so spare him the sight of them as he is away at Ventnor just now looking at stars through Dr. Mann's great telescope, but I expect him home on Monday.[4]

1. When Mrs. Elizabeth Tennyson moved from Twickenham to Hampstead, the furniture at Chapel House had to be removed. Woolner arrived at Farringford on the seventh. During his stay he made significant progress on both his Emily Tennyson medallion and his bust of the Laureate, "difficult work for Mr. Woolner as A. is not at all fond of having his face copied and will only spare a little while at night when Mr. Woolner has to take a candle in one hand and model as he can" (Journal, 28 February 1856).
    2. J. E. Tyler, *Henry of Monmouth, or the Life of Henry V,* 2 vols. (London: 1838).

3. William Holman Hunt (1827–1910) did come to Farringford in the spring of 1856, bringing Tennyson a gift of Latakia tobacco.

4. Tennyson returned on 6 February from his visit with Dr. R. J. Mann, the author of *Maud Vindicated* and an enthusiastic amateur astronomer.

47   To Thomas Woolner
Woolner, Thomas Woolner, *p. 111*

Farringford, 20 March 1856

Dear Mr. Woolner,
There is one I can answer for as half inclined to cry seeing so many kindly appropriate remembrances.[1] We feel there is one friend at least who does not find the Solent a Lethe. Accept our best thanks. The boys were as delighted as you could desire them to be. All the balls danced together and the license to whip Mamma was particularly charming.

The little stretcher Hallam appropriated as "mys" and began forthwith exercising himself. Apollo did not strike the lyre on the occasion of your departure but he mourned in sober earnest prose and said how sorry he was you were gone. Baby asked for you and Hallam said you were "gone over the great towns."

. . . We have had our noses taken according to order and A. has had his forehead and hand taken. . . .[2] "Merlin" goes on grandly. I think "Trust me not at all or trust me all in all"[3] has grown into an exquisite song. I hope your kind gifts will preserve many a precious scrap.

1. After leaving Farringford on 15 March, Woolner sent the Tennysons a number of gifts, including two "stretchers," presumably some sort of spring-operated exercisers, and an album for the poet's manuscripts.

2. For Woolner's Emily Tennyson medallion and his Tennyson bust.

3. See "Merlin and Vivien," ll. 382–96, 444–47.

48   To Julia Margaret Cameron

Ritchie, From Friend to Friend, *p. 8*

Farringford [March 1856]

It is tantalising to have a big smooth rounded down just in front of a large window and to be forbidden by the bitter winter blasts to climb it. It is a pity the golden furze is not in bloom, for when it is it makes a gorgeous contrast to the blue Solent. . . . Alfred has been reading *Hamlet* to me and since then has been drawn down to the bay by the loud voice of the sea. . . . There is something so wholesome in beauty, and it is not for me to try to tell of all we have here in those delicate tints of a distant bay and the still more distant headlands. These I see every day with my own eyes, and so many other things with *his,* when he comes back from his walk.[1]

1. Tennyson took at least two walks each day, and one of his favorite strolls was to Freshwater Bay, about a mile from Farringford, where he loved to watch the sea from the tall cliffs. C. V. Stanford remembered the methodical regularity of the poet's walks, even in old age: "The daily walk from 11 to 1 and the shorter stroll in the afternoon were timed to the moment. Sometimes on returning from his morning walk he would find that he had taken five minutes less than his fixed two hours, and would insist upon finishing the allotted period by pacing up and down in front of the door." See Charles Villiers Stanford, *Studies and Memories* (London: Constable, 1908), p. 92.

49   To Thomas Woolner

Farringford, 11 April 1856

Dear Mr. Woolner,
Could you without any great trouble let Mr. Palgrave have his Macaulay before long?[1] He has asked about it, this is why I ask. We hope soon to hear you find the studio good and filling with models. "Merlin" is all written down, and those who have heard it are astonished at its grandeur. . . .[2] Cowslips and oxlips and primroses star the field now, but it is yet uncertain whether this field or any other is to be ours. You may think we do not like this delay. Have I told you that if we buy, we have to have a sale in the house of the Seymour furniture before the 23rd of May, which is an additional reason for desiring a

speedy decision . . . ?[3] Alfred is suffering from his foot,[4] I grieve to say, but I hope poultices may set all right again. I have, or somebody has, nearly broken my chest expander. We both of us like our gymnastics very much and I think we shall always keep a supply of the stretchers.

    1. Francis Turner Palgrave brought his copy of the first two volumes of Macaulay's *The History of England* (1849–61) to the Tennysons on 27 December 1855, and they in turn lent the book to Woolner.
    2. Emily Tennyson recorded in her Journal, 31 March 1856, that Tennyson "read 'Vivien,' just completed, to Venables who pronounced it 'grand'." (H. Tennyson, *Materials for a Life of A. T.*, II, 161).
    3. The purchase of Farringford was assured on 14 April, when the Tennysons received notification that Mr. Seymour had accepted their offer. Emily Tennyson's Journal comment on the twenty-fourth, when the title had been approved and arrangements for sale completed, reflects her heartfelt satisfaction: "We have agreed to buy, so I suppose this house among the pine trees is ours."
    4. Tennyson was troubled by gout much of his life, and in later years he sometimes attributed to that affliction the despondency that had marred his young manhood.

50   To Thomas Woolner

28 April 1856[1]

Dear Mr. Woolner,
What a wonderful medallion you have sent.[2] Wonderful in delicacy! I congratulate you that after all your unheard of labours and misfortunes the result is so admirable. The only thing I would suggest is the scraping away of a little of the nose underneath the nostril all along to the point so as to shorten the nose a wee bit; if this would not bother you and if you think it right. . . . We were delighted to hear what Millais said and did.[3] I do hope that little statue of yours[4] will do great things for you. We shall look with warm interest for any proofs of appreciation.
    . . . We both of us went to the Grand Review in the little Solent and saw things very comfortably and well. The sight was magnificent. I wish you had been there. I got a ticket by mistake and so I came to be there. I am glad I went. The firing along the whole line when the Queen was saluted, the clearing of the smoke when ships and distant hills began to be seen

again, the long line of ships standing up still and grand like an avenue of sphinxes, the cheering, the manning the yards, the great ships turning in slow majesty one after the other. We are glad to have seen so grand a sight.[5]

Alfred's love. He and the boys are pretty well.

1. Amy Woolner dates the letter 18 April 1856 (*Thomas Woolner,* p. 112), but 28 April 1856 is unmistakably the date on the ms.
2. The brass Tennyson medallion.
3. Woolner wrote to Emily, on 15 April 1856 (*Thomas Woolner,* pp. 111–12), that no one else had admired his Tennyson bust quite so much as John Everett Millais, "who went into raptures at the sight of it, and told me to tell you he thought it 'splendid' he said no other word would express his feeling with regard to it."
4. The marble statuette of "Love" (1856).
5. The doubtful outcome of the Crimean War did little to dampen public enthusiasm for the Grand Review of the Fleet on 23 April 1856, the second such review in three years. The current militaristic ambiance is graphically illustrated by an excerpt from a *Times* article the following day: "On the waters of the Solent was yesterday displayed a fleet the like of which the eye of mortal man never beheld, compared with the vastness of the vessels of which even our own mighty armaments of other days were puny and insignificant, and compared with the powers of which the vessels that bore the victors of the Nile and of Trafalgar seem puny and innocuous."

The Tennysons traveled to Yarmouth and the Grand Review the morning of 23 April in the company of Drummond Rawnsley and Alexander Grant, both of whom had been at Farringford since the twenty-first. Emily thought the show magnificent and some of her Journal description of the spectacle is worth quoting:

> The yellow sands swarmed with people clustering like bees. Here and there red coats enlivened the mass. The *Victory* stood proudly in the midst of the harbour. We heard a salute, then the *Victory* manned arms and soon the royal yacht with its three tall masts, each bearing a flag, came out of harbour. Every ship saluted. The smoke curled along the whole line six miles long, I was told, and then cleared partly away and we saw ships and the distant hills beginning to appear. A beautiful sight. Soon the Queen's yacht passed us and the ships manned arms

and we heard the cheer of the *British Tar* and the *Solent*
cheered, too. It was pleasant to hear A's voice cheering.
I waved my handkerchief. As we passed at the head of
the lines I thought of the avenue of Sphinxes, the great
ships stood so still and grand.

Resolved to renovate the home which was now their own,
the Tennysons soon began preparations for extensive redecora-
tion. Emily spent several weeks choosing new furnishings and
packing books and other valuables for a temporary removal to
the "Red House," a little place near Freshwater, where they
stayed during the last two weeks of May. Tennyson read Chaucer
to his wife at night and occupied his days in the garden or
in the summer house, entering the house from time to time to
venture an opinion on the choice of new wallpapers. On the
thirteenth, into the midst of a house strewed with stacked books
and disarranged furniture, walked Prince Albert. Though the
Prince called at what must have seemed the most inopportune
of times, his visit indicated an increase of Royal interest in the
Laureate, and Emily wrote in the following letter to her sister
that he said he would soon return with the Queen. But despite
her intention and that of the Prince, the Queen never visited
Farringford, and Tennyson's introduction to his Sovereign had
to wait for another time.

51   To Anne Weld

The Red House, 15 May 1856

My dearest Nanny,
Such a strange week as we have had. On Monday the
Monckton Milneses and Simeons to luncheon. Tuesday Prince
Albert to call. Two rings at the door and Colonel Phipps or
somebody announced the Prince who had come to see the fort
and had heard Ally lived near and had come to ask if he would
speak with them.[1] I said I would go and fetch him and asked
the Colonel to show Prince Albert into the drawing room and
disappeared myself. He was very kind, shook hands with Ally
and talked to him very gaily. One of his gentlemen gathered a
huge bunch of cowslips which he took into his own hands and

said they were so very fine (and so they are) and that they make good tea. We hear this morning he said it was a very pretty place and that he should certainly bring the Queen. It will be a pity if we miss the great honour and pleasure it would be to receive her.

1. The Golden Hill Fort was located approximately a mile northeast of Farringford. Colonel Phipps was an equerry to the Queen at Osborne.

52 *To Thomas Woolner*

The Red House, 27 May 1856

Dear Mr. Woolner,

I ought to have answered your kind letter long ago but I have been in rather a distracted state of mind first with the packing and then with the removal here and various little annoyances which I need not specify. It is a fortnight tomorrow since we came here and now today Lambert, the landlord of Plumbley's Hotel, is bidding for us at the sale at Farringford. . . .[1] I think one might soon make the house comfortable again were it not for the ghastly appearance of the drawing room and dining room walls so woefully stained by pictures. Ally has a fancy for the drawing room paper and will not have it changed for he says whatever paper we had he should not be happy without red and flesh colour and bright frames. Can you recommend him to any pawn brokers for we must not look to finding our oil pictures in a more reputable quarter. . . . I have found out that Ally's big stretcher does quite well for me holding it shorter than the handles. . . . Have you seen any of the illustrations? I long to hear what you think of them. Some of Millais' seem to us very fine.[2]

1. The best hotel in Freshwater in its day, Plumbley's numbered Lewis Carroll among its regular patrons. The Tennysons bought a good deal of the Seymours' furniture at auction.
2. Millais, Rossetti, Holman Hunt, Arthur Hughes, Daniel Maclise, and Charles Horsley all worked on the *Illustrated Edition*. Although Tennyson liked Millais's illustrations, he found many of the drawings repugnant, and he disliked the project from its conception. Moxon's enthusiasm influenced Tennyson to permit publication, nonetheless, and the edition appeared in the spring of 1857. It did not sell as well as Moxon had expected, and the publisher absorbed a heavy loss.

53   To Thomas Woolner

Farringford, 10 June 1856

Dear Mr. Woolner,
I know you take so kind an interest in us that you will be glad
to hear we are here at last in our home for life, I hope. I know
we have your good wishes for all good to us in it. I am as you
may suppose a good deal knocked up, but I write now partly
because I am not sure whether you are waiting to hear from me
before you fulfill your kind promise of sending the medallion.
. . .[1]

Alfred has nobly stood out all the bustle and bother of the
removal, helping to unpack and himself to place the things.
The boys are charmed at getting back. Hallam said, "May I
stay?" He still retains so much recollection of you that he
persists in calling a stranger kind to him Mr. Woolner.

Alfred does not know I am writing or he would send kind
messages. Be of good cheer; the bad days are, I hope, behind
you. The night behind and only the day before you.[2]

1. In a letter of 28 May 1856, to Emily Tennyson (*Thomas Woolner,*
pp. 113-14), Woolner wrote of the recently completed medallion: "I
think it looks very well; I feel sure there is some of your character,
for various persons who have seen it remarked upon the extreme
sensitiveness it displayed, and some said it was the most sensitive face
they ever saw. . . ."
2. Woolner enjoyed little recognition and few commissions before
his great success with the 1857 Tennyson bust, the real turning point
in his career.

54   To James Spedding

Farringford, 27 June 1856

Dear Mr. Spedding,
If the "long-necked geese"[1] have deceived me I am glad. They
hissed in my ear that you abused "Maud." I said, treacherous
man, did he not stand by my cab a whole quarter of an hour
and did we not agree there were but those few things that were
not admirable in it, and did not my tormentors reply, "Ah, you
see, even Mr. Spedding cannot speak the truth always," upon

which I told them I was sure Mr. Spedding did speak the truth and would always speak the truth to me. (I did not mean to imply, but not to them. One is obliged to be so precise.) For the rest I do most heartily agree with you that a thing must stand or fall of itself, that in the end the great and good will assert its own rights. At least I think you think this and I am sure I do. So I was utterly against that Defense Vindication[2] as it was called, however kindly meant, and now I am not going to trouble you any more about it but I shall instead tell you how delighted I am you like "Merlin" and "Enid" more especially as you dare avow a change of opinion . . . not a determination to write a book proving the poet's home is a nest of demons or he could not have written this.[3]

Farewell. Much as I honour Bacon[4] I wish you were on our hills instead of amongst those proof sheets. Pray do not defend the beard; of itself it will surely fall.[5]

1. "Maud," I, 153.
2. Dr. Mann's *Maud Vindicated*.
3. Tennyson printed both idylls in the summer of 1857 under the title *Enid and Nimuë: The True and the False*. Their first publication, as "Enid" and "Vivien," was in the 1859 *Idylls*. Emily's remark calls to mind the anonymous critic of "Maud" who wrote: "If an author pipe of adultery, fornication, murder and suicide, set him down as the practiser of those crimes" (*AT*, p. 286).
Tennyson always regarded Spedding as an impeccable judge of literature, and both he and Emily from time to time solicited his opinion of the Laureate's work.
4. With R. L. Ellis and D. D. Heath, Spedding edited *The Works of Francis Bacon, Viscount St. Albans* (1857–74).
5. See Letter 64, below, for a further remark on Tennyson's beard.

55   To Alfred Tennyson

Farringford, 1 July [1856]

Many thanks, dearest, for thy note. . . . I must say I am puritan enough to be sorry thou shouldst have spent Sunday morning so. Maybe it was but a slip of the pen and yesterday meant the day before. My idea of Sunday as a day of high spiritual enjoyment thou knowest. Here is a note from Mother. Thou wilt I hope see her at Park House. Why hast thou forgotten the pleasant way of addressing my letters? The other looks cold and strange to me. "Sambo"[1] must take thee to the Milnes and the Boynes and Camerons and especially to the Venables and Chapmans.[2] Let us not seem to neglect our friends. Thou who art so true to them in reality should not seem otherwise. I had rather be without thee a little longer than that thou shouldst belie thyself to seem unkind.

I should like much to see the pictures. Some day when we have paid for this [Farringford] I want a frame to thy picture. I mean to wait for all I can until then. Hallam asks for thee. Baby is much more lively. He screamed with delight at some painted pictures of poultry last evening. Farewell, ownest own.

1. Unidentified.
2. Tennyson first became acquainted with Frederic Chapman (d. 1895), of the Chapman and Hall publishing house, at Park House in the early 1840s, while residing at Tunbridge Wells. A cousin of the founder, Frederic Chapman was a partner in Chapman and Hall from 1841 until 1880, and the managing director from 1880 until his death. Tennyson was in London the final week of June, returning to Farringford on 2 July.
For the Boynes of Brancepeth Castle, see above, Letter 6, n. 2.

56   To James Spedding

Builth,[1] 15 September 1856

Dear Mr. Spedding,
"Merlin" seems to me an awful tragedy. Do you not think that the higher and more imaginative the man, the more likely he is to fall, the lower he is likely to fall if he once yield ever so little to a base and evil influence. You think this, perhaps, but think also that in the case of Merlin, Nimuë[2] does not look, even at the beginning, enough the angel of light to have attracted him but it seems to me devotion or an appearance of it has more power over men than over women in itself. To a woman it is repulsive if she have no sympathy with him who pays it but I do not think it is so with men. Only I have looked at the world through such a very little chink all my life that I feel I have small right to give any opinion at all on the subject. And yet I felt it so kind in you to say what you thought, I am in a way constrained to say what I think, however foolish my

thoughts may be. Alfred is at Caerleon,[3] was when he wrote the letter I have today. He left me for it on Monday. Till then we have been wandering about together but our purse had grown so lean it seemed best for me to stay here with the bairns. We hope to be home at the end of the month.

1. In late July the Tennysons let Farringford for two months and traveled in Wales.
2. Tennyson's Vivien was modeled on Malory's Nimuë, chief Lady of the Lake, an ambiguous character who traps Merlin but has no enmity for King Arthur. See J. M. Gray, *Man and Myth in Victorian England: Tennyson's "The Coming of Arthur,"* (Lincoln, England: Keyworth and Fry, 1969), p. 23.
3. The reputed site of one of King Arthur's courts, Caerleon is purported to have a cave where many of Arthur's knights lie sleeping until the king return to lead them in reestablishing his realm.

57   To Alfred Tennyson

Builth, 17 September 1856

How art thou, dearest? Hallam was very much interested today when I told him thou wast gone to Caerleon, the city where King Arthur had his great round table where none but the good knights were to sit. Baby says, "Papa is gone to Becon."[1] The little creatures are well and very good and pleasant. . . .

I have made my way through some more of the *Hanes Cymru.*[2] The story of King Arthur gives me a feeling of awe reading it here alone. It is so grand and, in Welsh, seems so true. "The way of the soul."[3] No story in the world is to be compared with it I think. It is made for thee I am sure. Thou must take care of thyself and husband thy energies to spend them on this.

1. For "Brecon."
2. While writing "Geraint and Enid," Tennyson read the *Hanes Cymru* (the history of Wales), the *Mabinogion,* and Llywarch Hen's elegy on Geraint's death in the battle of Llongborth (Ricks, p. 1526).
3. Tennyson first used the phrase to describe *In Memoriam* and at one time considered it as a possible title for that poem.

58   *To Alfred Tennyson*

Builth, 20 September 1856

Dearest,
How good thou art writing to me every day. A thousand kisses
for it. . . . I am glad that thou shouldst see Caerphilly. The
city of ruins against the desolate mountains must be fine, for
they say the castle was so big the ruins look like those of a city
rather than a castle. Yesterday morning as I lay in bed I came
to the conclusion that our best plan is to let Merwood[1] have the
garden because he will let us have the first choice of vegetables
and all we want whereas Lambert[2] would have his own house
to think of. Besides Merwood, being in the farmhouse, could
look after it easily, and his people and himself seem to belong
to one more than anyone else at Freshwater. Then a good man
in the house would do all we want both in the house and
garden, with occasional help for moving, etc., and we could
dispense with a boy altogether and one servant less is many
cares the less, we both agree. . . .

I have written at last to Mr. Spedding to tell him my mind
about "Merlin," saying I thought it an awful tragedy, asking
whether it might not be that an imaginative and great man like
Merlin could fall lowest, were he once to yield ever so little to
an evil influence; saying moreover that if he (Mr. Spedding)
did not think Nimuë sufficiently an angel of light in the
beginning to attract Merlin. *I* thought devotion or the
appearance of it had so much power in itself over men that
this might account for it.

1. Merwood worked for the Tennysons as gardener and handyman
until April 1860.
2. Another hired man and tenant on the Farringford estate.

59   *To Thomas Woolner*

Farringford, 20 October 1856

Dear Mr. Woolner,
The photograph and the book[1] have deserved earlier thanks but
I have been by no means well and have been doing what I
could to hide the fact from the Patmores[2] so I know you will

not think me less grateful for my silence. The book is so noble Ally says he dare never write in it, so what do you think he proposes instead in his excessive reverence? Why to paste in pictures from the newspaper. Truly I think you will say this is a new proof that extremes meet. I for my part hope he will find none to paste in. . . . If you can come and stay with us when you want a little holiday, that is what you must do.

Only think of the lordly kindness of Mr. James Marshall who writes to know if there is a chance of having us as guests next year at Tent Lodge that he may dismiss his yearly tenants if there be! Of course we cannot think of such a thing, but I think instead we must ask people to look out for a comfortable house amongst some beautiful scenery in the Lakes that we may if all be well go there next year.[3]

The Patmores seem to me to have improved so very much in external things. One knows they were always as good as could be *almost* but they have gained in amenity of manner and he apparently in cheerfulness. Our bairnies look pale I grieve to say. I hope it is only teething.

1. Woolner had sent a photograph of the poet and an album for his rough drafts.
2. Coventry and Emily Patmore were at Farringford from the fifteenth until the twenty-third. The friendship between Tennyson and Patmore was strengthened by their wives' affection for each other, and during the late 1850s they were particularly intimate. Relations cooled in the 1860s, however, and after Emily Patmore's death in July 1862, the two poets never met again.
3. The Tennysons spent a long holiday at Tent Lodge in September 1857; the next autumn they journeyed through the Lake district into Scotland.

60   To Thomas Woolner

Farringford, 11 November 1856

My dear Mr. Woolner,
The beautiful boxful has arrived quite safely today. Accept our best thanks. Dr. and Mrs. Mann are here and are delighted as well as Alfred and myself with the delicate yet lofty beauty of the medallion and with the grandeur of the bust.

Do you know I have been taking great liberties with your

name just now? I have requested Aunt Franklin and another influential person that if there be a statue of Uncle Franklin by way of memorial in Lincoln Cathedral you may have the doing of it.[1] My aunt replied she thought there was no chance of a statue for want of funds. I replied that you being a young artist a statue might be possible with you as artist when it might not be another being artist. . . . I hope you will not think I have been over-bold.

Sir John Simeon was so pleased with his medallion and not less with the maker thereof if I may be permitted to say so. . . .[2] Our boys are well. I wish you could see them. I am so pleased the medallion and bust are such great successes. The bust is Alfred's favorite and mine also I think. The medallion strikes the Manns most at first.

1. Woolner never did a statue of Sir John Franklin, the Arctic explorer, Emily Tennyson's maternal uncle.
2. Woolner did a plaster bust of Simeon in 1872, now in the Royal Academy. The medallion mentioned here, however, is undoubtedly a copy of the second Tennyson medallion which Tennyson had given to Simeon.

61   To Thomas Woolner

Farringford, 6 December 1856

Dear Mr. Woolner,
Many thanks for your kindness in having remembered the medallion[1] for the Rawnsleys. They are charmed with it. I write now to ask if you will do me the favour to order a gold frame for it like ours when next you go to your framemaker. . . . We have read *Aurora Leigh*[2] and rejoice in its good and great and beautiful thoughts. But tell me, is it a poem or a novel in high verse? It seems to me not a poem and yet it may be, I know; one whose melody I have not yet learnt, but must learn from itself if I am ever to learn it at all. . . .

1. A copy of the second Tennyson medallion.
2. Mrs. Browning sent the Tennysons a copy of *Aurora Leigh* (1857) before publication. The Laureate pronounced it "very good lymph of poetry" (*AT*, p. 303).

62   To Thomas Woolner

Farringford, 16 December 1856

Dear Mr. Woolner,
I know how much you care for the Brownings so I am going to
tell you the good news we heard from Sir John Simeon
yesterday, that Mr. Kenyon has left them a good deal of
money.[1] If this brings them to live sometimes in the Isle of
Wight will it not be delightful! Many a happy meeting may
you have with them at Farringford. I want to stir you to look
after the Newton monument. I think I told you Alfred wrote
about you to Dr. Latham[2] who seems to be the acting man.
Now Ally is applied to for his subscription, so something is
going to be done I suppose. . . .
    Ally has taken to rolling the lawn. I must go out to him. The
bairns are well.

1. A cousin of Mrs. Browning's, John Kenyon had given the Brownings
a hundred pounds annually for some years before his death in 1856.
Kenyon left £4,500 to Mrs. Browning and £6,500 to her husband.
2. Dr. Robert Gordon Latham (1817-88), ethnologist, philologist,
author, and Queen's Physician.

63   To Thomas Woolner

Farringford, 24 December 1856

Dear Mr. Woolner,
This is Christmas Eve and the first in our own house. It is
saddened by Lionel's being ill as he was when you were here
nearly two years ago. He was recovering then. He has been
very unwell since Friday last, and this is why I have not been
able to answer your kind note before. . . .
    Dr. Latham directs his last letter from Greensford,
Middlesex. I do not know whether this is home now. Perhaps
from his position as Queen's Physician it would be not very
difficult to find out whether it is. If you should see him you
will mention Alfred's name will you not and say it is we who
preferred your looking after the statue.
    I am so glad you have made such good and pleasant friends
as the Trevelyans.[1] Next time they want change of air, and may

this be long if they only want it for health's sake, but when next they do want it, recommend Freshwater. I hope you are having a merry Christmas, and that a happy New Year is coming for you. . . .

I thought the Brownings had been poor or I should not so much have rejoiced over their acquisition of money.[2] I think it is a bad thing to get into the habit of over-prizing wealth, whether for one's self or others, and it seems an overprizing to desire more than food and raiment and Farringford.

1. Sir Walter Calverley Trevelyan, sixth baronet (1797-1879), naturalist, geologist, and liberal patron of the arts, and his first wife, the former Pauline Jermyn (d. 1866). In his letter of 17 December 1856, to Emily Tennyson (*Thomas Woolner,* pp. 125-26), Woolner set down his impressions of the Trevelyans and expressed his pleasure in the interest they evidenced in his artistic well-being when he visited them in London not long before.

2. Woolner wrote in response to the news of the Brownings' inheritance in his letter of 17 December: "That is fine fun you write of—the Brownings having plenty of money left them. I do not much care about it tho'; for they are very well circumstanced in these matters I believe" (*Thomas Woolner,* p. 125).

64   *To Thomas Woolner*

Farringford, 18 March 1857

My dear Mr. Woolner,
Our best thanks for the reviews. I cannot tell you how glad we are that the bust should be recognized not unworthily.[1] Sure this is the beginning of a happier day for you. . . . I wish the public could compel Alfred by act of Parliament to cut off his beard! We had the Simeons and Camerons here last night. I wished you could have met them. On Monday they assembled here also to keep Lionel's birthday, three years old.

1. Woolner informed Emily Tennyson in a letter of 8 March 1857 (*Thomas Woolner,* pp. 130-31), that Ruskin had pronounced the Tennyson bust "a triumph of Art," and in a letter of 16 March (pp. 131-32), he told of other admirers, the Charles Welds, the F. D. Maurices, and Carlyle, who "of all the persons who have been to see it . . . was the most delighted—said it was a thorough success, absolutely perfect, etc.—and made a great fuss."

65   *To Thomas Woolner*

Farringford, 13 April 1857

Dear Mr. Woolner,

But that I know you are among the understanding ones I
should have felt you had been day after day blaming one for
not having thanked you for papers and kind notes. You know
what it is to get into a crazy state from overwork. It is decided
that Mother and Matilda will not come to the wedding[1] nor the
Lushingtons nor the Turners, so instead of the expected
overflowing house is an empty one. We do hope that yourself
and Mr. Vernon Lushington[2] will be able to return with Alfred,
who I think will probably go to town from St. Lawrence on
Friday. He ought to have gone ten days ago for his teeth. . . .
We do rejoice in what is said of the bust.

1. Horatio Tennyson's marriage, 16 April 1857, to Charlotte Elwes,
daughter of Dudley Cary Elwes.
2. (1832-1912), fourth son of Sir Stephen Lushington (d. 1877), of
South Hill Park, Berkshire, judge and Secretary to the Admiralty,
1869-77.

66   *To Alfred Tennyson*

Farringford, 30 April 1857

Dearest,

A note from thee today was an unlooked-for delight. Bless thee
for it. I hope Cartwright will make thee comfortable. Do not let
anyone play tricks with that toe. I think it very likely from the
cold or from the state of thy general health. Thou dost not say
if thou left "Merlin" and "Enid" with Moxon or not.[1] These
days are always in a manner more sacred to thee than any
others because two or three years thou didst spend them with
me at Horncastle. The statute folk did them honour fiddling
and dancing then and now the dove coos in our own elm-tree.
. . .[2]

I do not send letters because there are none thou wouldst
particularly care to see but I keep them for thee. I have not
quite got over the chill yet but am better. I sent the lending
library books the same day or rather the next and a note to say

I had sent them. Shouldst thou buy books think of the servants please. Prescotts[3] would do for them.

1. Tennyson had gone to London to see both his dentist and Dr. Cartwright, who was treating him for gout, as well as to arrange with Moxon the printing of the *Illustrated Edition* and *Enid and Nimuë*. Emily described in her Journal the circumstances of a rather disorderly embarkation on the twenty-seventh. At the last moment Tennyson discovered that the carriage which was to take him to Yarmouth was too small to allow Emily, Hallam, and Lionel all to go to see him off. The boys were finally permitted to ride on their parents' laps, but the change of plans delayed Tennyson so much that he was late for the steamer and had to follow it in a rowboat for some distance in order to get aboard.

2. Tennyson undoubtedly paid occasional visits to Horncastle during the 1838-40 engagement. Statute fairs for the hiring of servants were held annually in many rural towns and villages.

3. Historical books by William Hickling Prescott (1796-1859), American historian and author of the *History of Ferdinand and Isabella,* the *History of the Conquest of Mexico,* the *Conquest of Peru,* and numerous other works.

67   To James Spedding

Tent Lodge, 14 September 1857

My dear Mr. Spedding,

We have been at the Marshall's own house for nearly a fortnight but here I am again this evening. Alfred, I hope, is at Wastwater with Mr. Marshall and Mr. Williams.[1] I would have answered your kind note the very day it came but I was very tired and Mrs. Marshall said, "Write only the business letters," and I felt they were all I could do, and other days came and we drove and talked and were very tired again. . . . Mrs. Marshall is as enthusiastic as you can be about Mrs. Shapcote.[2] I hope I shall like the music as well as you like both her and her music, and if I can like music to any part of *In Memoriam,* Mrs. Shapcote need not desire a greater triumph as far as I am concerned.

We have not been well here but, notwithstanding, there has been great enjoyment in our visits. One does so heartily love the Marshalls, to say nothing of all the pains they have taken to show us every day something beautiful. We have besides been having Mr. Venables here. I wish we could have had you too. Alfred means if possible to get over to Mirehouse for a call. We go away next week, I believe. Whether north or south I cannot yet say. The boys are well and laugh so loudly going up the hills in the postwoman's donkey cart that the neighbors come out to stare.

1. Unidentified.
2. Mrs. Edward Gifford Shapcote, a friend of the Speddings, who, in 1857, published a volume of songs entitled "Eleven Songs, words taken from *In Memoriam* and other poems by Alfred Tennyson." The songs were received by copyright deposit in the British Museum on 23 September 1857.

Tennyson had little opportunity to progress with his Arthurian project during the early summer of 1857. From the first of May until mid-July, the house was constantly inundated with visitors, including his mother, his sister Matilda, his brothers Horatio and Charles, Cecilia and Edmund Lushington, Vernon Lushington, the Archibald Peels, the Simeons, the Bradleys, Woolner, Lear, William Wilberforce, Bayard Taylor, the American writer, and George Coltman, an old Lincolnshire friend. Emily received her guests gladly, and when she was able, she delighted in conducting strolls about the estate. On 19 May she rambled with Woolner, Vernon Lushington, and Tennyson through "a paradise of flowers—blue hyacinths like the heavens breaking through the earth, crocuses, gorgeous crimson, grown in the pine trees. A. covered with sweet golden dust from them. The cedar brightening with the new leaves" (Journal).

In late July the Tennysons visited Charles and Louisa Turner at Grasby, and thence proceeded to Manchester where they met Woolner, attended Dickens's reading of "A Christmas Carol" in the Free Trade Hall, and went to see a fine exhibition then on view at the National Gallery which included an assortment of Turner sketches and works by Holman Hunt and William Mulready. By the end of the month they were at Coniston where they spent the remainder of their holiday. While there they visited with numerous old friends, among them Venables, Allingham, Franklin Lushington, Mary Marshall's brothers, Stephen and William Spring-Rice, Matthew Arnold, and Dr. William Whewell,

Master of Trinity, and they found a new friend in C. L. Dodgson (Lewis Carroll). The Tennysons protracted their visit until the end of September, spending much of their time boating on Coniston Lake and walking through the surrounding countryside. One day they went with the Marshalls and William Spring-Rice on a grand expedition to Dungeon Ghyll, some eight miles north of Coniston via Tilberthwaite and Fell Foot. From Fell Foot they followed the slope of Lingmoor Fell to Blea Tarn, supposed site of the Solitary's cottage in Wordsworth's *Excursion.* Emily shortly wrote in the Journal her impressions of the hills which rise just beyond: "What grand walls of rock this . . . and Lingmoor crouches magnificently like a lion at the foot of Langdale Pikes and what a fine sweep they make to the valley, the moraine just beyond!"

From Tent Lodge the Tennysons journeyed to Inverary to visit with the Duke and Duchess of Argyll, and returning to England by way of Glasgow and Carstairs, stopped at Park House for a week. On the morning of 3 November they went with Mrs. Cameron to see the Carlyles, who saw them despite Carlyle's strict mandate against morning visits, and the following day they began a more normal routine at Farringford after more than three months' absence.

68   To Elizabeth Barrett Browning
Wellesley College

Tent Lodge, 14 September [1857]

My dear Mrs. Browning,
There came a hearty smile of joy at your kindness although unhappily the question seems to have a somewhat graver answer. Alfred has not been well here. Our friends are so kind we have not liked to leave, as for health's sake we ought to have done a month ago. He has been better of late but still he is not well. We both of us sighed for the south and we ought to have followed the instinct which led us thither. . . .

Last year we were in cold wintery [?] Wales and now we are here and both years we had better have been in France or Italy. Whether we go still further north I cannot say. We are expected in Scotland but I have more faith in English doctors than

Scotch and for my own part I am not sure if mere change of air will restore Alfred and if he will not have to put himself under a London doctor. The country ones have done their best.

We do often think and talk of you and wish so heartily we could be with you. Yes, I love and admire Frederick so well myself I am very sorry for you that you are parted from him but still more am I sorry for him. I believe you scarcely know how much you were to him, as you are used to be to so many.[1]

You have faith in Alfred or I dare not say to you he has talked over and over again of writing to you about your poems. Then he said, "I had so much rather speak about them," and so the days and months went on and he never said one word of all the admiration he felt, no not even thanked you for your precious gifts. Do not think him ungrateful. You will not, I am sure.

I wish you had heard "Enid" and "Merlin." Mr. Browning's words were so encouraging to him but then the worst of it is, a grain of dispraise from almost anyone outweighs even your praise, and people come and say these old stories will not do and he so far believes them that he stops work for months perhaps for years and life is so short.

He bids me say how very much he felt the kindness of your enquiries. He is gone to Wastwater and desired I would write immediately or I would wait for a line from himself. Yes, I do hope to see your little boy[2] very soon. Our boys are healthy and merry and quite simple children with small inclination for anything but play. I feel it should at present be indulged that they may have what chance we can give them of gaining strength to bear the weight of over—very, I will not say over, sensitive nerves that may have descended to them and that many signs make me believe have descended and I cannot wish it otherwise. . . . I hope I may before long be able to write again and tell you he is well and at work.

1. The Brownings met Frederick Tennyson (1807-98), the Laureate's oldest brother, who had first gone to the Mediterranean in 1834, soon after their return to Florence in 1853. In a letter of 24 February 1853, to Joseph Milsand, Browning wrote, "I have a new acquaintance here, much to my taste, Tennyson's elder brother, a very earnest, simple, and truthful man, with many admirable talents and acquirements. He is very shy. He sees next to no company, but comes here and we walk together" (William H. Griffin and H. C. Minchin, *The Life of Robert Browning* [New York: Methuen, 1912], p. 189). Mrs. Browning was fond of both Frederick Tennyson and his poetry, and in a letter of

15 July 1853, to Mary Russell Mitford, she pronounced his verse "full of imagery, encompassed with poetical atmosphere and very melodious. On the other hand there is vagueness and too much personification. It's the smell of a rose rather than a rose—very sweet, notwithstanding. His poems are far superior to Charles Tennyson's, bear in mind. As for the poet, we quite love him, Robert and I do. What Swedenborg calls 'selfhood,' the *proprium,* is not in him." See Frederic G. Kenyon, *The Letters of Elizabeth Barrett Browning* (London: Macmillan, 1897), II, 123.

2. Robert Wiedemann Barrett Browning (1849-1912).

69   *To Edward Lear*

15 September 1857

Dear Mr. Lear,
Oh I am indeed glad you are to go to Corfu if all be well.[1] I hope Frank will be able to make things quite easy when you are once there. . . . I wish that we may be alone when you both come for that both will come I will hope, and I trust the sadness of the past will but deepen the delight of our hours together. I must warn you however that sometimes when with Frank I grow just as silent as he is, unless it happen that I am with him alone and then I can generally conquer the shyness which his silence brings, but I dare say you will do instead of being alone in this case and I shall be helped by your presence instead of my old friends the empty room or the sofa in the corner or the solitary drive. Between Ally and myself the sympathy is too intimate almost for us to help each other sometimes and we must rather be helped or hindered together. So, dear Mr. Lear, do both come and I will think we shall all be very happy together. Poor Ally is gone to London today to try to get his toothache cured. . . . He is gone with the Grants as far as Basingstoke. We have had many pleasant hours with them and we are sorry to part from them.

The bairnies are well except that baby suffers somewhat from his teeth. The dear little fellow folds his hands and says his grace after his fashion and the other night he was saying his prayers in bed a long while. . . . He dearly loves "Papa"—"Pretty Papa" as he has been known to say. Farewell. I hope the cough is gone.

1. Lear was in Dublin, Ireland, in the company of his friend, Chichester Fortescue, Baron Carlingford (1823-98), from the end of August until the beginning of October. He returned to Corfu in November without making his intended visit to the Isle of Wight.

70   *To Edward Lear*

Tent Lodge, 18 September 1857

Dear Mr. Lear,
How do we like Coniston? The people and the mountains very much, the hollows and the mists not at all. We always are and are not going to Scotland next week; which we shall do remains to be seen. We have been very poorly almost all the while here and I rather dread moving further north. . . . Mr. Venables was staying with the Marshalls about ten days and we were there also most of the time. He was extremely kind and pleasant. He had come from Park House but the account he gave was not very cheering. . . . Poor Frank seems to have quite as great a horror of Corfu as yourself. Oh dear, oh dear, why do we not keep him in England when we want him so much?

71   *To Edward Lear*

Farringford, 17 November 1857

My dear Mr. Lear,
All good be with you. We would rather have spoken it than written it but it was not to be it seems. Come back soon well and happy. . . . You were very right, I was quite worn out body and mind. We had scarcely been a day alone for about six months. I cannot tell you how glad I was to get home. . . . The boys were beyond measure glad to see their own home again, happy though they had been in most places during our absence. They went about saying, dear old Farringford, my own dear house, my own dear cart, and so forth. . . . Lionel's addition to the old woman who lives in a shoe is almost worthy

of you: "She gave them some medicine without any sugar."
What will our young lady neighbours say to me for having fed
them with false hopes of seeing you before you left![1] Alfred's
love.

1. Emily Tennyson's implication that the young ladies of Freshwater
will pine over Lear's absence is characteristically kind. Lear thought
himself too ugly to interest any woman, and, according to R. E.
Francillon, his "plainness of face was made the more emphatic by
his nearness of sight, awkward slouch, and a style of dress which can
only be called careless by courtesy" (quoted by A. Davidson, *Edward
Lear: Landscape Painter,* p. 105).

72   To Thomas Woolner

Farringford, 15 February 1858

My dear Mr. Woolner,
Many thanks for both the letters.[1] If you could have seen the
quiet smile at one moment, the shout of delight at another as
the letter moved them, I think you would have felt repaid for
the trouble of writing it. . . .

But for that bust it does seem a very great shame that it
should leave England. We had heard that Trinity College had
offered £200 for it. I do not know what the price fixed on it is
but I have that feeling for Trinity that as far as feeling goes I
would rather have it there than elsewhere, though I know it
ought to be in London. . . . Alfred says, "Tell him not to part
with that to America. He is sure to find a purchaser in
England."[2] I do hope you will soon come to us.

1. Woolner wrote to Emily from London on 11 February 1857,
enclosing a lace collar made for Hallam Tennyson by Pauline, Lady
Trevelyan.
2. Woolner had thought of selling the Tennyson bust to a Dr. Fellows
of Boston. But, as Emily Tennyson hoped, Trinity College purchased
the bust and placed it in the vestibule of the Library, the Library itself
being reserved for monuments to the dead.

Except for a brief trip to London to his dentist in late May,
Tennyson was home during the entire spring of 1858. As usual

there were many visitors, including John Henry Newman and Benjamin Jowett, each of whom came twice in April, as well as Algernon Swinburne and John Tyndall, the natural philosopher. When the Tennysons were alone, the poet spent most of his time writing in his Maiden's Croft summer house (see below, Letter 182, n.2); but he was continually interrupted by his sons' requests for his participation in activities ranging from playing battledore and shuttlecock to building castles and flying kites. Nonetheless, he wrote a draft of "Sea Dreams" and "The Grandmother" during these months, began "Lancelot and Elaine," and completed "Guinevere," which he presented to Emily at tea time on 15 March.

After dinner the Tennysons read nursery tales and rhymes to Hallam and Lionel. Then, when the boys had gone to bed, Tennyson read to Emily from his own poems, or from Goethe, Shakespeare, and Dante, and occasionally from Whitman or Béranger. Together they read from the Bible and from Plato, Lucretius, Hegel, Bacon, Kemble, and Motley's *Rise of the Dutch Republic*. These hours of reading and academic discussion alone with her husband revived in Emily "a feeling of the freshness of youth," along with memories of Henry Sellwood's reading aloud to her and her sisters in his Horncastle study so many years before. In the afternoons after tea or after their reading at nights Emily sometimes sang to Tennyson, and played when her hand would permit it, and his delight in her songs also recalled the pleasure her father had found in her music when she was a girl (Journal, 28 April 1858). The following letter, written after Tennyson had returned to London and his dentist on 9 June, reflects something of the love-charmed contentment which prompted Emily to write in her Journal on 14 April: "If it were not faithless I should be afraid of so much happiness as I have."

73   To Alfred Tennyson
(with a postscript from Hallam Tennyson)

Farringford, 13 June 1858

Own dearest,
I know thou dost not think of days so perhaps thou wilt not

remember this. Nevertheless, I kiss thee on our wedding-day and I say God ever bless thee and us and a great deal more I say that I will not and cannot write and a great deal more I feel than I could say if I would. Thou art so good and I am so happy that I can have but one wish, that we may grow ever more one with God in Christ and so whatever betide we shall be one for ever.

Here are a syringa and a bit of myrtle for thee. There is no mist today but it is a beautiful day, sunny with soft clouds. Our boys are better, though neither quite well, but well enough to get out a little and I think I shall get to church this afternoon. I never saw anything so beautiful by way of syringas as ours. They are almost as white as the hawthorns were. Even the poor rhododendrons look gay.
My dear Papa,

Love and Kisses. I hope you are well. I dreamt God a large head and a large face and hair like Lionel's.

Your loving little son,
H. T.

74   To Alfred Tennyson

Farringford, 16 June 1858

Own dearest,
It looks as if poor Milnes were sorry. I hope some day you will meet and have the matter out with him.[1] Though I do not as thou knowest very much care for what people say about thy things, being strong in the conceit of my own instinct, yet I will confess to a kind of pleasure when people are near going into "high strikes" over them. I believe it is the joy of sympathy. The children want to tell thee about their visit to Mrs. Prettyman[2] yesterday. The old butler's face at sight of them was worth a great deal. He took out the rocking horse and the stuffed gazelle on the lawn and made much of the bairns. Last night I began to think the "villainous centre-bit"[3] had come at last. I got up and listened and was more and more convinced, a distinct grinding of glass. I thought, shall I ring the bell to alarm the thieves? Wake the maids I know it will not. No, I will light a candle and hold it to the window. I held

it and grew bolder and went to the window myself and saw a
snail grinding the glass with its shell, and afterwards listened
with pleasure to the strange sounds it made sometimes like
some instrument of music. . . .

If it be convenient to thee some day I will ask thee to get a
dissected map of Europe for the boys. Their wildness is
unbounded. When they heard that Uncle Frank was coming
back,[4] they took to beating me and kissing me and pulling all
my hair over my shoulders calling out, "I am so glad, I am so
glad," in the most crazy fashion. I can scarcely fix them to
anything. The map would be something new.

1. Monckton Milnes had been critical of the 1857 trial volume, *Enid
and Nimuë*. Whether or not they "had the matter out," Tennyson and
Milnes remained on affectionate terms, although as they grew older
they saw each other less frequently.
2. A Freshwater neighbor.
3. "Maud," I, 41.
4. Franklin Lushington resigned his Corfu judgeship and returned
to England in August 1858.

75   To John Forster

Farringford, 31 October 1858

Dear Mr. Forster,
Sunday the post goes early; I must write a line of hearty thanks
for your letter. I copy the passage concerning you from
Bradbury and Evans telling you at the same time that I have
copied the whole letter for Charles Weld:[1]

"Before Mr. Forster went out of town we
consulted him as to the propriety of getting
forward with the Illustrated Edition of *The
Princess,* and by this post we send the first two
sheets, etc."

Upon which Alfred commented last night almost in the words
of your letter. He felt sure you could have given no such
advice. We will not interfere personally in anything concerning
this matter. All shall go through yourself and Charles Weld
since you with such exceeding kindness consent that so it shall
be. It seemed necessary to send some sort of answer to

Bradbury and Evans. Now Alfred desires that there should be a stop put to the illustrated edition of *The Princess* until something concerning it can be decided. I enclose a statement of facts respecting the illustrated editions. They must be taken as *mine* in which he as far as he remembers concurs.[2] You will see that there has been no arrangement whatever respecting *The Princess*. On the contrary we were utterly astonished when we heard that Maclise was in Italy or had been there drawing for it. Alfred of course will not come to town since you and Charles advise that he should not.

1. After Edward Moxon's death on 3 June 1858, Tennyson was never able to establish a satisfactory relationship with the Moxon heirs, though he remained with the firm until 1869, because of his affection for Moxon and for his widow. In October 1858, the Tennysons were shocked to learn that Moxon's intended to publish an illustrated edition of *The Princess,* despite the poet's dislike of the illustrations Daniel Maclise had done for the volume and his decision to cancel plans for its publication. Frederick M. Evans (1803?-70) and William H. Bradbury (1832-92), managers of Moxon's from 1858 until 1864, wrote to Tennyson in behalf of William Moxon, brother of the founder, informing him of the plan and contending that the publishing house had received Tennyson's sanction for the edition from John Forster. Charles Weld, who had been representing the Laureate in negotiations with Moxon's, wrote to Emily Tennyson in Forster's defense on 30 October (unpublished letter, T.R.C.): "Forster utterly denies having been ever consulted respecting the illustrated edition of *The Princess.* He has written to Evans, requiring an explanation."
Earlier in October William Moxon had informed Weld that any new financial arrangement between Tennyson and his firm would have to wait upon settlement of a debt of £8,886.8.4, which Tennyson owed the estate of the late Edward Moxon. In a letter of 27 October to the poet (unpublished, T.R.C.), Weld detailed Moxon's claim that "in consequence of *your* earnest solicitation his late brother had embarked in an unfortunate speculation of publishing an *Illustrated Edition* of your poems, of which he printed 10,000 copies and that 7,790 remained unsold. These are valued at £8,374.5; 2,080 copies of *The Princess* at £338; 400 of the *In Memoriam* at £76.13.4; and 600 of "Maud" at £97.10—making altogether £8,886.8.4." The eldest Moxon brother, Charles, did not support William Moxon's spurious claim, however, and it was dropped. Though he had been falsely accused and very nearly swindled, Tennyson nonetheless permitted the publication of Moxon's illustrated *The Princess,* inasmuch as the firm had already made extensive financial commitments to the project.
2. In the "statement of facts" (unpublished, T.R.C.), included in this letter, Emily Tennyson made it clear that the *Illustrated Edition* was entirely Edward Moxon's own proposal, and that Tennyson was "heartily sorry" for the failure of the speculation, though he had never been

optimistic about its chance for success. Emily concluded her statement to Forster with an assurance that her husband had never in any way consented to the publication of an illustrated edition of *The Princess:* "Alfred is certain he never agreed to *The Princess* unless it were by silence. I will of course copy anything, answer anything, do anything I can to lessen your trouble, dear Mr. Forster. Between ourselves, I will come up to Burlington House alone if it would be desirable to question me personally."

76   To Charles Weld

Farringford, 2 November 1858

My dear Charles,
Thanks a thousand for all your care and trouble. There was no written agreement or memorandum respecting the third of profit or any other publishing arrangement. Mr. Moxon offered the third to Alfred of his own accord in his own house.[1] 1848 is the earliest account we have of this but Alfred does not know that this was the first of this division of profits. This does not seem important to us as there is proof of the arrangement subsisting long before any talk of the illustrated editions.

We never came to any arrangement respecting the *Illustrated Edition* of the poems, except that which appears in the letters I have copied for you. In conversation Alfred stated that it was impossible for him to furnish funds to pay the artists and I think, as far as I remember, Moxon said, "Oh, we can manage all that."

1. Emily Tennyson nodded. According to their oral agreement, Tennyson retained two-thirds of all profits and allowed Edward Moxon one-third, plus five percent on gross sales of all Moxon editions. By the beginning of 1859 there were new terms which allowed the Moxon firm a commission of ten percent with no direct share of profits.

77   *To Charles Weld*

Farringford, 3 November 1858

My dear Charles,
As it is of great consequence to us that the Christmas sale
should be as little hindered as possible, and as we believe there
are now no more of the poems remaining except the *Illustrated
Edition,* we are anxious to get the matter settled as soon as
possible that the publishing of these may go forward. There
seems no safe ground upon which to act until some lawyer has
satisfied us as to the points of law in question. . . .

I hope, dear Charles, you will not be much annoyed by what
he [William Moxon] says. He is, I suspect, so angry that his
brother made a bad speculation that he does not know what he
says. I am only sorry you should suffer from his wrath as Ally's
representative.

78   *To Charles Weld*

Farringford, 6 November 1858

My dear Charles,
Many thanks. This is exactly what we wanted. It is indeed a
great satisfaction to find that the legal opinion corresponds
precisely with our own common sense view of the points in
question. . . . It is a great comfort to find that you have formed
so favourable an opinion of Mr. Nettleship.[1] We shall with
confidence place ourselves in his hands. . . .

Alfred would prefer coming up himself. As he says, no
agreement could be made without him. Having made myself
very ill two years ago he has a horror of my undertaking once
again.[2] However . . . I think he would still consent if when the
time comes you feel that I should be of any use.

1. Henry John Nettleship of Kettering, Northamptonshire, a solicitor.
2. Tennyson left for London alone on the eleventh, a bitter east wind
having sealed his resolve to leave Emily at home.

79   To Margaret Gatty[1]
Boston Public Library

Farringford, 8 November [1858]

Dear Madam,
Our Sunday post which returns immediately prevented me
from answering your kind letter yesterday. I dare not ask you
to run the risk of crossing the Solent on the slight chance of
finding my husband at home this week as we are bid hold
ourselves ready to go to town this week on important business.

   We regret to hear that you are out of health and if we do not
meet this time we hope that another time when you are in our
neighbourhood not for health but for pleasure we may have the
privilege of making your acquaintance.

   1. (1809-73), Emily Tennyson's friend and correspondent from the
time of her first visit to Farringford, in the Laureate's company, on
20 November 1858, until her death fifteen years later. The youngest
daughter of the Rev. Alexander John Scott, D. D., Lord Nelson's chaplain
in the *Victory,* Mrs. Gatty is best remembered for her popular children's
books. Although poor health permitted her few visits to the Tennysons',
she frequently sent them her husband's lectures and sermons, as well
as her own stories, to which Emily sometimes responded with critical
appraisals. Like his wife, the Reverend Alfred Gatty was an author
and a Tennyson enthusiast. On 6 December 1859 he delivered a lecture
entitled "The Poetical Character," illustrated from the work of the Poet
Laureate, which was published in 1860, and he later wrote *A Key to
Tennyson's In Memoriam* (1881).

80   To Margaret Gatty
Boston Public Library

Farringford, 29 November 1858

My dear Mrs. Gatty,
Many thanks for your kindness to us all. Hallam makes quite a
pet of his prayer book. We have read "The Poor Incumbent,"
my husband and myself.[1] We read it the evening of the day it
came and I saw he was touched and he told me that it was the
visit of the bishop that had so touched him and as for me this
and many other things in it touched me. . . .

   I wish I could tell you that Alfred's cold is gone but it is not, nor mine neither, but I can tell you that the publishing affairs are settled at a 10 per cent commission thanks to Charles Weld's kind exertion in our behalf.

1. Like Julia Margaret Cameron, Mrs. Gatty was forever showering the Tennyson's with presents. After her first visit to Farringford she sent an assortment of gifts, including "The Poor Incumbent," a story she published earlier that year, and a scythe, especially for the poet. Tennyson often mowed his own grounds, and he liked to assist the hired men at Farringford, and later at Aldworth, in rolling the lawns, cutting new glades, spreading gravel, etc.

81   To Margaret Gatty
Boston Public Library

Farringford, 6 December 1858

My dear Mrs. Gatty,
The scythe has arrived. A beautiful one it is and Alfred is very grateful for it. It looks as if even I might mow with it. . . . You are very kind to think of us as you do in all sorts of ways. Do you know I think I should have rewarded you by getting you hung for murder by slow poison had I gone on taking the Nux Vomica? Two doses of it on two nights following had so poisonous an effect on me. Why will not the homeopathists find some strengthening globules not poisonous?[1]
We both of us admire "The Hundredth Birthday."[2] It is very charming. I admit that you had a right to admire his old woman. He has read the other tales also. I, you know, have but very little time for reading.

1. Nux Vomica, literally the vomiting nut, a poisonous seed containing strychnine and brucine, was widely used in powdered form in the nineteenth century for treating indigestion and other alimentary disorders. It was considered particularly useful for people nervous and dyspeptic as the result of overwork and mental fatigue.
2. One of Mrs. Gatty's *Legendary Tales* (London, 1858).

82   To Margaret Gatty

Boston Public Library

Farringford, 7 December [1858]

My dear Mrs. Gatty,
I had meant to have written even if your kind letter had not
come for I remembered that I had stupidly forgotten to give
our best wishes about the Living. Heavy writing days and not a
few consequent aches and pains must be my excuse. I do not
know if I shall ever sufficiently overcome my dread of
homeopathic poisons to consult a homeopathic doctor. I thank
you not the less for your recommendations. Alfred's cough may
I think be said to have gone. . . .
   With our best thanks and remembrances for all your kindness
and a hearty commendation of the scythe which looks to me a
transformed sword and which Alfred pronounces so admirable
that once he is master of it there need be no slovenly lawns.

83   To Margaret Gatty

Boston Public Library

Farringford, 13 December 1858

My dear Mrs. Gatty,
Little Hallam says, "Why is Mrs. Gatty so kind to us?" and we
can do little else than echo the question. Two more gifts since
I last wrote! One does feel rather ashamed and very grateful.
   I have read "The Dragonfly" and think it fine. The chief
difference between the feeling of this and "The Sedge
Warbler" appears to me to lie in the change of state which
seems to make palpable the thin wall never to be pierced by
mortal eyes.[1]
   Do I like parables? Yes I do. I hold them one of the best
forms of teaching but then their amplifications, pleasant to
children, are to me trying except within very strict limitations.
I only enjoy them through the child when they exceed these.
Naturally, a hint, some Dantesque ellipse is that which
suggests most to me, I think.
   "The Model Lodging House" is very interesting to us both.
Alfred said, as you would expect, after reading it, "This is a

true parson." We do indeed like to know that the true parson cares for one whom I know to be the true poet. Would that they could see more nearly into each other's souls.

I am not so inhuman as you think. I provided two large bowls and a little one for my large sea family. They were none of them disturbed from their stones. Some of them have gone to the care of the cook, who has taken a fancy for them. You will think me a queer creature but having seen the life of these creatures I should at once put them back into the sea. I only take care of them for Alfred. Do not send him the pink one unless it is a creature with a different mode of existence. We shall have no one to take care of it when we leave home. They are only mesembryanthemums that we have. The pink one is at least twice as big as when you left.[2]

1. Both of these tales, actually entitled "A Lesson of Faith" and "The Unknown Land," are from the first series of *Parables from Nature* (London, 1855).
2. Margaret Gatty was intensely interested in the study of seaweeds and zoophytes, and in 1862 she published a book on *British Seaweeds*, which was supervised by her friend, Dr. William Henry Harvey, author of *Phycologia Britannica* (1846-51). Evidently Tennyson shared her interest, and Mrs. Gatty must have been delighted with his mesembryanthemums, or midday-flowers, bright-colored sea plants which often open their flowers only for a short time each day.

84   To Julia Margaret Cameron
Ritchie, From Friend to Friend, *pp. 15-16*

Farringford [1858]

It is like a book. All so perfectly happy, and yet I feel ungrateful for saying so, for so long as one believes in love and truth, so long must one believe in the possibility of happiness, and I myself, having so much of the reality, should most of all dare to believe in the possibility for others. Let them be married soon—I may be pardoned for a horror of long engagements.[1]

1. Mrs. Cameron's daughter Julia married Charles Norman early in 1859. Emily Tennyson's remarks call to mind her statement in "For Her Sons" that the long delay before she and Tennyson were married "may have been a mistake" (p. 100).

85   To Margaret Gatty
Boston Public Library

Farringford, 12 January 1859

My dear Mrs. Gatty,

Alfred has gone out for a long walk with Mr. Jowett,[1] so I must ask you to accept from me his best thanks for your beautiful copies of Blake which we all, Mr. Jowett included, admire very much. I must get them put in Alfred's study, I think.

I hope this new year has begun, as it will go on, happily with you, and I hope that you do not much regret the southern living.[2] The advantage of staying among those who have learnt to love and trust us seems to me so very great as to overpower most others, and I suspect when people are equally mated in any degree that society cannot in reality do so much for them as imagination sometimes whispers it might do. A good field of work is in this case, it seems to me, the greatest boon of life.

1. Benjamin Jowett arrived at Farringford on January sixth and remained until the eighteenth. Emily Tennyson wrote about his visit in her Journal: "We have had very interesting conversations with him and A. and he have had long walks and A. has read on different evenings 'The Grandmother,' 'The Maid of Astolat,' part of *The Two Noble Kinsmen* . . . some of Shakespeare's sonnets, Gray's 'Elegy,' Crabbe's 'Parting Hour' . . . and some of Goethe's poems." It was Jowett who suggested the subject for "The Grandmother," first published in *Once a Week*, 16 July 1859, as "The Grandmother's Apology." In a letter to Mrs. Tennyson in December 1858 (see *Memoir*, I, 432–34), Jowett said: "It always seems to me that 'old age' has been badly treated by poets. . . . Its beauty, its sadness, its peace, its faded experience of life are good elements of poetry. An old lady once said to me quite simply, 'The spirits of my children seem to hover about me.' Might not something of the kind be expressed in verse? If it could, like 'The May Queen,' it would touch the chords of many hearts."
   "The Maid of Astolat," published in 1859 as "Elaine," and in 1870 as "Lancelot and Elaine," was not quite complete when Tennyson read it to his wife and Jowett. On 8 February Emily Tennyson wrote about the poem in her Journal: "He has quite finished writing it down now, all but a little bit at the end, and brings it to me for I want to read it myself. It is well to read things to oneself without the glamour of his reading which may beguile one." It is interesting to note that Thomas Woolner had written to Emily Tennyson on 7 June 1858, encouraging her to persuade Tennyson to write an idyll about the "Maid of Astolat" (see *Thomas Woolner*, p. 149).
2. Though born in Essex, Mrs. Gatty lived all her married life (1839-73) in Yorkshire.

86   *To Thomas Woolner*

Farringford, 1 February 1859

My dear Mr. Woolner,
Mr. Cox[1] was so good as to send me the song, and I fully
meant to have acknowledged it yesterday but post time came
before I had done so, having as usual many other letters to
write. . . .

I think the music very beautiful. The wailing accompaniment
of the beginning especially so. If I dare I should object to the
long notes of the second stanza. "Well" is not according to the
metre of the poem. We both hope it will not be long before we
hear you sing it and then, who knows, perhaps I may give you
a hard task and ask you to sing mine too;[2] and you are not to
say I have stolen the theme because it happens to be strangely
like Mr. Cox's, though of course wanting much of the beauty
and all the science, because mine was done before my
marriage. Do not betray me or I might be thought conceited. I
have neither the power nor the wish to set up as a great
musician and I would not set up for a small one.[3] Hear! hear!
hear!

1. Cox gave Woolner singing lessons for a time, but when he told
his pupil that he would never be first-rate, Woolner discontinued his
lessons.
2. Possibly one of Emily Tennyson's several printed settings of her
husband's poems, including "The Song of the Alma River," "The City
Child," and "Minnie and Winnie" (Tennyson's "Child-Songs"), and
the songs presented in concert by Mlle. Janotha in 1891.
3. Emily Tennyson had neither the talent nor the desire to realize
the prediction later ventured by Mlle. Janotha in a letter to Emily, written
after the performance of her songs in concert at St. James's Hall, that
she would one day be "very very celebrated as a 'musique composer'"
(unpublished letter, 12 December 1891, T.R.C.).

87   *To Thomas Woolner*

Farringford, 6 February 1859

My dear Mr. Woolner,
It is a great pleasure to hear of your being so busy[1] and I hope
to hear that a dozen men in your studio are also busy under

your orders. Pity me! Behold my poor little note meant to be so courteous returned to me by some clown or the other named King who had joined the "W" and "K" together "WK" so that, being involved with the letters above, I took the name for "Whing."[2] I hope I do not often make mistakes in my letters to these strangers, at all events I have never been accused of any before. I do plead guilty to having looked at no more than the end of the letter. . . . You can understand this knowing how hard the labour of answering all the letters we receive. The name of the book I wrote from memory. . . . Alfred is so disgusted at this man King for having returned my letter that he will not let me write in his name and of course I will not sanction the man's impertinence by addressing him in my own.

1. Woolner informed Emily Tennyson in a letter of 16 January 1859 (*Thomas Woolner*, pp. 158–60) that "Hurrying, scurrying, worrying, toiling . . . and to be whirling like a distracted teetotum has been my fate since I left Farringford a week ago."
2. Emily included in her letter to Woolner her note to John William King (1792–1875), vicar of Ashby-de-la-Launde, Lincolnshire, from 1822 until his death:

> Mr. Alfred Tennyson presents his compliments to Mr. Whing and begs to thank him for his *Earnest Pilgrim* and for the kind words which accompany it. Mr. Tennyson hopes Mr. Burnard Neville is well and prosperous.

King wrote his indignant reply at the bottom of Emily Tennyson's note:

> Madam,
>   The name on the title page is
>   J: W: King
> The title of the book
>   *Earnest the Pilgrim*
> and the gentleman named in my note
>   Neville Burnard
> not Burnard Neville
>
>   I am Madam,
>   John: W: King

88   To Margaret Gatty
Boston Public Library

Farringford, 12 February 1859

My dear Mrs. Gatty,
You are not to be broken on the wheel this time or even

hanged, drawn, and quartered as a false traitor. I don't know whether Mr. Gatty has fled from us as only worthy of some such punishments. He says he wants the Sunday in London and if he be really honest and true he will prove it by bringing you another day. I think he wants a much longer holiday than he says he shall take. It is unfortunate he had such bad weather while with us. He had not seen the place at all in reality. I hope you will be so kind as to tell us how he is when he reaches home, as I need not tell you that little as we have seen of him we have seen enough to take a sincere interest in him.

He told me much that I liked very much to hear about Dr. Hook and your curate and the people about you and other things. He has been so good as to take charge of "The Grandmother," who is to be left at Burlington House prefactory to her introduction into the world in company with "The May Queen."[1]

My boys are with me and have only made me blot my letter. Lionel cried because he had not said goodbye to Mr. Gatty. I will not try to write more; they distract me so much asking me this and that.

1. Alfred Gatty was at Farringford from the tenth until the twelfth. A Journal entry reveals that he spoke to the Tennysons of the Very Rev. Walter Farquhar Hook, the dean of Chichester, and "of his own curate who has made forty youths deemed untamable obedient to him in all things. . . ." "The May Queen," first published in 1832, was not printed in *Once a Week* with "The Grandmother's Apology," but it did appear as an illustrated octavo in November 1860, and again, as a crown quarto, with chromolithographed illumination, in March 1861.

89   To Thomas Woolner

Farringford, 15 February 1859

My dear Mr. Woolner,
The box has arrived quite safely, and the contents give great delight. Alfred says of my medallion he does not see how it could be better, so you see he is not ungrateful for your generosity. Hallam seemed extremely pleased with it. You see I take this to be more of you than yourself for I begin with it. Your noble self is not so noble as I would have made it. We

had had the wit to find out what a fine engraving that is before
your letter came which pleased me. We thank you most heartily
for all. . . .[1]

I am sure you would love Sir Alexander.[2] I wish I might call
him Grant, man-fashion. What a pleasant chronicle your letters
always are. Is it true that you are going to do a copy of Alfred's
bust for Oxford?[3] I am glad they pay you the homage of
wishing it at all events.

The "Maid of Astolat" is quite finished now, all but last
touches; I do not think you will find her all unworthy of your
ideal. Alfred is better again and very cheerful. Mr. Gatty
proved to be an apparently open-hearted, kindly, sensible man.

1. On 12 February Woolner had mailed to Farringford a case containing the completed Emily Tennyson medallion, an engraving entitled
"Boädicea" by the illustrator Thomas Stothard (1755-1834), and a portrait
photograph of himself.

2. Woolner had seen Sir Alexander Grant at a dinner at Francis
Palgrave's home on 11 February, and he wrote in his letter of the twelfth
to Emily (see *Thomas Woolner,* pp. 161-63) that he felt he would be
"immensely fond" of Grant if he knew him better.

3. Woolner carved only two replicas of the 1857 Tennyson bust, one
for Mr. Charles Buxton of Maidstone and one for Mr. Charles Jenner
of Easter Duddington, who, on Tennyson's death, gave his replica to
Hallam Tennyson to place in Poet's Corner, Westminister Abbey.

90   To Margaret Gatty
Boston Public Library

Farringford, 16 February 1859

My dear Mrs. Gatty,
I cannot write much for I have had an illness two months, first
a cough, then great pain, but I am getting better. Not finding
good from other things prescribed I have tried your Bryonia
globules[1] and I fancy they have been of some use.

Alfred has been to town and has seen a great many people
and had great praise of his poems.[2] He went up in order to put
them in the publisher's hands but returned without having
done it, fresh troubles having arisen, or old ones revised.
Rumour of sale amongst them. Nothing has therefore been
done about the first edition either. We are expecting the Welds

tomorrow who may help us with one of the difficulties.

Alfred and the boys are pretty well. Your task must be interesting but it is not one which can excuse you for overwork.

1. Made from the root of the red-berried bryony and used in homeopathic pharmacy.
2. In June 1859, Moxon's printed 40,000 copies of the first series of *Idylls* at the published price of seven shillings per copy.

91   To Thomas Woolner

Farringford, 23 March 1859

My dear Mr. Woolner,
What a wicked woman I should be if I thought it a trouble! Why is it not a glory to be able to pay a tribute in any way however humble to a great work and to a great man. I have told Alfred that if you do not hear to the contrary before Sunday, you may conclude that the portrait may be exhibited and that his name may be put on the committee.[1] I entirely agree with what you say about the portrait. Mr. Watts thinks I want a particular expression, but it is not that I want, I *only* want what has scarcely yet been given in the world, the man at his highest stamp forever so long as canvas will last. You know the lines that exactly express what I do want,[2] so I hope will Mr. Watts some day. Nevertheless, the portrait is, as you say, "a high and noble work of art," and it ought to be known to the world for its own sake and the sake of the artist.

What you tell me of the poor Rajah's state is sad indeed, sadder for us than for him. He must feel that he has done a good day's work. We may well fear that when he is gone we have none left to do such another.

Have you quite perfected yourself in the song? I am sorry that your Watts is to leave England.[3] We cannot spare such men.

1. In his letter of 20-21 March 1859 to Emily Tennyson (*Thomas Woolner*, pp. 165-66), Woolner asked if the Tennysons would allow G. F. Watts to exhibit his recently completed portrait of the poet at the Royal Academy Exhibition that spring. Although the portrait did not present a view of Tennyson altogether satisfying either to himself

or to the poet's wife, Woolner said, it was nonetheless a just likeness which the public ought to have the opportunity to see. Watts himself considered this "moonlight portrait" of Tennyson the supreme work of his life.

Woolner also requested in the same letter that Tennyson sign a circulating appeal to the nation requesting governmental support for Sir James Brooke (1803-68), raja of Sarawak, Borneo, from 1841 until 1863. During the February-April 1857 Chinese rebellion in Borneo, Brooke lost his property and barely escaped with his life. Despite his requests for aid, the British Government failed either to offer personal assistance to Brooke or to legislate his recommendation that Sarawak be declared a protectorate. Woolner closed his letter to Emily with an apology for his petitions: "I am sorry to trouble you . . . but you who are high up in the world have to undergo these bothers in common course, the high branches are often stirred and blown about while the grasses and weeds below enjoy an enviable placidity."

2. Amy Woolner postulated (*Thomas Woolner,* p. 167) that the lines are from "Lancelot and Elaine."

As when a painter poring on a face,
Divinely through all hindrance finds the man
Behind it, and so paints him that his face,
Lives for his children, ever at its best (ll. 332-36).

3. Henry Edward Watts (1817-1904), journalist, author of *India Heroes,* and an old friend of Woolner's, had made plans to return to Australia to become editor of the *Argus.*

92   To Alfred Tennyson

Farringford, 26 March 1859

Own dearest,
So thou art in the Enchanted Palace once more.[1] I do not doubt that thou art happy and I hope it will do thee good. I saw by the papers that the Argylls[2] are in London, whether at their lodge did not appear but of course thou wilt see them. It was very good in thee to send me thy dear letter in spite of moving quarters. Take care of thyself. I think thou wilt consent to the portrait being exhibited because after all the horrible slanders of thy face I want people to see something truer to thee. I enclose the Literary Fund paper[3] which is interesting and deserves attention, does it not? . . .

There have been divine lights on down and sea. "Glorious lights" as little Lionel has more than once exclaimed. Love to the Principessa.[4] My pain is better, Hallam's cold nearly gone. God bless thee dearest.

Poor Charles. Perhaps we shall be able to do something towards convincing Louy but I fear not because she is fully aware of what has been so often said by others that abstinence is easier than moderation.[5]

1. While in London attending to preparations for publication of the first four *Idylls,* Tennyson visited at Little Holland House, Kensington, celebrated home of Henry Thoby Prinsep (1793-1878), the Orientalist and Indian civil servant. The Prinseps lavishly entertained the leading literary and artistic figures of the day, particularly Burne-Jones, and G. F. Watts, a permanent guest for nearly twenty-five years, and Tennyson rarely failed to stop at Little Holland House when he went to London.

2. George Douglas Campbell (1823-1900), eighth Duke of Argyll, scientist, poet, chancellor of the University of St. Andrews, Secretary of State for India, 1868-74, and Lord Privy Seal, 1852-55, 1859-66, 1880-81, and his first wife, Elizabeth Georgiana (d. 1878), daughter of Queen Victoria's beloved Duchess of Sutherland. From the time he and Tennyson first met at a Buckingham Palace levee on 6 March 1851, Argyll was of the utmost importance to the bard in his relations with the Court. It was Argyll who wrote to Tennyson on behalf of the Queen on 25 March 1862, only three months after Prince Albert's death, conveying Her Majesty's command for the Laureate's initial visit to Osborne. When Tennyson replied that he was "a shy beast," who would feel uneasy about the proper manner of salutation, retreat, etc., Argyll wrote again (27 March) to reassure and to advise him: "Don't let yourself be a 'shy beast' . . . Talk to Her as you would to a poor Woman in affliction—that is what she likes best" (*Dear and Honoured Lady,* ed. Hope Dyson and Charles Tennyson [London: Macmillan, 1969], pp. 68-69). Argyll was a dear, lifelong friend and a regular visitor at Farringford and Aldworth. He introduced Tennyson to the House of Lords in March 1884.

3. A "Report of the Anniversary of the Royal Literary Fund" was published in London each spring.

4. Mrs. Sarah Monckton Prinsep, the charming, energetic sister of Julia Margaret Cameron; one of the celebrated seven daughters of the Indian civil servant, James Pattle.

5. Apparently Charles Turner had begun using opium again. He must have righted himself quickly inasmuch as there is no record of his succumbing to the habit after his recovery in the mid-1840s.

93   To Arthur Hugh Clough

Bodleian Library, Oxford

*Farringford   [14] April [1859]*¹

Dear Mr. Clough,
I will take care that the books (*Llywarch Hen* and the
Gododin)² are returned by some friends who are to be here at
Easter if it will not matter to send them before. It is a shame
that your uncle and yourself should have had the trouble of
inquiring about them. I trust Mrs. Clough and the baby are
well.³

1. Dated by Frederick Mulhauser, *The Correspondence of Arthur Hugh
Clough* (Oxford: Clarendon Press, 1957), II, 641.
2. Clough had loaned the Tennysons from his library two works
eulogizing sixth-century Welsh warriors, *The Heroic Elegies and Other
Pieces of Llywarch Hen,* with a literal translation by William Owen
(London, 1792), and *Y. Gododin: A Poem on the Battle of Cattraeth,*
with an English translation by the Rev. John Williams ab Ithel (Llando-
vey, 1852).
3. A daughter was born to the Cloughs in February 1858. Tennyson
and Clough were good friends from the early 1850s until the younger
poet's death in November 1861. Their intimacy reached a peak in July
1861, when Clough met Graham Dakyns and the Tennyson family at
Mont Dore and spent the next month with them touring the Pyrenees.
Mrs. Clough subsequently wrote about her mortally ill husband to Emily
Tennyson, "He was so happy with you, and it was quite like adopting
another family, his interest about the boys" (quoted by P. G. Scott,
"Tennyson and Clough," *Tennyson Research Bulletin*, November 1969,
p. 68).

94   To Alfred Gatty

Boston Public Library

Farringford, 10 May 1859

My dear Mr. Gatty,
You might have done anything you liked with the poem,
keeping the name secret. Now, I fear, you may possibly be
disappointed seeing it in the *Times*.¹ Charles Weld went off
with a copy though it was written for you, but he went off with
a copy as I say and afterwards had leave to put it in the *Times*,
the T. not being supposed to mean Tennyson. We rather

thought you would at once have put it into a northern paper so that it would have appeared first in the north in that case.

Pray make Alfred's apologies to the editor of "The Constitutional Press." He has never received his letter. Alfred never did contribute to any periodical, has indeed refused many urgent requests to do so as you may imagine. Unless you consider "contribution" sending such a poem as "The Riflemen" on a special occasion.[2]

1. Published as "The War" in *The Times* on 9 May, this poem, written on the outbreak of the Franco-Austrian war, was adapted from an earlier poem Tennyson wrote along with "Rifle-Clubs!!!" in 1852. Tennyson sent Gatty a copy of the poem on 5 May, and that ms. included a stanza which was deleted before publication (see Ricks, *The Poems of Tennyson*, p. 1110). The poem was not reprinted until restored in 1892 as "Riflemen Form!"

2. Nonetheless Tennyson soon sold "The Grandmother's Apology" to *Once a Week*, and thereafter he not infrequently published in periodicals. In a 26 May 1860 letter to Mrs. Gatty (unpublished, Boston Public Library), Emily Tennyson wrote: "Perhaps you know I always disliked his sending poems to magazines. He sent the first away from home all unknown to me."

95   To Edward Lear

Farringford, 23 May 1859

My dear Mr. Lear,

Welcome to England once more! For is it not the best land after all barring bronchitis? Pray be careful while this east wind lasts and come to us whenever you will come when it is gone. You know how glad we shall be to have you. . . . If Ally go to town for a few days about the poems, I shall tell you if I can, because there may be a chance of your seeing him there and perhaps coming down with him.[1]

1. In April 1859, Cavour and Louis Napoleon began waging active war against the Austrians in Italy, and Lear left for England soon thereafter. The cold English spring soon began to tell on him, and within a fortnight his old respiratory ailment had returned. On 6 June Lear came to Farringford and spent a few cheerful days suspended from his dreary London routine. He sang to Emily and played after-dinner games with her and the boys, delighted in Tennyson's booming recitation of his new *Idylls*, and enjoyed himself thoroughly, despite his observation

that his hostess was overextending her strength and growing increasingly fatigued. Lear's exhilaration was shortlived, however, and on 10 June, two days after leaving Farringford, he wrote to Chichester Fortescue that he had felt "a heavy-post-happiness depression," from the moment he left Emily's presence.

96   To Thomas Woolner

Farringford, 25 May 1859

My dear Mr. Woolner,
What an interesting chronicle your letters always are![1] I have to go and look after A.'s room and see that it is made as comfortable as may be in its unfinished state for the evening.[2] It is a queer thing now with ceiling away, for which the builders excuse themselves with reasons to my unconstructive mind not good. In spite of this Alfred pronounces it a charming room and I quite agree. . . . Alfred is gone to Brooke.[3] The boys have just been in chasing each other with a mad glee born of the south wind perhaps. They are going as they fancy to gather all the daisies on the lawn.

1. See *Thomas Woolner,* pp. 170–71, for Woolner's letter of 13 May 1859.
2. Emily Tennyson was having the poet's attic study remodeled.
3. Tennyson had gone with the Argylls to visit Sir James Brooke.

97   To Margaret Gatty
Boston Public Library

Farringford, 3 June 1859

My dear Mrs. Gatty,
I ought to have answered your kind letters before but I have had a great deal to do in many ways and have not yet grown very strong so I hope you will excuse me, and now that I write I have not very good news to tell for poor Ally has, for this week past, been far from well having suffered both from swelled face and hay fever. He was to have taken his proofs up last Saturday but was not able. If he be well enough perhaps

he will go on Monday. He has been also vexed by hearing that the American edition of his works is sold at Paris for three francs. Certainly our descendants in the far west cannot boast of honesty as one of their good qualities. . . .

I wish we could lend you some of our company since you say you sometimes feel the want of a little more. The boys are pretty well, though changeable weather is rather trying for them. I hope you are all well in spite of it. Did I tell you of our making bay windows in three of the attics and raising two at least of the ceilings? Also of the platform Ally has devised at the top of the house to look at once on the two seas.[1]

1. When the carpenters first began to remodel the attic, which had done service as Tennyson's study, both the poet and Emily were saddened. They grew "quite sentimental" over the barn-like rafters which were removed, and on 10 May Tennyson talked "of all the pleasant evenings spent under its low ceiling, all the thoughts and all the feelings thought and felt there." By the time Tennyson returned from his 10-27 June trip to London, however, Emily was able to record the happy conclusion of the first major alteration undertaken at Farringford: "He comes. Never I think so happy a meeting for me of all the happy meetings. He likes all that is done. . . . I let the boys show him the new door from the study to the greenhouse according to my promise to them, and he is pleased with everything. The view from the new windows is a kind of drunkenness of delight" (Journal, 27 June 1859). From the new platform atop the house, Tennyson could see both Freshwater Bay and Alum Bay, some two miles west.

98   To Alfred Tennyson

Farringford, 22 June 1859

Dearest,
Is it not a grand thing for me that one of the wishes of my life has been fulfilled for thee instead of me or me in thee rather.[1] When I was a girl the only way in which I could console myself for not hearing greatest music greatly given ("The Messiah" to my mind always the crown of things in music) was by thinking that I should hear better still in heaven. I am full of joy that thou art so delighted with thy day and I kiss thee for thy thought of me then. I think thou oughtest *as thou sayest* to give Evans "The Grandmother" or to lend it to him, for I should wish it to be published in one of thy own books

some day if we live. Send it him for a year if thou wilt. I hope yesterday's dinner was pleasant and I trust Saturday will indeed bring thee back but do not come if there is anything for which thou wouldst wish to stay. . . .

Hast thou called on Maurice? And if not wilt thou not before leaving those parts of town. My love to them. Charles and Nanny are very pleased that thou wert pleased on Monday.

An Italian with——but Hallam is to tell. The Italian says they fight for France and Piedmont and that they do not trust in God so I understand him and so will not be able to make a kingdom for themselves.[2] I fancy Nanny gave up her ticket to thee. Wilt thou not get her one for another day?

1. On the afternoon of Monday, 20 June, Tennyson attended at the Crystal Palace a performance of *The Messiah,* presented as part of the 1859 Handel Commemoration Festival, which opened on the eighteenth and extended through the twenty-fourth.
2. The unidentified Italian evidently felt that the Franco-Austrian War was a product of the personal ambitions of Napoleon III and Piedmont's Count Cavour. The Italians were betrayed in July 1859, when Napoleon made peace with Austria behind Cavour's back.

On 28 June Frederick Tennyson, who was in England for a short time prior to his move to Jersey, arrived at Farringford, and he spent much of his six-day visit expounding Swedenborgism to the Laureate. Alexander Grant, Grant's wife, and his father-in-law came on 1 July in the midst of a furious storm which pelted the house with hailstones the size of walnuts and submerged the kitchen beneath three inches of water. That same day a maid of Mrs. Cameron's appeared unexpectedly to request the manuscript of "Guinevere," which her mistress unaccountably feared the Tennysons might give to the Grants. Emily persuaded her husband to keep the holograph "Guinevere" for the present and recorded the incident in her Journal: "A. does not care about his manuscripts. He gives them to anyone who asks. To me they are more precious than words can say. Every page almost a memory. . . . A. says Mrs. Cameron shall have it if anyone has it. One does not like to refuse kind and energetic Mrs. Cameron anything."

A fortnight later James T. Fields, the Boston publisher and author, later editor of the *Atlantic Monthly,* came from London with his wife Annie, at the poet's request. Arriving on the fourteenth at precisely 5 P.M., the Tennysons' dinner hour, Mr. and Mrs. Fields found Farringford "very large, rambling and irregular, full of comfort, beauty, quiet," and Emily impressed Mrs. Fields as "a holy woman" who diffused her own spiritual aura throughout her home and lifted all who came there "to a higher plane of Truth." In manners, in conversation, and in the minutest household arrangements, Mrs. Fields thought the Tennysons combined "the extremest simplicity and elegance" in a style indicating both intelligence and refinement. For three days Annie and James Fields were alternately invigorated by strolls about the estate and stimulated by dinner discussions and the poet's readings, and their visit lived in Mrs. Fields's memory as "a star in our firmament of happiness," the crown of their 1859 English vacation (quoted by Howe, "The Tennysons at Farringford: A Victorian Vista," pp. 449, 454).

The favorable reception of his *Idylls* (10,000 copies sold the first week after publication) so enlivened Tennyson's spirits and improved his finances that by August he felt free to take a holiday. In the company of Francis Palgrave he sailed for Portugal on 17 August and proceeded from Lisbon to Cadiz, then to Tangier, and finally up the Tagus River to the ancient city of Santarem. Disappointed by the scenery in Portugal and tormented by the flies and the heat in Spain, Tennyson and Palgrave returned to England on 12 September, without having fulfilled their intentions of seeing Seville, Malaga, Granada, and Gibraltar. Emily and the boys traveled to London from Park House on the twenty-seventh to meet him, and they journeyed home together the next day to meet Anne and Agnes Weld, who remained at Farringford the next three weeks. Emily was unwell during much of September, and her Journal, sketchy as always when she was indisposed, tells of no other visitors before the end of October.

99   To Thomas Woolner

Farringford, 20 October 1859

Dear Mr. Woolner,
It was very pleasant to hear from you again and I thank you for your welcome letter.[1] I should long ago have written to you

had I not been so ill this summer that the doctor forbade my writing which indeed part of the time was needless as I could not write nor can I much now though a great deal better than I was. Ally and the boys are pretty well. I do not think this year's voyage was as successful as the last though Mr. Palgrave did all that could have been done to make it so. However it has furnished some pleasant recollections besides those of his extreme kindness and care so we must not be ungrateful.

I am inclined to think a country gentleman's life a very wholesome one in many ways, so to me your holiday appears pleasant and good.[2] I and the boys spent all our time at the Lushingtons'. Days with them have their own peculiar charm to me and this was not wanting, only I was not in a state to enjoy it to the full. The boys liked the novelty of playfellows and got initiated in cricket and other things. . . .

The little bust[3] looked touching and beautiful in its place and I wished to have told you so then. I trust many more beautiful things are "in petto."

1. See *Thomas Woolner,* pp. 175-76, for Woolner's letter of 15 October 1859.
2. Woolner had spent his rural holiday "taking walks, bathing, shooting partridges, riding, playing billiards, smoking and dancing" (p. 176).
3. Woolner's marble bust (1859) of Edmund Lushington's son, Edward Henry Lushington.

100   To Thomas Woolner

Farringford, 26 October 1859

My dear Mr. Woolner,
Oh how sorry I am to hear of the evil that has befallen your group![1] Some Angel of beauty will dawn upon you some day and just such a one as you desire for your work. Poor Mr. Palgrave![2] Thunder, lightning, hail, frost, ice, wind, almost a hurricane, rain pouring in, trees blown down—Ally and the boys picking up sticks. Two maids gone to Newport to have two teeth out. I somewhat wearied with writing.

Dear Mr. Woolner, reading is rest to me. It is chiefly because I cannot read that I am weary. If the mind starve and languish, what hope for the body! What for the soul I had almost said but I do confess this ought to thrive whether the body and the mind starve or feed and flourish. No more today.

1. Unidentified.
2. According to the Journal, Francis Palgrave was visiting at Farringford on the twenty-sixth.

101   To Edward Lear

Farringford, 14 November 1859

Dear Mr. Lear,
We should like to know where you are and what you are doing and what you are going to do.[1] There has been an envelope addressed to you some time but we have had so many people and until the last week or two I have been so very unwell since our return at the middle of September and all the summer before I was so ill that the poor envelope had stared at me. . . . Such a still, delightful, old-fashioned, frosty day today! The air seems something good to eat for body and mind. . . .

When will you come to us! Soon, I hope, and then Alfred shall tell you himself the little he has to tell of Lisbon and Cintra and Santarem and this will be better than hearing it second-hand from me. He is pretty well and the boys are rosy and merry and hard to be tamed down to lessons. When people are here very docile, comparatively when they are not. Alfred's love and their love.

1. Lear was in London delivering paintings done the previous summer at St. Leonards-on-Sea, clearing his debts, and preparing to leave again for Italy. He sailed for Rome on 22 December.

102   To Thomas Woolner

Farringford, 16 November 1859

My dear Mr. Woolner,
If you are satisfied, we are, and so now there is nothing more to be desired but the advantageous light.[1] We are sorry to hear about Mr. Palgrave.[2] For the most part I agree with you about

religious books;[3] and yet, however dimly shadowed, there are ideas and truths in Mr. Maurice's book[4] that can only be ridiculed because too great for the comprehension of the mocker. As a man speaks of his friend and so kindles an ardour of affection in the heart of another man for the friend whom he loves and reverences, so some good men can speak of Christ and make Him seem more lovely than He would otherwise do to hearts stranger or estranged, and this is what we want to see—Christ as it were face to face[5]—to know Him heart with heart. The Word is the Word still, however abused, is it not? Pardon me, I am as bad as a religious book.

We had Sir John Simeon dining with us the day before yesterday and today he comes again with Mr. Charles Wynne.[6] We have had Kingsleys, Gattys, and others besides staying with us[7] and on Monday we expect Mrs. Cameron and her little boys. . . .

I wish you would give Alfred something to do. He is pretty well but for want of this.

1. Emily Tennyson alludes to settling the 1857 Tennyson bust in the vestibule of the Trinity College Library. Earlier in November Woolner had informed her that the lighting would be quite favorable in the vestibule (see Woolner's letter dated November [1859], *Thomas Woolner*, p. 178).

2. Francis Palgrave, who periodically lived with Woolner, had been unwell for some time, as Woolner informed Emily Tennyson in his letter of 13 November (*Thomas Woolner*, p. 180).

3. Woolner may have set down a low opinion of contemporary religious treatises in the 13 November letter. If so, Amy Woolner omitted that portion of her father's letter.

4. Probably *The Epistles of St. John* (1857).

5. In the recollections he sent to Hallam Tennyson after the poet's death, Benjamin Jowett recalled that Tennyson had once apprised him of his wife's declaration that whenever she prayed she saw the face of God smiling upon her (*Memoir*, II, 466).

6. Charles Wynne Griffith Wynne (1780-1865), member of Parliament for Carnarvonshire, 1830-32, and a friend of the Simeons.

7. The Gattys visited 31 October until 5 November; the Kingsleys, 8 through 10 November.

103   To Stephen Hawker[1]

Farringford, 2 December 1859

Neither the Laureate nor his wife disclaims the flattering lines.
How should they disclaim them? But both thank Mr. Hawker
for his kindness in sending them and send him all good
wishes.

1. Robert Stephen Hawker (1803–75), medievalist, necromancer, vicar
of Morwenstowe on the Cornish coast, and author of *Reeds Shaken
with the Wind* (1843) and *The Quest of the Sangraal* (1864), among
other volumes. Shortly before Emily Tennyson addressed her note, her
husband had written to Hawker to acknowledge a volume of verse
sent him by the author, together with a poem of lavish personal praise.
Tennyson indicated in that letter that although he appreciated Hawker's
lines about him, he thought them "too complimentary . . . to put faith
in" (H. Tennyson, *Materials for a Life of A. T.*, II, 242). Apparently
Hawker was affronted by Tennyson's letter, and Emily wrote to assure
him of their appreciation.
    Tennyson first met Hawker in the summer of 1848, when he visited
the parson poet at Morwenstowe. The two were much taken with each
other, and they spent an entire day discussing the Arthurian legends
and rambling about the rocks and the shore of Hawker's secluded village.
Hawker always remembered Tennyson's appearance as they bade
farewell, his garments covered with a Spanish cloak, and his long,
shaggy hair hanging around his face "in the midst of which his eyes
seemed not only to shine but to glare" (quoted by Charles Tennyson,
AT, p. 229).

104   To Thomas Woolner

Farringford, 23 December 1859

My dear Mr. Woolner,
How stupid and forgetful I have been. I have every day meant
to write to you, for I do not know how long, to say, do not be
angry with us for what we have done rashly in our wish to do
what we thought might be good and pleasant for you. We have
sent the photograph of your bust to Tauchnitz[1] as the best
portrait for his edition of Alfred's poems. It was done all on a
sudden and then afterwards I said, "We ought to have asked
Mr. Woolner first," and Alfred said, "So we ought." You ought
to have something for it and if you will tell us what we will
settle the matter. Alfred gets . . .[2]

1. Christian Bernhard, Baron von Tauchnitz, founder of the Tauchnitz publishing firm, which made its name chiefly through the *Collection of British and American Authors,* a series introduced in 1841. The inexpensive, paperback "Tauchnitz Edition" of Tennyson (1860) was especially popular in Germany and among English travelers on the Continent. Tennyson made what he termed "rather a bad bargain" with Tauchnitz, and when in 1868 the baron offered him an increased royalty, he gratefully accepted (see Tennyson's letter to Tauchnitz, 29 April 1868, *Memoir,* II, 54).
2. The remainder of the letter is missing.

105   To Margaret Gatty
Boston Public Library

Farringford, 23 January 1860

My dear Mrs. Gatty,

Our boys are on the heights of happiness just now, having walked into dinner each with a little girl hand in hand, Edith and Daisy Bradley.[1] I was forgetting that you know well about them.

I am glad that "Sea Dreams"[2] improves on acquaintance. It is only good things that can do so, as one needs not say it is so plain. . . .

I hope there will be one thing at all events in the *Cornhill Magazine* this next month which you will like—Ally's "Tithonus," a companion poem to "Ulysses."[3] 75,000 Mr. Smith said have been published for this month and were nearly sold when he wrote some days ago. I have much writing today and can only add our kindest regards.

1. Daughters of Granville and Marian Bradley.
2. First published in *Macmillan's Magazine* in January 1860, with the subtitle "An Idyll," and again in the *Enoch Arden* volume.
3. Written as a pendent to "Ulysses" in 1833, and entitled "Tithon" in its original, shorter form, "Tithonus" first appeared in the *Cornhill Magazine*, February 1860.

106   *To Frederick Goddard Tuckerman*
Harvard

Farringford, 25 January 1860

My dear Sir,
It seems to grow more and more impossible to my husband to
write letters, so lest you should have any cause to think your
welcome letter less welcome than it really was I must be
allowed for the present to thank you in his name, though he
has the intention of thanking you himself which I hope will
some day be fulfilled.

I am glad you like the *Idylls*. I think "Guinevere" is my
favorite but each differs so much from the other that it is
difficult to compare them. . . .

Our beautiful views will, I fear, be spoilt before long. People
are seized with a building mania. Already a bit of our sea is
built out from us and we are obliged to buy land at the rate of
a thousand pounds an acre merely to prevent more of the bay
being hidden by ugly brick houses. . . .[1] If our down were no
longer lonely we could not stay. We could only be here in the
winter when it is too stormy for visitors. . . .

Is there any chance of seeing you soon in England again? I
have often thought of writing to you, but I have been much out
of health ever since two autumns, one in Wales and the next at
the Lakes.[2] Last summer I was forbidden to write having been
taken ill when Alfred was away in Lisbon and Cintra three or
four weeks. The year before he went to Norway for three weeks
and was out in a great storm going. He liked his northern trip
much the best though he only went to see some waterfalls, the
Reichen Falls and others.

We have had the pleasure of making the acquaintance of Mr.
and Mrs. Fields, also of Mr. Charles Sumner,[3] this year and
you know that this must have been a pleasure.

1. The "roofs of slated hideousness" that mark an age of scientific
growth and Beauty's disappearance in "Locksley Hall Sixty Years After"
may perhaps be traced to the "ugly brick houses" which blocked
Tennyson's view from Farringford to the sea.
2. The autumns of 1856 and 1857.
3. Charles Sumner (1811–74), the senator from Massachusetts, best
remembered for his long and laborious support of slave emancipation.
Sumner's vehement opposition to the Fugitive Slave Law and the
Kansas–Nebraska Bill culminated in his Congressional speech, "The
Crime against Kansas," delivered 19–20 May 1856, which impugned

Senator Matthew Calbraith Butler of South Carolina and provoked an assault and brutal beating two days later by Representative Preston S. Brooks, a relative of Butler's, whose attack proved nearly fatal to Sumner. He spent much of the next three years in England recovering his health, and he visited Farringford 27-28 October 1859.

The Camerons settled at Dimbola, near Freshwater Bay, early in the winter of 1860, and by the first of February Mrs. Cameron was making frequent trips to Farringford. She arrived on 1 February with two legs of Welsh mutton, and she responded to Emily's efforts to discourage her characteristic generosity of bringing several rolls of costly wallpaper, decorated with a frieze from the Elgin Marbles, on her next visit a month later. Emily was stronger than usual during January and February, and she and Tennyson joined the new hired man Heard in a vigorous winter pruning of garden trees and shrubs. In March, however, Emily and both boys contracted whooping cough, and they were confined for more than a fortnight. While his family was ill, Tennyson worked at "Boädicea," a poem precipitated by Thomas Stothard's engraving, which he cast in the difficult galliambic meter to echo the *Attis* of Catullus. Tennyson recited the entirety of "Boädicea" to the Duke of Argyll one cold March day while walking through a field of stubble near Farringford. On 1 April, Emily came down to the drawing room, and by the twenty-seventh, when Tennyson read his revised "Boädicea" to her, she was well enough to begin supervising Heard's work in the terraces and the garden. By May she was fully recovered, and she even helped Tennyson mow the Farringford lawn.

107   *To Thomas Woolner*

Farringford, 20 May 1860

My dear Mr. Woolner,
Your account of Lady Byron was most touching both to Alfred and me.[1] Poor thing, one can feel no doubt but that her sad life has merged in a soul-satisfying happiness. One of her secretaries was once a governess at Somersby and I knew her

too and have heard delightful accounts of Lady Byron from
her. . . .

"Boädicea" is written down. Mr. Venables insisted on the
duty of writing it so strongly.[2] But you do not like it very much
do you? It is very fine, I think, though I would not have him
do many such things. I think all metres that properly belong to
a language are born in the minds of the poets of the land and
not adopted children. Love from Ally and the boys.

1. In his 17 May 1860 letter to Emily Tennyson (*Thomas Woolner*,
p. 193), Woolner wrote that the previous day he had taken a cast of
the left hand of Lady Anne Isabella Byron (1792–1860), the poet's widow,
who had died on the sixteenth. Lady Byron, he said, "looked as if
she were living, and had just dropped to sleep, and as proud as a
queen in all her splendour. I think there never was anything finer
than her brow and nose. . . . She seems to have been almost adored
by those about her."
2. Venables visited Farringford in the early spring.

108   To Henry Sellwood

Farringford [late May 1860]

Dearest Daddy,
I thought you would all like to see this letter which the Prince
Consort has written with his own hand to Ally, so I have
copied it:

Buckingham Palace, 17th May 1860

My dear Mr. Tennyson,
    Will you forgive me if I intrude upon your leisure with a
request which I have thought for some little time of making,
viz: that you would be good enough to write your name in the
accompanying volume of your "Idylls of the King"? You would
thus add a peculiar value to the book, containing those
beautiful songs, from the perusal of which I derived the
greatest enjoyment. They quite rekindle the feelings with
which the legends of King Arthur must have inspired the
chivalry of old, whilst the graceful form in which they are
presented blends these feelings with the softer tone of our
present age.

Believe me always, yours truly,
Albert
Buckingham Palace, 17 May 1860

Will you please not mention the Prince's letter to anyone lest it should get into some newspaper.[1]

1. Tennyson complied with the Prince's request; the signed copy of the *Idylls* is now in the Royal Library at Windsor. The Queen was as enthusiastic as Albert in her admiration of the *Idylls,* and in late May she wrote to Victoria, Princess Royal, in Germany, "I have just been reading Tennyson's *Idylls of the King* which I think you would delight in. They are so very peculiar, quaint and poetic. 'Enid' I think quite beautiful, and the latter part of 'Elaine' very touching, 'Guinevere' very fine—the early part quite sublime" (Dyson and Tennyson, *Dear and Honoured Lady,* p. 46).

109   To Rev. Alfred Gatty
Boston Public Library

Farringford, 7 June 1860

My dear Mr. Gatty,

Ally has no political poem of any kind or description and he fears he is not likely to have one (we have so many guests coming). If he should, however, we will send it to you.

Dr. Wolff arrived last night. His talk has an inspiration that cannot be withstood and he is so gentle and kind withal that one must like him as much as one wonders at him.[1] I am a good deal exhausted with the excitement for I have not yet recovered even my usual portion of strength, so excuse this short note. I hope Mrs. Gatty is better. I will write again when Alfred has considered the poems.

1. Dr. Joseph Wolff (1795-1862), the famous Anglican missionary to the Jews in the East, author of *Mission to Bokhara* (1845) and *Travels and Adventures* (1860-61), his autobiography, dictated to and superintended by Margaret Gatty. On 13 June, the day before his departure from Farringford, Dr. Wolff spoke in the Freshwater schoolroom. Emily Tennyson described the day in her Journal: "Mr. and Mrs. Isaacson [the Freshwater curate and his wife] . . . and Mrs. Cameron dine with us and all except myself go to hear Dr. Wolff's lecture. . . . A. walks with Mrs. Cameron and so is later than the rest of the party who drive. Mr. Isaacson tells the assembly that he only waits for A. and they cheer. Six pounds are collected for Dr. Wolff's church [Ile-Brewers, Somerset] and the boys when they hear of the church building rush off to their purses and give all they have except Grandpapa's sovereign."

110   *To Thomas Woolner*

Grasby Vicarage,[1] *28 August 1860*

My dear Mr. Woolner,
I am sorry that your little tour has been so spoilt by the
weather. We have generally had rain either by day or night and
this is the first day we have driven out but still our weather has
certainly not been so bad as yours.

I have read the greater part of your poem[2] twice through. I
am slow in making up my mind on poems and ought to read
yours oftener before I can pronounce any trustworthy
judgement, according to the measure of my trustworthiness in
such judgements, that is. Still I think I may venture to say that
some parts of it seem to me very fine, some beautiful, and that
with a little more time spent on retrenching and finishing, the
whole ought to be still finer and more beautiful. I speak with
great diffidence and more because I feel that it would seem
churlish to say nothing, rather than because I feel what I say is
worth reading. That bit about the hummingbird is very
beautiful and there are some grand lines worthy to be stored in
the treasure house of the wisest and best. . . . Two or three
words startle me——"fleckered" where I should have put
"flecked" and "gloared" which I do not know. The description
of the Father seems to me particularly good. The opening I like
very much but you will forgive me when I say that some parts
seem to me too long. I shall send it at once to Lady Trevelyan
for I am not now likely to have even so much time as I have
hitherto had to myself here.

1. Emily, Hallam, and Lionel Tennyson visited with Henry Sellwood
and the Charles Turners at Grasby during much of August and September, while Tennyson was vacationing in Cornwall. Tennyson and Woolner traveled through Bath, Bideford, Clovelly, Bude, and Boscastle, to
Tintagel and Travenna, where they were joined by Francis Palgrave.
The three then journeyed on through Camelford to Penzance, where
they met Holman Hunt and Valentine Prinsep, and the entire party
remained in the vicinity of Cornwall until mid-September, visiting,
among other areas, the Lizard and Land's End districts and the Scilly
Isles. The poet's wife and sons left Grasby on 16 September and, after
a brief stop in London, returned to Farringford on the twenty–second,
preceding Tennyson by only four days.
2. "My Beautiful Lady," first published in its entirety in 1863. Two
cantos of the work appeared in *The Germ* in January 1850. Woolner's
long, choppy poem bears the unmistakable stamp of the sculptor,
working, as it were, by chipping his lines one at a time.

111   To Margaret Gatty
Boston Public Library

Farringford, 10 November 1860

My dear Mrs. Gatty,
Thank you for your kind letter and for the interesting sea fact.
Alfred does know the western coast of Ireland and this and the
Cornish and Lincolnshire coasts are his three favourites. I wish
we could often fly over to one of them, for this place is
becoming far too public for us. Several houses have arisen
since you were here and several more are to arise they say.

Just now the boys are, I think, sweeping up leaves with
Alfred in the garden in honour of Grandpapa's birthday. (The
sweeping has turned to a chase I see). I am not able to go out
for I got knocked up by the damp journey home from Grasby
and have not been so well since. Moreover we have had a great
deal of company. . . .

We have set Mr. Bradley[1] and Mr. Jowett to work to find a
tutor for the boys. Their lessons are so perpetually interrupted
that it will no longer do for Hallam.

1. George Granville Bradley (1821-1903), headmaster of Marlborough,
1858-1870, Master of University College, Oxford, 1871-81, and dean
of Westminster from 1881 till his death. The Tennysons first became
acquainted with Bradley and his wife Marian in the summer of 1855,
when the Bradleys were vacationing at Alum Bay. Soon they were fast
friends, and in 1860 the Bradleys took a house near Freshwater expressly
to spend their holidays near Farringford.

112   To Thomas Woolner

Farringford, 7 December 1860

My dear Mr. Woolner,
We shall miss you very much at Christmas I need not say. Let
us know when anything is settled about Sedgwick,[1] please. I
heartily agree with you in your dislike of money affairs and I
become more and more convinced that money lies at the root of
at least half the sin and sorrow of the world. Beyond all price
to me would be a worthy subject for Alfred, one which would
fix him whether he would or no.[2] The boys' love and Alfred's.
The boys both shout out, "I hope he will come soon."

1. In March 1860, Woolner had completed his marble bust of the geologist Adam Sedgwick, and he was now looking for a proper buyer. He succeeded in placing his "Sedgwick" in the Trinity Library vestibule in February 1861.

2. Although Woolner replied on 5 December 1859 (see *Thomas Woolner*, p. 184), suggesting to Emily Tennyson that her husband "do the tale of the Sailor, which I told him of years ago," it was not until 28 September 1861 that Tennyson sent for a copy of "The Fisherman's Story." The tale arrived at Farringford on 11 November, and Tennyson completed "Enoch Arden" in March 1862. Tennyson was never content when he was not writing; once he declared to Granville and Marian Bradley "how much better he felt spiritually, mentally, and bodily while engaged in some long poem; and how often in the intervals he found time hang heavily, and a longing come for regular work" (*Memoir*, II, 51).

113   To Thomas Woolner

Farringford, 30 January 1861

My dear Mr. Woolner,
We have had a happy little glimpse of Mr. Jowett, and it is scarcely more for he says he must go tomorrow. . . . However, there is one comfort, he talks of coming back to Freshwater in the spring to work at Plato.[1] Alfred has been much better of late. He has begun his work again and looks bright in spite of the dull damp weather. I fear you have not recovered from your journey home; it was such a wretched day. Surely there are no broken fingers or toes or chipped noses or any other misfortunes in your rooms. Lionel has a small greeting to the "beautiful Sculptor with the golden beard," but I must leave him to send it himself. This damp makes me feel very tired so I will only say I hope you found Mr. Palgrave well and give you the boys' love and Alfred's.

1. Jowett did not publish his *Plato* until 1871.

114   To Edward Lear

Farringford, 14 February 1861

My dear Mr. Lear,

As to the pictures Ally is evidently much delighted.[1] He says he likes them very much and that they are grand. I wish I could see them. Did Ally tell you that we have secured a most highly recommended tutor for the boys? He is to come next Wednesday. His name is Dakyns.[2] He is about twenty-two, is said to be the most popular man in Cambridge, is highly spoken of by people who knew him there and at Rugby, and is recommended by Mr. Bradley, Head of Marlborough, and Mr. Benson,[3] Head of Wellington College. So one can only trust in God that he will do well for the poor bairns. Their love to you and they hope you will come soon. I hope you will come when it is fine.

1. In London from 7 to 13 February, Tennyson had been to Lear's rooms at 15 Stratford Place to see his most recent paintings.
2. Henry Graham Dakyns (1839-1911), poet, classical scholar, and tutor for Hallam and Lionel Tennyson from February 1861 until September 1863, when he became a classics master at Clifton College. At Clifton he formed an intimate attachment to John Addington Symonds, then a student at the newly founded college, and the two remained confidants for the next thirty years. As a young man, Dakyns was both academic and athletic, and that combination, together with an attractive simplicity and a fervent love of literature, made him "a man after Tennyson's own heart" (*AT*, p. 331). During his tenure at Farringford, Dakyns was particularly devoted to Emily Tennyson, and after her death he expressed to her son, his former pupil, something of his high regard: "How often has Jowett said to me, and I asserted, as who would not—that among great women she stood somehow apart in greatness" (unpublished letter to Hallam Tennyson, 13 August 1896, T.R.C.).
3. Edward White Benson (1829-96), first master of Wellington College 1859-72, bishop of Lincoln, 1868, prebendary of Lincoln, 1869, first bishop of Truro, 1877, archbishop of Canterbury, 1882 until death.

115   To Edward Lear

Farringford, 15 March 1861

My dear Mr. Lear,

I know that you must feel very desolate[1] and I wish we could do anything to make you feel less so. The memory of that calm and holy deathbed and that you were there to be to her what you have been through your life and what she felt you had been, is, I am sure, the truest comfort you can have at this moment.[2] Next only to that of the hope of meeting again not to part. You must come to us when you are equal to it. . . .

God bless you and comfort you! Whether they know it or not now, the holy ones who have left us do stretch out shining hands to help us to come to them. With Alfred's love, *believe me*,[3] and all best wishes and cordial sympathies.

1. Lear's elder sister Ann, who virtually reared him, died on 11 March 1861.
2. Among Ann Lear's final words were these: "Bless you my dear Edward! What a comfort you have been to me all your life!" (Noakes, *Edward Lear*, p. 183).
3. The emphasis on Tennyson's affection may indicate that Lear was unsure of the poet's regard for him. During his most recent visit to Farringford the previous March, Lear had been offended by his host's behavior during a walk across the downs, which he described in his diary: "AT was most disagreeably querulous and irritating and would return, chiefly because he saw people approaching. . . . After a time he would not go on—but led me back by muddy paths (over our shoes), a short cut home—hardly, even at least avoiding his horror,—the villagers coming from church. . . . I believe that this is my last visit to Farringford:—nor can I wish it otherwise all things considered" (Noakes, *Edward Lear*, p. 179). It is difficult to hold Tennyson responsible for Lear's displeasure, for the hypersensitive artist was always prone to distress and dissatisfaction for one reason or another. In a 4 March 1860 letter to Emily Tennyson (unpublished, T.R.C.), Woolner wrote that he had just received a letter from Lear full of his contempt for Rome which he now found completely unendurable. "But the curious thing," observed Woolner, "is that he hates every place, whether Rome, London, Thebes, Athens, Jerusalem; and I have no doubt that if he be *sous* Madagascar and the South Sea Islands he would hate those also."

116   *To Thomas Woolner*

Farringford, 10 April 1861

My dear Mr. Woolner,
I hope Mr. Clark[1] gave my message about writing to you or you would have good reason to wonder at my ingratitude for

the charming photograph.[2] Accept our best thanks which
would have come before had I not been very poorly and very
much oppressed with guests. Not because they were guests in
themselves oppressive; much the contrary, had one but had
strength for them and leisure for something of reading and
thinking to restore the elasticity of one's mind, now too like a
bow spoilt by long bending. . . . It was very pleasant to hear
him speak of Sedgwick as he did. I wished to hear more of
your work though he told me something. What a good and
pleasant man he himself seems to be.

You will be glad to hear that we like Mr. Dakyns (the tutor)
very much. He is very simple and kindly and intelligent and
most conscientiously anxious about the boys. Mr. Jowett left us
yesterday after a fortnight's visit and he thinks of him as we
do. Mr. Jowett is to return on Saturday week, if all be well. Do
you not think some of our neighbours will consider it a happy
thing for us that the dean of Chichester has also been our guest
lately so that there may have been an antidote to the poison of
heresy?[3] We have also had the Cloughs and Franklin
Lushington. Welcome guests these all have a right to be, but
then unfortunately more and more lodging houses spring up
and more and more strangers come with introductions so that
we have already begun to feel sure that we shall have to look
for another house. I think you would say we have improved
this by our new lawn where the stable was. I hope you will see
it before very long. The boys like their tutor very much. Next
week we expect their little cousins with Uncle and Aunt
Horatio.[4] Alfred has not been after his best fashion lately, but a
good deal troubled by people and things.

1. William George Clark (1821-78), essayist, Fellow of Trinity College,
Cambridge, and editor of the Cambridge Shakespeare, 1863-66. According to the Journal, Clark came to Farringford for a brief visit on 1
April 1861.
2. Woolner sent the Tennysons a photograph of his Adam Sedgwick
bust.
3. Jowett had suffered great blame for his unorthodox lectures at
Oxford and for his criticism of the Church. Like Jowett, Walter Farquhar
Hook, dean of Chichester, was a guest early in the spring of 1861.
4. Horatio and Charlotte Tennyson, the daughter of Dudley Cary
Elwes, had four children, Maud, Violet, Cecilia, and Bertram.

117   To Edward Lear

Farringford, 15 April 1861

My dear Mr. Lear,
You took so kind an interest in those unhappy affairs when you were here that I feel it is due to you to tell you the result of the Macmillan negotiation—Nothing. It is at an end. Evans declared that Ally's poems are the keystone of the arch to the Moxons and so the affair came to nothing.[1]

The offence is of the nature we believed it to be but we have had no particulars. Continual threats of self-destruction come to one and all at present in that quarter is dreary and dark. The only hope of improvement is in occupation and that under the circumstances is not easy to find.[2]

So much for ourselves, and what of yourself I wonder? I fear we cannot hope yet for much better news of you. It is only time that can fill up these voids do what one will. Mr. Jowett left us last week for an Oxford meeting. He is to return on Saturday to lodgings near us. On the 23rd we expect Horatio and all his to stay with us.

1. Lear visited the Tennysons in mid-March 1861. Tennyson first negotiated with Alexander Macmillan (1818–96), the publisher, in 1861, but he decided to continue with Moxon's at that time. See above, Letter 75, n. 1.
2. In April 1861, Charles Weld was implicated in some serious indiscretion at the British Institution, and he relinquished his position there. Not long thereafter he became a partner in a publishing house with Lovell Augustus Reeve (1814–65), noted conchologist and editor and proprietor of the *Literary Gazette*, 1850–56. There is apparently no record of the specific nature of Weld's offense.

Emily Tennyson's Journal entry for 15 May 1861 is a record of Tennyson's determination to give up smoking. En route to Cambridge with Emily and the children, to receive a degree, Tennyson suffered severe heart palpitations while staying in Weybridge at the Oatlands Park Hotel. The poet attributed the attack to smoking and resolved to abjure tobacco for the sake of his health. Taking his pipe up to the hotel Belvedere, he smoked it a final time, then broke it in half and scattered his tobacco to the wind. His resolution, however, was short-lived, as it had been at least once before when he attempted to stop smoking. On 12 December 1855, Emily had recorded that she and the poet made a bonfire and burned "the box with all the pipes in it, he having first put the last bit of tobacco into his study fire." Emily apparently accepted her husband's indulgence and left to him its regulation. Certainly she never felt anything like the disgust Jane Welsh Carlyle voiced in 1845, when she said of Tennyson, "He is unmarried and unlikely to marry, as no woman could live in the atmosphere of tobacco smoke which he makes about him." See David Alec Wilson, *Carlyle on Cromwell and Others* (London: Kegan Paul, 1925), p. 283.

Before they returned home, the Tennysons drove from Weybridge to St. George's Hill, which Hallam and Lionel scaled with their father to view Windsor Castle and Hampton Court. Stopping briefly at Winchester, they then traveled by rail to Lymington and arrived at Farringford on 22 May. Tennyson passed the remainder of May and most of June at home, with the exception of 4-6 June, when he went to the New Forest with Edmund Lushington. In late June the Tennysons decided to spend their summer vacation touring the Pyrenees. Both boys were still suffering the effects of whooping cough, and their doctor thought the mountain air would be beneficial. Also the poet felt the trip might be good for his own hay fever, and he was eager to return to the site of his Pyrenees tour with Arthur Hallam thirty-one years before.

The Tennyson party, including the tutor, Graham Dakyns, and, for a brief time, Anne and Agnes Weld, left England on 27 June and journeyed to Auvergne and then to Bourges, where Emily found the fourteenth-century St. Stephen's Cathedral magnificent in its grand simplicity. Next they visited Clermont and Royat, and Tennyson and Dakyns climbed to the summit of Puy de Dôme, famous for its ruins of a temple of Mercury and for the experiments undertaken there by Pascal. The party next drove to Mont Dore where they were joined on 21 July by Arthur Hugh Clough, who was en route to Florence. Though far from well, the genial Clough was a welcome addition to the Laureate's company, and he traveled with them periodically during the next month and a half.

Following excursions to Mt. Sancy and Mt. Capucin, the Tennysons left Clough at Mont Dore and journeyed on through Tulle, Perigueux, Bordeaux, and Tarbes to Bigorre. Tennyson had been provoked all along by the difficulty of obtaining rooms, carriages, and donkeys and by general hostility to the English, but he was stirred by the view of the Pyrenees, which Emily thought "glorious with a sort of spiritual clearness and distinctness." The Tennysons encountered Clough at Bagnères de Luchon on 17 August and again at Luz on the thirty-first. During the next fortnight Tennyson, Clough, and Dakyns daily walked or rode through the mountains, traversing gorges and ravines, topping crags and steeps, and pausing from time to time to muse before sublime cascades.

High in the Pyrenees they stopped at Gavarni and explored its famous *cirque* crowned with snow-fields and glaciers. Though it did not seem so grand as he had remembered it, Tennyson still thought Gavarni the noblest district in the Pyrenees. Thence they proceeded through the valley of Argellez to Cauteretz, with Clough, Emily, and the children riding, and Tennyson and Dakyns walking along an older road, the same one the Laureate had traveled with Hallam when he began writing "Oenone" in the summer of 1830. From Cauteretz the men climbed to the Lac de Gaube on 7 September, and on their return they described to Emily their amazement at the perfect stillness of the great purple lake with its reflection of the snow-clad Vignemale. Clough was exhausted by the excursion, and he remained behind on the eighth, helping Hallam and Lionel with their journals, while Tennyson and Dakyns walked through the valley of Cauteretz. By late evening that same day Tennyson had written and presented to Emily two stanzas of "In the Valley of Cauteretz."

On 9 September both Dakyns, who wanted to visit Sargé, and Clough, who was to meet his wife in Paris on the eighteenth, left the company. Emily was sad to see them go. Dakyns had proved himself "the most unselfish of mortals," she wrote in her Journal, and of Clough she said, "There could not have been a kinder . . . or more thoughtful companion than he." Leaving Pau, the Tennysons traveled north to Dax and thence to Amiens and returned to England and Farringford on the eleventh. The following letter, written from Luchon on 26 August, again evidences Emily's fondness for Clough as well as her concern for his health. Though he seemed improved when he left the Tennysons, it soon became clear that he was not to recover. Clough died in Florence on 13 November 1861.

118   To Mrs. Arthur Hugh Clough
Bodleian Library, Oxford

Bagnères de Luchon, 26 August [1861]

My dear Mrs. Clough,
We have been so very glad to have good news of you and to
think of you happy as you can be without your husband. . . . I
do really hope this long separation will be repaid to you when
you see the improved state of Mr. Clough's health. It seems to
me that even the Pyrenean illness which he has had has in one
way been satisfactory as proving increase of strength in his
power of recovery. Do not be over-hasty in coming to him. Be
tolerably strong before you undertake the journey, for his sake.[1]
It is a great pleasure to us to have him, I need not say.[2]

1. In early August 1861 Mrs. Clough had given birth to a third child,
Blanche Athena.
2. Emily Tennyson's veneration for Clough was undiminished ten
years later when Mrs. Clough and her daughter Florence visited Farringford. She wrote in her Journal, 18 July 1871, "Independent of all likings
for herself, Mrs. Clough and her children have for *his* sake a kind
of sacredness in our eyes."

119   To Thomas Woolner

Farringford, 8 October 1861

My dear Mr. Woolner,
Though not yet free from the cruel bondage of seventy or
eighty letters we found on our return, to which number there
have been daily additions, yet I cannot help saying we are so
very glad that you have a house fitted to your purposes, and in
a quarter likely to make you still better known than you are.
We rejoice too of the pleasant news of Mr. Palgrave and *The
Golden Treasury.* . . .[1]
We wish you could have seen the divine expression of St.
Firmin (I think it was) in one of the screens of the Cathedral of
Amiens.[2] The sword is uplifted over the martyr to strike and
certainly there is a heavenly glory in his face not to be
forgotten. And a wonderful drama too in the surrounding
group. They are statuettes, all coloured. Mr. Palgrave will

remember the Col d'Aspin and will know how we must have been charmed with this on so fine a day that we saw nearly the whole chain of the Pyrenees. He will remember enough of Luchon and Luz and Cauteretz and Pau to tell you that we must have distinct and pleasant pictures of each but do you know I will whisper this in your ear that the beauty of Farringford is dearer to me than that of any of those places where one could live. One could not live in the Col d'Aspin nor the Port de la Picade, where Ally saw so gorgeous a sunset that he said it was worth all the discomfort and suffering of the journey to have seen it.

1. In his letter of 5 October 1861 (*Thomas Woolner*, pp. 205–06), Woolner informed Emily Tennyson that he had taken a house in Welbeck Street, Cavendish Square, large enough for both his studies and his residence, "the result of about six years' searching." Francis Palgrave had already moved in, and Woolner followed before the end of December. Palgrave seemed cheerful, even hopeful, wrote Woolner, as a result of the astounding success of his recently published *The Golden Treasury*, a collection of his selection of the finest English lyric verse. The idea for the collection first occurred to Palgrave during talks with Tennyson, and the Laureate greatly influenced the final choice of its contents.
2. There are images of St. Firmin, patron saint of Picardy, all over the cathedral. She is talking about the high reliefs of the choir-screen.

120   To Edward Lear

Farringford, 10 October 1861

My dear Mr. Lear,
I rejoice to hear that you are somewhat better. Go on on the good road so that at least if we cannot see you we may think happily of you. . . . I wish I could give a good account of ourselves. Perhaps this is in the future, at present we have neither of us recovered from the illness which haunted us in France. The boys are nearly well and I think Hallam seems the stronger for the journey. Ally saw some things which he will delight to remember; so did we all though what the boys and myself saw was chiefly in passing from one place to another. . . . We were first in Auvergne. There Nanny and Agnes went with us, but as neither was well they did not go further. The drive from Clermont to Mont Dore was one of the things Ally

and I most enjoyed. We thought how beautiful you would make that beautiful plain with the hills beyond, the old dark Clermont on the height as foreground. The air was delicious, by far the most delicate of any I breathed in France.

The most glorious of all the views we all had was that from the Col d'Aspin when one looked over nearly the whole range of the Pyrenees and of one gorgeous sunset which Ally and Mr. Dakyns saw on the Port de la Picade. He said that it repaid him for all the discomfort and illness of the journey, so after that I was content. Before I was continually doubtful and anxious as to whether the whole was not nearly a failure and whether one had not better go back at once. We went by Bourges and came back by Tours and Amiens and Boulogne.

We are tomorrow to take the farm into our own hands. I hope Heard, who is to manage it, is a very good man. We have every reason to think that he is from what we have seen of him and we both like him very much. I cannot help hoping that Alfred will be better for this new source of interest. . . .

Nanny is just about getting into her new home, a very nice house on Notting Hill which they have taken for three years.[1] God grant that it may be a happier home than she has had before since leaving our father's! They were all a month with us I think you know before we left home. He the day we left got some appointment in this new exhibition-arrangement office.[2]

1. Anne, Charles, and Agnes Weld remained at Notting Hill, London, until 1865, when they moved to Bellevue, New Bridge Hill, near Bath.
2. In 1862 Weld was appointed a district superintendent for the International Exhibition, as well as general manager of the Exhibition's philosophical department.

121   To Alfred and Margaret Gatty
Boston Public Library

Farringford, 15 November 1861

My dear Mr. and Mrs. Gatty,
I am grieved to tell you that my husband has been nearly three weeks in town under a doctor taking chlorine baths, etc. He has not yet returned, neither is it certain when he will be

allowed to return and when he does the doctor says he will for sometime require great care, so I fear I cannot fix any time when he will be able to see guests;[1] otherwise, I should gladly have fixed a time for welcoming your friend.

I cannot say that we are any of us quite as we ought to be but the weather has been stormy and trying. The boys are highly delighted with following the plough and riding the horses and such things. I am glad yours go so well.

1. Tennyson left Farringford on 28 October and remained in town until 23 November, lodging first in Frank Lushington's temporarily vacant rooms in the Temple and then, when Lushington returned, in George Venables's chambers. When he came home, Emily noted in the Journal that he still did not "look as I would have him"; but she was gratified by the satisfaction he expressed with a number of minor improvements, indoors and out, which she had managed during his absence.

122   To Margaret Gatty
Boston Public Library

Farringford, 10 December 1861

My dear Mrs. Gatty,
Thank you for your kind gift.[1] I have already found amusement in it and I doubt not shall do more and instruction besides. But do you know I love not the Irish. I think them a nest of traitors with some honourable exceptions. In the course of conversation with a learned man yesterday I made it clear to myself that patriotism I love, nationality I love not. I wish conquered nations could take gracefully the married state upon them. . . .

He does not like to have his few lines called an ode. An ode must be a free song and not written because asked for and as asked for, and besides the fact of his having written the lines was not to be mentioned. There is as yet nothing finished and final as the lines and music must be one if they are to be at all.[2]

1. An advance copy of *The Old Folks from Home, a Holiday in Ireland in 1861* (London, 1862).
2. The "Ode Sung at the Opening of the International Exhibition" was published with music by W. Sterndale Bennett, 12 April 1862, and sung at the exhibition on 1 May. The poem was actually written

in October 1861, but Tennyson added three lines of reference to the Prince Consort (ll.7-10), as the originator of international exhibitions, after the first draft.

123   To Margaret Gatty
Boston Public Library

Farringford, 17 December 1861

My dear Mrs. Gatty,

I do not know to what you allude but I cannot allow the poor Queen to have any blame cast on her without saying that she never in any way deserved any, at all events as far as we are concerned. We have had nothing but kindness from her. She never asked for an ode and certainly we cannot think she would have done it in a wrong way if she had.[1]

I was only speaking in Irish fashion when I spoke of the nest of traitors. I doubt not there are multitudes of loyal hearts in Ireland but the disloyal bawl so loud that their modest voices are scarcely heard above the din, and I had just been made very wrathful by Smith O'Brien[2] and by Aubrey DeVere. It is so wicked in those who call themselves Christian gentlemen to keep up old grudges when they know very well that for years England has done all she can for those who are too little inclined to do anything for themselves. . . . It is just as rational for the Saxon to cry out against the Norman in England as for the Celt to cry out against the Norman in Ireland, Scotland, or Wales. . . .

I write this to beg you to unsay anything unkind about the Queen that may have been said. At all times it would be hateful to us to hear, most especially now.[3] Thanks for all your good wishes. We heartily send you the like.

1. Knowing Tennyson's aversion to writing to order, Mrs. Gatty had evidently expressed consternation that the Queen should have entreated a poem for the International Exhibition. However, the ode was written by request of the Committee for the International Exhibition, not by request of the Queen.
2. William Smith O'Brien (1803-64), Irish insurgent; member of O'Connell's Repeal Association, which he found too moderate and abandoned to lead the young Irelanders in the Repeal League. After the short-lived uprising of 1848, O'Brien was sentenced to death; in

1854 he was released on condition of not returning to Ireland, and in 1856 he received a free pardon.

Emily was undoubtedly incensed by a letter of O'Brien's which was printed in *The Times* on 7 December 1861. In that letter O'Brien expressed his opinion that the English government might take advantage of the secession of the Confederate States of America to declare war on the Union government. England, he argued, was not above assailing any nation in a situation unprepared to defend itself. O'Brien predicted, however, that in the event of such aggression England would find herself vigorously opposed at home by five million Irish "who pant for an opportunity of avenging the wrongs of their race."

3. In the wake of Prince Albert's death, 14 December 1861.

124   To Margaret Gatty
Boston Public Library

Farringford, 2 February 1862

My dear Mrs. Gatty,
I enclose the Dedication by way of token of all our good wishes.[1] Last night I dreamt of the *Dean* and when I, being pleased to see him, held out my hand with great eagerness, he withdrew his, and, I thought, this is because I only sent Dr. Mann's book instead of writing about *Maud*![2]

Hallam is reading to me—forgive my blunders. Ally is, I am thankful to say, much better. You will be pleased to hear that the Queen and Princess Alice like their lines exceedingly and have thanked him in the warmest terms.[3] You will not let the Dedication out of your own hand before it is published, please.

1. Tennyson completed his "Dedication" of the *Idylls* to the memory of the Prince Consort early in January 1862 and sent copies to the Duchess of Sutherland, to her daughter, the Duchess of Argyll, and to Princess Alice. The "Dedication" first appeared in the fourth edition of the *Idylls* (1862).

2. Evidently Emily Tennyson had sent Dr. W. F. Hook, dean of Chichester, a copy of *Maud Vindicated*.

3. On 15 January 1862, Princess Alice wrote to thank Tennyson for the "Dedication": "If words could express thanks and real appreciation of lines so beautiful, so truly worthy of the great spirit which inspired the Author, Princess Alice would attempt to do it;—but these failing she begs Mr. Alfred Tennyson to believe how much she admires them, and that this just tribute to the memory of her beloved Father touched her deeply." Princess Alice also conveyed the Queen's "warmest thanks"

for the lines and her assurance of "how much moved she was in reading them, and that they soothed her aching, bleeding heart" (Dyson and Tennyson, *Dear and Honoured Lady*, p. 65).

125   To Thomas Woolner

Farringford, 11 February 1862

. . . The "Fisherman" is to have a previous training I think in his boyhood. Alfred has been talking to Captain Hamond[1] about it. There would not be sufficient bettering of his condition in a mere sailor's pay. This is why the boatswain is important. I hope you were not vexed by trouble thrown away as much as I was vexed that you should have thrown it away.[2] Though no good and kind act is ever really thrown away, is it? Alfred varies but on the whole is better. He and the boys send love.

1. Sir Graham Eden Hamond (1779–1862), of Afton Manor, Norton, was made a captain in the Royal Navy in 1798; he became an admiral of the fleet in 1862.
2. Although Tennyson altered various details and greatly expanded the ending, "Enoch Arden" is essentially "The Fisherman's Story" made over. It was not until the summer of 1862 that Emily Tennyson wrote to FitzGerald to ask what training Enoch might have needed to obtain a job as ship's boatswain (see the *Memoir*, I, 515).

126   To G. F. Watts

University of Virginia

Farringford, 17 February 1862

My dear Signor,[1]
I rejoice to hear that your beautiful and touching portrait is now in a form to be known and delighted in by many.[2] Alfred will, of course, send his signature since you desire it.

Thinking you may like to have the Dedication we send a copy for you and one for Mrs. Prinsep if she also cares to have it, with all kind words.[3] I trust that this winter has dealt gently with you and that you are growing stronger and stronger.

Alfred is not well, but thanks to Dr. Jackson's kind care he is certainly in some ways better.[4]

1. The Thoby Prinseps's pet name for Watts, by which his close friends often spoke of and to him, as something less formal than a surname and less familiar than a Christian name.
2. Evidently Watts's "moonlight portrait" of Tennyson (1859) was reproduced for public sale.
3. A copy of the "Dedication" of the *Idylls* remains with the ms. letter, in the Tennyson Research Centre.
4. Dr. Jackson of Freshwater often ministered to Tennyson's minor complaints.

127   To Margaret Gatty
Boston Public Library

Farringford, 7 May 1862

My dear Mrs. Gatty,
I have for a long time been meaning to ask after your daughter and to express a hope which I most sincerely feel that the scarletina did not spread. Now I have more to say for I perceive by the *Times* that Dr. Wolff[1] is gone and I know how much you will miss him. Surely we have lost a very remarkable man. One who should have lived forever as the world will scarcely see his like again. How thankful you must be that you accomplished your labour of love in writing those books for him. . . . Ally I hope will come home today. He has been in town but not at the Exhibition, in spite of the minute description given of his appearance by some of the papers.

1. See above, Letter 109. Dr. Wolff died in Somerset on 2 May 1862.

128   To Thomas Woolner

Farringford, 10 July 1862

My dear Mr. Woolner,
The story is very grand and very finely told we think.[1] The arrangement and form are so good. Best thanks for it. Yes, Mrs.

George Patmore wrote to me simply announcing the death.[2] It is a terrible thing for him indeed. Do you know that your name was almost the last word she spoke?

. . . I feel that I have not half enough thanked you for having taken so much trouble about the story, nor expressed what I think of its grand capabilities. I hope he will do it.

1. On 5 July 1862, Woolner sent Tennyson "The Sermon" (see *Thomas Woolner*, pp. 219–25), a story he had heard as a child from his grandfather and an old rustic. Tennyson subsequently reworked the tale into "Aylmer's Field," which he completed in December 1863.

2. Emily Patmore died of consumption on 5 July 1862. Mrs. George Patmore was the wife of Coventry Patmore's brother.

On 18 July the Tennysons arrived in London to begin their summer holiday. During their two weeks in town they spent considerable time with James Spedding, Francis Palgrave, and W. H. Brookfield, a man, they concluded, unequaled for "freely flowing wit and humour" (Journal, 1 August 1862). The poet and Emily also saw Gladstone, Woolner, F. D. Maurice, George Venables, the Duke of Argyll, Lord Monteagle of Brendon, and Sir Stephen (Vere) De Vere, and they had a private tour of the International Exhibition, for Emily the high point of their visit. After a brief stop in Hampstead with Tennyson's mother, they left for Lincolnshire on 5 August, and, passing through Lincoln, they reached Grasby Vicarage two days later.

Tennyson left Emily and the boys with the Turners in mid-August and, with Palgrave once again his companion, traveled through northwest Derbyshire to the Peak and Dovedale and then to Rowsley and Haddon Hall, ancient seat of the Avenel family. From Haddon they proceeded to Castleton and Buxton, where they met Monckton Milnes and the Charles Trevelyans. Turning north to Yorkshire, the poet and Palgrave visited Leyburn and Middleham, stopping to view the ruins of Middleham Castle, once owned by Warwick, the King Maker, and they paused again at Bolton for an excursion to the twelfth-century Augustine abbey on the bank of the Wharfe.

Tennyson returned to his family at Grasby about 10 September, and on the thirteenth the Tennysons were back home with "the old life . . . walks, letters innumerable, and farm accounts."

In the more than two months intervening between the return to Farringford and the date of the following letter, they entertained few guests, and the poet worked diligently at "Aylmer's Field" and other poems for his next volume. His routine, punctuated by nightly star-gazing, was interrupted only by G. F. Watts's occasional calls to work on Emily's portrait, and by brief visits from Edmund Lushington and from Woolner, who was, of course, gladdened by Tennyson's employment.

129   To Thomas Woolner

Farringford, 5 December 1862

My dear Mr. Woolner,
I rejoice to hear that you are so busy.[1] You must not spend spare minutes in writing when reading is so much better for you. Yes, Alfred is going on with the poem. He takes walks often now that the tourists are gone. I think the beginning of the poem very fine; my chief objection to it is that it must necessarily be so indignant in its tone.

1. See Woolner's letter of 2 December 1862, to Emily Tennyson (*Thomas Woolner*, p. 229).

130   To Elizabeth Tennyson

Farringford, 15 January 1863

Dearest Mother,
I had copied this[1] for thee yesterday after Lady Augusta Bruce[2] who brought from the Queen the copy of *The Prince Consort* (a book containing a sketch of his character and his speeches) had left. It is in the Queen's own writing, a superscription to the book. . . . I am thankful to say Ally has been much better this autumn than last. He has had a headache these few days but only, I hope, in consequence of company.

The Queen has also sent him a beautiful and touching photograph of Herself, the Princess Royal, and Princess Alice, and I think Prince Alfred, with those lines from Ally's dedication: "May all love, etc."

Dearest Mother, thy prayers we count among our most precious blessings and one of thy notes as among the best gifts the new year can bring. Also the Queen has sent a copy of the prayers used by Her morning and evening on the anniversary of the Prince's death and the sermon preached before the Princesses and Princes.

> To Alfred Tennyson, Esquire
>   Who so truly appreciated
> this greatest, purest and best of men
>   from
>   the beloved Prince's
>   broken-hearted widow
>   Victoria Rg.
> Osborne, 9 December 1862

1. The superscription the Queen had written in a specially bound volume of *The Principal Speeches and Addresses of His Royal Highness the Prince Consort with an Introduction Giving Some Outlines of His Character* (London: John Murray, 1862), which Emily Tennyson copied for her mother-in-law at the end of this letter.
2. (1822–76), lady-in-waiting to the Queen who, in 1863, married Arthur Penrhyn Stanley (1815–81), liberal theologian, then Oxford Professor of Ecclesiastical History, and dean of Westminster from 1864 till his death.

131   *To Drummond Rawnsley*
Harvard

Farringford, 26 January 1863

My dear Drummond,
We have had a house full of company or I should not so long have delayed returning the Greek iambics. Ally and our guests both agreed in thinking the song not fitted for Greek iambics so I fear if you think it is you will be disappointed at hearing that Ally does not admire the translation. I suppose there is no need to tell Mr. Thring[1] more than the first.

Hallam and Lionel have not begun to think about dancing but I have great sympathy with all young things that love it having liked it so myself once in a day.[2] Many a time even since here I have danced in a room alone for the pure pleasure of it, so has Ally if not for pure pleasure, for pleasure and exercise.

Yes, he has been reading Stanley to himself and me but we were interrupted by the arrival of friends before I at least had seen much. This and his *Eastern Church* seem to me peculiarly valuable to our British world at this juncture.[3]

Ally bids me say what he thought would interest you as Lionel's godfather that the Queen has asked him to bring them to see her in the spring when she returns.[4] You will not mention this, I know, or anything of the kind we may tell you. We have such a horror of newspapers. We are all to go. Lady Augusta Bruce was spared to bring over a copy of *The Prince Consort* for Ally with a very kind inscription in the Queen's own hand. Hallam gathered some snowdrops and this is what Lady Augusta writes:

> Pray say to your dear Hallam that I gave almost all the snowdrops, a few I could not part with, to the Queen. They were the first Her Majesty had seen this year and by the Queen's desire were kept carefully in a glass on Her writing table for a week I am sure. The Queen was much pleased to know that the name of the gatherer was "Hallam" and that he had such good and great godfathers[5] and also that he has such a nice little brother whose usefulness in acting as a pioneer Her Majesty was much pleased to hear of. . . .

Which means that he went with Ally and Lady Augusta to the bay to tell Ally what, alas, he is too blind to know for himself, the names of the people he meets.

We are all pretty well, I am beginning to shiver at the idea of school for the boys. I suppose they must go in little more than a year if all be well. We like Mr. Bradley so much that perhaps they will go to Marlborough.[6] With kindest love to you all from us all and a hope that you will come and see us before long.

1. Edward Thring (1821–87), headmaster of Uppingham grammar school, County Rutland, from 1853 till his death; author of *Education and School* (1864) and *The Theory and Practice of Teaching* (1883), as well as numerous poems and translations, one of which Rawnsley evidently sent to Tennyson for his appraisal.
2. Emily Tennyson indicated in "For Her Sons" that she and Tennyson

often attended balls in the Somersby neighborhood, and that Tennyson "was fond of dancing and especially of waltzing, and he waltzed well and was a coveted partner."

3. The Tennysons had been reading Arthur Stanley's *Lectures on the History of the Jewish Church,* vol. I (1863). Emily also refers to his *Lectures on the History of the Eastern Church* (1861).

4. On 9 May 1862, the whole family visited Osborne, and Hallam and Lionel Tennyson were presented to the Queen.

5. Henry Hallam and F. D. Maurice.

6. Tennyson expressed his high regard for Granville Bradley in 1866 when he dispatched his elder son to school with the comment, "I am sending Hallam to Bradley, not to Marlborough" (*AT*, p. 362). The intimacy between Bradley and the Laureate was encouraged by the friendship of their wives. Though Emily and Marian Bradley apparently wrote personal letters confiding the minutiae of their lives, only isolated scraps of their correspondence have survived. But Mrs. Bradley set down several descriptions of her friend in her diary, which is preserved in the British Museum. In 1856, during the early days of their acquaintance, she wrote: "Mrs. T. is middle-aged quiet and gentle with a sweet expression of eyes. She is a first-rate wife to him practical and devoted and fully able to sympathize with the Poet." And again, "Mrs. T. is charming, a beautiful combination of the intellectual and practical and earnest goodness with a manner at once warm and gentle—there is a very spiritual look about her clear brown [*sic*] eyes . . ." (Richardson, *The Pre-Eminent Victorian,* p. 181).

When she came to Farringford in January 1863, Lady Augusta Bruce apparently informed Tennyson of the Queen's desire that he compose some lines honoring Princess Alexandra of Denmark, who was to marry Albert Edward, Prince of Wales, later Edward VII. Tennyson sent his "A Welcome to Alexandra" to Osborne on 6 March, but he missed the wedding four days later because his ticket for admission was not sent to Farringford in time. Following a short visit by Mrs. Gatty from the eleventh till the fourteenth, Tennyson and Emily went to Osborne on the sixteenth to express their good wishes for the Prince and Princess.

On 1 April Charles Weld came, on behalf of the International Exhibition, to present to Tennyson an urn and salver inscribed to acknowledge his "Ode Sung at the Opening of the International Exhibition." Tennyson read a completed draft of "Aylmer's Field" to Emily on the tenth, and at night he read aloud from Shakespeare and Comte. Emily liked "his own beautiful poem" best of all, "a great refreshment" after dreary Comtist philosophy.

Several new guests, including Thomas Littleton, fourth Baron Lilford, and the Swedish photographer Rejlander, occupied the first week of May prior to the visit to Osborne on 9 May, which is described in detail both in the Journal and in the following letter to Anne Weld.

132   To Anne Weld

Farringford, 12 May 1863

My dearest Nanny,
I wanted to write to you yesterday but a Queen's messenger came with books for Ally, "The Meditations" and Guizot's *Prince Albert* and another in which Ally was to write a poem and letters from Lady Augusta which had to be answered, so I could not.[1]

I must tell you a little now and more when we meet. We lunched at one with Lady Augusta, after that drove with her about the grounds, and on our return she was sent for by the Queen and came back to fetch us into the drawingroom. Soon there was a quiet shy opening of the door and the Queen came in. I found myself on my knee kissing the hand which was given to me but I do not know how I came there.[2] Ally talked eloquently and I never felt so little shy with any stranger nor spoke so freely. The Queen laughed heartily sometimes and sometimes was sad. Her face is really beautiful now in its childlike simplicity and its vast love. Quite a small face beaming all over. We saw all the Princes and Princesses. All were very kind and shook hands kindly. The boys had their little talk aside with Prince Leopold and we gave Princess Beatrice a volume of the poems in answer to her request for "poetics." More when we meet. Our kindest love, dearest Nanny. Do be vaccinated. We mean to be.[3]

1. The Queen sent Tennyson François Guizot's *Meditations and Moral Sketches,* translated from the French by J. Butler, Marquis of Ormonde (Dublin, 1855), and Guizot's *Le Prince Albert, Son Caractère, Ses Discours* (Paris, 1863).
    In response to the Queen's request that he write a poem in the album she sent him, Tennyson set down "In the Valley of Cauteretz," which the Queen previously had praised to the Duke of Argyll.

2. In his diary Hallam Tennyson also described his mother's, and his own, first meeting with the Queen: "Her Majesty shook hands with Mamma and Mamma very courteously went down on one knee and kissed the Queen's hand and the Queen shook hands with Lionel and myself and we shook hands with all the Princes and Princesses except Princess Louise: she only shook hands with Mamma" (Dyson and Tennyson, *Dear and Honoured Lady,* p. 77).

3. Emily Tennyson may have meant to be vaccinated, but it took Julia Cameron an entire day of beseeching and cajoling to persuade the poet to submit to vaccination on 19 May along with the rest of his family. Evidently Tennyson's vaccination was given incorrectly, and he felt unwell for some time as a result. Indeed he blamed his vaccination for the ill health he suffered most of the remainder of that summer.

133   To Margaret Gatty
Boston Public Library

Grayshott Hall,[1] 10 June 1863

My dear Mrs. Gatty,

The cards have followed me to our Hampshire farmhouse. We sincerely wish all good and happiness to the bridegroom and the bride[2] and for yourselves all the happiness that can come of this after the little bit of allowance that must be made for personal loss even to the most unselfish. How has this third winter dealt with you? We had snow even this far south on the 22nd of May, and at Farringford there was ice, we heard. Both our boys are with us; Hallam very much stronger but still not yet quite recovered. Lionel well and much improved in speech.

We have not yet secured a plot of land in this neighbourhood as we had hoped to have done. Until yesterday, he has had not the slightest bit of hay fever. He was walking about five hours yesterday and this, I fear, brought it on, for he has been very unwell since and now that we have no longer the inducement to remain here that we had so long as he was well, I trust that we may soon be gone home, for this undrained house is very trying to one who is shut up in it so much. They have been driving out a good deal for we have the pony carriage here and two swift ponies instead of the old ones. The heathy wilds all about are beautiful and will be more so.

    1. The Tennysons had recently leased Grayshott Farm, near Hasle-mere, where they went for short stays over the next few years, 1863–67, thus avoiding some of the Isle of Wight tourist traffic while they searched for an appropriate location for a permanent summer retreat.

    2. One of the Gatty children was soon to marry. In a letter of 14 August 1863 to Mrs. Gatty (unpublished, Boston Public Library), not included here, Emily Tennyson again wrote about the marriage: "May all possible happiness come to the young bride and bridegroom and the first and greatest that they may be speedily married. I like not, nor have I, as far as human eyes can see, any reason to like, long engagements."

134   To G. F. Watts
University of Virginia

Farringford, 24 June 1863

My dear Signor,

"This is one of the great pictures that future generations will look at" was one of the exclamations which greeted yours on its arrival.[1] I can only feel ashamed when I think how much of your time and thought have been spent on me and when I know that it is a picture of myself and such a one that a lady (Lady Grant, Sir Alexander's mother) said this morning she almost felt in sitting near it that it could speak to her. I do not know how such a beautiful picture has come, but you are a subtle alchemist, a great magician, that I do know. He hopes to thank you in person tomorrow.

    1. Watts's portrait of Emily Tennyson, painted, for the most part, during November 1862, captures both her loving tenderness and her strong will. When the picture arrived at Farringford the following June, the Argylls and others present agreed that it looked like a Gainsborough.

Tennyson was not equal to much traveling during the summer of 1863, but he was away from home for nearly three months nonetheless. He left Farringford on 27 June for London where Sir James Paget, Surgeon-General to the Queen and the most renowned pathologist of the age, treated him several weeks for a gouty infection. Emily and the boys left home on 26 July

145   To Alfred Tennyson

Own dearest,

How I wish I could have a telegram from thee tonight telling me the result! When I read those insulting taunts from the French papers I longed so for one of thy trumpet blasts which should make every soul in the land feel that not for all the scorn and reproach that can be heaped on us will we be moved to do that which seems to us wrong and not for all the suffering which may come from a war in which we should stand alone as helpers will we be moved from doing what we feel to be right.

Lady Grant and Tiny[1] have been here to luncheon. The hay is going on beautifully. I must get out a little for it is late. Such a perfect hay-making day! I went to communion yesterday and spoke to so many people. Croziers, Franklins, Miss Hamond, and all so kind. Our best love.

1. Tiny Cotton. See above, Letter 19, n. 3.

On 6 August the Tennysons left England for Boulogne and a seven-week tour of northwestern France, much of it through Brittany. Traveling quickly south from Boulogne, they passed through Paris and on the eleventh arrived at Chartres, where they visited the magnificent Gothic cathedral three times before proceeding to Le Mans. They toured the grand cathedral dedicated to St. Julien in Le Mans, and Emily later recalled "the jeweled splendour of the windows in the gloom of the high springing pointed arches" and the enormous upright stone, supposedly a menhir, between two buttresses to the right of the west portal.

On the way to Nantes they stopped at the Castle of Angers and inspected everything in that once-grand military construction, from the seventeen round towers to the dungeons with their prisoners' rings still in the walls. Then, following the Loire, they visited the remains of the chateau of the infamous Gilles de Rais, the original "Blue Beard," and, of course, the Nantes cathedral. By mid-August they reached the seaside resort of Carnac, whence they went to see the prehistoric Alignements of Carnac, 3,000-odd standing-stones arranged in the form of a quincunx, on the moor half a mile north of the town. And on the road to Locmariaquer they saw the Men-er-Hroeck ("stone of the fairy"), a menhir originally seventy feet high, and the three dolmens known as the Mané-Lud, the Col-ar-Marc'hadowrien, and the Mané Rutual. Tennyson thought the megaliths "not nearly so fine as Stonehenge," but Emily found the great, fallen Men-er-Hroeck, the Dolmen de Caesar, the Table des Marchands, and all the other stone works fascinating. She and the boys mounted the Caesar dolmen and viewed from its top the Morbihan and the Ile de Gaur'inis.

Proceeding through Quimper and the picturesque town of Morlaix, the Tennyson family paused again on 22 August at Pleyben, a village, like so many Breton villages, remarkable for its church. The Tennysons thought the Pleyben church with its celebrated "parish enclosure" and its incredibly intricate pattern of arches particularly fine. The next day they continued to Lannion, then to Mont St. Michel and Avranches, and on 2 September they arrived at Bayeux where, in the small museum in the public library, they viewed the 230-foot-long Bayeux Tapestry illustrating the events which led to the conquest of England by William in 1066. A favorite opinion of the origin of the tapestry ascribes it to Matilda, wife of the Conqueror, and Emily credited Matilda in her Journal with "a good wife's deed." On 6 October they reached Rouen by boat, and Tennyson was reminded of the same boat trip once made with Arthur Hallam. They spent the night of the eighth at Dieppe and journeyed across the channel to Ryde on the ninth; that same evening they were back at Farringford.

146   To Thomas Woolner

Farringford, 11 July 1864

My dear Mr. Woolner,
I cannot tell you how sorry I am that my intention of writing to you the very day Ally returned has not been fulfilled till now. . . . I rejoice at the happy account he gives of you and the family so soon to be nearest to you.[1] I hope it will not be later than September. The months of our short life are precious.

Why should they drag wearily with absence when they might go winged with presence, which sentence I take to be worthy of Queen Elizabeth herself in its elaborateness or whatever else it might be called.

It is so blue and beautiful today here. So wine-dark the sea. Ally is gone over it in a little boat manned by five stout soldiers to Key Haven, the port at which one lands for Aubrey House where my sister Anne Weld now lives.

I hope you think he has given your stories well. I wish he would give mine now and do the "San Graal" for me, not but that I heartily adopt "Enoch Arden." The boys are gone to be photographed, poor chicks! or they would send their kindest love.

1. While in London Tennyson evidently visited the George Waughs, parents of Woolner's fiancée.

147   To Margaret Gatty
Boston Public Library

Farringford, 13 October 1864

My dear Mrs. Gatty,

I have been meaning to write to you and say that we found no inscriptions on dials in our journey.[1] Indeed I only noticed one dial and that was on the wonderfully beautiful church at Le Mans close to the Druid Stone which is built up in the wall. The dial was borne by a shadowy skeleton angel.

Many of the old churches we saw were very glorious and the Druid stones at Carnac and Locmariaquer are interesting and weird-looking; the Bayeux Tapestry also extremely interesting. Brittany itself is wild Wales in miniature, Normandy fine and bold and rich.

Ally bore this journey much better than the last and the boys were very well. I unfortunately got a cough and I have had a bad one almost ever since I came home five weeks ago. . . .

Our poor peregrin falcons are both taken and in captivity. They are getting very tame but I cannot bear the thought of their being prisoners. Our boys wanted to sell watches to make five guineas to buy them that they might set them free, poor little souls. However Ally said they would be sure to be caught again or shot so that there was no use in it. I must not say more than our kindest regards.

1. Mrs. Gatty's interest in sundials eventually resulted in her publication of *The Book of Sundials* (1872).

148   *To Thomas Woolner*
Bodleian Library, Oxford

Farringford, 4 November 1864

My dear Mr. Woolner,

Mr. Wilson arrived yesterday and he has kindly taken the boys for me this morning, so I will not let it pass without a few lines of thanks for your welcome letter,[1] and of affectionate congratulation from us on your marriage, which all who have the pleasure of knowing your bride think so very happy. May it indeed be so ever more and more. We looked for you both at the appointed time, and now we will look for you whenever you bid us do so, and let it not be long.

Perhaps just now that all is so new and strange you find you cannot work much but my hope is that when you have become accustomed to the new order of things you will work all the better for having one to take pride and pleasure in all you do, ever by you.

Thanks for what you say about the new poem,[2] but for you it would not have been. Do you like the idea of the selection in sixpenny parts for the working man?[3] And I wonder whether you would approve of my notion of having headings and tail pieces, if had at all, made out of flowers, emblematic of the colonies by way of telling the world that one considers that the colonists too are among the people of England. Each colony ought to have its flower or tree emblem but as far as I can make, it has not. . . .

We hope that in consideration of our being so far away from town, you have chosen a tankard or gold bracelets or whatever you will by way of memorial of our good wishes and will send the like to us, or had you rather we should ask Mr. Palgrave to do this for us? With love and best wishes from Alfred and the boys to yourself and all kind greetings from us all to your Alice.

1. See *Thomas Woolner,* pp. 255-56, for Woolner's letter to Emily Tennyson dated 3 November 1864.

2. In his 3 November letter Woolner wrote of "Aylmer's Field": "I do not find that my experience agrees with the Bard's opinion of his 'Aylmer's Field'; for he thought it was and would be regarded as the least effective of the new poems, whereas I hear good judges say quite the contrary. Froude, by no means a light authority, told me the other day he thought it the finest piece of writing that Tennyson had ever done."

3. In January 1865, Tennyson published, under the title *Moxon's Miniature Poets, A Selection from the Works of Alfred Tennyson,* an inexpensive, two-volume "People's Edition" which he hoped would reach the workingmen of England to whom it was dedicated. The edition was not well received, and no more volumes were published.

149   *To Anne Weld and Henry Sellwood*

Farringford, 6 February 1865

My dearest Daddy and Nanny,
I must tell you about Mrs. Cameron's "Time." She was talking on an interesting subject with Mr. Pollock[1] when suddenly she rushed out with extended arms, "Stop him! Stop him! There he is, Time." An old man was brought in with white hair. According to Hallam, he was undressed, had no shirt on. Wanted scrubbing very much. Mrs. Cameron wraps him up in best shawls, puts an egg cup in his hand, turns him into "Time," but talks to him so much about his beautiful face that he is supposed to have grown very conceited at last. . . .

1. William Frederick Pollock, see above, Letter 37, n. 2.

150   *To Mrs. Thomas Woolner*

Farringford, 11 February 1865

My dear Mrs. Woolner,
We shall be delighted to welcome Mr. Woolner and for as long a time as he can stay, yourself also if you change your mind.
. . . Lionel was the other day singing the sweetness of the days that were past, when the sculptor with hair like a torch was

here, in Latin verse—so Mr. Woolner will perceive he is of a
constant mind. Hoping that we may send him back quite well,[1]
believe me, very truly yours.

  1. Woolner was suffering from an eye inflammation.

151   To Edward Lear

Farringford, 17 February 1865

My dear Mr. Lear,
I am sorry your winter has not been so pleasant as one could
have wished it.[1] In spite of the beauty of its situation I took a
dislike to Nice. Poor Frank and Katie, you know of course of
their loss. A kind of awful doom seems to hang over that
family.[2] A sort of martyr fate. It is hard to rejoice in suffering
for others, even when one looks upon it as a crown of glory for
them. I hear Katie bears her loss very well. . . .

  Ally has been far better this year than last I am thankful to
say. We have at last seen two of the eight sixpenny numbers
fairly launched into the world but the world at present has not
shown itself very grateful. However one has the satisfaction of
feeling one has done what is right in this small respect.

  We are having another fight for our view, this time fighting
with the elements, trying to get up a bank in the [illegible] to
shut out some hideous houses built or building in the field on
the opposite side of the road;[3] then we have at last nearly got
up a coach house which we have been without except at the
other house,[4] ever since we pulled down the old one to make a
lawn.

  We are expecting poor Mr. Woolner here alone. Do not be
alarmed, he is not parted from his wife, whom every one I hear
name her, praises, but he is coming in the hope of getting rid
of an inflammation in one of his eyes. . . . We are hoping to
have the Grants here before long, also Mr. Jowett. He spent a
fortnight with us at Christmas and was more cheerful than I
have ever seen him, I think. Mrs. Cameron is making endless
Madonnas and May Queens and Foolish Virgins and Wise
Virgins and I know not what besides. It is really wonderful
how she puts her spirit into people. . . .

The boys are strong notwithstanding the colds they have had. Football, chess, cricket are passions with them but they are not bad about their lessons either. Hallam seems to have gained a great deal in this year. I wish I might keep Lionel another year for I know it would be good for him. Ally has been very patient about tutors. I must not try him further. Our kind love to you.

1. Lear spent the winter of 1864-65 in Nice, which he found lonely, expensive, and every other way wretched. The weather was bitterly cold, and he was even disappointed in what he saw—"Obscure torrents, and unpleasant villages: roaring sea:—but no peacock hue bays nor any other pleasure" (Noakes, pp. 204-05).

2. The Frank Lushingtons' first child was born dead, Henry Lushington died in his prime in 1855, and the Edmund Lushingtons lost their only son in 1856. Fate continued to deal harshly with the Lushingtons, particularly the Edmund Lushingtons. Their oldest daughter, Emily, died in 1868 at the age of nineteen, and their youngest, Lucia Maria, died five years later at age twenty-one. Only the second daughter, Zilly (Cecilia), lived to adulthood. See Charles Tennyson, "The Somersby Tennysons," *Victorian Studies* (Christmas Supplement 1963), p. 53.

3. The Tennysons actually raised a bank, upon which they planted wagon-loads of trees, in order to block out the "new red brick houses" the poet despised (H. Tennyson, *Materials for a Life of A. T.*, III, 5).

4. Probably the Terrace, a house on the Farringford estate owned by the poet, which the Horatio Tennysons occupied during the late 1860s.

152   *To Alfred Tennyson*

Farringford, 25 February 1865

Own dearest,
Thou knowest how I am with thee in spirit. God bless thee, mine own, and give thee strength to bear up against this sorrow.[1] Pleasant and lovely is it to think of the holy beauty and sweetness of her life, of the perfect love for you all. Anything so divine cannot die, one knows that it is one with God and Christ and must live forever. God bless thee, dearest, and make us all like her in life and death, one with her and one with Himself ever. I would I were with thee. Bring Tilly home with thee if she likes to come and thou to bring her, or

Harriet and Arthur,[2] if thou wilt. I have proposed a plan for her future life which I have written to Louy, subject, of course, to thy approval.[3] She is only to show it to thee or at least first to show it to thee and only to thee unless thou approve. . . .

I think, dearest, that if we were to help towards keeping on Rosemount till September it would be best, if Tilly like it, because of Aunt Mary Anne.[4] We ought to help, ought we not? Our boys are gone to Cowes today with Mr. Lipscombe.[5] It looks a lovely day. Soft clouds on a blue sky, calm and tender. My best thanks for thine.

1. On 22 February 1865, Tennyson received word that his mother was seriously ill, and he immediately set out for London. She died before he could get there.

2. Tennyson's brother Arthur (1814-99) and his wife, the former Harriet West.

3. The plan provided for Matilda Tennyson's dividing her time between Farringford and the Charles Turners' Grasby Vicarage. Actually she spent most of her time with the Tennysons, and she became so passionately attached to the poet that she would never again visit Farringford or Aldworth after his death. From 1892 until her death she lived at Park House with her sister, Cecilia Lushington.

4. Mary Anne Fytche survived her sister by only a few days.

5. The tutor for Hallam and Lionel Tennyson who replaced Mr. Wilson on 11 November 1864.

153   To Thomas Woolner

Farringford, 20 March 1865

My dear Mr. Woolner,

Ally would immediately go and look at St. Mary's[1] had he but money at present to buy it. Very likely he will go and look though he could not buy just now however well he might like it . . . My fear is the western climate. I cling to the Surrey hills as my natural home. Alfred always laughs at me about my Hale Paradise.[2]

It is extremely kind in you to remember the annuity tables. I should like to set all the bells in England ringing so much do I rejoice over this first gleam of hope for our labouring class.[3] I wish I knew any good Nimuë who could work a good charm on Mr. Gladstone; then he should be compelled to steal a little of his surplus every year to make a fund to augment the small annuities of the labouring class. I prophesy that this would in a great measure swallow up the poor-rate, rendering it soon almost a forgotten name and I think it could not fail to raise proportionally the tone of the people. . . .

Mr. Paul's[4] boys do not reassemble before the third of May. Ally says that had he known Mr. Lipscombe would have stayed another year he would have kept Hallam and Lionel at home, but I fear their doom is sealed now and that they could not be kept at home without ill-treating Mr. Paul. . . . When are we to have Mr. and Mrs. Carlyle here?[5] They always seem to glide by us however much hope we may have from time to time that now they are really coming. Ally successfully to work now!

1. A house near Seaton which Woolner suggested as a possible summer home for the Tennysons. They visited St. Mary's in July 1865, but decided against purchase.

2. When she married, Emily Tennyson was living with her father at Hale, near Farnham, West Surrey. As a young girl she often visited with Sellwood relatives in Somersetshire, and her fondness for that "delightful country" influenced Henry Sellwood to build at Hale in 1848 ("Recollections," p. 7).

3. In March 1864 Gladstone introduced The Government Annuities and Assurances Bill, which provided for the insurance of lives with the government and the purchase of government annuities with returns in the form of a future monthly allowance. The bill, which Gladstone and other proponents felt would introduce a new era of self-help and respectability to the poor, encountered stiff opposition, but Gladstone's hand was firm and in due time the bill became law. On 4 March 1865, the *Times* announced the issuance of tables of regulations regarding purchase of the insurance and annuities.

4. See above, Letter 34, n. 1.

5. Woolner wrote on 24 March (see *Thomas Woolner*, pp. 258–59) that he believed the Carlyles were heading directly for Scotland and would have no opportunity to come to the Isle of Wight.

154   To Edward Lear

Farringford, 12 May 1865

My dear Mr. Lear,
Ally hopes to be in town in the beginning of June and then he will thankfully receive the Canaletto and look through the gallery with delight I am sure. . . .[1]

We have been in a distressed condition about the boys. Three times we have begun preparation, expecting to go at once with them to Mr. Paul and three times whooping-cough there has prevented us from going. It is very unsettling and makes all things very difficult especially as we had let the tutor[2] accept a mastership at Winchester. The Pauls now talk of a week or ten days as the probable time of our going. The boys are sadly spoilt by their ugly dress.[3]

1. Lear had an exhibition in London in May 1865. Evidently he had secured for Tennyson a painting by Canaletto, the Venetian artist, who had spent several years in England and drawn many English landscapes.
2. Mr. Lipscombe.
3. Like all the students at Kegan Paul's, Hallam and Lionel Tennyson were required to wear tunic-like costumes with high, stiff collars.

155   *To Aubrey DeVere*

Memoir, *II, 22–23*
(A postscript accompanying Tennyson's letter)

Farringford, 15 May 1865

He[1] was one of the five of his friends I knew before our marriage, and the third (the other two Arthur Hallam and Henry Lushington) who has left us.[2] No new friends can be like the old to him or to any, I suppose, and few of the old were so dear to him as he. May I too say all that is kind and sympathizing? How does his father bear his loss? It seems a long time since we met.

1. Stephen Spring-Rice (1814–65), whose recent death Tennyson lamented in his letter to DeVere.
2. Charles Kingsley and Edmund Lushington were probably the other two friends.

156   To Richard Owen[1]
British Museum

Farringford, 16 July 1865

Dear Mr. Owen,
We are, I fear, obliged to leave home this week to see a very
sick aunt. We hope that you are thinking of next week as that
in which you intend to come to us. We have so often wished to
see you here, we hope really to have this great pleasure at last.[2]

1. (1804-92), the famed naturalist and anatomist who, in 1856, left
the Royal College of Surgeons to become superintendent of the natural
history department of the British Museum.
2. From 18 to 21 July the Tennysons were at Cheltenham with Mrs.
Elizabeth Russell, the poet's aunt. Emily Tennyson had a long intimate
talk with Mrs. Russell, and she noted in her Journal that Tennyson
refreshed the old lady's spirit with a tale "of primeval dragons and
particularly of that not far from Farringford which Professor Owen
was coming to see." Owen did visit the Tennysons before the end
of July, and Tennyson took him to Brightstone to see the fossilized
remains of the dragon he had told Mrs. Russell about. Owen fitted
the bones together to simulate the original dragon.

157   To Thomas Woolner

Farringford, 24 July 1865

My dear Mr. Woolner,
Many thanks for your kind letter and our best wishes for the
beautiful Fanny[1] and Mr. Hunt. I trust that the marriage will
not only make them happy but add, if possible, to your own
happiness and Mrs. Woolner's. Do you know we went round
by St. Mary's? We had to hurry back to see Professor Owen so
there was no possibility of trying to find Lady Ashburton.[2]
Will Mrs. Woolner some day say how sorry we were for this?
The place is indeed very finely situated but what do you think!
We have discovered that there is a mortgage of £2,000 on it, so
imprudent as to purchase. . . .
    Our boys are with us and well. Great is the joy of having
them as you well know. They are very brown and a good deal
altered considering the short time. But they keep their old
simplicity though somewhat of the old grace is gone, only for a
time, I hope.

1. Fanny Waugh, Mrs. Woolner's elder sister and the first wife of William Holman Hunt.
2. Louisa Lady Ashburton (d. 1903), second wife of William Bingham Baring (1799–1864), second baron, statesman; postmaster-general, 1845–46.

Soon after the boys' return from their first school term in late July, Tennyson took his family on a holiday tour to Belgium and Germany. Sailing on 9 August, they first visited Brussels, and then on the twelfth they reached Waterloo. There the poet interviewed an old English sergeant and, aided by maps and books, he carefully examined the battlefield, pointing out to Emily, Hallam, and Lionel the bush close to which Lord Raglan lost his arm, the spot where Sir William Ponsonby fell, the Lion Mound commemorating the wounding of the Prince of Orange, and the red wall at Hougoumont which the French mistook for British Redcoats. From Waterloo they journeyed to Luxembourg and Trèves, and early in September they visited Weimar and the shrines of Goethe and Schiller. On the ninth they reached Brunswick and went to the Church of St. Jean to see the crypt containing the coffins of the nine Brunswick dukes. Tennyson and Emily thought Brunswick particularly quaint and comfortable, but they pushed on to Hanover the next day, feeling that they had already been away from responsibilities at home too long. They swept through Aix-la-Chapelle on the eleventh, sailed for Ryde the following morning, and arrived at Farringford by mid-afternoon, where they were greeted by Heard, Mrs. Cameron, and an alarming accumulation of unanswered letters.

158   To Thomas Woolner

Farringford, 16 September 1865

My dear Mr. Woolner,
We are at present in a very knocked-up state. It is nearly ten and I am ordered to go to bed as soon as possible so I must not say much except that instead of Swiss mountains we have seen Waterloo, Trèves, Weimar, and Dresden, Magdeburg,

Brunswick, and Hanover, and Aix-la-Chapelle. I hope he has
stored some recollections that will be pleasant when the (to
him usual) unpleasant accompaniments of continental travel
have worn away.

159   *To Thomas Woolner*

Farringford, 5 October 1865

My dear Mr. Woolner,
I wish some good soul would make you so rich that you need
not live in roaring smoky London.[1] We have not yet had much
chance of rest having had so large a party in the house.[2] Nine
is a not inconsiderable addition to one's family to say nothing
of occasional guests. My cough besides will not let me rest.

We will take the greatest care of Mrs. Woolner if you will
trust her to us. I wish you could come too for I fear, no, I
ought not to *fear,* but I know Mrs. Woolner will find the island
a kind of prison without you.

The other day we had yet another story told us . . . like
"Enoch Arden."[3] It makes one fear the women do not wait so
long as they should. I like better that old German story, where
the faithful baroness is dispensing of her goods to the poor and
one bold beggar embracing her is about to be knocked down
by an attendant, when the beggar says, "My friend there is no
need of that, behold your Master!"

1. On 3 October 1865, Woolner wrote to Emily Tennyson (see *Thomas Woolner,* pp. 265-66): "I have just returned to Babylon and its horrid roaring, having been touring in the Highlands and other places for 17 days."

2. Queen Emma of the Sandwich Islands and her attendants were guests of the Tennysons from 28 September to 2 October. The Queen and her late husband, King Kamehameha IV, had planned a trip to England before his death in 1863, and the young dowager subsequently made the intended visit, hoping that travel might serve to dull her grief.

3. In his letter of 3 October Woolner related a story with a plot similar to that of "Enoch Arden."

160   *To Hallam and Lionel Tennyson*

Farringford, 4 November 1865

My darlings,
I hope you have been enjoying these beautiful days.[1] Yesterday
I went in the donkey chaise with Papa, Heard accompanying
and Aunt Tilly going a little way with us, to see the Middleton
farm house[2] now tenanted by Hiscock. . . . The Hiscocks
looked all radiant for Hiscock had the day before gained the
first ploughing prize in the class, three pounds. Little George
showed me his new shoes, and Mrs. Hiscock told me with
delight that out of the three pounds she had bought Hiscock
and all the children winter shoes. . . . I think I told you we
were expecting Mr. Barnes, the Dorsetshire poet,[3] to dine and
sleep on Wednesday. We thought Mr. Barnes very good and
simple and interesting.

    1. Hallam and Lionel Tennyson left for their second term with Mr.
Paul on 21 September. They returned to Farringford on the twenty-eighth
to meet Queen Emma and left again for Dorsetshire on 3 October.
    2. The Middleton house was about a third of a mile from Farringford.
    3. William Barnes (1800–86), the pastoral poet, known for his idylls
in the Dorset dialect and for his rather fanatical attempts to Saxonize
English. Barnes's three volumes of verse were published in 1879 under
the title *Poems of Rural Life in the Dorset Dialect.*

161   *To Thomas Woolner*

Farringford, 8 November 1865

My dear Mr. Woolner,
I do not doubt that Mr. Patmore will make a good use of his
riches. He was very generous as a poor man and I do not think
he will be less so as a rich.[1] Stepmothers must in modern story
be made always good instead of bad, as they used to be. I think
one hears of so many good ones. For instance, Lady Simeon.[2]
Sir John has just left us having paid a bachelor visit while his
wife is away with her little boy for change of air. He is looking
better than I have seen him for years.
    I am so glad you have a bit of imaginative work to do,
though not one you would perhaps have chosen, yet it must be

a relief from the busts of dead men or living either. You are rather vicious about the "National Ode,"[3] but I shall hand you over to Mrs. Woolner for punishment. Tell her for once she must forego her nature.

1. On 18 July 1864, Coventry Patmore married Marianne Byles, daughter of a large Gloucestershire landowner. William Allingham wrote in his diary entry for 19 November 1865 that he and Tennyson had that day walked on the High Down with Woolner, who told them of Patmore's wealth by his second marriage, his new estate in Sussex, and his magnificent wines (Allingham and Radford, *William Allingham's Diary*, p. 128).

2. Catherine Dorothea Colville, who married Sir John Simeon on 2 October 1851 and became stepmother to his four surviving children by his first wife.

3. "National Song," first published in 1830 and ultimately adapted for Act II of *The Foresters,* which Tennyson completed in 1881 and published in 1892.

162   To Alfred Tennyson

Farringford [December 1865][1]

. . . Henry Taylor thinks that Colonel Eyre has been quite right.[2] He has worked at the Jamaica affair from four in the morning till late in the evening and has been up through storms and mist every day to office. Sometimes falling asleep on the rug quite worn out when he came home.

Lionel says he is very happy at Mr. Paul's now. He tells me that after all his day work he goes out on certain evenings to a night school. One likes to hear this, does one not?

1. The first part of the letter with the salutation and date is missing. Tennyson went to London in the company of Woolner on 1 December, visited with the Woolners and the Palgraves, was formally introduced to the Royal Society, and returned to Farringford on the nineteenth.

2. The conduct of Colonel Edward Eyre (1815-1901), governor of Jamaica, 1862-66, in suppressing the native rebellion of October 1865 was both violently attacked and vigorously defended by the English press and public. During the period of martial law he declared while crushing the rebellion, some six hundred persons were killed or executed. Like Henry Taylor of the colonial office, always a strong voice for strict order in the colonies, the Tennysons supported Eyre. The poet sent a subscription to the fund for Eyre's defense against the prosecution for murder pressed for by the Jamaica Committee headed by John Stuart

Mill. And when Gladstone attacked Eyre's actions at Woolner's dinner in December 1865 (see *AT*, p. 359), Tennyson let it be known that he thought Eyre entirely justified in the severe steps he had taken.

163   To Thomas Woolner

Farringford, 19 December 1865

My dear Mr. Woolner,
Now you must let me write myself to say that Alfred has arrived safely this morning by the 12:30 boat, having slept at Lymington and dined and breakfasted with Mr. Allingham, and tell you how grateful I feel to Mrs. Woolner and yourself for all the enjoyment you have given him. His letters have always had such a happy tone that I am sure that none of the trouble you have taken to amuse him has been thrown away. Unfortunately we have five people to dinner today so we miss the first day of him to ourselves and on the second day it does not seem half so easy to tell all that has befallen.

The boys are already looking much better. We have got a second and bigger pony for them. Before they drove with me to meet Ally they rode together to Alum Bay and home by Totland, changing ponies at Alum Bay.

164   To Robert Browning
Yale

Farringford, 20 December 1865

My dear Mr. Browning,
He came home yesterday and brought me your kind gift doubly dear to me as your gift and a memorial of one who in a few short hours could plant herself in the heart for life.[1] Accept my affectionate thanks I pray you.

It rejoices me that he has seen you and I hope you know what a large portion of his pleasure in a visit to town consists in seeing you. May the good day some day come when we shall have the privilege of welcoming you here.

1. Emily Tennyson was devoted to Mrs. Browning from the time of their initial meeting in Paris in July 1851. Mrs. Browning died on 29 June 1861.

Hallam Tennyson left Farringford for his first session at Marlborough on 20 January, and within a fortnight his father took Lionel and Emily to London for a lengthy visit. The Tennysons took the opportunity of seeing many old friends, including the Carlyles, the Gladstones, the Argylls, the William Brookfields, the F. D. Maurices, Edmund and Franklin Lushington, Woolner, Palgrave, Spedding, Froude, and Browning. Emily and Lionel were particularly pleased with their visit with Browning on 13 February, and Browning found Emily "just what she was and always will be, very sweet and dear" (*AT,* p. 363).

Emily was unwell much of the spring of 1866. Tennyson took her to a London doctor in May, and she returned by herself the first week of June. On her return home she found, as always, more letters than she could well manage, and soon she had a houseful of visitors as well. Woolner, William Allingham, Henry Taylor, and Archibald Peel were all guests at Farringford in early June, and on the nineteenth Emily wrote to Lear that she could at present receive no more.

165   *To Anne Weld and Henry Sellwood*

2 Upper Gore Lodge,[1] *22 February 1866*

My dearest Daddy and Nanny,
I hope people will leave me a little time in which to tell you how exceedingly we enjoyed our great dinner with Mr. and Mrs. Gladstone and Lady Gertrude last night.[2] He talked to me nearly all dinner time most eloquently. I am delighted to have seen him for fine as his speeches are when one reads them they give one but a faint idea of the power and intensity of the man. He is quite affectionate in his manner to us. Mrs. Gladstone said to me, "Doesn't he look happy?" when he was talking with Ally. Lady Gertrude said she had never enjoyed anything so much in her life.

1. Kensington residence of Emily Tennyson's Aunt Franklin, the widow of Sir John Franklin, the Arctic explorer. In 1866 the Tennysons were at Gore Lodge from 3 February until 23 March.

2. Emily Tennyson preserved in her Journal a record of dinner on 21 February with Mr. and Mrs. Gladstone and Lady Gertrude Talbot, the wife of Gladstone's friend, Edward Talbot, bishop of Rochester, 1895–1905. Emily thought Gladstone's talk that night "full of interest" and Gladstone himself illumined by "a glow and intensity in his whole being."

166   To Edward Lear

Farringford, 19 June 1866

My dear Mr. Lear,

I have been waiting to write until I could say that we had a room to offer you but I do not like to wait any longer, so now I write, though we have not one, to tell you that we shall probably leave home on the 3rd of July as Hallam returns on the 27th of this month.[1] He is as happy as one can desire, I hope, at Marlborough. The Bradleys are most kind and the other masters are also very good to him. . . .[2]

It was very good in you writing. I have had such an ill winter and spring of it that I have not been able to write at all so you must not think hard things of me because I have not answered.

1. Although the Tennysons took no prolonged tour in the summer of 1866, they did go to Lyndhurst and the New Forest for several weeks in July.

2. Granville and Marian Bradley were always devoted to Hallam Tennyson. In January 1868, Emily Tennyson set down Bradley's avowal "that if he searched the whole world over he could not have found a more satisfactory boy or one who promises to be a more satisfactory man" (Journal, 23 January 1868).

167   To Margaret Gatty
Boston Public Library

Farringford, 26 July 1866

My dear Mrs. Gatty,
I have often been wishing to know how you are and often have
meant to write but you know how it is with me. The letters that
must be written today jostle aside the letters that may be
written on another day and so many other days come before
they are written. But how are you? Strong again I do hope.

My sister is in her house and is delighted with it though in
the midst of the horrors of painting a house that has not been
painted these fifteen years nor repaired either apparently since
there is two months' work on it; not all absolutely necessary
work, for part goes to beautifying, putting in oriel windows,
etc. Nevertheless, as I say, she is delighted and so is Agnes.
Mr. Weld loves gay cities better. Eternal winters in the eternal
city would be more to his taste, I suppose, for he seems to have
been gayest of the gay this last winter when there.[1] My sister
admires the church very much too and finds the climate very
delightful and the people very pleasant as far as she has had to
do with them. At present, of course, she can see but little
except tradesmen and the neighbouring farmer and his wife
who give her the best of milk and butter.

We are now waiting to receive Dr. Stanley[2] and then alas! we
are off ourselves, whither I scarcely know, but probably to
Brittany and I hope certainly to Grasby. Ally needs change
though he is better this year than last. How is Stephen? The
boys are sometimes admitted to help the Freshwater cricket
club, so they are getting on in the world.

1. Charles Weld had spent the previous winter in Rome.
2. Arthur Stanley, Dean of Westminster.

168   To Lionel Tennyson

Park House,[1] 27 August 1866

My own darling,
I am very glad to hear that the boil is better. There is one
passage in your letter that makes me uneasy. Speaking of the

half-glass of beer not being enough for anyone in this hot weather, you say you "buy some." Does this mean beer or what do you buy? I scarcely know what to recommend but I should think seltzer or soda water would be best. Certainly not beer as half a glass is as much as is good for you. . . .

I can scarcely believe that it is only a week, it seems so very long. How sad life would be if one might not look to spending an eternity with those dearest to us and meanwhile what a help it is to one to bear absence that one may from the distance encourage each other in the work that God has given us to do. God bless thee, mine own. Our best love. Try and write as distinctly as you can that Papa may not have difficulty in reading the letters. He is very much interested in reading them, and it is a pity to spoil his pleasure.

1. On 20 August 1866, the Tennysons took Lionel to Hastings to place him under the tutelage of a Dr. Hunt, and they subsequently stopped at Park House for about ten days. Lionel at that time spoke somewhat haltingly, and Dr. Hunt was known for his success in helping children with speech difficulties.

169   To Lionel Tennyson

Park House, 4 September 1866

My darling,

I hope that you will study your subjects well and make your speeches with as much in them as possible. If you remember, we all agreed what a useful thing, rather I should say what a necessary thing, it is for men to be able to form clear ideas on different subjects and arrange them in due order and express them in the best possible language. . . .

It is a great comfort to hear that you are well and that you sleep well. Do you go on with meat three times a day?[1] . . . This rainy weather makes it very difficult to know what to do. Nothing but home seems tempting and Freshwater is so full, Heard says, that I am sure Papa would want to leave it again as soon as we got there. . . .

You do not seem to have any lessons at all. Be sure to keep up Greek and Latin and French as much as you can. God bless thee darling. Our best love. Papa says to you, "Pray write with ink." Aunt Tilly has bought you a very pretty mother-of-pearl paper cutter and for Hallam a goose's head to hold papers together. I think I had better keep the paper knife for you as you have one already and this might get broken by post.

1. Lionel had complained to his mother that he could not eat as much meat as he was served at school.

170   To Lionel Tennyson

The Red Lion, Petersfield, 16 September 1866

My own darling,
Here we are thinking of thee. The rain pours but Papa has been out all morning notwithstanding. Twelve-and-a-half today thou art, beloved one, getting on fast in years which makes one all the more anxious to hear how the stammering is. Lady de Gray's son was cured in a month, so I hope a month has done a good deal for you.

We could not well stay at Haslemere, partly because the best rooms were taken. We had a glorious drive yesterday and at last Papa has actually been on the Devil's Jumps. . . .[1]

It makes me very anxious to hear of cholera so near, but I feel sure Dr. Hunt will send you home without a moment's delay if he judge it prudent. I know that it is only God who can keep us, still there's something for us to do. Be sure you do not take uncooked fruit or anything unwholesome. . . . Have you seen that the very synagogue in Capernaum where our Saviour preached is said to have been discovered? How much one would like to see it. . . . God bless thee, own darling. Our best love. No chloroform remember on any account whatever, supposing you have the tooth drawn. I entirely forbid it.[2]

1. The Tennysons were still searching for land suitable for a permanent summer retreat. They had been told of a tract near the Devil's Jumps, five miles northwest of Haslemere, but when they went there, they found the location unsatisfactory.
2. Emily Tennyson's fear of chloroform may perhaps be traced to an incident she records in "For Her Sons." In July 1850, while she and Tennyson were in Clifton on their wedding trip, the poet injured one of his nails and had a minor operation to repair it. Before surgery the doctor gave Tennyson chloroform, with grievous results. "I was turned out of the room," Emily remembered, "and heard him shout

as if hallooing the hounds. His poor mouth was blistered, for the chloroform was not of the best, but no other evil came of it" (p. 103).

171   To Lionel Tennyson

Farringford, 15 October 1866

Own darling,

Thou wouldst spare thy mother many tears and perpetual anxiety couldst thou but send her two or three words every day in an envelope until those words were, "Thank God quite strong and well," and then thou must promise to let me know at once if thou art at all ill after this.[1] You cannot tell, my boy, how much anxiety both Papa and I suffer on your account. Neither would we have you know it, for such things come chiefly by experience but still imagination can do much and we must try to imagine the feelings of others that we may minister to them as need requires, must we not, my own?

My things are ready for packing that I may come to you if you want me. Unless we are wanted from illness we shall not leave home at present and Mr. Grove and Mr. Sullivan[2] (a great musician) have fixed to come to us on Wednesday.

Papa took me out into the fields yesterday in my little carriage and to see the great barley stack. It was a clear, beautiful day and it did me good. Mrs. Cameron called afterward. I hope to send you some more grapes. Perhaps it would scarcely be wise to send the cakes yet. God bless thee beloved. Our best love.

1. Lionel had been troubled by a severe cold as well as a toothache. On 13 October Emily Tennyson wrote about his condition in the Journal, "Continued news that Lionel is very weak. Day and night the thought possesses one."

2. George Grove (1820-1900; knighted 1883), editor of *Macmillan's Magazine,* and author of the four-volume *Dictionary of Music and Musicians,* 1878-89; and Arthur Seymour Sullivan (1842-1900; knighted 1883), the composer, a partner in Gilbert and Sullivan from 1875 onwards. Grove and Sullivan came to Farringford on 16 October 1866 to attempt to induce Tennyson to write a song-cycle which young Sullivan would set to music. Tennyson consented and within a few days he completed a draft for "The Window," sometimes called "The Song of the Wrens." Alexander Strahan published the song with Sullivan's music in December 1870.

172   To Lionel Tennyson

Farringford, 16 October 1866

My own Darling,

. . . The Mr. Sheridan Knowles[1] who made the ~~short~~ [*sic*] King Arthur Legends short (where should the short be? I don't like to cut the King short of his lordly proportions!), well anyhow, Mr. Knowles has this moment been here. We have lent him Layamon's *Brut* to see if he could popularize the legends there before King Arthur. He thinks he may and perhaps that Macmillan will publish them in his magazine. I trust that your friend has returned. You never answered my question as to whether you are allowed to go out and whether you would like a daughter of DeQuincey's and a friend of Uncle Edmund's to call and take you out.[2] Our best love.

1. James Sheridan Knowles died in 1862. Emily Tennyson meant James Thomas Knowles (1831-1908), architect, founder of the Metaphysical Society, editor of the *Contemporary Review*, 1870-77, founder of the *Nineteenth Century* and its editor from 1877 until his death. In 1862 Knowles published a little volume entitled "The Story of King Arthur and His Knights of the Round Table," dedicated to Tennyson, and after the poet's death he wrote the memorial poem "Apotheosis: Westminster, October 1892." Knowles's friendship with the Tennysons was confirmed in June 1867 when he agreed to design the summer residence which was to become Aldworth. He persuaded Tennyson to agree to a less modest dwelling than the four-room cottage the poet originally had in mind, and the design "grew and grew as it was talked over and considered, the details being all discussed with Mrs. Tennyson, while [Tennyson] contented himself by pretending to protest against any addition and improvement" (H. Tennyson, *Tennyson and His Friends*, pp. 246-48). Gordon Ray observes that Knowles brought "a current of fresh air" into Tennyson's life. From the late 1860s until his death Tennyson periodically went to London with Knowles. Occasionally he accompanied Knowles to meetings of the Metaphysical Society (see Letter 238, n. 2), of which Knowles was founder and Tennyson a charter member. Tennyson was apparently devoted to his cheerful, energetic young friend. "You certainly are a jolly good fellow," Tennyson once told Knowles. "You do encourage me so much." And later he added, "I'm very glad to have known you. It has been a sort of lift in my life." See Gordon N. Ray, *Tennyson Reads "Maud"* (University of British Columbia, Vancouver, 1968), p. 16.

2. Probably Emily, DeQuincey's youngest daughter, who never married. Edmund Lushington's friend is unidentified.

173   To Anne Weld and Louisa Turner[1]

Farringford, 2 February 1867

My dearest Sisters,
Will you tell Daddy with our best love that there is a command
from the Queen today that Ally and I should go to Osborne.[2] I
hope I may be able to get off as I have been shut up for so
many weeks. She gives us our choice of days from the 7th to
the 20th of February, but I have not yet been out. I have been
meaning to go the first opportunity as my cough is much better
though in other respects I am not at all well just now.

1. Mrs. Charles Turner was visiting the Welds helping to care for
her father, Henry Sellwood, who in late January 1867 had suffered
a stroke which left him partially paralyzed.
2. On 28 January 1867, Tennyson sent to Osborne a copy of his
"Elaine," with illustrations by Gustave Doré, which Alexander Strahan
had recently published. Tennyson did not much like either the illustrations or the form of the book, but "Elaine" was a favorite of the Queen's,
and she at once "commanded" that her Laureate and his wife come
to Osborne. Emily Tennyson was not up to the trip, and so on 14
February Tennyson visited the Queen alone.

174   To Anne Weld, Louisa Turner, and Henry Sellwood

Farringford, 8 February 1867

My dearest Daddy and Sisters,
I thank you both for your deeply interesting letters. I earnestly
desire to see our dearest Daddy when he is equal to seeing me
without any chance of overfatiguing him and when I shall not
be troublesome to you. Our boys are gone today.[1] A very dreary
day in all senses of the word. . . .
    Generally the boys and I go into the study and read after
dinner when we are alone but last night Ally wished the boys
to stay with him so we stayed and they sang to him all the
evening. They sing some things very sweetly together. Ally was
very much charmed with some of the singing. Hallam has still
a sweet boy's voice as well as a deep man's voice for singing.
Ally made a bowl of weak punch and gave them a little. Is it

not strange to think that if Hallam go on well he may have
reached the top of the school and leave it honourably in two
and a half or three years? If it should be so and all prosper
with us we must give him the advantage of learning modern
languages abroad before going to college.[2]

1. Hallam and Lionel Tennyson were at home from mid-December
until February, when Hallam returned to Marlborough, and Lionel,
no longer under Dr. Hunt's therapeutic care, returned to Kegan Paul.
2. In August 1872, Hallam Tennyson went to France with his parents
and remained there for some weeks to study French. The next August
he accompanied his father on a tour to the Engadine and the Italian
lakes.

175   To Lionel Tennyson

Farringford, 11 February 1867

My darling,
I got up early this morning to see Mr. Sullivan off.[1] He played
three exquisite little bits of Sebastian Bach's. I wish you could
have heard them. Is it not delightful that Hallam is promoted?
Dear old fellow, it will make him very happy. As I tell him[2]
the house seemed very still and sad without you, my darlings.
. . . Louy Simeon[3] who came on Saturday and is going today
has been talking so long with me that I can only say God bless
thee, darling. Our best love.

1. Arthur Sullivan arrived at Farringford on 8 February. During his
three-day visit he talked with Tennyson about their song cycle, "The
Window," played a good deal of Bach on Emily Tennyson's piano,
and sang for her his own songs, "Sweet Day," and "O Mistress Mine."
2. Emily Tennyson must have written regularly to her older son at
Marlborough, although no 1866 or 1867 letters to Hallam have been
found.
3. The Tennysons treated Sir John Simeon's daughter Louisa like
their own child, and she often stayed at Farringford when her father
was away in London or elsewhere. Shortly before her death Louy (then
Mrs. Richard Ward) recalled her feelings as a young girl for Farringford
and for Emily Tennyson: "I was sometimes allowed to drive over to
Farringford with my father, and, need I say, I looked forward to these
as the red-letter days of my life. Not only were the talk and intellectual
atmosphere intoxicating to me, but I became passionately attached to
Lady Tennyson. Praise of her would be unseemly; but I may quote

what my father was fond of saying of her, that she was 'a piece of the finest china, the mould of which had been broken as soon as she was made.'" She was, Mrs. Ward concluded, "so helpful, so tender, full of the wisdom of one who had learnt to look upon life and all it embraces from one standpoint only, and that the very highest!" (H. Tennyson, *Tennyson and His Friends*, pp. 309–10).

176[1]   To Lionel Tennyson

Farringford, 16 February 1867

My darling,

I should have written yesterday to have thanked you for your welcome letter but I thought that you would rather that I should wait until today to tell you about Papa's visit to Osborne. It was a cold, east-windy day and rained so as to make William and Butler[2] wet on their return, but I hope that no one is the worse for it. The Queen was looking well and seemed merry. She asked about you both and desired Papa to express to me Her regret that I could not come.

Papa made her laugh when talking about the Cockneys and our going to the farmhouse.[3] She said, "But we are not much troubled here by them," and Papa replied, "Perhaps I should not be either, Your Majesty, if I could stick a sentry at my gates."

She inquired what was doing in poetry. Papa spoke of Browning and Swinburne and added, "But verse-writing is the commonest accomplishment in the world now, everyone writes them. I dare say Your Majesty does." Upon which She said, "No, that I do not. For the life of me I never could make two lines meet."

She told Papa that she liked Queen Emma very much and remarked that she was so lady-like. Papa burst forth into indignation at this rich British people not having done more for her than they had done. £4,000 instead of the £40,000 she wants.[4]

The poor Queen said that she has no time for books. She asked Papa why he did not do some great work. And he said that it was *such* an age and they talked about the age a little and he said that he feared universal suffrage and vote by ballot would be our ruin. She told Papa that she wanted to thank him for the handsome book and they talked about this and Doré[5] and Frenchmen and hexameters, English, German, and classic, for Mrs. Gordon[6] was there, Caroline Herschel . . . was and her father's hexameter translation of the *Iliad*[7] was naturally named. Papa was glad to see Mrs. Gordon again. She was in the room all the time and Papa asked her to come here and she said that she would. The Queen told Papa that she had heard that Marlborough was the best school. . . .

I hope you will have a better sermon tomorrow. Certainly nothing can be more unprofitable than invective against those who differ from us. The safest way for us all is to abide in the religion of our forefathers unless we see some overpowering reason for leaving it, and with respect to others if we are moved in spirit to testify that they are wrong or to us that they seem wrong (for there is a right and a wrong though the boundary may sometimes be difficult to find), we should try to prove it meekly from God's own book, should we not? God bless thee, darling. I know that you will keep what I have said about the Queen to yourself.

1. For Emily Tennyson's very similar, though slightly briefer, letter to her father and her sister, Anne Weld, which I do not include, see Dyson and Tennyson, *Dear and Honoured Lady,* pp. 84–85.

2. William Knight, the coachman, who first came to Farringford as a stableboy in 1853 and remained with the Tennyson family until his death in the 1920s. Sir Charles Tennyson observes that the vivacious snub-nosed coachman was "as great an original as his master." He was "a wizard with horses," and with the Tennyson children as well, and, despite his lack of formal education, a homespun philosopher and occasional poet (Charles Tennyson, *Stars and Markets* [London: Chatto and Windus, 1957], pp. 30–36). Butler, who evidently accompanied Knight when he drove Tennyson to Osborne, was another of the Tennyson's domestic employees.

3. The Tennysons intended to go to Grayshott Farm, Haslemere, which they had hired in November 1866, in early March, but Hallam fell seriously ill at Marlborough and they consequently deferred their plans until mid-April.

4. While she was in England, Queen Emma enlisted support for the recently established Episcopal Mission in the Sandwich Islands.

5. Gustave Doré (1833–83), the French painter and illustrator. Doré illustrated works by Dante, Rabelais, Balzac, and La Fontaine, as well as Tennyson's *Idylls.*

6. Caroline Gordon; otherwise unidentified.

7. Sir John Frederick William Herschel (1792–1871), the astronomer, in 1866 published a translation entitled *The Iliad in English Accentuated Hexameters.*

177   *To Lionel Tennyson*

The Lodge, Marlborough [March 1867]

Own darling,
Dr. Symonds thinks very favourably of our Hallam.[1] He was so
very, very good. He came all that long way last evening . . .
and he had to go by seven this morning. . . . No words can
express the goodness of the Bradleys to us and we are all
bound forever to them. Without my having said a word to him
about it he exclaimed against the excessive exercise common in
this day and the beer and stimulating things which are thought
to be made necessary by this. He said boys do not want it and
besides he said exactly as I have so often said to thee, beloved,
that this overexercise exhausts the brain. So be warned in time,
darling, for these are the words of one who is esteemed the
wisest doctor of the West, who is called to Devonshire one day,
to Wiltshire another, into Wales another. He asked a good deal
about you, told us that Mr. Dakyns is still at Clifton.

Dr. Symonds would not take a farthing by way of fee though
his fee is twenty pounds or something of the kind. He said he
thought coming not merely a pleasure but a privilege.

1. On 1 March 1867, the Tennysons received word from Marlborough
that Hallam was seriously ill with congestion of the lungs. Immediately
they telegraphed to Bristol for Dr. John Addington Symonds (1807–71),
Benjamin Jowett's "Beloved Physician," father of John A. Symonds,
the writer and historian. Although Hallam's illness was critical, it was
brief, and on 26 March he went home to Farringford.

178   *To William Allingham*

The Lodge, Marlborough [14 March 1867]

My dear Mr. Allingham,
I would not let Mr. Bradley write, he has so much to do. I have
returned late from our boy and can say no more than thank you
for your inquiries. We have the unspeakable comfort of seeing
him gain strength from day to day. We left home a fortnight
ago on Friday summoned by telegraph and found him
perilously ill with pneumonia and low-feverish symptoms. You
know what we must have gone through. . . . The tenderness

and devotion of all here is not to be told. He could not have been better nursed and cared for.

179   To Lionel Tennyson

The Lodge, Marlborough, 14 March 1867

Many, many happy returns of the day[1] to thee, my own darling. God ever be with thee and bring thee nearer and nearer to Himself and then we are sure that thy life will be full of blessing to thyself and to others. It will be a happy sight for thee—our Hallam's handwriting—and not at all shaky, you see. He lies on his sofa in a pair of loose, eastern-like, purple and gold-coloured trousers, and a jacket of dove-coloured cloth, and his new flannel pouncha bound with red over this, and his nurse is evidently proud of him for she said, "Doesn't he look nice?" and, "I should so like Mrs. Bradley to see him." Mrs. Cameron has sent him these and two little Japanese trays and a hot-water plate and a tea pot for his food, with her usual generous kindness.

The doctor still hopes that we shall get our Hallam home next week. At present he cannot stand but Mrs. Bradley says she never knew of any boy's recovering so rapidly and she thinks it a sign that he has a very good constitution. We have everything to be thankful for have we not, my darling?

1. Lionel's birthday, 16 March.

180   To Lionel Tennyson

Farringford, 29 March 1867

Own darling,
Our Hallam slept well after his drive yesterday[1] and his reading of the first two scenes of "As You Like It" with me, each taking a part. Picture us with a big Shakespeare on a little table near the fire in your room, for there we two sat side by side reading after dinner. Is it not a great advance that he can read aloud as much as this without hurting himself?

Today we have been driving part of the way up the Needles Down. Yesterday the two houses of Cottons, Sir Andrew Hamond[2] and Lady Hamond, Mrs. Cameron, Mr. Atkinson[3] all came to inquire after our Hallam. All but Mr. Atkinson and the Benjamin Cottons saw him. Everyone is exceedingly kind.

Papa's cold we think a little better today. I feel better too. God bless thee, darling. Our best love.

1. According to the Journal entry for 28 March 1867, Emily Tennyson that day took Hallam for a drive on the Needles Down and home by Colwell Bay, about three miles northeast of the Needles.
2. See above, Letter 142, n. 6.
3. Freshwater's Anglican vicar.

181   To Lionel Tennyson

Farringford, 30 March 1867

My darling,
We have been driving to the New Hotel today. Wicked Hallam would insist upon driving up to the hotel and enjoyed seeing the butlers look out of the stables and the landlord, apparently, send away to the house and the waiter dart out to open the carriage door. . . . He is very merry. Today he was amusing himself by calling out, "Coachman," in a small voice supposed to be mine and by inventing all sorts of imaginary remonstrances about "not shaking the poor invalid" and "bumping my poor boy," also supposed to be mine. All the while laughing until he almost tumbled off the seat.

182   To Lionel Tennyson

Farringford, 6 April 1867

Own darling,
You will be thankful to hear that our Hallam has ridden both yesterday and today on Fanny,[1] more than an hour each time, I think. Besides he has this afternoon been out with Papa and me. Papa drawing me in my little carriage, Hallam being of

course forbidden either to draw or to push. We went by Maiden's Croft[2] and [illegible] and instead of returning straight by Abraham's Mead and the farm we made a little diversion into the hilly field which joins Middleton to see the pretty bank that is now where a hedge used to be. He says that he is not at all tired and Hardinge[3] is with him now. I am always rather hopeless about photographs of any of us. I don't think that we photograph well.

When I was out of the room this morning Hallam received a box looking like a pill box. . . . When I came in I found him contemplating the contents and what do you think they were? Grandpapa's two beautiful seals and the ring with Grandmamma's[4] pretty golden hair in it, his gifts to Hallam. Grandpapa wished me to take the seals long ago at Grasby but I did not like to rob him of them. Now he gives them to Hallam as the eldest son. Is it not good in him?

1. The Tennyson children's pony which sometimes pulled their mother in her wheeled garden chair; remembered by Edith Ellison, the Granville Bradleys' daughter, as "one of the fattest of white ponies." In *A Child's Recollections of Tennyson,* Mrs. Ellison described an occasion in her girlhood when Fanny was for her the cause of severe mortification: "For some reason that I do not recall she was sent over for me to ride one day, and I had hardly proceeded a quarter of a mile before the saddle quietly described a half-circle and I was deposited in one of the ditches that always ran on either side of a Freshwater lane. I was furious. Never had such a thing happened to me before. To think that I should be thrown—and by fat Fanny too!" (pp. 65–66).

2. A meadow adjacent to the Farringford lawn, Maiden's Croft was named by the monks of the Abbey of Lyra, Normandy, who owned the land before Walter de Ferringford acquired it in the fourteenth century. Arthur Paterson pictured it as "a very quiet and sheltered spot far from habitable places, facing the lonely Town, and sheltered by the trees to north and east, . . . a favorite haunt of Tennyson's" (Allingham and Paterson, *Homes and Haunts,* pp. 9–10). Tennyson built the summer house in which he did much of his writing very near Maiden's Croft.

3. Hardinge Cameron, son of Charles and Julia Margaret Cameron and namesake of first Viscount Henry Hardinge (1785–1856), who served as governor general of India from 1844 until 1848.

4. Sarah Sellwood, Emily Tennyson's mother.

183   To Lionel Tennyson

Farringford, 7 April 1867

My darling,

It seems that we were all wrong about the seals and ring yesterday in thinking that because they were addressed to Hallam that they were all meant for him. One seal was meant for you and the ring for me and our old darling is very glad that it is so. . . . God bless thee, darling. Our best love.

I am afraid that we are being bullied into a war with Spain. Hallam and I greatly approved of Lord Stanley's curt and decisive letter.[1]

1. In a letter to the Spanish Government, reproduced in *The Times* on 5 April 1867, Edward Henry Stanley (1826-93), afterwards fifteenth Earl of Derby, the Secretary of State for Foreign Affairs, demanded the immediate restoration of the British coasting vessel *Queen Victoria,* seized in 1866, as well as "proper pecuniary indemnity to her captain and crew; accompanied by an expression of regret addressed to Her Majesty's Government for the outrage committed on the British flag," lest the matter "assume the proportion of a serious difference between Great Britain and Spain."

184   To Henry Sellwood and Anne Weld

Farringford, 15 April 1867

My dearest Daddy and Nanny,

Mr. Cotton[1] has rather a Greek face, that extremely low growth of hair over his forehead, rather a handsome face with hair that is reddish, the eyes of an enemy more than of a friend, his face freckled, middle height. Very considerable ability, but a Comtiste, believing nothing that cannot be proved from experience. It was his worship of Nature that made him [decide to] marry Mary Ryan. He saw that photograph of her as Cordelia kneeling before Mr. Henry Taylor[2] as King Lear at Mrs. Cameron's photographic gallery and thereupon determined to make her his wife.

Did I by the by ever tell you that Mr. Lear was imprisoned as a spy in Austrian Italy during the war there and on producing his passport was released with immense civility and congratulation on bearing the name of the British King Lear. Best love to you all.

1. Henry Cotton, only son of Sir Arthur Thomas Cotton, the distinguished engineer with the Indian civil service, who married Mrs. Cameron's pauper maid and model, Mary Ryan, on 1 August 1867. In mid-summer Emily Tennyson wrote of plans for the wedding, which took place in the little village church at Freshwater: "Mr. Cameron says he will give [Mary] away, but he quakes so at the idea as the day comes near that it is doubtful whether he will find courage when it actually arrives" (quoted by Brian Hill, *Julia Margaret Cameron: A Victorian Family Portrait* [London: Peter Owen, 1973], p. 117). In his account of the romance in *Julia Margaret Cameron* (London: Fountain Press, 1948), Helmut Gernsheim mistakenly identified Cotton's bride as Kate Shepherd, another of Mrs. Cameron's parlor maids. The mistake is corrected, however, in the new edition of Gernsheim's book (London: Da Capo Press, 1971).
2. Henry Taylor frequently posed for Mrs. Cameron's pictures.

185   To Henry Sellwood and Anne Weld

Farringford, 25 April 1867

My dearest Daddy and Nanny,
Mrs. Cameron and Charlie[1] were here last night. Mrs. Cameron has made some magnificent photographs, clear and smooth as well as picturesque. Ally says no Titian is so fine as that of Blumenthal.[2] He is a little man and, as usual with her little men, comes out a grand one. She wants Ally to go today for a trial. He has been but I don't know the result.

1. Charles Cameron, another son of Charles and Julia Margaret Cameron.
2. Jacob Blumenthal (1829–1908), the German pianist and composer who took up residence in London in 1848 and subsequently became pianist to Queen Victoria and a very fashionable teacher. Blumenthal came to Farringford on 15 April 1867, sang for the Tennysons his song "The Days That Are No More," and was photographed by Mrs. Cameron. The photograph of Blumenthal is presently in the Gernsheim collection in London.

On 29 April, after Hallam had recuperated at home for a month, the Tennysons left for Grayshott Farm. Two months of relaxation there were disturbed only by excursions to Blackdown, the highest hill of the Sussex North Downs, to view Black Horse Copse, the site Tennyson and Emily had decided upon for their long-envisioned summer house. The Drummond Rawnsleys, Sir John and Louy Simeon, Jowett, and Lear came to Grayshott, but no one remained more than a day or two, and the Tennysons returned to Farringford on 29 June refreshed and invigorated by the prospect of a permanent summer retreat. Two weeks later James Knowles followed them to present preliminary sketches for the Blackdown house.

By late August Tennyson was again eager for travel. He left home on the twenty-third and traveled to Lyme Regis where Francis Palgrave and his family were vacationing. The poet persuaded Palgrave to extend his holiday, and the two set off on a walking tour which took them along the Devon coast to Exeter, Dartmouth, Kingsbridge, and Thirlestone, and then back through Ivybridge and Exeter to Lyme. Tennyson returned to Farringford on 12 September, and two days later left again with Emily, who was summoned to Lymington to her father, who died in his sleep the morning of 15 September. Though he had spent most of his time since Emily's marriage with the Turners and the Welds, there had always been a special bond between Henry Sellwood and his oldest daughter. He had long been ill, but the end came suddenly, and Emily was shocked and deeply saddened for months. She wrote few letters during the remainder of 1867 (apparently none have survived), and her Journal entries for October through December are sketchy and wearisome, with the exception of a touching tribute to her father's grand simplicity of character, to his undaunted cheerfulness, and to his unselfish love. By Christmas time, nonetheless, she was composed, and the Tennysons welcomed their regular holiday guests Jowett and Woolner, who were followed by Allingham, the Simeons, and the Bradleys soon thereafter.

186   To Edward Lear

Farringford, 10 January 1868

My dear Mr. Lear,
Every day since that on which I received your kind letter I have been wishing to write to you but what with people and

everyday work and Christmas work added, it has not been
possible. Now, if there be anything in atmosphere spiritual, my
letter ought to be of the best and wisest for Mr. Jowett sits by
the fire, his Plato[1] on a little table at which he works
diligently. But alas that one so sensitive to earthly influences
should be so insensible to the unearthly, that any should feel
the cloudy sky and the snow and the frosty mist and be
stone-dead to the other.

I hope you are really tolerably comfortable and happy at
Cannes. I am really better than usual as far as my cough goes.
Ally is not quite the thing in health but very cheerful. . . . He
has been reading Hebrew, which is good for him. . . .

Mr. Digby[2] came on Tuesday. He seems good and simple
and . . . sensible. I trust that he may do well for the boys. We
have however no intention of keeping either permanently at
home. The doctors recommended that Hallam should not spend
the winter at Marlborough, but if all be well he will return
after Easter. . . . What is to be done with Lionel I do not
know. He still stammers when overdone. . . . What is it that
you say about a house at Cannes?[3] I do think it a good thing to
have a house somewhere certainly. There is a dearness in the
old room and the old chair that is something worth, and I
suppose one ought to wish that you should find that something
worth under a sunny sky.

1. See above, Letter 113.
2. The new tutor who arrived on 7 January was apparently a favorite
with Hallam and Lionel. The Journal has several references to the three
playing football and croquet together.
3. Lear did not buy a house until 1870, when he established his
Villa Emily at San Remo.

187   To Thomas Woolner

Farringford, 6 March 1868

Joy to you, my dear Mr. Woolner, on your great good fortune![1]
May it be only the beginning.

I wish you were here to advise us. We are sorely troubled by
Mr. Payne's advertisement of a new edition. We don't know
how to divide the poems into four volumes and there are not

many new poems and the whole affair is hateful.[2] Ally will
have to go to town to consult his friends about it soon, I think;
so he will, I hope, see the beautiful pictures and hear that you
have a good nurse. It is very bad for Mrs. Woolner being
without a proper nurse, I am sure. Ally is charmed with the
"Ophelia" even more than with "Elaine."[3] Love from Ally and
the boys if they knew I was writing.

1. His acquisition of a painting. Woolner began about this time to
buy pictures, and he eventually amassed an excellent collection.
2. Tennyson rejected the Moxon proposal for an edition of his collected
works. In 1872–73 Alexander Strahan published the six-volume *Imperial
Library Edition.*
3. Woolner completed the marble statuette "Ophelia" in 1868. He
had exhibited "Elaine" the year before.

188   To Thomas Woolner

Farringford, 10 March 1868

My dear Mr. Woolner,
About this edition. The exceeding annoyance has made me
both ill and wretched at times. What I do really care for is that
my Ally should stand before the world in his own childlike
simplicity and by this he would be made to appear a mere low,
cunning tradesman and it shall not be if I can prevent it.[1] I say
I, but he hates it all, of course, as much as I do, only he does
not see the consequences as clearly as I do, perhaps not having
turned his mind to the subject. The first thing to be done is to
say that this edition will go on in the old plain-sailing fashion,
I hope, and we can then enforce simple advertisements. The
next, that we must insist upon a little volume of new poems in
the type of the old, for those who have the old edition.[2]
   A thousand thanks for your really friendly offer of
hospitality. I want a few strong-willed friends to carry him
through this for I feel that his good name will be injured and
moreover without the poor consolation of any worldly good (if
consolation that could be called), for Mr. Pollock says that in
this respect even it is a bad bargain for him. . . . Forgive me,
but I perceive that you so entirely agree with me that I speak
out by way of thanks for your friendship in having done so.

1. The same day that she addressed Woolner for the second time about her dissatisfaction with the proposed edition, and with Frederick Evans's mode of advertisement, she elaborated on the subject in the Journal: "Very much annoyed by Mr. Payne who cannot understand our love of absolute simplicity in advertisement business arrangements so that we may be free to take thankfully what comes in this way. Be it much or little. What grieves me is that his love of excitement may mislead the public as to A., who has nothing to do with these matters."

2. That is, *A Selection from the Works of Alfred Tennyson* (the *Miniature Poets Edition*), 1865, the last Tennyson volume Moxon's published.

189   To Thomas Woolner

Farringford, 24 March 1868

My dear Mr. Woolner,
The stone is not to be laid for a month[1] to come so that he will, I suppose, try to manage the Payne business by letter. He bids me ask you if you will kindly put him in the way of procuring some of the 1847 port which you told him could be had at so moderate a price. I am sorry to say anything which involves your giving an answer, though to say the truth it is a treat to read such letters as you write; for instance, when you have a beautiful picture to write about. . . . I cannot express to you the beauty of the flowers this spring. It seems as if all the glory of one's youth had come back into them. How pleased Ally, who is studying Hinton,[2] would be by this last part of my sentence; only he seems more apt to talk of the shadow that comes from oneself than the glory.

1. The foundation stone was laid at Blackdown (Aldworth) on 23 April 1868.
2. James Hinton (1822–75), the philosopher and aural surgeon. Hinton's *Life in Nature* (1862) and *The Mystery of Pain* (1866) greatly interested Tennyson, and it was at Tennyson's suggestion that Hinton was asked to become one of the earliest members of the Metaphysical Society.

190   To Thomas Woolner

Farringford, 26 March 1868

My dear Mr. Woolner,
The magnificent looking wild boar ham has arrived. I mean to
prove myself no "bird of Paradise,"[1] if this needed proof, by
partaking of what has always seemed to me a romantic dish.
How should it not be, when it recalls to one *The Odyssey* and
all sorts of beautiful myths and actual wilds and forests
besides! . . .

I beg you without a moment's delay to insure your pictures if
you have not already done so. One is positively afraid of some
Nemesis after so much good fortune. No, I am not. I have a
kind of feeling that good fortune is good for you, and if so, I
am sure that you will have it, for have we not all what is best
for us? With our love and best thanks.

I mean to have the ham cooked in wine and kept for some
choice occasion if possible.

1. "Epilogue [The Day-Dream]," l. 7.

191   To Benjamin Cotton
James O. Hoge

Farringford, 2 September 1868

My dear Mr. Cotton,
I must not take anything but a white sheet to thank you for
your delightful letter. Most heartily do we reecho the "Bless
you" and yours. It is most kind in you to give this first news of
Tiny yourself. She has our very affectionate wishes I need not
say. May the Captain[1] prove in every way worthy of her (and
that is saying a great deal in our estimation), and may they be
happy as heart can dream.

Is the little Alamayo to stay with them? If so she will have a
task almost as anxious as it is interesting except that I hope
Tiny is wise enough not to be over anxious but to do her best
and cast her care upon the One who alone can prosper even the
best. With all kindest remembrances and once again our
assurance of the great pleasure your Sunday's visit gave us.

Captain Speedy has been here and I am charmed with the way in which he speaks of Tiny and his own hopes.

1. On 15 December 1868, Tiny Cotton married Captain Tristram Charles Sawyer Speedy, who had served with General Napier in Magdala, Abyssinia, in 1867, and had acquired custody of Prince Alamayahu, son of the Emperor Theodore, after the death of the prince's parents. Speedy returned to England in December 1867 and took the prince to his home near Freshwater. During the months prior to Speedy's marriage to Miss Cotton, Alamayahu several times visited the Tennysons and played in their garden, where he is said to have cautioned, "Take care: there will be an elephant in that jungle" (*Memoir,* II, 56). Three years after Speedy married, his guardianship of Alamayahu was challenged by Hormuzd Rassam, author of *A History of the Abyssinian Expedition* (1869) and the personal attendant of the Abyssinian queen at the time of her death. In a letter printed in *The Times* on 11 March 1872, Rassam charged that there had been "a great mistake as to the alleged request of the Queen of Abyssinia that Captain Speedy should take charge of the Prince." In fact, Rassam continued, "a few days before her death the Queen complained . . . twice of the importunity of Captain Speedy regarding the custody of her son." There is no record of the Speedys' reaction to Rassam's letter, and it is difficult to judge the validity of his allegations. In any case Alamayahu remained the Speedys' ward. He attended Cheltenham College, Rugby, and Sandhurst, and died of pleurisy in November 1879.

192   To Lionel Tennyson

Reading, 24 September 1868

Own beloved,
I must make this worst of pens write thee word that we are safely so far. . . . It grieves one's inmost soul to think of thy dear, sad face up there in the lonely garret but soon it will not be lonely but there will I doubt not be many a pleasant and affectionate companion to cheer thee. So often things that seem to be all wrong turn out far better than what would have seemed best could have done. . . .[1]
Thou hast been a good and loving boy and I look with earnest hope to seeing any little want of discipline there may have been corrected now, and there is nothing on earth Mother desires so much (for there is nothing on earth worth caring for in comparison) as that we should all grow day by day better and more like our divine Master and for this we must all pray,

must we not, my own darling? May God ever bless thee and may we be kept in health and safety for a happy meeting at Christmas. Papa's best love.

1. On 23 September 1868, the Tennysons took Lionel to Eton for his first half. When they stopped the following night in Reading, Emily wrote in her Journal, "It is desolating to see our poor boy weeping alone in his garret. . . . He takes the wrong books which spoils his Greek, but Mr. Hornby [the Rev. James J. Hornby, the new headmaster] kindly promises A. to make allowance. He drives with us to the station and we part there and we see him alone in the Fly."

193   To Lionel Tennyson

Reading, 25 September 1868

My own darling,
I trust that the work has gone well today and that thou art feeling happier. Get out as much as possible, always open your window when you leave your room, and in every way take care of your health. If we are parted bodily we are one in spirit, beloved, and must be forever whatever come if only we are one in Christ. . . .

Mother's wits were so bewildered yesterday that she sent for the carriage at the wrong hour, 12:30 instead of 3:30, so poor Papa had to telegraph, which is doubly provoking as an impertinent woman came up to him yesterday and asked his name, "Is your name Tennyson?" He said, "Why, what matter?" She replied, "Oh, I only wanted to know."

Be sure to say how thou art. I will keep this to post from home if we reach it in time. If not, from Yarmouth. God bless and protect thee, beloved.

194   To Lionel Tennyson

Farringford, 26 September 1868

Own darling,
Pray beg Mr. Stone,[1] or perhaps I had better beg him, to get the proper books of reference: Smith's classical dictionary,

ancient and modern Atlas, etc. Kalends, Nones, and Ides were divisions of the Roman months. Kalends the first day of the month, Nones either the fifth or seventh, Ides exactly eight days after, marking the middle of the month. You remember how Caesar before his death was told to "Beware the Ides of March," don't you, my boy? But you will think you are in school. Still if I write such things, I need not say how anxiously we look for the result of the examination. Anxiously in one sense but certain that however it is, it will be for the best, since our boy has done his best.

Papa last night said, "Feel the want of the voices," and we could not but agree how changed and sad the house seemed, silent to us though sounds of revelry came from the hall where, because of the rain and storm, the men were having their dinner. . . .[2]

Such a large grand bird sailing just now close by the cedar. I should have thought it a peregrine falcon only that I believe they are too wild to come so near a house. . . .

Are there any nice books in the library? Don't read novels, darling. It was very good in Mr. Stone having thee. God bless thee, own beloved. Our best love. Write to us both together.

1. Edward Daniel Stone (1832–1916), assistant master at Eton from 1857 till 1884. Lionel lived at Mr. Stone's house during much of his residence at Eton.

2. On their way home on 25 September the poet and his wife crossed the Solent "in the roughest gale of the year," and they were "tossed like shuttlecocks, as A. says." At Farringford they found a large party of farm laborers at a harvest home supper in the servants' hall, but the sounds of revelry failed to drown "the heart stillness of the house" which oppressed the Tennysons when they first returned. On the twenty-eighth they were comforted by a letter from Lionel, and by the next day Emily Tennyson seemed more reconciled to his absence. "One's heart cannot but yearn towards one's boys," she wrote on the twenty-ninth, "but surely I, if anyone, ought to be thankful for my lot."

195   To Mrs. Thomas Woolner

Farringford, 1 October 1868

My dear Mrs. Woolner,
We got back last Friday from taking our Lionel to Eton so now

we are quite alone but we have the comfort of hearing that the boys are well and happy except that poor Lionel partly from nervousness in examination is placed so low that he has to go over again with work that he did long ago which is very disheartening to him. However, we are given to hope that this will be rectified in November and meanwhile he is getting accustomed to school ways.

We rejoice to hear that you have had a good holiday though we wish it could have been made still better and happier by Mr. Woolner's sharing it. However, it is a grand thing to have accomplished satisfactorily the most important part of a national work[1] which will hand his name down worthily as long as it lasts and moreover bring, I hope, more interesting objects to his studio. . . .

We have never heard a word from Mr. Peel[2] since his marriage. Perhaps they are aggrieved by Ally's not having gone to the wedding. . . .

He is sorely bothered too about his publisher and feels the need of advice which he cannot get here. But one must expect bother in this world and no doubt it is good for one in some way or the other. He is very cheerful notwithstanding this. I have recovered from a somewhat sharp illness, and now I think I have nothing more to say except that we heartily rejoice in the good news of Mr. Woolner's work and in all good news about you. With love from us.

1. The designs for the Manchester Assize Courts, which Woolner began in 1863. He did figures of Alfred the Great, Henry II, Edward I, Randolph de Glanville, Judge William Gascoigne, Edward Coke, Thomas More, Matthew Hale, and others.
2. Archibald Peel, the son of General Jonathan Peel of Marble Hill. Peel first became acquainted with the Tennysons in 1851, and he was their occasional guest thereafter.

196   To Lionel Tennyson

Farringford, 21 October 1868

Own beloved,
Annie Thackeray[1] came to us yesterday. She is very delightful and we agree in our notions of how to do good in the world, I

think. Last night we made a great circle with the Ritchies,[2] Prinseps,[3] etc., and had "Russian Scandal," and "Earth, Air and Water," and "I Love My Love,"[4] and the girls said they had enjoyed themselves very much.

Mr. Allingham is come again today to walk with the whole Ritchie party to the Needles, all at least who do not drive with me, Annie Thackeray, and Mrs. Ritchie.

1. See above, Letter 139, n. 2.
2. Anne Thackeray's cousins, Augusta, Eleanor, and Emily Ritchie.
3. Probably including Annie, Alice, May, and Val Prinsep, frequent guests of both the Tennysons and the Charles Camerons. In 1874 the Henry Thoby Prinseps abandoned Little Holland House and moved into "The Briary," a house adjoining the Farringford estate largely designed and paid for by G. F. Watts.
4. Victorian parlor games. "Russian Scandal" is a whispering game involving the passing of a scandalous message from one player to another. "Earth, Air, and Water" may begin with one player throwing a handkerchief at another and calling out, "Air!" The person hit with the handkerchief must respond with the name of some bird, i.e., a creature belonging to the air, before the first player can count to ten. A forfeit must be paid if the player names a creature that does not live in the air, or if he fails to speak quickly enough. The second player then throws the handkerchief at another and calls out, "Earth!" or "Water!" The game then proceeds in similar fashion. "I Love My Love" commences with a player arbitrarily choosing one letter of the alphabet to begin words which provide information about his "love." For example, a player might say, "A. I love my love with an 'A,' because he is admirable. He comes from Afton, lives on apples, and his name is Alfred." All the other players follow suit with the same letter before going on to the next letter.

197   To Alfred Tennyson

Farringford, 19 November 1868[1]

Own dearest,
My best thanks for the precious booklet. I don't quite like to see thy "Holy Grail" in such common guise[2] for it does not seem honour due. I have read it through as best I could but my brain is too heavy to enjoy it as I shall do when more at leisure. It is my treasure to myself now and I can pore over it at will. I long to hear what Tilly and Horatio say of it.[3] May I let the boys see it and Mr. and Mrs. Bradley? I do so hope that

Sir John will not send for thee,[4] the journey is so troublesome to thee and I am so anxious thou shouldst have a little pleasure before returning.

The children take a great interest in the old shepherd. They have been out this morning to the park to give him the gloves and half a pound of gingerbread each, which I gave them for him. Last evening he greeted Horatio with, "Bless the man he is come again!" he was so rejoiced to see him. He tried to make him promise to come and hear the psalm singing before the funeral[5] but Horatio could not quite bring himself to this.

Take care of thy back, dearest. My cough is getting better.

I have heard of a "treasure of a cook" from Mr. Digby, by name "Happy Holiday." If she deserves her name, she will be a great contrast to our poor, good, doleful Andrews,[6] who is still resolved on going. . . . Kindest regards to Mr. and Mrs. Knowles. God bless thee dearest.

I wrote to Mr. Taine[7] the day of thy leaving us and had a very courteous reply.

1. Tennyson visited with the Knowles at Clapham from mid-November until 19 December. While in town he negotiated with Alexander Strahan, and on 31 December severed all official connections with Moxon's.

2. A trial edition of "The Holy Grail." When Emily Tennyson read the first draft of the idyll she had long yearned for her husband to write, she felt her own desire "more than fulfilled." And on 18 May 1869, when Tennyson read a corrected version of "The Holy Grail" to her, she again expressed her satisfaction: "I doubt whether the 'San Graal' would have been written but for my endeavour, and the Queen's wish, and that of the Crown Princess. Thank God for it. He has had the subject on his mind for years, ever since he began to write about Arthur and his knights" (*Memoir*, II, 65).

3. Horatio Tennyson's first wife Charlotte died in October 1868. He and his two daughters came to Farringford on 7 November and remained until the thirtieth.

4. Sir John Simeon ran for reelection to Parliament in 1868, and he relied heavily on Tennyson's advice and influence. Sir John was M. P. (Liberal) for the Isle of Wight from 1842 till 1851, and again from 1865 till his death.

5. The old Freshwater shepherd's wife had recently died (*Memoir*, II, 59).

6. Mrs. Andrews continued to cook for the Tennysons for many years.

7. Hippolyte Taine (1828–92), the critic and historian, author of *De l'ideal dans l'art* (1867) and *Histoire de la littérature anglaise* (1863-64), among numerous other works. In the *Histoire* Taine labeled Tennyson the greatest English poet of his time; but elsewhere he wrote that "neither Tennyson nor any other nineteenth century poet, with the exception of Byron, has anything to equal" Mrs. Browning's *Sonnets from the*

Portuguese. See *Life and Letters of Hippolyte Taine,* translated by Mrs. R. L. Devonshire, vol. 1 & 2, and E. Sparvel-Bayley, vol. 3 (London: Archibald Constable & Co., 1908), III, 184.

198   To Alfred Tennyson

Farringford, 20 November 1868

Own dearest,

It is so unlike thee to be shut up all day except twenty minutes that I fear thou must be very far from well. I shall get thee to put on the red shirts again for the winter. . . .

Pray do not let the poems go into "Good Words." As to people having no reason to complain if they were, there I differ, for part of the object of those who have thy other poems would of course be to have these as a volume in the series. And when it is taken into consideration that *Enoch Arden* in one year brought in about £6,000 it is perfectly absurd to think of £700. . . .[1] Make a stand at once; it may save future trouble. Do thou not think so? Put it on me if thou wilt, for I do entirely object not only on these grounds but on the ground of the unpleasant position it puts thee in with regard to other magazines. There is now for instance an entreaty from Dallas[2] through Mrs. Cameron. He says he will give anything asked by thee for "Property"[3] for *Once a Week* this Christmas. . . .

Better give the poems to the edition allowing the single volume a start then let them go into *Good Words* in a money point of view. But I don't suppose it is in this point of view one so liberal as Chatham[4] regards them. It is probably only as a tribute to his own fondling. Louy Simeon has been here all the afternoon. They think that they have a majority of 120 promises! Old Sam drives her about canvassing and says, "Me and my young lady knows what to say to them."

1. Early in 1868 Tennyson published several poems in periodicals: "The Spiteful Letter" in *Once a Week* and "The Victim" in *Good Words,* in January, "Wages" in *Macmillan's Magazine,* in February, and "Lucretius" in *Macmillan's* and in *Every Saturday,* in May. For "The Victim" *Good Words* paid Tennyson £700, a large sum for a single poem; but the poet's wife obviously felt he squandered any poem he published in a periodical. Tennyson took her advice and published no more in periodicals for several years.
2. E. S. Dallas (1828–1879), editor of *Once a Week.*

3. "Northern Farmer. New Style," which first appeared in *The Holy Grail and Other Poems* (1870).
4. Evidently an assistant editor of *Good Words*.

199   To Alfred Tennyson

Farringford, 22 November 1868

Own dearest,
I am sorry that the Simeons did not write to thee about the letter. Of course I should have told thee about it had I known they had not. They are working so hard canvassing, that is why. It is published in a Hampshire paper, I think. I very nearly telegraphed to desire that it should be printed "My Dear Simeon" (I knew I might). Somehow or other it begins "Sir John," which he regretted.[1]

I am afraid that they will be horribly disappointed at thy not coming tomorrow. They have an idea that thy influence will do so much for them. It is a very great nuisance to have to come down and go up again assuredly, but I fear, dearest, that at the present, there is so little possibility of quiet here that it is really better to be obliged to be away a little.

Poor Horatio has such a complication of troubles. Both servants ill at Cheltenham—one very ill with the same sort of fever apparently that Anne has.[2]

. . .[3] quiet and companionship of the great of old as we used to have them did so much for both of us. Well, it is no use pining for the past as I often do. One must make the best of the present. It is a joy to hear that Browning thinks as I do of the "Grail."[4] Horatio and Tilly also are charmed with it. Horatio says it seems as if the power of language could go no further. He has read it aloud to us.

1. Evidently Sir John Simeon had published Tennyson's 17 November letter (*Memoir*, II, 60), in which the poet assured Simeon of his support of his candidacy for reelection as M. P. for the Isle of Wight.
2. Anne Weld was ill, apparently with some sort of nervous disorder, during much of the autumn of 1838.
3. An entire leaf is missing here, and the extant manuscript resumes below in mid-sentence. A portion of the final page is also lost.
4. When Tennyson read "The Holy Grail" to Browning in London on 19 November, Browning called it his "best and highest" (*Memoir*, II, 59).

200   *To Anne Weld*

Headon Hall,[1] *24 December 1868*

My dearest Nanny,
A Merry Christmas and a Happy New Year to you is one of the
dearest wishes of my heart! I have been hoping for the little
box this morning but I am sorry to say that it has not come. I
wanted to have put the pictures by their bedside tomorrow
morning in the old accustomed fashion of Christmas morning.
However little they may have of their Father's genius they bid
fair [?] to have the childlike simplicity of his nature. It is quite
touching to see my boy of 5 feet 10-1/2 inches kneel by my
knees to say his prayers just as he has always done. Lionel too
is just the same. . . . I am sorry that Hallam has had to come to
this extremely stormy place but we mean to try and get back on
Saturday for we have had our clerk of the Greenhill works
down at Farringford to examine the drainage, etc. He says he
can see nothing in the house that would cause illness and as
we have made the drains ourselves and are so exceedingly
particular in attending to them we expected this to be his
verdict and cannot but believe that the disease originated in the
girl herself who used to go out at night after her kitchen work
and who we know was with Roger's son (who, *I believe,* had
had both scarlet and typhoid fevers himself and whose sister
died of them), for Heard found him lurking inside our grounds
in the dark and heard her talking to him. Of course we have
had her bedding removed and are having the room
lime-washed.

1. Emily, Hallam, and Lionel Tennyson stayed at a Mr. Bird's Headon
Hall, Alum Bay, from the eighteenth until the twenty-eighth. One of
the Farringford maids had contracted scarlet fever, and Tennyson insisted
that the house be completely scoured and disinfected and that the
drainage be inspected for possible sources of contamination. G. M.
Young notes that sanitation as we know it was in its infancy in Victorian
England and that those responsible for the installation of drainage
systems were so ignorant of proper precautions "that it is no wonder
that in the novels and memoirs of the day 'the fever' plays a striking
part." See *Early Victorian England,* ed. G. M. Young (London: Oxford
University Press, 1934), I, 84.

201   To Anne and Agnes Weld

Farringford, 20 January 1869

My own Nanny and Agnes,
You know that in spirit I shall be with you and that I grieve
that none of us are there bodily.[1] A nervous affliction that Ally
had years ago has been upon him of late. He could not face the
sadness, I know. You will forgive him seeing that it is because
he feels and not because he does not feel. He wants to have
you at the Terrace,[2] wished that you should have it at once but
I knew that you would on no account allow this, Horatio
having been promised it until April. . . .

Our Lionel has gone back to Eton today. I am sorry to say
that he is thinner and his roses have faded a good deal these
holidays. I suppose it is because of the damp.

1. Charles Weld died suddenly on 15 January 1869.
2. See above, Letter 151, n. 4.

202   To Edward Lear

Farringford, 6 February 1869

My dear Mr. Lear,
I want to tell you myself about poor Nanny and Agnes because
you have always been so kind about them. Is it not a blessing
that the last year was so much the happiest that has been for
many a year. He was quite changed. Never once lost his temper
the whole year. At the communion on Christmas day not only
Nanny but the officials noticed his extreme devotion. It was
only a few days before that Friday that we learnt that the
doctor had pronounced this pain in the side and shortness of
breathing from which he was suffering to be from enlargement
of the heart.

All day he had been well and extremely kind. They went to
bed about ten, about eleven he rang, my sister who was in the
study close by was with him in a moment, Agnes too. One
quarter of an hour of terrible agony and he died in Nanny's
arms having begged forgiveness and granted his and blessed
them both. He had written a very nice letter to me about her
not long before. The Turners are with them and are as good
angels to them.

203   To William Gladstone
British Museum

Farringford, 14 February 1869

Dear Mr. Gladstone,
You listen so patiently to all,[1] please listen to me one moment
. . . . Is it not possible to throw all land and all money
produce, whether of mechanic skill or of brain, into one great
mass to be taxed and rated and tithed equally for general
purposes, leaving the special to be specially dealt with (such as
lighting of cities)?

Money in this case would take rank with land in its form of
interest not of principal (3 for 100), which, I think, might solve
many difficulties. (Perhaps my thoughts have been often before
thought.) The whole country to be divided into districts, each
district to be under the charge of a steward, a gentleman of
standing and education, to be as irremoveable as the judges
who shall register, collect, and administer somewhat after the
theory of some native Indian administration, I think.

Pardon me and do not of course waste one moment in
answering me. With all most earnest wishes that you may have
wisdom given you to rule this great land, for great I still
believe it, thank God.

1. On 23 November 1868, Gladstone was elected to the first of his
four terms as prime minister.

204   To Hallam Tennyson

Reading, 1 May 1869

Own beloved,
I do not think that I am so ungrateful as thou wert half
disposed to have me for the great delight of that glimpse of
thee and for what must ever be a privilege to any ever so little
worthy of it, a few hours with Mr. and Mrs. Bradley.[1] The
lovely forest too that is now to me "a joy forever."[2] I have been
continually thinking of thy poem. I hope it is fairly copied out
and that "The Master" will be pleased with it despite its
imperfections of which thou art as fully sensible as anyone.
. . .

Wilt thou say to Mrs. Bradley that I hope to write to her when we reach home, probably tomorrow. This is the Sunday letter which must not be omitted for thy sake or for mine.

And now, beloved, think out carefully every thought and do not be content without finding the connection of each sentence of the longest passage. If it be a passage worth reading there is one as surely as there is between the heart and every member to the very smallest of the body. And God prosper thee in thy work and in all things and bless the blessing of thy Father and thy Mother upon thee. Our best love to thee. Kindest love too to Mr. and Mrs. Bradley.

It would be very good exercise to take some one rather difficult passage and see how each thought grows out of the other and put down the connection. Perhaps thou hast scarcely time for this at school, but to be able to do it is the glory of man intellectually.

1. The Tennysons visited at Marlborough 26-29 April.
2. Keats, *Endymion*, l. 1. She refers to the New Forest through which she and her husband drove en route home.

205   *To Hallam Tennyson*

Farringford, 11 May 1869

Own beloved,

I trust that there is nothing amiss. Thy Sunday's letter has not come. This makes one the more anxious as thou art no longer at the Lodge.[1]

Our two or three nights alone have been a great treat to me. Last evening Mr. and Mrs. Andrews, a Lincolnshire clergyman and his wife living not far from Grasby and knowing Uncle Charlie, came here on the strength of their acquaintance. Papa read them the "Northern Farmer" and they promised to pay attention to its dialect when they get home and compare it with what they hear. She is a sister of Mrs. Lewis Fytche. . . .[2]

Papa has been out driving with me today as it was fine enough to have the carriage open. He has read to me and talked in the evenings and is cheerful and pretty well, I am thankful to say, though still suffering sometimes from the solar plexus.
. . .

I know that my letters are very stupid. The cares of this life engross me so much, what with our own affairs and Uncle Horatio's and Aunt Nanny's. I long to know what you will say to Papa's proposal.[3] Lionel makes no comment. He is thinking perhaps of his visit to Mr. Jowett. I send his letter lest he should not have time to write to thee. God bless thee, beloved one. Our best love.

1. Hallam Tennyson no longer lived with the Bradleys.
2. Lewis Fytche was Tennyson's cousin.
3. Tennyson offered to invite Anne and Agnes Weld to come to live at Farringford.

206   To Hallam Tennyson

Farringford, 18 May 1869

Own beloved,

. . . Wilt thou remember to make some comment on the plan of Aunty's living with us. Of course what you and Lionel feel about it makes a very great difference and I fear that Aunty and Agnes will feel slighted if you say nothing at all to me. There cannot but be an anxious risk in such things and in this case when the furniture has to be moved and what is far more important when there are so many very strong individualities to be thought of, all should weigh well before deciding. . . .

Papa has been very cheerful since Mr. and Mrs. Knowles have been here. He has a great fancy for them. I am thankful to say that Mr. Knowles has the power to encourage him in his work.[1]

Thou art right, my boy, not to build upon the prize. To pray to be able to put oneself absolutely in God's hand, having tried to do one's best, is our highest wisdom and to attain to it the highest good, is it not? No letter from Lionel today. God bless thee, beloved. Our best love.

1. Emily Tennyson observed in her Journal entry for 11 November 1871 that Knowles's "active nature . . . spurs A. on to work when he is flagging." Tennyson himself acknowledged that without Knowles he might never have completed the *Idylls of the King.* Hallam Tennyson recalled that his father would sometimes point at Knowles and say, "I was often urged to go on with the *Idylls,* but I stuck: and then this beast said, 'Do it,' and I did it" (*Memoir,* II, 110).

207   To Hallam Tennyson

Farringford, 28 May 1869

Own beloved,
It was very pleasant to see the Americans[1] enjoy themselves so
much. The place, the cooking, all appeared charming to them,
and not less so, Mrs. Cameron. She made photographs of Mr.
Fields and of Miss Lowell who seems a nice, simple girl
thoroughly the lady in feeling and not *very* American in
speech. Tell Mrs. Bradley that her Grandfather Spence was
banished because of his love for England and her Grandmother
always closed her shutters on the 4th of July (the day of the
Declaration of Independence, thou knowest) and put her
knocker in crape. Papa said he should drink her health after
dinner. God bless thee, beloved. Less than a month now to the
day when I may hope to see thee. Our best love.

1. Mr. and Mrs. James T. Fields and their companion, Mabel Lowell
(b. 1847), the daughter of James Russell Lowell, were at Farringford
25-27 May.

208   To Rev. Stenton Eardley[1]
Indiana University

Farringford, 3 June 1869

Dear Mr. Eardley,
He is not very well today. If you will allow him he will write
to you from town at the beginning of next week and tell you
whether he will be able to go with you, if all be well, to
Mürren. We trust that this delay will not inconvenience you.
All I have heard and the little I have seen of you make me sure
that I could not entrust him to a kinder and better guide, and
as I know that I should only be in the way so high in the
mountains I am indeed thankful that you undertake him. I only
ask you to remember how very blind he is in spite of his seeing
so much that most others do not see and I know that you will
grant my request.
   I most heartily hope that the pleasure and profit of the
journey will not be less to yourself than to him. Pray thank
Mrs. Eardley for her goodness in sparing you.

1. (1823–83), vicar of St. Stephen's, Birmingham, from 1849 until 1854, when he became vicar of Emmanuel Church, Streatham, a living he held until his death. During June and July 1869, Eardley traveled through France to Switzerland with Tennyson and Frederick Locker (afterwards Locker-Lampson), the father of Eleanor Locker, who in 1878 married Lionel Tennyson.

209   To Hallam Tennyson

Farringford, 8 June 1869

Beloved one,
I had such a touching interview with the old shepherd[1] yesterday. He came to me for he said that he could not abide any longer without seeing me. He talked of his wife and of you both. The way in which he bowed down when he said, "God bless you," as if in the very presence of God (and was he not), asking for the blessing, was sublime. . . . I had another interview too, one with an adoring American, for so he may be called having lived thirty years there though a native of this island. Not being able to wring Papa's hand he wrung mine instead. Then I had one with Miss Vernon[2] which I will tell thee about if all be well when we meet. God bless thee, darling.

1. See above, Letter 197.
2. Governess for Horatio Tennyson's children.

210   To Alfred Tennyson

Farringford, 16 June 1869

Best beloved,
I have written thee two little letters and sent one to Dover and one "poste restante Mürren," but both have gone on a bootless errand, I suppose. Pray tell Mr. Locker that he has my affectionate thanks for the Folkestone letter.[1] Thou knowest how precious thy little word is and the letter written by thee from York Gate. Mrs. Palgrave was so good as to give me news

of thy leaving them in excellent spirits and saying how they missed thee.

But now I must tell thee of myself and of the boys. Good news from both of them. Hallam says that a poor fellow who was to be expelled for billiards and drinking had sent for him and told him he was in such despair at thought of his father's grief and at the little brother, who had always looked up to him, finding him one of the greatest blackguards in the school that he was just going to throw himself out of the window when Bright came in, so he got in bed instead. With thy leave I would have him here for two or three days, should Hallam think this would be of use to him. The first time he went to billiards he said to the boy with him, "This will be my ruin for life." It seems he looks up to Hallam very much. Lionel has been distinguishing himself at cricket and says that there is just a chance of his going in for the 5th form trials,[2] but only just, he fears.

There is a very kind letter from Lord Hatherley saying that he will certainly bear in mind Mr. Vernon and that if he could make any way with his list he should be very glad to put a case recommended by us on his special list. . . .[3]

We have all of us an invitation from the Prince of Teck, as President, and the other officers of the Regent's Park Botanical Gardens for today. I did not know whether it was a card that had to be answered so I sent an answer to Louy Simeon to forward or not as her father advised.

The Archbishop of Canterbury seems to have made a very wise speech last night,[4] Lords Stratford de Redcliffe and Carnarvon[5] following his lead. They advise that the bill should be read the second time and amended. The debate continues.

I am more furious than ever with Bright, he has written such a revolutionary letter.[6] I do think the ministers should forthwith eject him from the cabinet. A proper punishment for having admitted him there, having to do this!

. . . God bless thee, ownest own, and fill thee body and soul with His own spirit in the mountains whether He is indeed they or they but shadows of Him as the work of His hands, as we poor mortals say.[7] The work of His will I suppose we mean. Commend me to Mr. Locker and Mr. Eardley. I do hope the three get on pleasantly together. I shall be very anxious to hear. I am recovering from my fatigue.

1. Tennyson, Locker, and Eardley left Folkestone on 14 June. They arrived in Mürren on the nineteenth.

2. The term examinations for advancement to the fifth form, the second most advanced student level at Eton.

3. William Page Wood, Baron Hatherley (1801-81), was Lord Chancellor under Gladstone. Mr. Vernon, the father of the Horatio Tennysons' governess, may have been involved in a case which Hatherley agreed to give top priority because of the Tennysons' interest; but it is impossible to be certain.

4. In his 15 June speech to the House of Lords the Archbishop advised the peers to pass the long-contested Irish Church Bill and to attempt to reconstruct it in committee. The Queen had long realized that the disestablishment and disendowment of the Irish Church were inevitable, and her opinion of course influenced the Archibishop. The Lords subsequently passed the bill by a vote of 179 to 146.

5. Stratford Canning, first Viscount Stratford de Redcliffe (1786-1880), ambassador to Turkey during the Crimean War, and Henry Howard Molyneux Herbert, fourth Earl of Carnarvon (1831-90), colonial secretary under Lord Derby and again under Disraeli. Tennyson wrote an "Epitaph on Lord Stratford de Redcliffe" which he first published in *Tiresias and Other Poems.*

6. John Bright (1811-88), the radical statesman famous for his opposition to the Corn Laws and for his support of the Reform Act of 1867, wrote a letter designed to taunt the House of Lords into passing the Irish Church Bill. "The Lords are not very wise," he affirmed, "but there is sometimes profit to the people even in their unwisdom. If they should delay the passing of the Irish Church Bill for three months, they will stimulate discussion on important questions, which, but for their infatuation, might have slumbered many years . . . ." Quoted by Sir Spencer Walpole, *The History of Twenty-Five Years* (London, New York, Bombay, and Calcutta: Longmans, Green & Co., 1904-08), II, 363.

7. In an account of his travels with Tennyson (see the *Memoir,* II, 66-80), Frederick Locker-Lampson recorded a similar thought expressed by Tennyson in language very close to his wife's. In Mürren, on 19 June 1869, Tennyson looked toward the higher Alps and remarked to his companions, "Perhaps this earth and all that is on it—storms, cataracts, the sun and the skies—are the Almighty: in fact, that such is our petty nature, we cannot see Him, but we see His shadow . . ." (p. 68).

211 To Charles and Louisa Turner

Blackdown,[1] *10 August 1869*

My dearest Charlie and Louy,
I send you one word of best wishes for your great day as a

token of those wishes for you and for your work which cannot be uttered.[2] May the new church be ever a fold for Christ's lambs and no hireling fervence ever pollute its walls but one faithful shepherd follow another to the end of time each in blessing you as he enters eternity, and for yourselves may you ever give God the glory of this work and every work of your hand.

Our boys are doing the work of homey hands here on terrace and road. Some day I hope they will help the building of a church both here and at Farringford. At present we are very desolate for want of one because Lord Egmont will not let us have a road,[3] and Mr. Duke has not finished our stables, and the churches are a long way off for walking. We get on slowly inside and out.

On Friday our Hallam has to leave us. He is a most dear boy. Just as simple and pure as ever and growing I hope daily in strength and faithfulness. I never had so little enjoyment of his holidays because of having been so beset by work of many kinds.

I am writing too much so I will only add our best love and God bless you! I am glad poor Nanny's purchase is at last completed and the work of the house fairly begun.[4]

1. The Tennysons moved into their new summer home within a few days of Tennyson's return to England on 11 July.
2. The Turners completed a new church at Grasby in the summer of 1869.
3. The Tennysons' neighbor, George James, sixth Earl of Egmont (1794–1874), refused for some time to permit the opening of an access road through his land.
4. Anne and Agnes Weld had a new home built on the Isle of Wight, not far from Farringford.

212   To Hallam Tennyson

Blackdown, 27 August 1869

Own beloved,
Papa does not get reconciled to his room at all; though we keep it quiet for him the windows and the ceiling are as displeasing to him as at first. He has had three walks with Lionel but he is chiefly occupied in watching the men.[1]

Uncle Charlie and Aunty Louy talk of going to Oxford tomorrow and to Farringford on Monday, thence here. Aunty Nanny sits for hours watching the digging of the stone and finds herself very much the better for it, so I do hope her new home will suit her and it is pleasant to find that the Hamonds and herself take to each other so much. . . .

Lionel takes me out about five into the little wood and we laugh and say that it is Mrs. Tennyson and her son so weary of the loneliness of the place that they go to the gate to see the villagers go home from work in hope of a chat. He has been very good and contented copying music and learning little bits of Beethoven and Mozart, etc. God bless thee, darling. Our best love.

1. Though initially he may have watched the hired laborers, Tennyson subsequently worked along with them to make the Blackdown terrace garden and the little hidden lawns cut out of the surrounding copse.

213   To Edward Lear

Blackdown, 1 September 1869

My dear Mr. Lear,
Thou ask me how I like Blackdown. For my own private opinion I much prefer Farringford as to its beauty. The absolute solitude of this place at present is not displeasing to me or would not be if there were not so many workmen about . . . and if the terrace were green instead of a waste of sand and if there were flowers growing instead of lime and trees instead of . . . boards and shrubs instead of stones. But all these things will be in time, let us hope. Meanwhile, the great plain is fine, no doubt, and I don't care so much for want of the road which Lord Egmont denies as most people would, I suppose, even though I have more reason to care having not the power to walk. This to my Lord with my compliments.

My Lionel has drawn me into the little wood every evening. Thank God he is the same dear innocent child as ever. We have sent him off with his gun to Farringford today. He has been so good and contented with the absence of all amusement that he deserves some. My sister and Agnes are at Farringford and perhaps the Turners too. Nanny is building a house near

Farringford. We have good accounts of our Hallam. He too was perfectly contented here and he too is just the same childlike creature! Greater comfort to me than I can say. I find the furnishing rather a troublesome affair, not having the strength necessary for looking after much myself. . . . His love. He is pretty well.

214   To Hallam Tennyson

Blackdown, 28 September 1869

Own beloved,
It is astonishing how little time we have alone here on what seems our lonely hill. This evening and tomorrow I hope we may calculate on, for Mr. Lear has gone this morning and Mr. Knowles does not come before Thursday or Friday.[1] Mr. Lear very much regretted not having seen you both and over and over again charged me to send love to you both. Many thanks for names of books. Papa has been reading the *Life of London*[2] and Crabb Robinson's *Diary*[3] and Wallis' *Malayan Archipelago*,[4] which rather disappoints him by absence of all enthusiasm for tropical scenery though it abounds in it for the natives of those islands he visits and has wonderful accounts of animals and birds and insects. Mr. Lear will, I hope, see Lionel sometime in this month. It distresses one to find him in for another cold. I am afraid he must be imprudent.

I hope you have some time ago received fruit from home. I have sent many messages about it. The blackberries here are better than the mulberries, I think, but we have had too many in the house to think of gathering them for preserves unfortunately.

Aunt Nanny and Agnes had a bad passage but a warm welcome to make up for it. I think Auntie is now quite convinced that I intended the best in opposing their living with us [and] did the best, which is of course a comfort great in proportion to the trial of her first misunderstanding and difference of opinion. . . . I do feel it a great relief not to have the daily pressure of three separate families however glad I hope I am to do what I can for Uncle Horatio and Aunt Nanny. God bless thee, own beloved. Our best love.

1. During September the Tennysons entertained Frederick Locker, Alexander Strahan, the Charles Turners, and Anne and Agnes Weld, in addition to Lear.
2. Probably Pierce Egan's *Life in London* (London, 1821).
3. *Diary Reminiscences and Correspondence of H. C. Robinson,* selected and edited by J. Sadler (London, 1869).
4. Perhaps Samuel Wallis's *An Account of a Voyage Around the World in the Years 1766, 1767, and 1768* (London, 1773).

215   To Hallam Tennyson

Blackdown, 5 October 1869

Own beloved,
The terrace is nearly shaped and tomorrow we hope to see seven wagons laden with turf from our Farringford down.[1] I feel rather compunctious in taking so much thence however much I like to have it here. Seven wagons were to take it down to the little boat which was to leave Yarmouth with it for Southampton early yesterday morning. I tell Papa people will call him the mad poet on the hill. By the first boat this morning the trees from our Farringford nursery were to be taken to Lymington to be packed with such as we have ordered there from Miller. These we hope to have tomorrow and also to see Heard plant them. . . .

I have had time for reading the last few days—a great refreshment I need not say. I have finished Pressensé[2] and have been reading some sermons of Martineau[3] and some interesting articles in reviews. . . . An article on St. Paul in *Macmillan's* I have read. Renan's *St. Paul*[4] being the book reviewed.

1. On 7 October the first turf from Farringford was laid for the Blackdown lawn.
2. Edmund de Pressensé, *The Critical School and Jesus Christ: A Reply to M. Renan's Life of Jesus,* translated by L. Corkran (London, 1865?). In her Journal entry for 29-30 September Emily Tennyson set down her high appraisal of Pressensé's book, which, she said, had enabled her for a time "to live with Christ in His earthly life."
3. James Martineau, *Essays Philosophical and Theological,* 2 vols. (London, 1869).
4. Volume three of Renan's *Histoire des origines du christianisme.*

216   *To Hallam Tennyson*

Blackdown, 15 October 1869

Own beloved,
Poor Lionel has set his dear little heart on coming home. It grieves mine more than I can say that Papa does not wish him to come. The breakdown of the engine[1] made him nervous about railway journeys. He is in town now. Yesterday there was a letter telling that his privately printed little "Window" had actually been published by Payne so he had to go to town about it. He went last night to Mr. Locker's.[2]

Dr. and Mrs. Acworth[3] and her maid are coming tomorrow, not to my delight. . . . She is a so-called spiritualist! This morning I have been out ever since breakfast or rather since post-time planting. I don't much like having all the responsibility but this is a grumbling letter thou wilt say or at best a "don't like" letter.

Own darling, if ever in times to come thou shouldst be tempted thou wilt remember how that great and good master besought thee with tears not to yield.[4] It is rather strange, Papa had been reading in the *Westminster,* I think, a fearful account of the effect of immorality and how the effects lasted as it were forever from generation to generation. He said he never read anything so awful.[5]

1. On 10 October 1869, an accident on the Midland Railway at the Long Eaton Junction, near Nottingham, resulted in the death of seven persons.

2. J. Bertrand Payne sanctioned the inclusion of Tennyson's privately printed "The Window" in D. Barron Brightwell's *A Concordance to the Entire Works of Tennyson* (London, 1869), which Moxon's published without Tennyson's knowledge. Emily Tennyson set down Tennyson's reaction in her Journal: "A. annoyed by the concordance of his works. It seems to him that the world must think it an assumption to have one published during his lifetime but he knew nothing about it. He finds 'The Window' in the concordance published by Moxon, another breach of trust on Mr. Payne's part." Tennyson went to London on 14 October and spent two days with Frederick Locker, who informed him that the concordance was being "sold underhand."

3. James Acworth (1798–1883), president of Baptist College from 1835 until 1863, and author of *The Internal Witness to Christianity* (1856). Emily Tennyson recorded the Acworths' visit in her Journal entry for 19 October: "Dr. and Mrs. Acworth come. A. and Tilly much amazed by raps on the table in the middle-room. In A.'s study a table heaves like the sea. Mrs. Acworth is a great medicine though a delicate little

creature with very bright eyes. Something there must be in [spiritualism].
What I cannot say, but it seems to me a power more liable to abuse
than others."

4. Perhaps Granville Bradley had lectured Hallam and other Marlborough boys about sexual temptation.

5. Tennyson had read in the July 1869 *Westminster Review* (pp.
82–107) an article entitled "Prostitution in Relation to the National
Health," a report by the Select Committee of the House of Lords on
the 1866 Contagious Diseases Act. The report attests to the prevalence
of syphilis throughout the world, gives a detailed account of its consequences for future generations, and calls upon wise and well-meaning
women to rescue men from dangerous and demeaning sexual dalliance.

217   To Lionel Tennyson

Blackdown, 15 October 1869

Thou poor little darling, hast thou not received my letters? I
dare not send the carriage for thee tomorrow. Papa went to
town yesterday on account of that wretched Payne and he will
want it to bring him home. I told thee in my last that the
breakdown of the engine had made him nervous. I cannot tell
thee how it grieves my heart to disappoint thee, thou darling.
Thou knowest it is from the carefulness of love that Papa
objected. On seeing me so much disappointed he afterwards
agreed to it in a way, but it is all in vain now for he is not
here.

Dr. and Mrs. Acworth are to be here on those very days to
my non-pleasure. She is a spiritualist and I dread her. I should
see nothing of thee wert thou here. I have been out all the
morning looking after the planting and must go again. It is a
great responsibility to have all the ordering of it to myself.

218   *To Hallam Tennyson*

Blackdown, 19 October 1869

Own beloved,
Thou wilt be glad to hear that Aunt Tilly leaves me much more
to myself than she used to do. She fortunately greatly prefers
the dining room to *our* room, as I call the library . . . and
moreover I fancy someone must have spoken to her about
leaving me alone, and Papa and me too, for she often says,
poor thing, "Don't come with me," after dinner, but of course I
do generally. . . .

I am beginning Lecky's *European Morals*[1] and I so cordially
agree with him as to the intuitiveness of conscience, for which
he does stout battle in the beginning of his book, that I hope
the more to be interested by it throughout. I remember how my
wrath was roused as a girl by Paley's utilitarian greatest
happiness morality, though I had, as I suppose most young
creatures have, a thorough belief in happiness and a wild
longing for its topmost heights in this world. Yet I never
dreamt of pursuing it for myself, though, strange contradiction!
It seemed then and it seems still lawful to seek to give it to
others, if it be but of the right kind. Perhaps I am wearying
thee with such talk, for perhaps thou hast scarcely time to
think on them [*sic*] and such things are a weariness when
presented by others if one cannot think them out for oneself.
God bless thee, beloved. Our best love.

1. W. E. H. Lecky, *History of European Morals from Augustus to
Charlemagne* (London, 1869).

219   *To Thomas Woolner*

Blackdown, 23 October 1869

My dear Mr. Woolner,
We have been told by Mr. Lear that you have another little
girl[1] and that she and Mrs. Woolner are well. Accept our hearty
congratulations and good wishes. We hear too that you have
Millais' great little picture.[2] We give you joy on that too.

As for ourselves we have been living for more than two
months in the midst of a sandy desert, wheelbarrows

continually coming and going and sometimes carts and often the strokes of the joiners' and masons' tools and later of the stone carvers. . . . We shall not finish furnishing our house this year, the finishing of the house and shaping of the grounds having taken so much longer than we expected. . . . We have no road yet to our house, Lord Egmont having started objections to it entirely unforeseen by us and proportionally annoying. . . . Now having said so much about ourselves let me add that I hope work is prospering with you and all other things.

1. Second of the Woolners' six children.
2. Unidentified. "Lorenzo and Isabella" (1849) was evidently the only Millais painting owned by Woolner, but it is by no means a "little picture."

220   To Hallam Tennyson

Blackdown, 2 November 1869

Own beloved,
No doubt if the poison acted on the lungs I should think blowing into them might revive an apparently dead creature, as it does in cases of drowning. Such things serve to press on one with special force the great and inscrutable (as I believe) mystery of life—do they not? I mean of mere vegetable and animal life which some would now reduce to a mechanism. I often think that those laws of the Pentateuch which seem to us so strange about not mingling things, such as wool and linen, for instance, are a warning against confusion of ideas. Moreover it seems to me that there are, as it were, tidal waves of this confusion so that ordinary confusion becomes compounded at certain epochs. Now, as it appears to me, mechanical discoveries and inventions, striking to the imagination, have confused all high ideas, even of spirit, in some minds and robbed life of the awe and mystery which belong to it of right and ennoble it, nay rather are the very life of life in this our mortal state.

Physiology seems to me extremely interesting, as far as I know anything of it, but if seems as if man were only in the portals yet of this great science. With the small leisure for similar studies which school gives, I suppose you can only hope to glean such an inkling of what they are as to look to pursue them with more profit in future years than if you had never had an idea given you of what they are.

Tell me, own darling, if such a letter as this wearies thee. Papa talks of going home in about three weeks. I think it is quite wise to stay here until the leaves are gone at Farringford. . . . I feel happier today than I have felt here. Papa is so divinely good to me.[1]

1. On 1 November Emily Tennyson expressed her joy in having time to spend alone with the poet: "A very happy day. . . . A. and I sit reading. We talk together over the fire in our room at night."

221   To Hallam Tennyson

Blackdown, 5 November 1869

Own beloved,
There is a rumour that displeases and news of a petition that pleases me in the *Pall Mall* today. The rumour is that the Queen is to be prayed to give up our colonies; the petition that she would form them into one empire and proclaim herself Queen of this as she proclaimed herself Queen of India. I can see from Lord Carnarvon's letter about New Zealand[1] that he shares our feelings regarding the colonies and I am glad except that Gladstone seems born to carry all before him, even his opponents more than subserving his will.

The *Idylls* are now in their two books as they are to be, one containing both old and new *Idylls*, eight in all, the other the new *Idylls* for the sake of those who have the old. To these are added "Property," "Lucretius," and a few little poems.[2] Already twenty-six thousand of this last volume are bespoken, thirty-one of the other. Papa is now correcting preparatory to final publication. . . .

I have read poor Auntie Nanny's *Burgundy*[3] and I think she has managed wonderfully well with it. It is really interesting for that sort of book. Is it not strange? Some days ago she was at Harold's Cross, an old place of the Welds' where indeed some of the family still live. . . . There had been a fire there which amongst other things had partially destroyed the portrait

of a certain Puritan-looking Agnes of some generations back.
. . .

God bless thee, own darling. Our best love. Papa has been
fairly cheerful of late. I am pretty well.

1. In his 3 November letter to the *Times* Carnarvon wrote of his
concern that native unrest in New Zealand might trigger a full-scale
insurrection. He felt the Mother Country had made a grave mistake
in allowing New Zealand to attempt virtually total self-reliance, and
he recommended that financial assistance be sent to the colonists to
help them establish proper means of self-defense.
2. Issued by Strahan and Co. in December 1869, *The Holy Grail
and Other Poems* includes "The Coming of Arthur," "The Holy Grail,"
"Pelleas and Ettarre," "The Passing of Arthur," "Northern Farmer. New
Style" ("Property"), "Lucretius," "The Golden Supper," "The Victim,"
"Wages," "The Higher Pantheism," and "Flower in the crannied wall."
3. Charles Weld, *Notes on Burgundy,* edited by Anne Weld, with
a memoir of the author (London, 1869).

222   To Hallam Tennyson

Blackdown, 12 November 1869

Own beloved,
I hope Mr. and Mrs. Bradley and thyself are as much fired as I
am by the hint of giving up the colonies and by the hope that
comes out of it, through the petition of some working people of
England for a more intimate union, that the nation may rise as
one man and demand that the Queen shall weld us and our
colonies into one great empire indivisible save by civil war.
Then will one dream of Papa's life and mine be in course of
fulfillment.

I do hope that next year if we live we shall see something of
the most intelligent of our statesmen. I feel that Papa's words
should not fall powerless on them. This reminds me that when
he went to Haslemere Station he was addressed by an elderly
gentleman, "Very cold this evening, Sir." "Rather." "Pardon
my impertinence but are you Mr. Tennyson?" "What matters
my name? What is yours?" "Stratford de Redcliffe."
Whereupon they shook hands and so did the lady with him,
probably his wife, and Papa was asked to go to town in their
carriage but he professed a wicked inclination for the smoking

carriage and promised to renew the acquaintance, upon which they said, "Really?" and he answered, "Really." I hope it will be "really" as he must have much to tell which would interest Papa, and I am very anxious to enlarge the borders of his circle which from death and other causes is growing painfully narrow, and surely great talk is a great help.

223   To Hallam Tennyson

Blackdown, 16 November 1869

Own darling,
I am in a great hurry this morning. Someone has been sent by Mr. Strahan with the new book[1] to be corrected, and Mr. Estcourt[2] is coming to luncheon so thou wilt forgive a hurried scrap. Papa came home to dinner yesterday and is to go up to the Metaphysical dinner tomorrow, I think, and to return next day with Mr. Knowles, Mr. James Martineau, Mr. W. G. Clark, Mr. Locker, and perhaps Lady Charlotte and Eleanor.[3] The last two or four to remain.

    1. *The Holy Grail and Other Poems.*
    2. A. Harbottle Estcourt, Deputy Governor of the Isle of Wight.
    3. James Martineau (1805-1900), the Unitarian divine. Lady Charlotte was Frederick Locker's wife, and Eleanor was the Locker's daughter.

224   To Hallam Tennyson

Blackdown, 30 November 1869

Own darling,
Aunt Tilly begins to "rue" as to crossing the Solent twice and to think that she will go to Edinburgh instead. Whether she really will or not I cannot say, or whether Aunt Nanny and Agnes will come before Christmas or after I cannot say. Certainly a little time alone with Papa and our boys would be very precious but no doubt that which is kindest to other people is in fact best for ourselves though it may not seem so. God alone can order the hearts of men though Fathers and Mothers are often made his instruments and are indeed most blessed when so honoured. Nevertheless they must not repine if God give them less of this power than they would fain have,

and after all one knows that in this that which most tends to the strengthening of each individual soul is best for to his own Master each must stand or fall. This thou wilt say is a sermon not a letter.

Aunt Tilly and I have been alone since Friday. Last night she interested me by telling me how she and Aunt Mary were walking one autumn evening just before Arthur Hallam's death and saw a tall figure clothed in white which disappeared through a hedge where no gap was, for they went up to it thinking that perhaps Farmer Baumber's white goat had been walking on its hind legs and how she was so awed that on reaching home she burst into tears. Then she spoke of the day when being at the dancing school at Spilsby she brought back the letter announcing the death, which she gave to Papa when he was seated at the dinner table, which I need not say he left, and how poor Aunt Emily was summoned to have the news broken to her. Then she told how the little ones (not very little neither) used to "roar" when Papa, Uncle Charlie, and Arthur Hallam went to college but chiefly for Papa who was kindest of all to them though Arthur Hallam was so good to them that they were all in love with him. God bless thee, darling.

225   To Hallam Tennyson

Blackdown, 7 December 1869

Own beloved,

Mr. Pollock was very much delighted with the place notwithstanding the snow and he expressed himself very pleased by having so early an opportunity given him of seeing it. I know that this letter of Lionel's will please thee, so I send it, and I know too I shall have all his letters safely home when I see thee, my own. . . .

I heard such a pleasent thing of the Queen from Mr. Pollock. He was at some copper merchant's house not long ago and saw in different rooms sketches of the Princesses and letters from the Queen's family and photographs of them. On asking what this meant it appeared that the Father of the copper merchant's wife had been on more than one occasion very useful to the Duke of Kent[1] and the Queen never forgets this but the birth of every child has been announced to her and the merchant and his wife have been invited to see it. When the Crown Princess of Prussia[2] was in England they were asked to see her and her children and always they are treated as friends of the family. God bless thee, darling. Our best love.

1. Queen Victoria's father.
2. Victoria Adelaide Mary Louise, the Queen's eldest child; later Empress, mother of Kaiser Wilhelm.

Lionel returned from school for Christmas vacation on 17 December, Hallam arrived four days later, and soon Farringford was teeming with their young friends. Anne Thackeray and her cousins, Augusta, Emily, and Eleanor Ritchie, came for Christmas, and the first of the year they were joined by W. H. Brookfield's daughter, Magdalene, and by Margaret and Edith Bradley. The boys were now old enough to enjoy dinner parties and dances, as well as female companionship, and they attended several holiday gatherings at the William Croziers' and elsewhere in Freshwater. A few days after Christmas Hallam contracted chicken pox, and he remained home until March under doctor's orders. During Hallam's protracted absence from Marlborough Tennyson devoted himself almost exclusively to his son, instructing him in his regular school work, strolling with him on the High Down, and reading to him from Shakespeare, from Arthur Stanley's *Lectures on the History of the Eastern Church,* and from his own poems. On 15 March the Laureate left Farringford for Blackdown and thence went to London, where he took new rooms in Victoria Street and remained for two weeks visiting the Lockers and renewing old acquaintances.

226   To Charles Lutwidge Dodgson[1]
Yale

Farringford [March 1870]

Dear Sir,
It is useless troubling Mr. Tennyson with a request which will

only revive the annoyance he has already had on the subject and add to it.

No doubt "The Window" is circulated by means of the same unscrupulous person whose breach of confidence placed "The Lover's Tale" in your hands.[2] It would be well that, whatever may be done by such people, a gentleman should understand that when an author does not give his works to the public he has his own reasons for it.

1. "Lewis Carroll" (1832–98). The Tennysons first became acquainted with Dodgson in September 1857 during their holiday at the Marshalls' Tent Lodge. In the spring of 1859 Dodgson visited Farringford, hoping to hear or see something of the *Idylls*. However, though he received Dodgson kindly, Tennyson refused to display any unpublished work. As Sir Charles Tennyson suggests (*AT*, pp. 316–17), the Laureate's caution may have been prompted by his remembrance of Dodgson's incisive parody of "The Two Voices," which had appeared in *The Train* in 1856.

2. See above, Letter 171, n. 2. In November 1867 "The Window" was printed privately by Sir Ivor Guest, with the subtitle "The Loves of the Wrens," and with the twelve songs untitled. Despite his compliance three years later with Sullivan's desire to publish "The Window," Tennyson never much admired the songs, and he is said to have offered Sullivan £500 to cancel the arrangement shortly before their publication in December 1870. For information on "The Lover's Tale," see below, Letter 310, n. 1. The copy Dodgson had seen must have been one of the original few Tennyson permitted to circulate among friends.

227   To Alfred Tennyson

Farringford, 21 March 1870

Own dearest,

It was a great joy to have thy letter this morning. The one drawback was that thy hoarseness was not gone. The boys have been doing their Horace this morning and are now working together at their Herodotus. . . .

I hope thou hast seen all the accounts of the wonderful things that are being done and are going to be done, such as the Russian illumination of the body so that bullets may be seen and extracted afterwards, if they have any steel in them, by magnetism; the new tunnel under the Thames that is, and that under the Channel which is to be; the canal from the Bay of Biscay to the Mediterranean which is proposed; and the new balloting machine.[1] I hope thou wilt go to the House and hear and see besides all that is best worth hearing and seeing elsewhere. I will do my best with the boys and though we cannot but miss thee exceedingly, we all feel that it is desirable that thou shouldst have society and society thee. Our best love to thee. God bless thee dearest.

Now that the American postage is so much less letters come nearly every morning from America. I think they will keep and so I do not send them.

1. A faithful reader of each day's *Times,* Emily Tennyson was as aware of scientific developments as she was of the political and social nuances of her time.

228   To Alfred Tennyson

Farringford, 22 March 1870

Own dearest,

Pray, pray, get a call boy. I cannot bear to think of thy being there alone with no one to supply thy very few and simple wants.

Last evening Mrs. Cameron said that she would like to come but did not like to pay the Fly, or rather did not feel that she ought, so we sent the carriage and she and her three adopted daughters[1] came. A heavy evening, I am sorry to say, but there were no gentlemen for the young ladies thou knowest.

Our boys are good. They work several hours in the day. Lionel was at his Horace an hour and a half before breakfast (late thou knowest this is now). I sent him some of my coffee as he is not strong enough to fast long. Hallam is asked to dine at the fort[2] tomorrow but he has refused saying that he is bound in honour to work during thy absence, so I suppose he thus by anticipation declines the dance which is to be on Friday.

I am so sorry to have had those troublesome letters to send thee but I send those about which I think it will be a relief to thee to consult thy friends.

I have told Annie Thackeray of thy being in town so I dare say she will come and see thee. Do subscribe to Mudie's[3] and get books to amuse and interest thee. There is a club[4] card for

March 29. This day week is it not? Lord Clarendon[5] presides. I mean to send thee some fresh butter in a day or two. I will send the spectacles that want mending with it.

1. Mrs. Cameron's photographic models.

2. The Golden Hill Fort.

3. In 1870 Tennyson joined Mudie's Lending Library, founded in 1860.

4. Tennyson was a member of the Sterling Club, a popular literary society which also included in its membership Carlyle, Thackeray, Dickens, Walter Savage Landor, and Leigh Hunt.

5. George William Frederick Villiers (1800-70), fourth Earl of Clarendon, Secretary of State for Foreign Affairs, 1865-66, under Earl Russell, and 1868-70, under Gladstone.

229   To Alfred Tennyson

Farringford, 25 March 1870

Own dearest,

I have been thinking if there is anything I could send thee to help the dinner but I have come to the conclusion that certainly at some restauranteur's or the other thou canst do better than could be done by cooking things here to have them recooked there. . . .

Thou hast not remembered to answer about Hallam. Two of the Fraser-Tytlers[1] are to be at the dance this evening so it is rather a temptation to him to go. . . .

Tell me how thy dinner prospers. I hope the little box of butter and biscuits has reached safely. God bless thee, dearest. Our best love and best thanks for thy letter.

1. Freshwater neighbors whose three daughters were contemporaries of Hallam and Lionel. In 1886 Mary Fraser Tytler became C. F. Watts's second wife.

230   *To Alfred Tennyson*

Farringford, 27 March 1870

Own dearest,
Best thanks to thee for thy dear letters. There was another very
depressed letter from Mrs. Bradley yesterday. The little
Franklin[1] is gone. They thought he was recovering but he sank
and was dead in a few minutes from exhaustion. What sad
news for his poor parents in India. Mrs. Bradley gathered some
spring flowers for the lonely grave and we sent some too
yesterday and Hallam has written to the colonel to tell him that
he doesn't believe there was a purer, innocenter, better little
soul in the world, and it was his own thought doing it. . . .

The dance was on Friday—gay with flags and twelve or
thirteen ladies, I believe. Some from the other side of the
water, but I don't think Hallam minded very much about being
there.

I trust thy dinner will go off well today. What I chiefly want
to know was whether it is thy wish to have the Blackdown
rooms papered this year (the sitting rooms), and then I
mentioned Silas Tucker as the man recommended by Mrs.
Cameron and the one from whom we had our Grayshott
papers. I mentioned him also to Mr. Knowles, asking him if he
approved of him, but he only said something about not
repapering the bedroom yet, and of course we did not think of
doing it. No matter about it though. If thou art content to trust
me, I will do my best for the rooms, supposing they are to be
done.

1. Son of Colonel Charles Trigance Franklin (1822-95), of the Royal
Artillery, who served at Mhow in Central India from June 1869 until
the end of 1870.

231   *To Alfred Tennyson*

Farringford, 28 March 1870

Own dearest,
I cannot help fearing lest thy throat should be suffering from
this black, bitter weather. Mrs. Cameron has gone all the way
to Ventnor today to see Henry[1] run races, which, as she was

quite knocked up by Friday's walk, seems very imprudent.

Yesterday it was sunny though cold. In the afternoon as they[2] were returning from church they saw Miss Lane's[3] carriage with apparently a very gay party of ladies. Hallam took off his hat as is duty bound, when on coming close it proved that they were Cameronian maids. Miss Lane has lent them the carriage and after the fashion of their mistresses they had driven up to the fort. The officers hearing the bells all ran down thinking to see Miss Lane, when behold it was the French maid and her English companions so they departed disappointed and left the coast clear for the privates who gave the ladies an invitation to tea. Away they went to get leave and Hallam met them on their way back, leave being had.

Oh dear, this seems very silly now I have written it. Hallam is gone to the Needles again . . . having finished his novel. But I should add that he got up and did some Horace before breakfast. Lionel is gone out to try and shoot a magpie at the double petition of Heard and the shepherd, the magpie being a torment to the lambs. He has been doing some of the *Heracleidae.*

I hope thou will enjoy thyself this evening. Mr. Knowles said that thou went to dine with him.

1. Henry Herschel Hay Cameron ("Punch"), the Charles Camerons' youngest son. Though he long dreamed of a career on the stage, Henry Cameron eventually became a professional photographer with a studio in London near Cavendish Square. Among his more notable sitters was Aubrey Beardsley, who pronounced the resultant portrait of himself "superb" (see Hill, *Julia Margaret Cameron,* p. 174).
2. Hallam had not yet returned to Marlborough, and Lionel had come home with a bad cough on 9 March.
3. The Lanes lived outside Freshwater, very near the Camerons.

232   *To Hallam Tennyson*

Farringford, 15 May 1870

Our beloved,
Yesterday after I had given orders not to admit people I saw Mrs. Cameron and Miss Lane on the lawn bringing a parcel in her hands (Miss Lane, I think). I opened the drawing room

window and let them in. They were both very pleasant, Mrs. Cameron very affectionate, and Miss Lane less stiff than I have often seen her. The parcel contained many photographs of Pinkie,[1] some as a Queen in the Marie Stuart cap and ruff, the Narcissus one, and others. This last is a Flora I think and not a Ceres. The mouth is the failing part in all but they are otherwise very fine studies. Then there were to my astonishment still finer ones of Miss Bridges and there were some of Miss Quail who is too evidently attitudinizing. . . .

Miss Vernon[2] paid me a long visit apologizing much for it. A sad account altogether of poor Uncle's state. The reason the two girls[3] were so pale on Friday was that they had overheard him speaking angrily to Miss Vernon as he so often does after a letter and they both cried very much about it. . . .

Burn this my child, will it not be better? I trust that thou art well, beloved, and that thou art having a happy Sunday and hearing words which will strengthen thee to do bravely and to bear patiently after the pattern of our Master.

1. Emily Ritchie, another of Richmond Ritchie's sisters.
2. See above, Letter 209, n. 2.
3. Horatio Tennyson's daughters, Maud and Violet.

233   *To Hallam Tennyson*

Aldworth,[1] *24 May 1870*

Own beloved,
We arrived here last night and thy dear letter is a welcome greeting. My kindest love to Mrs. Bradley and thanks for hers. A very sad parting from Farringford for but an hour before we left we heard the news of our dear friend Sir John[2] which the papers have probably told you before this. . . . I know, darling, this will grieve you. Few people took so much interest in thyself and Lionel as he. I hope to write about other things another day.

We have lost one of our dearest friends. Papa's dearest I think and most trusted, but one must not think of this in the face of the far greater sorrow at Swainston.[3] As for poor Lady Simeon I can fancy few states more forlorn than hers except that she has the love and the full confidence of her stepchildren. But what a family to be thrown upon her with not ample means moreover.

God bless thee, darling mine. I need not bid thee pray for them. One is so shocked not to have prayed more for one's friends when they are as we believe beyond the reach of prayer. Our best love.

1. For their summer home Emily Tennyson chose the name of the old Sellwood family seat, the little town of Aldworth in Berkshire.

2. Sir John Simeon died on 23 May 1870. On 27 June Tennyson wrote about Sir John to Lady Simeon: "He was the only man on earth, I verily believe, to whom I could, and have more than once opened my whole heart and he also has given me, in many a conversation at Farringford in my little attic, his utter confidence. I knew none like him for tenderness and generosity" (*AT*, p. 389).

3. The Simeons' home, Swainston Hall.

234   *To Hallam Tennyson*

Aldworth, 31 May 1870

Own beloved,

Papa has gone by the 9:52 train this morning on his sad journey.[1] I hope all went off well yesterday, darling mine. I send thee this letter of Lionel's as he desires. I am sure it will vex thee as it does us. We could not have thought that Lionel would have given in to such ungentlemanly, unchristian ways. I certainly should not think of writing to his tutor. It is much better for him that he should take the consequences of his conduct. The master is the master God appoints for him whatever he is and there is assuredly the best of reasons why he should be however it seems to us. This thou knoweth, and that it is by faith in the wisdom of God's daily providence in small things that we are trained to that faith which conquers death through Christ.

Aunt Tilly arrived yesterday and she is looking very well and is very cheerful and she thinks Papa is looking well and so do I.

1. To Swainston for Simeon's funeral.

235   *To Hallam Tennyson*

Aldworth, 1 June 1870

Beloved,
Papa arrived safely before nine last evening and had a little
dinner. . . . Dreadful as was the day he would not for anything
not have gone, they were so very grateful to him for going.
Both Lady Simeon and Louy saw him and I believe saw no one
else except the brothers. Poor Louy seized his hand and kissed
it and Lady Simeon said, "Do not forget me for the sake of him
that is gone." Johnnie[1] looked very good, Papa says, and as if
he meant to do what is right. He is to remain in the army. As to
the rest I don't know that anything is settled. The shrieks and
sobs were dreadful. Lady Simeon embracing the coffin in the
vault and Louy on the bench. . . . Nightingales were singing,[2]
beautiful roses were all about the house and gardens and lilacs
were in full bloom, and the contrast only added to the sadness.
. . .

1. John Stephen Barrington Simeon (1850-1909), fourth baronet,
M. P. from 1895 till 1906.
2. Both Sir John and the nightingales are immortalized in the lovely
lines "In the Garden at Swainston," which Tennyson wrote while waiting
for the funeral procession to leave Swainston:

> Nightingales sang in his woods:
>   The Master was far away:
> Nightingales warbled and sang
>   Of a passion that lasts but a day;
>   Still in the house in his coffin the Prince of
>   courtesy lay (ll. 6-10).

236   *To Hallam Tennyson*

Aldworth, 13 June 1870

Beloved,
I begin my letter to thee today because today Papa and I have
been married twenty years. It is a beautiful day. Papa is going
to stay dinner here I am glad to say but is to go up by the 8
o'clock train with Mr. and Mrs. Knowles to his own rooms. . . .
  You remember Sir Henry Taylor's son Aubrey.[1] I am grieved

to say he died on the 16th of May. His mother and sister
Eleanor went to meet the ship and were met by the sad news.
Mrs. Cameron told me of it. As I say to Lionel I thought I
would not tell you of it on our wedding day, but God so
ordered that it should come to us and there must be a message
to us in it, if it be only of thankfulness that he has spared us so
long to each other and of watchfulness as to whether we have
done or tried to do all we ought to have done for each other.

1. (1845–70). Despite a variety of lifelong infirmities, young Taylor
had shown great intellectual promise.

237   To Alfred Tennyson

Aldworth, 14 June 1870

Own dearest,
We have a delightfully warm day here today and a brooding
mist which makes the landscape very soft and beautiful as far
as one sees it.
  I was so afraid afterwards that what I said about a week
seeming so long when thou art away might sound as if I in the
smallest degree grudged thy being away and did not as thou
knowest I do with my heart rejoice that thou art in the way of
seeing people who may interest thee.

238   To Alfred Tennyson

Aldworth, 15 June 1870

Dearest,
I am afraid it is very hot for thee in town. Here the change is
delightful. . . . Certainly we have most zealous workmen. They
were up at three or four this morning, I believe, doing the
drains, making the old connection good.
  By slow degree the house is getting sweeter. Tilly is, I am
glad to say, better today so I hope she may be persuaded not to
go to a London doctor; though, of course, if he will set her

right more quickly she had better go being so nervous about herself as she is.

It was very good in thee to grant my request and see Paget. One has a horror of such a thing establishing itself.[1] I shall think of thee at the Metaphysical Club[2] tonight.

1. Tennyson was afflicted with eczema on his legs and back during much of the summer of 1870, and he was treated several times by Sir James Paget.
2. Tennyson was a charter member of the Metaphysical Society, an organization founded by James Knowles for the purpose of investigating religious and philosophical questions relating to the spread of positivism and agnosticism, from its formation on 21 April 1869 until a few months before its dissolution early in 1880. In his "Prefatory Sonnet to the 'Nineteenth Century,'" first published in the first issue of *Nineteenth Century,* in March 1877, Tennyson treated the relationship between the Metaphysical Society and the two magazines Knowles successively edited, *The Contemporary Review* and *Nineteenth Century.*

239   To Alfred Tennyson

Aldworth, 20 June 1870

Own dearest,

Mr. Grote's book on Utilitarian philosophy[1] is sent thee by the editor. There is nothing more to tell thee except that Tilly is better though still very wretched, poor soul. The piano[2] has been of great use as I have played as much as my arm will let me and music is the only thing she really cares for or at least the thing she cares most for as thou knowest. She also cries out at the dearth of novels in the house and wants especially to see *Lothair.*[3] Canst thou bring it? I, for my part, should like to read *Ginx's Baby* . . . .[4]

I am quite certain that no error is to be corrected except by a "counterblast" of truth apparently irrespective of it. The most by way of battle that can be admitted is an indignant apostrophe and even that not against opinion but only against practice.

However thou art too occupied to want to read long letters.

1. John Grote, *An Examination of the Utilitarian Philosophy* (of J. S. Mill), ed. J. B. Mayor (Cambridge, 1870).
2. Tennyson gave his wife a new piano for Aldworth in June 1870.

3. Benjamin Disraeli, *Lothair* (London, 1870).
4. J. E. Jenkins, *Ginx's Baby: His Birth and Other Misfortunes* (London, 1870).

240   To Hallam Tennyson

Aldworth, 1 July 1870

Own beloved,
I must write thee a few lines, but we have had guests in the house for so long now that I am very stupid. . . . We are still knee-deep in guests to be and Papa is going again to town. . . .

Aunty Nanny and Agnes go tomorrow. Mr. Jowett has been here since Wednesday and I do not know when he goes and I should not wish to know except that Lady Simeon is to come on Tuesday and desires to be alone with us. Louy is to come the Monday following. The Leaders[1] must if possible be packed in before the 15th. . . . Papa does not settle here one bit, so things are altogether rather embarrassing. God bless thee, beloved. Our best love.

1. A Mrs. Leader and a Miss Leader, possibly the wife and daughter of John Temple Leader (1810-1903), were at Aldworth from 18 to 22 July. Emily Tennyson wrote about their visit in her Journal: "I am glad to have seen so much more than I have done before of Mrs. Leader, being as she is an old friend of A.'s family." John Temple Leader's wife was Italian and might have been an "old friend" of Frederick Tennyson, who lived in Italy from 1835 until 1859.

241   To Alfred Tennyson

Aldworth, 14 July 1870

Own dearest,
How art thou and how is the poor leg? I have good news for thee. The agreement for the road is signed by Lord Egmont's agent and by ours and our bit of road may be begun any day. . . .[1] I have asked Mr. Simmons and Mr. Burdon[2] to lunch here to consult about the road on thy return for Lord Egmont has conceded so much that any trees necessary for making the road

may be cut down, and Mr. Simmons will not have them cut without first consulting thee. He and Mr. Albery[3] called in the morning and I saw the little man (Mr. Albery) might too easily yield, so I told him I had no idea of yielding to a crotchety old man and my parting advice was please hold your head a little high and Mr. Simmons has acted on it and has been "very stiff" as he expresses it. First Lord Egmont demanded that thou shouldst make the road thyself and that the parish would afterwards take to it and keep it in repair. Then besides he required that thou shouldst abandon for thyself and for all others the right of insisting on a good road down to the valley.

The road Mr. Simmons in thy name positively declined to make and said that thou wouldst not for a moment think of undertaking for others not to move about the road down to the valley though thou wouldst undertake not to move in the matter thyself. . . .

Lord Egmont's agent seemed rather astonished at the ground taken but I have no doubt this is the way to deal with my Lord and his agent.

1. See above, Letter 211.
2. Mr. Simmons was Tennyson's solicitor and Mr. Burdon represented Lord Egmont.
3. Simmons's assistant.

242   *To Alfred Tennyson*

Aldworth, 15 July 1870

Own dearest,
May the ten days do all for thee that Paget hopes and then I shall indeed rejoice in spite of thy absence. For myself thou knowest I have more faith in lying up on our lawn with the down breezes all around thee. I hope thou are not to be in bed.
. . .

Louy says she must go to her Uncle Cornwall's[1] tomorrow. I have felt as I used to do in old days talking with her for I can only talk when I may say just what I like, and to her I can, and I know that she likes it. I have grown too diffident of myself to think that anyone else does, having a strong feeling that one must have rosy cheeks, etc. to make one's talk generally acceptable. Thou wilt say that this is cynical. Perhaps it is. . . .

God bless thee, best beloved, and make thee soon well and happy meanwhile. Louy's love. Is Lord Houghton accepted?[2]

1. Cornwall Simeon (1820-80), Sir John Simeon's brother.
2. Richard Monckton Milnes was nominated by Tennyson and seconded by Sir John Lubbock for membership in the Metaphysical Society, but he was not elected when balloted for on 13 December 1870. Later Milnes did gain membership, evidently in July 1871.

243   *To William Allingham*

Aldworth, 8 August 1870

My dear Mr. Allingham,
We are delighted to hear that you are happier in town than you were in Lymington. All good happiness be yours for the future!

He has eczema again and has been under Paget, but I hope he is getting better. Only two months of the summer he has been unable to walk and a great part of the time a prisoner to bed and sofa, which is a pity. However one is sure it is all well some way.

244   *To Thomas Woolner*

Aldworth, 4 October 1870

My dear Mr. Woolner,
Would that some creative brain of some great statesman could devise a mode of vital union between England and her colonies that they might indeed be one. First, I would have every man among us trained to arms that we might keep the peace; then I would have everyone taught to read and write and sing and cypher, whether he would or no or whether his parents would or no; then I would have one great council formed by men from all the colonies of England, or rather Great Britain. These should originate legislative measures for discussion in a really imperial Parliament, which should, I hope, decide how best to give most to each other, not how to

keep most each for himself or his colony or his island.

But I shall weary you, and soon I hope you will come and talk to us about these and other matters. I am exceeding weary. We have had such an uninterrupted stream of guests and now our house is very full and will be yet for some time to come. All our relations, or many, want to see the new place. How are you still? Kindest remembrances to Mrs. Woolner and to "Guinevere"[1] whom Alfred admires much.

1. Woolner's half-lifesize statuette in marble, exhibited at the Royal Academy in 1872.

245   To Hallam Tennyson

Aldworth, 18 November 1870

Own beloved,

It is a fearful thought that we are just on the brink of war with Russia. Surely never even among savages was there so insolent a repudiation of a treaty as that contained in Gortschakoff's communication to our government and others concerned.[1] May God avert the war. The longer I live the more insufferable does war seem, though of course I would have instant war if the dispatch is not retracted. . . .

Papa declined the Cadiz journey. He felt that he was expected to make a poem about it or rather it had been expressly stated that he was and this, of course, he was very unlikely to do.[2] Moreover he is not well.

1. By the eleventh and fourteenth articles of the 1855 Treaty of Paris, ships of war of every nation, except for a few light police vessels, were thenceforward excluded from the Black Sea. Russia was bound to challenge the restrictions sooner or later, and, as a result of the encouragement of Germany's Count Bismarck, she did so in November 1870, when Price Gortschakoff declared that the Czar now felt himself obliged to reject Russia's prohibition from the sea. Although popular feeling against Russia ran extremely high, English statesmen realized the enormity of going to war over a provision which ultimately would be impossible to enforce, and on 7 February 1871, the restriction was annulled by the British Government.
2. The Royal Society astronomers who were planning a trip to Cadiz wanted the Laureate to go along in order to write a poem on the eclipse they expected to view. Tennyson of course rejected the proposal for

an assigned poem on a designated subject as " 'a thing absurd and out of the question' " (Journal, 20 November 1870).

246   To Alfred Tennyson

Farringford, 11 December 1870

Own dearest,

Mrs. Cameron and Annie Prinsep[1] came here last evening to tea. She[2] says that the Poet Laureate could not have had more honour paid him at Oxford than she had. She asked by one to dinner, by another to tea, by another to luncheon, and to a party at Dean Liddell's,[3] where the whole room was adorned with her photographs and many of the three or four hundred people there were saying, "Have you seen Mrs. Cameron's photographs? She is here tonight herself." "Oh, I should like to be introduced." So many were praising Hardinge, so many thanking her for this and that favour done to this and that relative at Freshwater that at last she scarcely knew what to do. A confession not common for Mrs. Cameron certainly. Mr. Cameron has been so very well, but he went out yesterday without an overcoat and got cold. It is very cold here but bright today. Yesterday rather misty. God bless thee, dearest.

1. A daughter of Henry Thoby and Sarah Prinsep.
2. Mrs. Cameron.
3. Henry George Liddell (1811-98), domestic chaplain to Prince Albert from 1846 until the Prince's death; headmaster of Westminster School, 1846-55; vice chancellor of Oxford, 1870-74; professor of ancient history at the Royal Academy, 1882 until his death; and compiler, with Robert Scott, of the well-known *Liddell and Scott's Greek-English Lexicon* (1843). It was for Liddell's daughter Alice (later Mrs. Reginald Hargreaves) that Charles Dodgson wrote *Alice's Adventures in Wonderland.*

247   To Hallam Tennyson

Farringford, 14 February 1871

Beloved,

Many thanks for thy most welcome letter. That we shall look

anxiously for news of work and play and of all things that
concern thee I need not tell thee. My first request is that thou
wilt not keep on wet clothes. The rain on Sunday made me
very sad thinking of my boys. Remember, in thy strong
fatalistic feeling, that it is preordained that I am thy Mother
and that thy Father is not less anxious than I about thee, and
moreover that however the facts may be reconciled (and I fully
admit that we know nothing of the mode of reconciliation),
man's will is free in Christ. Let us shut our eyes to the rest
until we have light to see clearly.

Now I will tell thee my little home story. Sunday was too
rainy for a walk. In the evening Papa read me a good deal of
Westcott's *Church of the Resurrection*[1] and then two passages
in Shakespeare. Yesterday was warm and sunny and delightful.
Mrs. Cameron came up in the morning. . . . After luncheon
Papa took me to the sunny corner, the little nursery garden by
the back gate and afterwards I walked three or four times up
and down before the study window. Then we sent the carriage
for Mrs. Cameron and she and Annie[2] came up in it, but only
Mrs. Cameron drove with Papa. They went the Yarmouth
round, home by the long way that is.

1. Brooke Foss Westcott's *The Gospel of the Resurrection* (London,
1866).
2. Annie Prinsep.

248   *To Hallam Tennyson*

Farringford, 16 February 1871

Beloved,
The styles of [Seneca and St. Paul] seem to me to indicate the
difference of their natures for though of course every man
living is too complex a being for it to be said of him he is
simply this or that, yet that he has a tendency to this or that
must be said of every human being or as far as we see he could
not have what we call character, the elements differently
mixed, that is, I suppose.

St. Paul	Seneca
Love: Devotion of the whole man	Admiration: Half to the world, half to goodness
Discipline of the whole man *for God's sake in Christ*	Partial discipline *for Seneca's sake*
St. Paul's style that of a man lost in his subject, the passion of it creating the style	Seneca divided between subject and style, Seneca always superintending the style

May we not learn from a study of the two men how much we owe to the revelation of the personal God. How much strength lies in the possibility thus afforded of self-devotion to a living Being higher than our highest thoughts, more loving than the most loving heart can divine, wiser than the wisest can forbode, juster than the justest, in the place of that diffused impersonal nimbus-like existence, however beautiful and glorious, Seneca's ideal. Be sure the central fire of man is in the heart kindled by the heart of God, if I may so speak. No intellect, however glorious, unwarmed, unvivified by this can attain to the real greatness of man. None can be so warmed in whom the spirit of God does not dwell but of the times and degrees and measures and modes of this indwelling it becomes not us to speak. I doubt not that not only among the Jews holy men of old spoke, moved by the Holy Ghost. I think Seneca affords a warning especially needed by this age drifting as it seems to be into Comtism.[1]

God bless thee, darling. Our best love. Take care of thyself this damp weather I entreat thee.

1. The Tennysons frowned upon materialist philosophies and found Auguste Comte's *Philosophie Positive* especially repugnant.

249   To Hallam Tennyson

Farringford, 17 February 1871

Beloved,

. . . Papa is still busy transplanting. I walked to the triangle
and to the front door yesterday in an interval of comparatively
clear sky but I could not do more. It was odd and yet not odd,
Papa said last evening much the same I had said to thee about
the deadly curse of these days, the loss in so many of the belief
in a personal God and in the human soul. He feels that we are
on the edge of a mortal strife for the life of all that is great in
Man and that this will be the cause. Pray God we may hold
fast to the faith delivered to the saints, one and all of us, and
be ready to fight the good fight for it.

Mrs. Grosvenor Hood[1] said of thee, "I do love that boy." She
had tears in her eyes when she spoke of thee. She said thou art
so truthful. So let no smallest breath of untruth dim thy
sincerity. God bless thee, own darling. Our best love.

1. Mr. and Mrs. Francis Grosvenor Hood lived at Heathfield, Norton,
near Yarmouth. Mrs. Hood was a good friend of the Tennyson family
and was particularly fond of Hallam and Lionel.

250   To Hallam Tennyson

Farringford, 21 February 1871

Beloved,

Couldst thou have seen poor Lady Elcho's[1] face on Saturday
thou wouldst know that sons ought to take care of themselves
now, even if thou hadst not known it before. I never saw
anything sadder. She had a restless look of always looking for
something. His manner has a boyish joy about it that reminds
me a little of Sir John Simeon. I fancy him sad beneath this.
. . .

Yesterday Papa and I went in the closed carriage to call at
the Terrace and then we went to the Camerons and saw all the
alterations. Wonderful improvements they are. Afterwards he
and Mrs. Cameron went in the open carriage to Yarmouth. Mrs.
Cameron drove up in a Fly soon after five on Sunday. She
dined with us. We talked gravely and heard the Ceylon letters[2]

which are good, and she said she had a delicious evening. . . .

As to army organization, I suppose thou wilt say thou takest it for granted that as it may be the duty of every son of England to help defend her if invaded, it must be the duty of the state to provide that each of her sons should be instructed in this duty.

Secondly, that England having advanced so far on the road of Christian civilization as to have come to recognize the fact that wars of ambition are unholy wars, and that therefore it is only wars of defense . . . that can be Christian wars, the inquiry as to army organization must be chiefly limited to the question, how the best defensive army can be formed and each son of England best fitted to take his place in it should the dire need rise:

To begin with, compulsory drill for every son born to England rich or poor as long as he is at school.[3]

Voluntary enlistment without bounty that there may be no bribe. Pay improved. . . .

Libraries in every fort and barrack. Morning and evening prayers, very short.

Every sort of trade and art necessary to the outfit of the army, its food, shelter, clothing, taught, as well as all military arts. . . .

Each [soldier] should . . . have the option of taking part of his retiring pension in the way of help to a colony and land there. . . . The aim should be to lift the soldier up to a sense of the true dignity of his post in itself and devotion for the good of others.

1. Anne Frederica, Lady Elcho, and her husband Richard, tenth Earl of Wemyss, visited Farringford on 16 February. The Elchos lost their first son, Francis, on 22 July 1870. Another son, Arthur, died in 1847, and a third, Alfred Walter, lived only until 1873.

2. Letters from Charles Hay Cameron, who was in Ceylon managing his estates most of the time.

3. In 1885 the Tennysons saw their dream of a school designated to educate and train young men for commissions in the Army realized in the "Gordon Boys' Home." The poet was instrumental in founding the home on the Isle of Wight, and he served as its first president. Emily Tennyson helped plan the home, named in honor of General Charles George ("Chinese") Gordon (1833-85), with whom her husband had discussed his idea for such a home, in 1879, and she wrote two songs, a morning hymn and an evening hymn, which the boys sang each day. The "Evening Hymn," in particular, evidences her unshakable faith in an ever-present, personal God:

Great God, who knowest each man's need
Bless Thou our watch and guard our sleep;
Forgive our sins of thought and deed
And in Thy peace Thy servants keep.
We thank Thee for the day that's done
We trust Thee for the day to be;
Thy love we learn in Christ Thy Son
O May we all His glory see.

Tennyson wrote an "Epitaph on General Gordon" for the "Gordon Boys' Home" which was first published in *The Times* on 7 May 1885.

251   *To Edward Lear*

Farringford, 22 February 1871

My dear Mr. Lear,
It is a very long time since I wrote to you or you to me but I do not think that you have failed to think of us more than we have of you. The time has, I fear, been a troublous one with you[1] from what I have heard, and it has not been untroubled with me though, as Hallam says, we must not complain of anything so long as we four are left to each other. Dear old boy, you would love him, I am sure, and say that he has grown up the same honest, faithful, affectionate, or rather I should say, deeply loving nature that he was first. Old Lionel too is much the same as when he scampered about the house with his hair flying behind him only instead of dancing and singing all to himself he plays on the piano. He is having a few music lessons at Eton and Hallam has had singing lessons at Marlborough and is considered to have a fine bass voice. They are both about six feet. . . .

Poor Ally has had a dreary eight or nine months rather from eczema in the leg and the treatment for it. He is better but not well. Much more languid than I like to see him. He has never got over our loss in May. Knowing Sir John, you may know something of what he was to us. So much sympathy, love, and knowledge of the world joined to so tender a friendship we are scarcely likely to meet again. . . .

Park House seems to be much as usual. Unutterably sad. Edmund, Cecilia, and Lucy[2] were with us more than a fortnight at Aldworth and liked the place. . . . For six weeks Ally was kept entirely to bed and sofa. Most unwise considering his nature and the slightness of the ailment in the leg.

1. During the autumn of 1870 Lear lapsed into a long period of depression, and he almost abandoned his plans for building a new house at San Remo.
2. The Edmund Lushingtons' third daughter, Lucia Maria (1851-73).

252   *To Hallam Tennyson*

Farringford, 24 February 1871

Beloved,

Poor Mrs. Cameron has been in bed two days from cold taken we fear in the open carriage. She sent Papa the new volume of Swinburne poems.[1] He says it is blasphemous so we think it is just as well that it should not be sent to Ceylon,[2] its final destination if not found too bad to be sent.

1. *Songs before Sunrise* (1871).
2. Mrs. Cameron intended sending the poems to her husband.

253   *To Hallam Tennyson*

Farringford, 28 February 1871

Beloved,

I have walked again to Maiden's Croft. I am decidedly stronger than I have been for some years at this season I am thankful to say. Papa is pretty well. He is still busy transplanting which is a good thing for him. . . .

I have had an invitation from Lady Stanley of Alderly[1] to go to her house for the presentation of the little "homage" to Carlyle—the clock which I helped to give,[2] but of course I could not have gone even if the note had reached me in time.

1. Henrietta Maria Stanley of Alderley (1807-95), widow of Edward John, second Baron, one of the original lady visitors of Queen's College, London, in 1848, and in 1886 a leader of the Women's Liberal Unionist Association.

2. In October 1870, Anne Thackeray asked Emily Tennyson to join in a little conspiracy to give Carlyle a gift. A clock was subsequently purchased, and it was presented to Carlyle at Lady Stanley's home on 27 February 1871. Emily Tennyson signed the "paper of signature," now preserved in the Carlyle Museum, Chelsea, which also included the names of Louisa, Lady Ashburton, Henrietta Froude, Anne Farrar, Juliet Pollock, Mrs. Oliphant, Anne Thackeray, Lady Stanley, and others.

254   To Hallam Tennyson

Farringford, 7 March 1871

Beloved,

I am indeed delighted that thou hast been enabled to succeed with the essays, and if any hints of mine have been of any use, of course this is a new source of pleasure and thanksgiving. My own feeling is that the *influence* of philosophy was greatest about the time of our Lord's birth. It was then a religion to so many or at least a moral guide. The intellectual interest in it was not less I suppose in the days of the Realists and Idealists but I think that it has had to weld itself to Christianity for any deeper interest. . . . Few have seen that there was no welding needed, that they were in fact one. Philosophy being included in Christianity as the lesser in the greater. Origen I believe and some of the early Neo-Platonists knew this more fully than it has generally been known since. . . .

We have now reverted to the old plan for Papa's room. The lower room is to be treated as a hall with the stairs running in it which will make it more spacious for dancing or acting, and when this and the greenhouse are lighted the suite of rooms will be very pretty, I hope.[1]

1. Sir Charles Tennyson explains that in the spring of 1871 Tennyson built, under a Mr. Waterhouse's direction, a large library with a playroom or ballroom under it, on the south side of the house. The new library was normally approached from the main Farringford staircase, but Tennyson had a turret staircase built on the south side leading into the garden, supposedly to afford a rapid exit when undesirable visitors were advancing on him (C. Tennyson, *Stars and Markets*, pp. 16–17).

255   To Hallam Tennyson

Farringford, 21 March 1871

Beloved,

. . . If more labour were spent in trying to teach people to follow in the steps of Christ and less in squabbling about dress or straining after definitions of subjects beyond our grasp it would be better for us. "If ye continue in my word then are ye my disciples indeed. And ye shall know the truth."[1] People do not seem to understand the distinction of seeing so much of God as shall draw up our souls in adoration and of seeing so much as shall enable us logically to detail the awful wonders of His Being as though we were anatomizing a human frame. One shrinks from writing such words, but they represent the feeling of many in these days only too truly, I fear.

Darling mine, we should certainly have a feeling of security in having you with Mr. and Mrs. Bradley . . . but on the other hand the first spirits of the day among the young are, I suppose, at Trinity and you will have Mr. Clark and Mr. Maurice and I hope also Mr. Westcott[2] as friends though there can scarcely be the same nearness of friendship with any of them as with the Bradleys.

You might grow up stronger by being forced to rely more on yourself in God. Strength is that in which the age is preeminently deficient. We would fain see a greater measure of it in our boys than we see in others.

1. John 8: 31-32.
2. Brooke Foss Westcott (1825-1901), Regius Professor of Divinity at Cambridge. In 1883 he became Canon of Westminster and in 1890 Bishop of Durham.

256   To Hallam Tennyson

Farringford, 2 May 1871

Beloved,

I quite agree with thee that death perfects the individuality not destroys it. Though perhaps one cannot quite see how this should be, believing that death makes one more like to God. I suppose it is only part of the old mystery of the relation between Finite and Infinite, the Relative and the Absolute. On our side of the question the best illustration is that of branches of the vine, members of the body, but on God's side if I may so speak this seems to tend to pantheism which the more strongly one feels one's own individuality the less one can accept, though in one's blindness and one's ignorance one can shape nothing in its place beyond the vague sense of personality. I have sometimes thought that even with God there may be a distinction between the actual person of personality and its presence. I have a feeling that my person is not diffused through a room for instance though my presence is. One is forced in these days on trying to reconcile conflicting ideas, but I believe the thing most wholesome for us is to acknowledge the impossibility, as I believe the wisest must do when he has in some degree taken the measure of humanity. . . .

Annie Thackeray went yesterday. . . . Papa read "Sir Tristram"[1] to Annie alone one day and last night to us all. It is very grand. He also read "The Holy Grail" to us and Béranger's "Napoléon" to us on Sunday. . . . We are thinking of getting together people who agree with us about the colonies or rather Mr. Knowles is thinking of it. We have quite converted him to our view.

1. Tennyson first published "The Last Tournament" in *The Contemporary Review* in December 1871.

257   *To Hallam Tennyson*

Farringford, 12 May 1871

Beloved,

I have made such small corrections in language as seemed to me desirable.[1] I have only read a little bit of the book but thy notice gives me an excellent idea of a whole and of the whole, as I believe, and leaves me at least with the desire to read the whole for myself and will leave others also I hope with the same desire.

It seems to me very well done as far as it goes, with the exception of a few colloquial inaccuracies, such as I think no gentleman should admit in conversation even and certainly not in print unless by way of satire on language. Papa found the same fault. "English undefiled" be thy motto as far as our language goes! I have numbered the pages as they have to be read. Glad indeed shall I be if they are of any use. Speaking of Matt Arnold, couldst not thou add "and others we might name still oftener," or some such sentence which would reserve thee from the implication that Matt Arnold is the crown of poets in these days. Of course what it wants as a critique is a little more of why the poem is good, whether the verse is good and why and so on.

1. Hallam had sent his mother his critique of Arnold's *Poetical Works* (2 vols., 1869).

258   To Hallam Tennyson

Aldworth, 13 June 1871

Beloved,
This is our wedding day so I write though I scarcely think thou wilt get the letter before thy return, but it is a day of thanksgiving for me and I know therefore that it is one for thee too if thou remember it, thou darling who hast so great a part in the thank-offering of my life and who will by God's help have an even greater and greater.

My boy, we had chosen for thee the lowlier and safer lot of a small college and had quite given up Trinity. I know not how it came to pass that thou hast thought otherwise unless it be that it seemed useless to speak of what was not to be till January, as we thought, and so perhaps we had silently made up our minds. Well, now I suppose it will be otherwise[1] and I suppose there are strong reasons for the decision to which Mr. Farrar[2] and thyself have come. May they be of God! God bless thee, thou best beloved. Our best love.

1. Hallam entered Trinity College, Cambridge, in October 1872.
2. Frederick William Farrar (1831-1903), headmaster of Marlborough from 1871 till 1876, archdeacon of Westminster, 1883, chaplain to the House of Commons, 1890, and Dean of Canterbury, 1895 till death.

259   To Alfred Tennyson

Aldworth, 7 July 1871

Beloved,
We think from thy message that it is under the impression that
Hallam would like to go to the party that thou hast said he may
come, so he follows his own inclination and does not come. He
says that Mr. Gladstone will only say in his heart, "What an
ugly boy," and turn his back and think no more about him so
he says he had better not present himself to the world in this
the least favourable period of his life while he is shy and
shaggy. He telegraphs however that if it is really thy wish that
he should come he may still do so. I at first pressed his coming
but finding him so averse from the garden party, I have agreed
to his telegraphing, thinking also that perhaps it is better he
should not be too soon taken into society but only see what he
can at home though he is not a young lady.

260   To Alfred Tennyson

Aldworth, 12 July 1871

Own dearest,
I rejoice to think that everyone makes so much of thee and I
trust that thou wilt return as confident as thy wife in the love
people have for thee. I will write to the d'Eyncourts[1] in case
thou shouldst not be able to call. . . . Hast thou been to the
Palgraves and the Woolners? God bless thee, dearest, and bring
thee home safely. Our best love to thee.

1. The family of Louis Charles Tennyson d'Eyncourt (1814-96), of
Bayons Manor, the son of Tennyson's Uncle Charles.

On 7 August Tennyson and Hallam set off on a ten-day tour
in North Wales, stopping first at Llanberis, a convenient starting
point for the easiest ascent of Mount Snowdon. From Llanberis

and Snowdon they proceeded to Beddgelert, near the southern base of Snowdon, and thence to the Vale Gwynant, where they viewed Moel Hebog and Llyn Gwynant looming in the distance. After a visit with the Archibald Peels at Wrexham, the poet and his son returned to Farringford, arriving unexpectedly on the sixteenth. Soon Hallam left for Marlborough, and Tennyson again journeyed into Wales, this time visiting the George Howards (afterwards Lord and Lady Carlisle) at Naworth Castle, usually associated with "Belted Will Howard," who is described by Scott in the "Lay of the Last Minstrel." In mid-September he visited his cousins' Brancepeth Castle which, he informed Emily, wanted the simple grandeur of Naworth with its ancient pictures and its medieval armor and tapestries.

261   To Hallam Tennyson

Aldworth, 29 August 1871

Beloved,

. . . Papa will not walk with Lionel. I got him to take Mr. and Mrs. Barlow[1] down the hill yesterday, and on Saturday he walked home with Mr. and Mrs. Lewes. . . .[2] I called there and stayed some time and then left him and he read some of "Maud." Mrs. Lewes said that his reading ought to be taken down in notes recitative-wise, but that will not give his magnificent voice with its delicate intonations. God bless thee, own darling.

1. Freshwater friends of the Tennysons.
2. During the summer of 1871, George Eliot and G. H. Lewes, who had been living together since 1854, resided at Shottermill, near Haslemere and the Tennysons. The *Materials for a Life of A. T.* and some few copies of the first edition of the *Memoir* contain Emily Tennyson's account of her visit with "Mr. and Mrs. Lewes," but Hallam Tennyson subsequently canceled the entry. George Eliot's letter of 5 November 1880 to Mrs. Tennyson (unpublished, T.R.C.) acknowledges another attempted visit and testifies to her appreciation of the Tennysons' acceptance: "The regret I felt in finding your cards that my drive had happened when I might have had the pleasure of seeing you has been deepened by my own inability to get to Aldworth. . . . I cannot bear to seem unmindful of any friendly sign made to me by you and yours."

262   *To Hallam Tennyson*

Aldworth, 20 September 1871

Own darling,

Papa has returned seeming well and in excellent spirits. He only stayed Sunday, from Saturday to Monday that is, at Brancepeth. He greatly prefers the old bare border castle[1] where all is bright and simple. . . .

I write today to tell thee of Papa's return and also to say, hast thou well made up thy mind about Trinity? for this letter to the master must, of course, be a final settling of the matter.

Papa saw remains of old Roman inscriptions about the wall and the valleys and in all directions there are battlements, even on the farmhouses. Papa is very glad to have had this little peep into the Borderland. They were going to have a ball for all their tenants and the gentry round in the great hall ninety feet long where all were to dance together as in old times, and Mrs. George Howard was laughing over a letter from a great squiress near who said that it was all very well for her daughters to look on but that they must keep their position. . . .

I fear it will never do for Lionel to go up to Trinity but that is not sufficient reason for thy not going. God knows whether it is best for you to be put together at college or not. I have longed for you to be together but Mr. Bradley will take care of him.[2] I think Lionel's name had better be put down at University to show our feeling towards Mr. Bradley. He is so sure that he can do nothing in mathematics or arithmetic, and I am doubtful whether Mr. Bradley's supervision during the whole of his stay, as we may hope, would not be better than thy help and care for only a part of the time. . . .

Our Lionel goes tomorrow. I am glad he should get out of the way of this frequent sporting which is bad for him if only that he will sometimes go without anything but beer all day. He is shooting at Vale Wood today and of course he reads nothing, but I shall sadly miss the old darling who is very good to me.

1. Naworth Castle.
2. The Tennysons intended to send Lionel to University College, Oxford, where Granville Bradley was master from 1870 till 1881, but he went instead to Trinity College, Cambridge, in the autumn of 1873.

263   To Hallam Tennyson

Aldworth, 28 November 1871

Beloved,

We rejoice in thy prizes,[1] darling, I need not say. Mr. Farrar wrote us a most kind note of congratulation on thy success and I congratulated him on having instituted the prize. What a pleasure it will be to hear thee read thy scenes, old darling, if we are spared to see thee three weeks hence.

I think certainly Papa had better write to the master of Trinity[2] and say that we have resolved on employing thy time till October either at Marlborough or abroad,[3] seeing they object to having thee at Christmas and that we feel it best on consideration that rules should not be broken for thee. . . .

Thou wilt be glad to hear that Papa has done a little song about the day of our dear Sir John's burial. It is not quite finished yet, perhaps, so I will not send it but I will keep it for Lionel and thyself. . . . Do not get cold in these last weeks but come home well if possible. Our best love.

1. Scholastic awards, possibly for a play Hallam had written.
2. Dr. William Hepworth Thompson (1810–86), an ex-Apostle, became master of Trinity College in 1866, after the death of Dr. William Whewell.
3. In August 1872, Tennyson took his wife and sons to France, and Hallam remained a month at Fontainebleau to study French with a Protestant clergyman named Pasteur Brand.

Tennyson and Emily left Aldworth on 5 December after an unusually long stay there, to be met at the Lymington Station by Mrs. Cameron, who rushed to greet them with open arms. Lionel joined his parents at Farringford on the fifteenth, and he was followed by Hallam four days later.

264   To Hallam Tennyson

Farringford, 8 December 1871

Beloved,
Sweet would it have been to thy ears to have heard Papa say
when [the Camerons] were pressing him to go to Ceylon with
Hardinge, "But I shall not see Hallam." He feels very much
tempted to go and indeed is chiefly held back from going by
the feeling that after all it will not be the West Indies, his ideal
of the tropics. Hardinge would wait until the 23rd if he would
go, and he would return with the governor.[1] I would he had
not this longing for the tropics. God bless thee, beloved. Our
best love to thee.

1. Sir Hercules Robinson, first Baron Rosmead (1824-97), governor
of Hong Kong, 1859-65; of Ceylon, 1865-72; and of New Zealand,
1879-80; and high commissioner of South Africa, 1880-89.

265   To Hallam Tennyson

Farringford, 3 March 1872

Beloved,
Thy letter is very interesting to me. I love to hear the thoughts
that come to thee on reading books and I think I have more
than once told thee that to my mind the highest fruit they can
yield to each man is the thoughts they awaken in himself. . . .
    I have this morning finished the thick volume of de
Pressensé.[1] I always knew my inclinations were Eastern
Church not Western but I did not until I finished this volume
know how Eastern my Christianity is either as to degree or
mode. "The witness of the Soul" being more essentially
Eastern than I knew and the ecclestiastical form more
essentially Western than I knew. . . .
    Lionel has sent me a really admirable essay. . . . Papa has
just read aloud two sheets of it and intends to finish the
remaining two and a bit. Lionel has also had the highest mark
for his verses three times this half so I do hope the poor old
laddy has at last aroused himself from his H.H.H.C. stupor or
torpor.[2]

1. *Heresy and Christian Doctrine,* vol. 3 of Edmund de Pressensé's *Histoire des trois premiers siècles de l'Église Chrétienne,* translated by Annie Harwood, 6 vols. (London, 1869-77).
2. Henry Herschel Hay Cameron was noted for his academic delinquency. Emily Tennyson found him lacking both in industry and in character, and she told Mrs. Cameron in February 1873, when Henry went to London to seek an acting career, that she feared he had not the energy either to do great things on stage or to prevent himself from being led into imprudence by his associates.

266   To Hallam Tennyson

Farringford, 15 March 1872

Beloved,

. . . Louy Simeon asked to come yesterday as Johnnie[1] was out. She slept here and is now walking with Papa. Uncle Charlie and Aunt Louy intend to stay until next Thursday.[2] Uncle Charlie has grown so wonderfully like Grandpapa in expression and sometimes in manner too. The theological discussions are not stormy now. No one can be more loving than both Uncle and Auntie are. I believe myself that being here has been an excellent thing for him. He seems quite to enjoy Mrs. Cameron and Louy Simeon, for instance. God bless thee, own beloved. Our best love to thee. It is most kind in Mr. Farrar but it is quite out of the question my leaving home at all events and I don't think Papa would be likely to go without me.

1. Sir John Simeon's son, John Barrington Simeon.
2. When Charles and Louisa Turner departed on 22 March, Emily Tennyson wrote in her Journal: "These partings are solemn now. Charlie looks so fragile it makes one count the days with him" (*AT,* p. 396).

Hallam left Marlborough on 3 April for the final time, to be greeted at home by Frederick Pollock, Mrs. Cameron and her son Charlie, and Lionel, who had arrived on 28 March, in addition to his mother and father. On 20 June the Tennysons left for Aldworth, where they remained until August, when they set off for a holiday trip to France, their fourth together. Tennyson spent his days at Blackdown working on "Gareth and Lynette," but he devoted his nights to his wife and sons, reading Shakespeare to them after dinner every evening except Sunday. On 4 July he went up to London to take a draft of "Gareth and Lynette" to press, and he remained there, perhaps to resolve confusions resulting from a poor transcription, until the fifteenth, when he returned to Aldworth with Mrs. William Brookfield. By the end of the month the Tennysons were also entertaining James Spedding, James Knowles, and Willingham Rawnsley, but they were free in time to sail for France on 7 August.

In Paris Emily was most gratified by her visit to the Sainte Chapelle with its magnificent stained-glass windows depicting eleven hundred and thirty Biblical scenes, but she sorrowed for the French citizenry who looked sad and subdued. On 14 August the Tennysons left Hallam with Pasteur Brand at Fontainebleau and journeyed into Burgundy, pausing at the historical capital, Dijon. Next day Tennyson, Emily, and Lionel visited the Chartreuse de Champmol, founded in the fourteenth century by Philippe le Hardi, and the thirteenth-century Cathedral of Saint-Bénigue. Continuing southward they went to Lyon and Mâcon, and thence to Vienne, rich in Gallo-Roman ruins, including the Corinthian temple, built in the early first century and dedicated to Augustus and Livia, which became a Christian church in the fifth century. Emily was particularly impressed by the temple and by the ancient Christian tombs in the churches of St. Maurice and St. Pierre, and she described in her Journal a certain sarcophagus with "two places in it and two skulls side by side," adding that she would like Tennyson and herself to lie thus together in their grave. En route to Grenoble the family stopped at Valence, where Emily addressed Hallam at Fontainebleau.

267   To Hallam Tennyson

Valence, 18 August 1872

Beloved,
I had thought to have written thee from Grenoble after having, as I had hoped, received thine but Papa was slightly deranged yesterday by a hot walk . . . so we thought it more prudent to

take a shorter journey and came here. It is now by no means
the primitive place we found it twenty-one years ago,[1] but one
in which I am thankful to rest today.

Before leaving Dijon where my last was written we drove
round the Chartreuse to the principal churches, Lionel ordering
our progress through them in very creditable fashion, he
having previously walked to them with Papa and alone. As it
was the Feast of the Assumption we had a touch of divine
strains and were very sorry, Lionel and I, that we could not
stay and hear more. On Friday we went by boat to Lyon from
Mâcon where we slept on Thursday. From Lyon we went by
rail to Vienne. A very interesting city on account of its early
Christian history, as thou knowest, and also by the remains still
to be seen there. Whenever they dig at all deeply they come
upon mosaics and walls of Roman houses.

I cannot tell thee the pleasure it was to see the ancient
Christian tombs. . . . They are in an exceedingly old church,[2]
some part of it, they say, of the fifth century! It is now being
restored. It reminded me somewhat of the Church of St.
Ambrose near Milan, though that is of brick, I think, this of
stone. . . . Papa is I hope quite well today and slept
notwithstanding our having had a wedding party in the house
last night dancing and singing and making loud mirth. Our
best love.

1. The Tennysons passed through Valence en route to Italy in July
1851.
2. Probably the twelfth-century church of St. André le Bas.

268   *To Hallam Tennyson*

Grenoble, 20 August 1872

Beloved,
We have received both thy dear letters and we are most
thankful for them I need not say. Papa said yesterday that it
was the best day we had had and we agreed. Certainly the
drive along the valley of the Isère made one long especially for
thee. There was such a dreamy magic light on the huge crags
which stretched in a long vista. Here and there gold-coloured
patches and streaks made the effect peculiarly rich and then at

the base of the bare crags came the richest valley clothed with vines and fruit trees and crops, the Isère running through them and here and there picturesque houses and villages. . . .

Papa is, I think, very well considering we should all be better if we were not pursued by fêtes of one kind or another. However they will make one value the quiet of home all the more I hope. I rejoice to hear that thou art gaining words and that thy accent is said to be good.

269   To Hallam Tennyson

Aix les Bains, 31 August 1872

Beloved,

Papa and Lionel did not arrive till after eleven from the Dent du Chat having accomplished their 1875 metres bravely and this on a mountain steeper than any part of Mont Blanc. The guide praises them both as good "montagnards" but Lionel, he says, is like "un oiseau." He is out today with the guide in honor of the first day of La Chape.[1] He wants him to hunt chamois with him. Yesterday Papa and he went to see the tombs of the Dukes of Savoy,[2] but they are quite modern and disappointed them altogether, but they liked their row on the lake.[3] Papa was so good as to let me have a row of half an hour first.

This morning Papa has been looking at the different antiquities fished up from the lake, some of the Stone some of the Bronze Age. Vases of the Stone Age were the only things he had not seen before elsewhere. . . . Altogether this has been a very good part of our journey, I hope, for Papa. . . . I shall write when I can fix the day when we hope to meet thee if not before. We all wish Louy Simeon all happiness I am sure as heartily as anyone can wish it.[4]

1. A French holiday in honor of Saint Martin.
2. The chateau of the Dukes of Savoy is in Chambéry, only a few miles south of Aix-les-Bains.
3. Aix-les-Bains lies on the bank of Lake Bourget.
4. Louy Simeon married Richard Ward on 29 October 1872.

Leaving Aix-les-Bains on 2 September, Tennyson, Lionel, and Emily traveled through Geneva and Lausanne to Fontainebleau, where they visited the Château of Fontainebleau and the famous royal forest, and were rejoined by Hallam. Thence the family returned to England, by way of Amiens and Boulogne, and reached Aldworth on the twelfth. Soon Lionel returned to Eton and Hallam left for his first term at Trinity College, where his mother, as usual, kept him informed of affairs at home. Although there were likely also many letters to Lionel, few have survived, and it is the Hallam letters almost exclusively which inform us of activities at Aldworth and Farringford during the early 1870s.

270   *To Hallam Tennyson*

Aldworth, 25 October 1872

Beloved,

The Peels[1] left yesterday. They were very affectionate and much wanted Papa to gratify Lord and Lady Russell[2] by going to Pembroke Lodge. They begged me to go too but this will not be and I fear Papa will scarcely go though it would be good for him to have a talk with the old statesman once again. . . .

Papa is pleased with the review in the *Times* yesterday.[3] It is certainly meant to be complimentary though I cannot consider it altogether appreciative. I hope thy copy reached thee. Say if thou art content to give the brooch with Lionel to Louy Simeon.[4] It is very pretty, I think.

Oh, I must tell thee that there are books[5] sent to the Bradleys, Mr. Jowett, Mr. Bright,[6] Mr. Farrar, Mrs. Cornish,[7] Annie Thackeray, Mr. Stone,[8] and Mr. Clark, in addition to the Master of Trinity's copy. . . . I have had two delightful evenings with Papa. On one we talked. Last evening he read me part of Ford's *Broken Heart*. Mr. Knowles comes tomorrow. Rather a pity that he should come when Lionel is here but it cannot be helped. God bless thee, beloved. Our best love.

1. The Archibald Peels of Wrexham.
2. John, first Earl Russell (1792–1878), prime minister from 1846 to 1852, and again in 1865, and his second wife, the former Frances Anna Maria Elliot, daughter of the second Earl of Minto.

3. The general tone of the 24 October review of the *Gareth and Lynette* volume, published earlier that month by Strahan and Co., is indicated in the following excerpt: "The title of this small volume is *Gareth and Lynette, Etc.*, but the Etcetera is somewhat deceiving, for it includes nothing more than the reprint of *The Last Tournament*. We have not so much as one lesser song or poem of any sort, and it is greatly to be regretted that such poets as Mr. Tennyson and Mr. Browning should have so little time or care for that minor music which makes up a large part of the fame and work of some of our greatest singers. . . . Busied with antique webs spun out of their own fancy, the poets of our time . . . pay little attention to what is happening in the world around them. . . . But without pursuing these sad reflections let us come to 'Gareth and Lynette' which is a truly charming story of British chivalry, not equal in power and passion and in analysis of human nature to the elder *Idylls of the King*, but in its clear and admirable diction, in its well-continued and simple plot, and in its refined and poetic imagination of knightly and womanly character well-worthy of the poet-hand which has written it."

4. See above, Letter 269, n. 4.

5. Copies of the new *Gareth and Lynette* volume.

6. Probably the John Bright who was Lionel Tennyson's housemaster at Mr. Paul's.

7. Blanche Warre Cornish (d. 1922), best remembered for her novel *Alcestis* (1873).

8. Possibly Edward Daniel Stone (1831-97), the assistant master at Eton. See above, Letter 194, n. 1.

271   To Hallam Tennyson

Aldworth, 29 October 1872

Beloved,

Our life and strength come mainly from within and we must have time to talk with ourselves and to realize in the depths of our souls the talk of others and above all to hold communion with God if we would grow as we should grow. . . .

Mr. Farrar wrote to Farringford and so did the Duchess of Argyll. Both very kind letters. Mr. Farrar says:

> Pray accept my very hearty thanks for your
> noble "Gareth and Lynette"! It is full of those
> great moral teachings which I for one regard as

the brightest function of the poet when he works with a conscience and an aim! Your *Idylls* now form a glorious picture-gallery for which every Englishman ought to offer his most grateful thanks.

I hope Hallam is happy at Trinity. With best wishes always for him and kind regards to Mrs. Tennyson, I am, dear Mr. Tennyson, with sincere respect,

Most faithfully yours,
F. W. Farrar

The Duchess says, "Grateful thanks for 'Gareth.' How fine the allegory. 'The Last Tournament' is very grand." I thought thou wouldst like to see the impression that "The Last Tournament" makes on a lady who must be called fastidious.

I suppose "the vision splendid" of stanza V is the delight he has relinquished and "Another race hath been, and other palms are won" refers to the life he has since lived, while he hath kept watch o'er man's mortality and found the meanest flower that blows hallowed by the human heart, its tenderness, its joys and fears. Perhaps "Another race hath been" also glances at the generations which have passed by beside him, their struggles and their victories. What Papa calls the "shot-silk" of poetry, its double meanings.[1] But I will ask him.

1. Evidently Hallam had asked his mother to interpret some lines of Wordsworth's Immortality Ode. She speculated that perhaps "Another race hath been" is an example of what Tennyson called the "shot-silk" of poetry, the evocative vagueness that gives it an imprecise meaning which may shade into other meanings. Once when Boyd Carpenter, Bishop of Ripon, asked Tennyson if they were right who interpreted the three queens in "The Passing of Arthur" as Faith, Hope, and Charity, the poet replied, "They are right and they are not right. They mean that and they do not. They are three of the noblest of women. They are also those three Graces, but they are much more. I hate to be tied down to say, 'This means *that*,' because the thought within the image is much more than any one interpretation." Sometimes in reference to the many meanings of poetry, particularly the *Idylls*, Tennyson would say, "Poetry is like shot-silk with many glancing colours. Every reader must find his own interpretation according to his ability, and according to his sympathy with the poet" (*Memoir*, II, 127).

272   To Alfred Tennyson

Aldworth, 1 November 1872

Own dearest,
The sun shines today and I hope it is cheering thee on to do
something pleasant. It makes the view very beautiful here and
if there is any faith in the new moon it will last for thee. . . .

Many thanks for having called on Aunt Franklin.[1] I hope
that by help of Mr. Knowles she will find a suitable house. It
is very good in Mr. Knowles, looking after the sonnets. As far
as my poor opinion goes I advise Charlie to take any sum
offered, be it ever so small, provided the expense of
publication is taken off his hands.[2]

I have told Eleanor Locker that thou wilt see them and fix
the day for their coming down. Hallam reports thee as having
been very "affable" at the wedding[3] and himself as very well
after his wanderings. God bless thee, dearest. Kindest regards
to thy host and hostess.

1. While he was in London correcting proofs for the *Gareth and
Lynette* volume, Tennyson visited his wife's maternal aunt, Mrs. John
Franklin.
2. Charles Turner's 342 sonnets were published by C. Kegan Paul
in a collected edition in 1880, a year after Turner's death. In the opinion
of Sir Charles Tennyson, these sonnets "are all sincerely felt and
sensitively finished; a third of them, at least, reached a high poetic
standard" (C. Tennyson, "The Somersby Tennysons," p. 16).
3. The Ward-Simeon wedding.

273   To Hallam Tennyson

Aldworth, 3 November 1872

Beloved,
I have never answered thy question about prayer. What I
would have added is first that it helps to keep up the idea of a
personal God. Secondly that it encourages trust in that personal
God and trust being so great a part of love and love of God
being the highest possession of any being, that is a great reason
for praying. It seems to me that the discipline of life is mainly
meant to teach us trust.

Then again it makes one know of one's own knowledge that personal God at least in part. One learns His tender sympathy for His creatures in spite of all in this world that seems to tend to the contrary and one gains if not distinct ideas of His attributes yet that sort of undefinable yet irreplaceable acquaintanceship which comes to one of a friend through intercourse and makes one know his inner essence a something not to be defined, but which makes him dearer to us than another and which necessarily makes God dearest as being beyond words infinitely worthy to be so.

Then at least for the time we pray our conversation is in Heaven and I have learnt to think much of moments spent in high converse even with men like ourselves, dead or living. For if we do not distinctly remember a word that is said we are so much greater in ourselves for having had so much of our lives great thoughts. It is by having them and having them and having them that one learns to have them always and to be at last great. That is why the "Du bist der Augenblick,"[1] is it not that Goethe calls it, is so unappreciably important, that is why one should spend as little as possible of one's life in frivolity. I do not say cheerfulness and wholesome relaxation but if possible let these be great of their kind. They are necessary I believe from my heart in some sort. God bless thee, own beloved.

1. Literally, "You are the moment." In all probability she has in mind the famous lines from *Faust I, Studirzimmer,* ll. 1701-04:

> Werd ich sum Augenblicke sagen:
> Verweile doch! dur bist so schön!
> Dann magst du nich in Fesseln schlagen,
> Dann will ich gern zu Grunde gehn!

Bayard Taylor translates these lines in the original meter in his *Faust* (Boston and New York, 1870):

> When thus I hail the moment flying;
> Ah, still delay—thou art so fair!
> Then bind me in thy bonds undying,
> My final ruin then declare!

Faust has similar lines in the Second Part, Act V, scene 5, ll. 11,581-82:

> Zum Augenblicke dürft ich sagen:
> Verweile doch du bist so schön.

Then dared I hail the moment flying:
Ah, still delay—thou art so fair!

274   To Robert Browning
Yale

Aldworth, 3 November 1872

Dear Mr. Browning,
It would indeed have been to us a single misfortune had we
been staying a month at Fontainebleau and not your month.[1] I
think it quite bad enough that we were there a few days and
not your days. It was our Hallam who was there a month and
what would he not have given to have set eyes on you even! I
must tell you that he reads some of your poems exquisitely and
you are not to laugh at me one bit for saying so.

My husband's patience having been tried beyond endurance
by certain proof sheets[2] he has rushed off with Mr. Knowles to
look after them from his house. He will be most pleased by
your kind words about his "Gareth"[3] and will, I am sure, not
only for your sake but for the sake of the poem itself, from
what one has heard of it, feel much sympathy with Mr. Domett
and I hope so much that his tongue may be moved to express
it,[4] but that is not rare with him, so I should rather say that his
pen may be moved to record it, which is very rare by way of
letter-writing. That you may not wish it were even so with his
wife I will say farewell. All good be with you ever.

1. In his 2 November 1872 letter to Emily Tennyson (unpublished,
T.R.C.), Browning expressed his regret that he had recently been to
Fontainebleau and had not seen the Tennysons there.
2. For *Gareth and Lynette, Etc.*
3. In the 2 November letter Browning thanked the Tennysons for
his copy of "Gareth and Lynette," which he termed "so beautifully
subtle and delicate."
4. Also in the same letter Browning recommended to the Tennysons
Alfred Domett's new 14,000-line *Ranolf and Amohia, a South Sea Day
Dream*. Browning was an intimate friend of Domett's, and his genius
is indirectly eulogized in the poem. Tennyson did like Domett's poem,
and he subsequently "said handsome things of it" (Griffin and Minchin,
The Life of Robert Browning, p. 248).

275   To Hallam Tennyson

Aldworth, 5 November 1872

Beloved,

Thy dear letter cheered me much. I have been very happy on the whole but my spirits flag a little sometimes in the storm of wind and rain and mist that rages almost ceaselessly and not knowing when Papa is likely to return. His proofs had not come again yesterday. Today he is to dine with Mr. Allingham at the Kensington Museum, tomorrow with Aunt Franklin. But I have my precious ones to think of and to pray for and this fills me with ecstasy sometimes. Oh, Dr. Vaughan[1] is so right in bidding one "shelve all in Christ." It is all so safe there but then it is so difficult to be humble enough to believe, to ask God to give one faith, and yet how strange that it should be us that are the creatures of His hand.

I believe that the highest enlightenment of any faculty brings with it some enlightenment of all others. . . . For instance, how often it has been remarked that when a man or a woman is in love his whole being is transformed, glorified as it were. Then again how religious the greatest physical philosophers have been, the Newtons, the Galileos. . . .

Didst thou see, yes, I think thou didst, that argument of Father Dalgairns[2] in proof of God, that the heavens were found to be after the pattern, as it were, of the forms and truths of pure mathematics worked out independently of the human brain. So that it is hard indeed to resist the influence that one great Being was the creator of both. . . .

I had a most happy letter from Louy saying that every corner of her life is so filled that she can scarcely believe her happiness . . . and also that Papa was so kind and genial[3] that he warmed everyone and that thou wert thyself and "what could one say more," she adds.

Lady Pollock seems well pleased with her future daughter-in-law, Miss Deffell.[4] Was she not Pinkie's[5] travelling companion once? They are not to be married for two years at least.

1. Charles John Vaughan (1816–97), the famous Anglican divine and headmaster of Harrow, 1844–59, credited with introducing to that school the same standards of excellence Thomas Arnold had established at Rugby. The memoirs of John Addington Symonds, who was a schoolboy

at Harrow from May 1854 until August 1858, describe a side of Dr. Vaughan unknown to the Victorian public. Vaughan's resignation from Harrow was forced by young Symonds's discovery that the educator was involved in a love affair with a schoolboy named Alfred Pretor. Four years later when Vaughan accepted the Bishopric of Rochester, Symonds's father, the renowned physician, threatened public exposure, and again he resigned. In 1879, eight years after the elder Symonds's death, he accepted the deanery of Llandaff.

2. Joseph Dobree Dalgairns (1818–76), superior of the London oratory from 1863 till 1865, and author of "The Personality of God," "The Spiritual Life of the First Six Centuries," and many other treatises and essays.

3. At Louy Simeon's wedding.

4. Frederick Pollock, third baronet, married Georgina Harriet Deffell on 13 August 1873.

5. Emily Ritchie; see Letter 232, n. 1.

276   *To Hallam Tennyson*

Aldworth, 26 November 1872

Beloved,

I got up early to see Mr. Locker off so I take this quiet time before breakfast to write to thee. I shall certainly send thy letter to Mrs. Cameron.

Whatever may be the mystery of our free will as reconciled to God's foreknowledge, sure I am that there is an unravelling of it hidden with Him for that the two coexist it is impossible for me to doubt, and I who have searched a good deal into many things with such power as God has given me am now so content to rest in mystery which seems not contrary to reason.
. . .

Eleanor has grown such a charming girl, not brilliant nor beautiful but so good and wise and sympathetic and with a sweet touching picturesque face. Poor child, she is very sad.[1] She wants much to come to us at Christmas and I thought it would be very pleasant for her to meet the Bradleys. . . . Lady Simeon came yesterday and remains until tomorrow. One ought to be thankful to be able to give a little comfort to these mourners. She says it is her one pleasure, coming here.

1. Eleanor Locker's mother, Lady Charlotte, died in April 1872.

277   *To Robert Browning*
Yale

Farringford, 19 December 1872

My dear Mr. Browning,
I wish I could tell you the exceeding pleasure of your goodly
gifts but could you have seen the gleam in Hallam's face this
would have told it better than I can. Take the thanks of the
four, for are we not, thank God, one.

He and I often say to each other that you were at Hallam's
christening and to the then babe there is now more of nectar
than champagne in the fact that you so kindly recall it.

I think *he* feels that little is wanted but "limitation" to make
your friend[1] a very considerable poet and it would give us both
great pleasure to see him should he ever care to come and see
us. Is it beyond hope that you yourself will someday bring him
either here or to Aldworth? With love and homage from us all.

1. Alfred Domett. See above, Letter 274, n. 4.

278   *To Hallam Tennyson*

Farringford, 3 February 1873

Beloved,
Papa has been walking with the Herberts[1] part of their way to
Yarmouth. . . . We shall miss them. Poor Papa has not a soul to
speak to now for Mr. Ward[2] is gone away for some weeks. I
must do my best. He has mounted up to thy bedroom now for
a temporary smoking-room while the weather is so cold. . . .

What a pity that Liddon[3] and Kingsley are taking this line
about the Athanasian Creed! Instead of its being a sign of
unbelief wishing that it should be read, it is just those who
believe most earnestly in the Father, Son, and Holy Ghost who
may shrink from having a faith so full of mystery forced into
words of definition, however grand, feeling that although
certain attributes of God may be sufficiently intelligible for all,
sustaining comfort and guidance to man made after His image,
yet when one comes to the very essence of the Being of Being,
what can be done by the greatest of creatures but to bow and
adore. . . .

I have not been out since last Monday. The snow lies in patches here "lurking for more," as the Lincolnshire folk say. Our best love to thee and God bless thee.

1. Auberon Herbert (1838–1906) and his wife, Lady Florence. Herbert was a prominent journalist, a fellow of St. John's College, Oxford, 1855–69, and M. P. for Nottingham, 1870–74. In 1885 Hallam Tennyson joined Herbert and a Mr. Albert Grey in founding a company for buying land and reselling it at a low price to landless agricultural laborers.

2. William George Ward (1812–83), Roman Catholic theologian who from 1863 through 1878 edited the *Dublin Review,* using that publication to oppose every hint of liberalism in the Church. In 1858 Ward inherited a sizable property at Norwood, Cowes; however, he spent little time on the Isle of Wight for the next thirteen years, and he and Tennyson did not become acquainted until 1871, when he built a home at Weston, a mile or two west of Farringford. During the winter of 1873 Ward and Tennyson became close friends, despite their great differences in religious belief, and the bond between the two men was strengthened by Ward's reverence for Emily Tennyson, whose conversation, he said, reminded him of John Henry Newman "in its sincerity and fine simplicity" (*AT,* p. 406). After Ward's death Tennyson wrote "In Memoriam—William George Ward," which was first published in *The Athenaeum* on 11 May 1889.

3. Henry Parry Liddon (1829–90), vice-principal of St. Edmund's Hall, Oxford, 1859; select preacher to the University, 1863; and canon of St. Paul's, 1870. In 1871 Liddon refused to agree to any change in the authority of the "Athanasian Creed," which represented orthodox Trinitarian doctrine, and it was in protest against any tampering with the Creed that he spoke at a meeting in St. James's Hall on 31 January 1873. The Tennysons' old friend, Charles Kingsley (1819–75), canon of Westminster, was in full accord with Liddon's insistence upon an inviolable Creed.

279   *To Margaret Gatty*
Boston Public Library

Farringford, 12 February 1873

My dear Mrs. Gatty,
He was very much touched by sight of your handwriting and all the suffering it betokened and all the effort.[1] Glad indeed should we be to learn that you were better.

He sends you these lines[2] in the form in which they were printed for the Queen with his love and mine and all kindest remembrances to Dr. Gatty and you all. . . . This is Lionel's last term at Eton and Hallam's second at Trinity so the world does not stand still with them either.

1. During the last few years of her life Mrs. Gatty was almost completely disabled by paralysis.
2. The dedicatory epilogue "To the Queen," which Tennyson completed on Christmas Day, 1872, and included in the 1873 *Imperial Library Edition*.

280   *To Hallam Tennyson*

Farringford, 18 February 1873

Beloved,
I am delighted that thou hast had such glorious music. I should like some day to hear Tityens[1] myself; it is a great privilege. Thou must certainly have the Handel. I would order it at once only I should not know what key to get it in. Handel is to my mind the archangel of composers. I know that some in these days would think me a benighted creature for saying so.
. . .

I am glad those two well-beloved friends like the "Epilogue." I hope thou will have received the copies I sent by Papa's special desire yesterday to give away among thy friends. Will the Master like one? Mr. Clark also should have one. Thou must tell him that this is the form in which they were printed for the Queen.

Papa has had a vote of thanks notified to him today from the Royal Colonial Institute which has made him honorary member.[2] Macfie, one of the council, has sent him his pamphlet, "A Glance at the Position and Prospects of the Empire,"[3] which advocates our view of these subjects. It would be a grand thing if Papa should have helped to establish a federation of Great Britain and her colonies. Surely each would be so much greater and more powerful as one in such a federation than as a separate nation that it cannot but be manifestly for the interest of all to found without delay the beginnings of such an union. Why are our ministers so blind on this subject? If it were always as cold as it is now, I should not wonder at any amount of blindness or stupidity.

The Lockers are so exceedingly kind. They actually want me

to go and stay with them two or three weeks as well as Papa. He will go I think shortly but I of course shall not. He and Agnes have gone with volumes V and VI[4] as a birthday gift to Mrs. Cameron.

1. Therèse Tietjens (Titiens, Tityens) (1831–77), the German soprano who came to London in 1858 to sing at Her Majesty's Theatre. After that theatre burned in 1867, she went to Drury Lane and later sang at Covent Garden and at the Drury Lane company's new house in the Haymarket just before her death.
2. Tennyson wove into his epilogue "To the Queen" a denunciation of the idea, epitomized in a *Times* article of 31 October 1872, that it would be to England's advantage for Canada to sever her connection with Great Britain. In appreciation for his concern for the unity of the Empire, Tennyson was selected to be the second honorary member of the Royal Colonial Institute (now the Royal Commonwealth Society), an organization founded in 1868 by a group including A. R. Roche and Hugh E. Montagomerie, for the purpose of providing in the mother country a meeting place and a center of information for all those connected with the several colonies.
3. Robert Andrew Macfie published the pamphlet in London in 1872.
4. Final volumes of the *Imperial Library Edition.*

281   To Hallam Tennyson

Farringford, 7 March 1873

Beloved,

Thou doest not know how ill poor Mrs. Cameron is. . . . Dr. Dabbs has solemnly warned her that she must go to town for that she was dying of anxiety[1] and has also written to beg that I would urge it upon her. . . .

I thank thee, my own, for our Lionel's letter. He is beginning "to feel his feet" as the nurses say of children when they begin to walk alone. I do think the old laddy will make a grand man some day.

Thou wilt like to hear that Papa and Mr. Locker had half an hour's talk with Mr. Gladstone when they called the other day.[2] He was very kind and pleasant apparently.

I am very glad that thou hast had a walk with Butler.[3] What does he think of the Irish University Bill?[4] I cannot help feeling that legislators ought to take a much higher stand than they do in these matters and teach what they deem right to be taught "in scorn of consequence."[5]

1. Mrs. Cameron grew sick from worrying about her son Henry, who was attempting, unsuccessfully, to find a place in the London theatre.

G. R. Dabbs, who was Tennyson's Isle of Wight doctor, attended both the poet and Lady Tennyson during their final illnesses.

2. Tennyson also went to Windsor on 6 March to visit the Queen, who wished to thank him in person for his gift of Volume VI of the Library Edition, containing the completed *Idylls,* and also to express her particular appreciation for the dedicatory epilogue.

3. Henry Montague Butler (1833-1918), Charles Vaughan's successor at Harrow, where he served from 1859 till 1885, when he was appointed dean of Gloucester. In 1886 he accepted the mastership of Trinity College, Cambridge, and in 1889 he was appointed vice-chancellor of that university. A dear friend of the Tennysons, Butler wrote of visiting them at Farringford and Aldworth in his "Recollections of Tennyson" (H. Tennyson, *Tennyson and His Friends,* pp. 206-21): "To go to either of Tennyson's beautiful homes, to see him as the husband of his wife and the father of his sons, was to me and mine for many years a true pilgrimage, both of the mind and of the heart" (p. 221).

4. In early March 1873, Gladstone's Irish University Bill, which proposed to provide for a university for the whole of Ireland open to men of all creeds, was defeated in the House of Commons by 287 votes to 284.

5. "Oenone," l. 150.

282   To Hallam Tennyson

Farringford, 8 March 1873

Beloved,

. . . The secretary of the Hakluyt Society[1] is to meet Papa at Mr. Knowles's tomorrow to tell him of Sir Richard Grenville who in one ship, the *Revenge,* fought 153 Spanish ships of the time for fifteen hours. Thou knowest Froude's essay about it I dare say. I do not. Papa wants to make a ballad of it which is excellent news is it not?[2]

Victor Hugo's ballads have stirred Papa up to the idea of writing some himself. Mr. Knowles wants him to make a drama of Lady Jane Grey. The Court circular only says the Queen and Princess Beatrice went out this morning. So it seems one must be careful how one talks of the visit to the Mausoleum.[3] I have told the Camerons because they would naturally wonder why Papa had not returned.

1. The Hakluyt Society was founded in London, on 15 December 1846, for the purpose of publishing accounts of early voyages and travels. Mr. Clements Markham was secretary of the society in 1873.

2. Tennyson read about the heroic 1591 fight of the *Revenge* against the entire Spanish fleet in J. A. Froude's "England's Forgotten Worthies" in the July 1852 *Westminster Review.* He published "The Revenge: A Ballad of the Fleet" in the *Nineteenth Century,* March 1878, under the title "Sir Richard Grenville: A Ballad of the Fleet."

3. Tennyson visited Prince Albert's Mausoleum with the Queen and Lady Augusta Stanley on 6 March.

283   To Hallam Tennyson

Farringford, 14 March 1873

Beloved,

Papa has had a most interesting letter from a Canadian by name Kirby of Niagara.[1] It begins: "While thousands of Canadians thank you in their heart of hearts for your noble rebuke of *The Times* for their persistent and unprovoked insult to the people of this Dominion not many probably will express their thanks to you personally. I for one however cannot refrain from doing so. It is due to you and to that 'True North'[2] which you so splendidly indicate, that Canadians show their deep sense of the obligation they really feel." At the end he adds that Canadians would give Papa "a reception that royalty itself might be proud of." I write somewhat hurriedly today, Hallam mine. Papa is very cheery. Oh what a delight to have him. Such precious minutes I had with him yesterday evening. God bless thee, own beloved. Our best love to thee.

1. See *Alfred, Lord Tennyson and William Kirby: Unpublished Correspondence,* ed. Lorne A. Pierce (Toronto: Macmillan, 1929).

2. At the time Tennyson's phrase ("To the Queen," l. 14) had wide currency both in England and in Canada, particularly in Canadian patriotic literature.

284   *To Hallam Tennyson*

Farringford, 18 March 1873

My beloved,

Mr. Locker is very confident about you both getting work. The Duke of Argyll is going to write his name for Lionel at the Athenaeum.

Perhaps ministers were rather vexed with Papa at first [1] but I do hope they will feel by degrees that his is the right view of things and be grateful to him in the end and what is much more act in his spirit. . . .

Professors Tyndall, Huxley, and Hooker were here yesterday.[2] Professor Tyndall sent all kinds of remembrances to you both and asked about you with much interest. He first called with Huxley and then came in the evening with Hooker.

1. For seasoning "To the Queen" with personal political opinion.
2. John Tyndall (1820–93), the scientist, superintendent and later honorary professor of the Royal Institution, was a frequent guest at Farringford and Aldworth. Joseph Dalton Hooker (1817–1911), president of the Royal Society, 1873–78, and the leading botanist of his day, was a friend of the Tennyson family from the time he and the poet first met in London in December 1865.

Thomas Henry Huxley (1825–95), the biologist, natural historian, expounder of Darwinism, and self-named "agnostic," was an intimate friend of the Laureate's, despite the obvious disparity in their fundamental beliefs. Huxley respected Tennyson as the most genuinely scientific poet of the age, and after the bard's death he wrote a poem to him entitled "To Tennyson: The Tribute of His Friends."

285   *To Edward Lear*

Farringford, 19 March 1873

My dear Mr. Lear,

Only think, Lionel was nineteen last Sunday and sometimes it seems but such a little time since you gave the Roman Catholic doll to Hallam and corrupted his faith at Seaford. . . . Well, he certainly has recovered from that now. You will I am sure be glad to hear that the best and most intellectual of his fellow students are his companions at Trinity and that the master and his wife speak of him in most satisfactory terms to our common friends.

Lionel's last half-year at Eton is now drawing to a close. It is a pity, I think, that they should have made their new rule, for from Easter to October is a long time for one of Lionel's age to be left to himself in a private tutor's house and not desirable seeing that it is generally filled with boys who have to be crammed just to pass. Probably for part of the time we shall send him where Hallam was last year to Pasteur Brand of Fontainebleau. . . .

Ally walks now most days with Agnes Weld who is at present only too fat and as merry as a bird. She is full of all sorts of information and her Uncle finds her a good companion.

Poor Mrs. Cameron has had a sad time of it lately. Her son Charlie had a dreadful operation to undergo in order to remove part of his jawbone, and this gave such a shock to her nerves weakened by his long previous illness and her persistent disregard of all rules of health for years past that she has been seriously ill. But for this I believe she and Mr. Cameron would have been off to Ceylon with their son Henry. It seems so impossible for her to part from this last son who is a comfort to her and his best hope of work is in Ceylon though his inclination leads him to try the English stage. Imagine, in our London theatre almost all the actors are gentlemen and I have heard of two ladies going on the stage, one because she is poor and the other from pure love of acting. . . .

286   To Hallam Tennyson

Farringford, 12 May 1873

Beloved,

Mr. Browning has written a most sweet letter to Annie saying that he is too used to abuse to care for it as he believes others do and the only pain he could feel from it is of pain to her.[1] This is the gist of [his] letter signed "Affectionately yours."

Annie told us thou wert probably with the Brookfields yesterday in their Cambridge lodging. She walked with us in the park to look at the newly planted trees whither Papa and Lionel took me in my little carriage yesterday and she also went to see the apple blossoms in the orchard—a lovely sight which Papa and Lionel had taken me to see on Saturday. I cannot well express the refreshment of these wanderings about the fields in the old fashion.

Annie dined with us and Papa at her request read some chapters of "Isaiah" and of himself and the "Song of Deborah," and our Lord's "Woe to the Scribes and Pharisees."[2] We watched the moon in the mist. It looked to me like a smile passing over a face when the mist cleared a little. Then we admired the wondrous veil of mist over the tender green at the end of the avenue. Annie seemed very happy. So I think she was on Friday when Mrs. Cameron and Annie Prinsep were also here and Papa read some Milton. He is very cheerful I am thankful to say.

I have not said half enough about thy journal. The two leading articles are clever, I think, and that on the tyranny of prejudice also. . . . Be very careful about thy language, old darling—no slipshod above all things. Go as far as possible into the innermost depths of thy being. What comes there expresses itself naturally in clear forceful language.

1. Browning indicated in his letter of 9 May 1873 to Anne Thackeray that criticism of his "Red Cotton Nightcap Country" troubled him only in that it might wound Anne, who had suggested the title for his poem (see Ritchie, *Records of Tennyson, Ruskin, and Browning*, pp. 178, 181).
    2. Matthew 23.

287   To Sophia May Eckley[1]
Harvard

Farringford, 18 June 1873

My dear Mrs. Eckley:
We sympathize with you most sincerely in your great loss. No one, we know, can replace for you this lifelong friend. May you be comforted in thinking of all his goodness in the hope of meeting again where parting is no more.[2] I need not tell you that Mr. Tennyson and myself have most kind recollections of your brother and he must ever retain one of the foremost places among American guests who have done honour to their country and whom it is good for us to have known.

1. Sister of Frederick Goddard Tuckerman, who died of heart disease on 9 May 1873.

2. Emily Tennyson never wavered in the complete faith in immortality she expresses here to Mrs. Eckley. "About a future life we know hardly anything," she once remarked to Benjamin Jowett, "but that little is enough" (*Memoir,* II, 467).

On 11 August, the day of Hallam's twenty-first birthday, he and his father set off for Pontresina and thence traveled to the Italian lakes, Val Sesia, and Val d'Anzasca. On 4 September Hallam noted in his journal that Tennyson had begun a new lyric, "The Voice and the Peak," inspired by the torrent in the Val d'Anzasca, in the poet's opinion the grandest valley in all the Alps. Passing through Ponte Grande, Bauer-Sierre, and Neufchâtel, the travelers then returned to England, arriving at Aldworth on 11 September.

During the next three weeks the Tennysons entertained the Bradleys and two new guests, Julia Lady Lennard, Arthur Hallam's sister, and the poet and critic, Roden Noel. When they were alone, the boys and their parents entertained each other, landscaping and planting shrubs together during the day, and at night alternately reading aloud. Shakespeare was, as usual, the favorite choice, and *Pericles, Henry IV,* and *Henry VIII* were all read before Hallam and Lionel departed for Cambridge on 13 October. "A. wanders forlorn," Emily wrote the day they left, "and one feels forlorn enough, the four being separated for even so short a time."

288   *To Lionel Tennyson*

4 Seamore Place,[1] *13 November 1873*

Beloved,
Yesterday Mr. and Mrs. Knowles and their brother Mr. Hewlett dined with us and Mr. Locker came early and sat with Mrs. Knowles and myself in the drawing room. The American, Moncure Conway,[2] came up with Papa and Papa went with Mr. Locker and him to the Cosmopolitan. Before they went we

had a discussion on the Resurrection of our Lord—Mr. Conway
maintaining that when St. Paul says, "He was seen of Cephas,
then of the twelve, and then by five hundred brethren at once,
last of all he was seen by me,"[3] that he speaks in *all* the
instances of a spiritual vision as he does in the case of St. Paul
himself. Without the context this might possibly be tenable;
with it, it cannot be, can it?

    1. At the end of October the Tennysons went to London to spend
some time with Emily's aunt, Mrs. John Franklin.
    2. Moncure Daniel Conway (1832–1907), American clergyman, social
reformer, and abolitionist. During the Civil War Conway went to England
to lecture on behalf of the Union, and he remained there as minister
to a liberal London congregation until 1884.
    3. A paraphrase of 1 Corinthians: 5–8.

289   To Edward Lear

4 Seamore Place, 27 November 1873

My dear Mr. Lear,
If you should chance to have been thinking of us it has been
no doubt as in one of our quiet homes but here we are instead
in the centre of Mayfair. People are very kind and we see a
good many of them but for my own personal likings nothing
short of the Premiership and the modest confidence of genius
befitting could make me happy in London, I think, unless it
were the fact that our boys had found work suited to them here
and that their home was with us, or that I saw my Ally really
the better and happier for being here. On the contrary he has
been but poorly here and out of spirits and at Aldworth he was
well and cheerful. However or notwithstanding he is convinced
that it is good for him to be here. I suppose it is and so here I
am content to be, though glad to think that he wishes to go
home to Farringford for Christmas.
    On Saturday your Daddy[1] was so good as to give us a card
for his great picture[2] and we had the pleasure of shaking hands
with him and he put me into the best place for seeing the
picture, and if he did not see that the wonderful expression in
those eyes brought tears to mine he must have thought me
stupid and ungrateful. The picture haunts one so that no doubt
it is greater even than one knows. The all but uniform

brilliancy needed no doubt for the shadow has a novelty for northern eyes which needs to be overcome.

Ally has been to Cambridge to see the boys. Mrs. Cameron and Henry and Mr. Knowles went with him. Hallam gave a splendid banquet to his Father. A palm tree adorned the table and the Trinity cook no doubt did his best and Hallam assembled those most likely to interest his Father and he was interested and thoroughly enjoyed himself and had the satisfaction of hearing all both at the lodge and elsewhere speak in the highest terms of our boy. Our Lionel had only been there a few weeks and so of course was almost a stranger but he develops satisfactorily I hope. Farewell! May your journey[3] be in every way prosperous and your return equally so.

1. Lear never aspired to the Pre-Raphaelite brotherhood, but he felt himself qualified to be called a son of that company, and he christened Holman Hunt his "Daddy."
2. "The Shadow of Death" (1873), first exhibited in London and then sent to Oxford. Pious extremists in London denounced the picture as blasphemous because of its representation of Christ as a very real and simple carpenter.
3. Lear sailed from Genoa on 25 October, docked in Bombay on 22 November, and subsequently went northeast by train through Jabalpur to Lucknow.

290   To Robert Browning
Yale

4 Seamore Place, 6 December 1873

My dear Mr. Browning,

Having seen you once we are all the more greedy of seeing you again during our short stay here. May we hope that you will give us this pleasure by dining with us on Tuesday, December 16th at seven o'clock?[1]

1. Later the same day Emily sent a second note to Browning (unpublished, Yale), asking if he could come to them on the seventeenth or eighteenth, since Tennyson would be obliged to dine at the Metaphysical Society on the sixteenth.

291   *To Hallam and Lionel Tennyson*

Farringford, 4 February 1874

Beloved ones,
You must promise to tell me faithfully about yourselves and
the fever. How I wish I could be at Cambridge to make your
rooms comfortable for you! . . . Papa's cold is better, I think.
He has read *Henry IV* to me both evenings. He has had
paregoric at night and walked with Agnes in the mornings[1] and
been tolerably cheerful. He went last evening to sit in thy
room, my Hallam, it being so much warmer than the big study.
He is going to remain there a little while.

1. After 1869, when she and her mother moved to the Isle of Wight,
Agnes Weld was Tennyson's favorite walking companion when Hallam
was away from home.

292   *To Lionel Tennyson*

Farringford, 12 March 1874

Beloved,
It is delightful news that the people seemed struck with thy
paper on Browning. In a certain way, no doubt, however
dramatic the poet, he gives himself in his works. The mistake
people make, who do not understand what a dramatic poet is,
is that they think his poems a kind of catalogue raisonné of his
very own self and all the facts of his life, not seeing that they
are often only a poetic instinct or judgment on the facts and
spirits of other men real or imagined no doubt based on the
poet's own nature and from hints in his own life.

293   *To Hallam Tennyson*

Farringford, 13 March 1874

Beloved,
I am afraid the snow and the absence of men spoilt the entry[1]
very much not only for Papa but for everyone. He says he

thought the Princess large and imperial-looking and that those who could see better than he pronounced her if not very pretty not plain. Mr. Knowles had taken seats in Regent St., so Papa was well placed. He says that the people were very enthusiastic and that the Queen and the Princess wagged their heads for miles as if their necks had been made of India rubber. . . .

I am sorry to say people tell Papa that the accent is on the antepenultimate of Alexandrovna which I think a little spoils the chorus but this thou wilt not feel so much not liking the chorus at all. . . .

Before Papa left home I had got him to begin reading the *Idylls* aloud to me straight through in the *Library Edition.* I am delighted to find how one heightens the other read so. Unfortunately we only got to the end of "Enid" so far. I could not but thank God that it is such a noble and beautiful work. The only failing point I see in any of Papa's works is in the violent scenes. They are evidently not of him as must be seen by the purblind. To me they always ring just a little false on that account. I am thinking of the old men's rage in "Dora," "Aylmer's Field," and parts of "Maud." He is made for passion and indignation not for rage, rage belonging to small natures. But perhaps my criticism is false and it is that I have never seen rage. Still, I think the hardest of all things is for a great nature to give a little one because this is not merely lesser than itself but alien to itself. Of course for a small nature to give a great one is simply impossible.

1. On 12 March 1874, Alfred, Duke of Edinburgh, returned to England with his bride, Marie Alexandrovna, only daughter of Czar Alexander II of Russia, whom he had married in St. Petersburg on 23 January. At the Queen's request Tennyson greeted the young Grand Duchess with his "A Welcome to Her Royal Highness Marie Alexandrovna, Duchess of Edinburgh," published in *The Times* on 7 March.

294   To Alfred Tennyson

Farringford, 17 March 1874

Best beloved,
I do not doubt that thou art enjoying thy little visit to our aunt.[1] I send the cards and the ballot of the club.[2] Thou will be

almost inclined to dine there for the sake of balloting for our
two friends Henry Taylor and Lecky.[3]

Assuredly the race of publishers cannot stand high with us as
far as our experience goes. May better things be in store for the
future. It is well that there is a prospect of something coming
in at all counts. . . .

Hast thou been to see the Lockers? It would be a great
charity to go, he has been so ill and low; and Annie Thackeray
hast thou seen her? And the Campden Hill House that they
want us to buy, but that will be on the way to the Argylls.
Lady Simeon too canst thou see? . . .

What sum shall I send to the Mansion House fund,[4] my
own? Thy name is so revered in India that it must not be
missing in the list which is, so precious to India, a proof of
sympathy.

1. Mrs. Franklin.
2. The Sterling Club. See above, Letter 228, n. 4.
3. William E. H. Lecky (1838-1903), historian, essayist, and liberal
Irish politician, M. P. for Dublin University, 1895-1902.
4. The Bengal Famine Relief Fund established in a public meeting
at the Mansion House early in 1874 in the face of the Indian famine,
which appeared too devastating for the Indian government to handle
alone. Funds poured in and eventually totaled more than £125,000.

The enormous popular approval of historical drama evidenced
in the London response to W. G. Wills's *Charles the First* in
1873 and to Henry Irving's production of *Hamlet* in early 1874
stirred Tennyson's interest in the theater, and he determined,
at the age of sixty-four, to undertake his first mature experiment
in dramatic writing. He thought of writing a play about Lady
Jane Grey, or perhaps one about Queen Elizabeth, and James
Knowles suggested that he choose the Armada as his initial
subject. By 10 April, however, he had settled upon the life of
Queen Mary. He read J. A. Froude's *Mary* and the account in
Holinshed to Emily, researched a variety of ecclesiastical his-
tories, including Foxe's *Book of Martyrs,* and began work in
earnest on his own *Queen Mary* by the end of the month.

In August Tennyson once more took his family to France.
They visited Paris, where they attended the Théâtre-français,
and subsequently stopped at St. Germain and Tours, where Emily

and Lionel remained, while Hallam and his father traveled on to the Pyrenees. There Tennyson matched his son's pace of twenty miles a day, climbed nearly to the cleft peak of the Pic du Midi d'Ossau, and passed through the valley of Cauteretz for the final time. Shortly after the return to Farringford in early September, Emily fell seriously ill, and it soon became apparent that she had suffered a complete physical breakdown. Her own account of her collapse, dated simply September 1874, appears as the last regular Journal entry for more than a decade:

> I had to answer many letters from unknown corre-
> spondents, asking advice from A. as to religious questions,
> and desiring criticism of poems, etc., and I became very
> ill, and could do but little, so my Journal ends here.

Hallam subsequently kept a diary, but his mother wrote nothing more of any consequence in the Journal until 1886.

It is impossible to determine just why Emily collapsed when she did. Undoubtedly she came home from France exhausted, and she evidently spent her little remaining strength answering her husband's accumulated letters. It seems likely that Emily's lifelong frailty was partly the result of a hypersensitive disposition, and twenty-two years of painstaking ministration to Tennyson must have been an emotional as well as a physical strain. Though she was always tired, she never knew when to stop working. For more than two decades she had held herself almost solely responsible for managing Tennyson's obligations, for seeing to his private requirements, for entertaining the hordes of guests and relatives who inundated Farringford and Aldworth, and for handling the bulk of the poet's correspondence. Shortly after Emily fell ill, Tennyson wrote James Knowles of the unhappy effects of his wife's constant letter writing:

> She has overwrought herself with the multifarious corre-
> spondence of many years, and is now suffering for it.
> I trust that with perfect quiet she will recover; but it will
> never again do for her to insist upon answering every
> idle fellow who writes to me. I always prayed her not
> to do so but she did not like the unanswered (she used
> to say) to feel wroth and unsatisfied with me (quoted by
> James Knowles, "Aspects of Tennyson," *Nineteenth Cen-
> tury*, 33 [January 1893], 187–88).

Emily improved very slowly, and Hallam had to abandon Cambridge and come home in order to assume his mother's duties as secretary and reader to the poet. On 16 October Tennyson wrote to Francis Palgrave that his wife was "still obliged to lie flat" and that she "must not exert herself in any one thing, the doctor says, if she be to recover" ("Draft for Materials for a Life of A.T.," III, 226). By the first of the year Emily finally began to show signs of recovery, and in late February she went with Tennyson to London, where they spent a considerable part of each spring from 1875 onwards. She wrote nothing at all, however, and as late as 20 April 1876, when Tennyson addressed Browning to thank him for his favorable report on the staging of *Queen Mary,* he reported that Emily had planned to write but that she was still unable to "put hand to paper" (*Materials for a Life of A. T.,* IV, 372).

Grave and protracted as Emily's illness was, it had little effect on her relish for life or her physical appearance. She remained remarkably youthful-looking, retaining both her auburn hair and her perfect complexion, and by mid-1876 she was again in charge of her household, directing its affairs largely from her sofa or her reclining chair. Finally in 1877 she returned to her letters, though from then on she wrote only personal letters, limited primarily to the family.

Very few of the letters Emily wrote during the late 1870s are extant. Hallam, her principal correspondent during the boys' years at school, was of course now at home, and Lionel was never as particular about saving his mother's correspondence as was his brother. The following note to Lionel, who in 1876 had taken an appointment in the India Office in London, is the only surviving 1877 letter. There is then another long gap until October 1878, when Emily began writing regularly to her sister, Louisa Turner.

295   To Lionel Tennyson

Farringford, 28 January 1877

My own beloved,
The voices of the lambs are pleasant in one's ears. What a pity that all work cannot be done in the country, one feels! But

what a good thing that work is dearer than even the country. This is what I feel when I think of my darlings shut up in London. Some good work, please God, they will do.

296   To Louisa Turner

Aldworth, 26 October 1878

My darling,
I don't think we shall go to Farringford very early this year unless we are frozen out here. Ally's study is so light here and so much less drafty than at Farringford that this is a great temptation to stay and besides to say the truth I hear of so many fresh people at Freshwater where already there were far too many for our taste that I am in no hurry to encounter them, and I don't think Nanny and Agnes miss us much seeing there are so many.

If thou wert but at the top of this hill so that we might see thee every day that would indeed be a comfort![1] I am so stupid I will not write more. Only take care of thyself for Uncle Charlie's sake and for ours and say every day to thyself for my sake, "God is love."

I remember well the wondering joy with which I first fully realized, I mean fully as my powers could, the words, "The Lord is loving to every man and His mercy is over all His works." One can beat this into one's brain when one is too dull for anything else cannot one, my sweetie. God bless thee ever.

1. Charles and Louisa Turner lived at their Grasby vicarage until their deaths in 1879.

297   To Louisa Turner

Aldworth, 27 October 1878

My darling,
Thou must be of good cheer for Dr. Manning[1] seems to have spoken very hopefully about thee. Take all the nourishment thou canst and then the poor brain which has been so long

exhausted and overworked will recover by degrees, please God, and become an honest servant to the soul. Remember, Louy, what a joy and blessing it would be to Charlie and to us to see thee well and try thy best to be so.

1. Evidently Louisa Turner's Grasby doctor. Her emotional illness late in life seems to have originated in the mistaken idea that she had failed her husband during his battle with opium soon after their marriage when his own emotional stability was threatened. See below, Letter 299.

298   To Louisa Turner

Aldworth, 5 November 1878

My darling,

The beautiful scarf has arrived. My most loving thanks for it. I shall keep it all my life and I ought to have no more painful glands with such a deliciously warm comforter. Hallam will, I hope, soon see thee and pay my debts for the wool and for the making of the dress. . . .

We are having Hallam's and Lionel's christening robe washed for the new Lionel or Lionella,[1] but I am so greedy over it that I only lend it. The rest of the things I have divided having given some to Eleanor, kept some for Hallam's Eleanor—whoever she may be.[2] He seems in no hurry to choose her and we cannot be very sorry that he is not, dear old darling. God forbid we should stand in the way of his marrying when he does wish it.

1. Alfred Browning Stanley Tennyson, first son of Lionel and Eleanor Tennyson, was born on 20 November 1878. He was named for his grandfather and for his two godfathers, Browning and Dean Stanley. Lionel had married Eleanor Locker, daughter of Frederick Locker and his first wife, Lady Charlotte Bruce, on 25 February 1878.

2. Hallam Tennyson married Audrey Boyle in June 1884.

299   *To Louisa Turner*

Aldworth, 13 November 1878

My darling one,
Who among the sons of men is worthy? But thou by the very
feeling of unworthiness provest thyself worthy with such worth
as man can have—the worth of coming like a little child to God
in Christ and doing what he bids or striving to do it.

My darling, try to think always that one's sins are blotted
out. Try to forget those things that are behind and to reach
forward unto those which are before . . . and doubt not that
after this long weary warfare the crown of victory will be thine.
Forgive me who am so much less worthy than thyself for
presuming to advise thee, my own darling. I could have no
hope but in doing as I say.

300   *To Louisa Turner*

Aldworth, 16 November 1878

My darling,
I must edge in a line to thee between the departures and
arrivals. Lewis and May Fytche[1] and Giovanni[2] and his wife,
the Lady Ortense, have just gone and I am hoping in a few
minutes to have our Lionel and then a college friend of theirs,
Walter Leaf,[3] whose name is so well known in all charitable
things. Poor Ortense must have had rather a dull little visit as
one's Italian has grown very rusty and she does not speak
English, but as it only lasted about two hours it does not so
much matter. . . . He is very gentle and jovial and she looks
very nice but perhaps thou knowest her. They were at the
Walters[4] of Bearwood this morning and got up at six o'clock to
come to us and are going on to Paris tonight. . . .

1. Lincolnshire cousins of the poet.
2. A relative of Frederick Tennyson's wife, the former Maria Giuliotti.
3. (1852–1927), the Homeric scholar, author, translator, and banker.
An intimate friend of Hallam and Lionel at Trinity, Leaf was Sir Charles
Tennyson's godfather.
4. John Walter (1818–94), the owner of Bearwood, was, like his father
before him, chief proprietor of *The Times* for many years.

301   To Louisa Turner

Farringford, 9 December 1878

My darling,

I am sorry that Ally and Hallam do not believe in poor little Agnes' plan for the good of the people here, for I should have liked if they could have helped her.[1] I cannot conceive of anyone more entirely absorbed in the welfare of others than she is. A most truly Christian love she has I do believe. Her whole face and form are lighted up with it.

How cheerful I should be if it pleased God that she should find a worthy companion for life. It is most good in Nanny making so great a money sacrifice without her hope, I fancy, in the cause. God bless thee, Louy mine.

1. Agnes Weld was active in charitable work on the Isle of Wight. Although the poet had little faith in the efficacy of charities, Emily Tennyson often worked with her niece in her generous projects to assist the poor. She was also active in the Blackdown area, devoting most of her efforts there to orphaned children from Dr. Thomas Barnardo's Stepney-Causeway Charity in London. Some of the waif children boarded temporarily in homes at Haslemere and in the surrounding neighborhood, and the poet's wife visited them regularly, often taking them presents as well. The eulogy to Lady Tennyson in the 11 August 1896 *Star* testifies to her kind efforts in behalf of the Stepney-Causeway children: "When changes were necessary, and some of the little ones had to return to town, or others were to be received in the country, the widow of the late P. L. would make arrangements for their departure or arrival, frequently writing half-a-dozen letters on the subject in as many days, and although not strong herself, the weather was seldom so bad as to prevent a visit to these humble little folk."

302   To Louisa Turner

Farringford, 14 January 1879

My darling,

It is an immense comfort to hear that the poor leg is better. Thou dost not know what a grief it is not to be able to help thee at all. Louy mine, thou art always far too favorable a judge of me. It is rather a hard fight now to keep my head above the waves but I have support that I do not deserve in a thousand ways, so no more of myself. . . .

Our little bairnie has his fine name of Alfred spoilt in one way by the addition of Browning and Stanley, the names of his godfathers which it is now considered etiquette to impose. However as I believe the godfathers are very pleased one ought not to regret the fact. Stanley has been a very kind friend and Browning is the most brotherly of poets. He has had a great trial in Ally's great popularity and his comparatively little popularity. God bless thee, my Louy. Our best love.

303   *To Edward Lear*

Farringford, 15 January 1879

My dear Mr. Lear,
I did not mean to have let so many days of the New Year go by before writing to you our affectionate good wishes for it and thanking you for yours and for your congratulations on the grandchild, but you will I know make all due allowances and a great deal more than due for the infirmities of the grandmother—poor old thing! . . .
  You would like to see Hallam taking his place by his sleeping nephew as a matter of course while nurse is attending on Eleanor. He passed his Roman law and is reading English law but law is not to his taste as it appears in law books however reverently he regards it in practice.
  Ally walks through all the snow and frost and rain and storm never shortening the morning's walk. He is generally extremely cheerful. Lionel gets on well with his work we are told and is much esteemed by his superiors and devotes himself quite passionately to all studies likely to make him a better public servant.

304   *To Louisa Turner*

Farringford, 31 January 1879

My darling,
Mrs. Greville[1] has gone today. I would thou couldst have

heard her recite "The Grandmother" as she did for Agnes. She drew tears from hundreds of eyes the other day, I believe. She has been staying at Sandringham. Her brother-in-law (and cousin) Sir Dighton Probyn[2] being Master of the Prince's Household, the Royal Family are always running in and out. All the little girls have been learning "The Grandmother" since she left and one of them thinks she could imitate Mrs. Greville.

She says that the Prince grieves greatly over his sister's loss.[3] He cannot even bear that the children should have their music lesson. The first thing he did I believe on the Sunday morning after was to receive early communion. Some time before her death she became for a short season quite rationalistic but the preparation of her daughter for confirmation quite restored her old faith by God's blessing. The last words she said I think were, "I did not know it was so beautiful." (She had apparently had some vision.)

Hallam will like his scarf about two yards and a quarter long please, my Louy, and done in white wool like my violet one only a little wider.

1. Mrs. Sabine Greville, a great admirer of Tennyson and his verse, which she was in the habit of reciting all over London. Though she was not especially gifted or intelligent, Mrs. Greville was a sincerely devoted friend to the Tennysons, and she helped fill the void left by Julia Margaret Cameron's removal to Ceylon. Perhaps she was accurately described by Henry James, who praised her "genius . . . for friendship" and concluded, "I can't praise her better than by saying that though she is on the whole the greatest fool I have ever known, I like her very much and get on with her most easily . . ." (*The Letters of Henry James*, ed. Percy Lubbock [New York: Scribner's, 1920], 1:71).
2. General Sir Dighton Macnaghten Probyn (d. 1924).
3. Princess Alice died of diptheria on 14 December 1878.

305   *To Louisa Turner*

Farringford, 2 February 1879

My darling,

. . . Mr. Cotton began his canvassing[1] by asking for Ally's vote and was told by Hallam that Ally would vote for him if he voted at all but that he would not vote and then Hallam went with Mr. Cotton to canvass Mr. Ward who promised his vote and agreed to be on his committee provided he was not required to speak or write or ride or drive or be on any committee for him. . . . Mrs. Ward turned to Hallam and said, "But why do not you stand, Mr. Tennyson?" Hallam pointing to Mr. Cotton replied, "Because there on that chair sits a worthier."

Ally's play *Becket*[2] is going through rather a strange ordeal now, that of being read aloud to Mr. Ward whose patron saint he is.[3] Hitherto it has stood the ordeal well. Mr. Ward says he is "quite a hero, a canonized saint. Very fine . . . how well he [Tennyson] reads it!"

I hope I do not tire thee with my small written chatter, my Louy. I would I could try what I could do with my spoken chatter! God bless thee.

1. In 1879 Benjamin Cotton was selected as Conservative candidate for the House of Commons from the Isle of Wight. On 28 April 1880 he lost the election to the Liberal Evelyn Ashley (1836-1907) by thirteen votes.

2. Tennyson had a short version of *Becket* printed in 1879, but he did not publish the final version until 1884.

3. Though Ward generally had little use for poetry, he was a zealous student of the drama.

306   To Louisa Turner

Farringford, 26 February 1879

My darling,

Best thanks! Hallam's remark was, "This is first rate." Very warm and beautiful he thinks it. He is only afraid that the fine sketch must have tired thy eyes and he bids me ask if it has not. If it has not, nothing could be better for Ally, I thank thee my Louy. But remember his is to be done only at odd times.

. . .

Nanny will tell thee all about those sad letters from Ceylon,[1] so I will not repeat. We are not likely to find one to take her place so loving and strong in her woman's way and so childlike in her faith. I am so glad that she was so happy here last autumn and that she had had such a happy week with all of those she loved in Ceylon at Henry's beautiful splendid new estate before the fatal attack.

1. Julia Margaret Cameron died on 26 January 1879. She and Mr. Cameron had returned to the Isle of Wight for a short visit in the autumn of 1878, having been in Ceylon with their sons since 1875. Shortly after their return to Ceylon Mrs. Cameron fell ill, and she died ten days later.

307   To Louisa Turner

Farringford, 27 April 1879

My darling,
Thy beloved One has gone to the rest he so much desired and thou wilt joyfully follow him in God's own good time.[1] May He ever be thy guide and comfort!

1. Charles Tennyson Turner died on 25 April 1879. He had been failing for some time, and his final illness was probably aggravated by his wife's poor health and chronic depression. Louisa Turner died less than a month later.

308   To Louisa Turner

Farringford, 30 April 1879

My own darling,
Thou hast been ever a perfect sister to me and let it not be forgotten that that true loving simple Christian soul . . . called thee his "Guardian Angel" and that to thee has been granted this exceeding blessing that through thy help he came out of a state, brought on chiefly by illness, from which scarcely any other human being has been known to be freed[1] into that state of patience and faith and love and hope which has been an example and a delight for all.

Doubtless, my sweetie, thou wilt accuse thyself of many things in the course of this fierce trial to him and to thee but all the more glory to God for the result, even if thy self-accusations were not mostly due to an overworked brain, overworked in doing what seemed to thee right or what was right and what has been to him a blessing beyond human conception.

I sent a box of primroses and forget-me-nots yesterday by post. I knew that he would have liked to have had some from Farringford and I knew that thou wouldst have wished him to have them. God ever bless thee. This darkness will pass, as God is just and loving, it will pass.

1. Evidently Charles Turner was not dependent on opium after 1849.

309   To Louisa Turner

Farringford, 1 May 1879

My beloved one,
I would that I were by thy side. Letters come speaking of him as among sweetest memories. . . . The Bishop of Lincoln [1] sends thee through Edmund his Christian sympathy and expresses his highest regard for Charlie both as a man and a poet. Mr. Spedding says: "When your friend is gone, though for his own good and to a better condition, you would still feel, as I feel now, how idle you have been in not making more of him while he lived. To think how many hours during the last fifty years I may say I have really *spent with* Charles Turner, for his little volumes have always been on my table and many of his sonnets and poems have been constant companions in my memory, and yet how long it is since we had any conversation with each other even by letter! I feel this the more because I had it for a long time on my conscience that I had neglected to tell him how much I was delighted with his last volume,[2] though I was recommending it and making presents of it to other people." Then he says, "It was only a few weeks since I was helping Edward FitzGerald to a complete set of his poems, 'a beautiful poesy of wild flowers' he called them."
     I copy these bits my darling, because Edmund said that we were to return the letter. Others that have come to us I can send when Hallam has seen them. I cannot write more today.

1. Christopher Wordsworth (1807–85).
2. *Sonnets, Lyrics and Translations* (London, 1873).

310   To Louisa Turner

Farringford, 7 May 1879

My darling,

Is it not rather a strange fate of one of Ally's very early poems printed when he was about 19? When two parts of this "The Lover's Tale" had been printed he withdrew them thinking them too imperfect for publication. Arthur Hallam admired them very much and distributed a few copies among their common associates. Somehow one of these or some others must have got abroad, for two parts of the poem have been pirated and the other day a copy (the original one, I believe) was sold for forty-one pounds and so Ally is advised to print the whole poem with his own corrections and the sequel "The Golden Supper" and our Hallam has in consequence taken up a copy for the publisher.[1]

Tell me, darling, if I bother thee telling of our doings. Thou art too loving not to read what I write but I will not write if it wearies thee. God bless thee. We look anxiously for news of thee. Ally says that the sonnets are like Greek epigrams they are so graceful and so perfect and that the more he reads them, the more he admires them.[2]

1. Tennyson prepared the first two parts of "The Lover's Tale" for his 1833 *Poems,* but he withdrew them because of what he considered imperfections, against the vehement objections of J. M. Heath and those of Arthur Hallam, who thought Tennyson "point-blank mad" to suppress so fine a work (*AT,* p. 129). Some time in 1833 Tennyson distributed several copies of the poem to his dearest friends, with a headnote admitting that it contained "nearly as many faults as words" (Ricks, *The Poems of Tennyson,* p. 300). But it was another copy, which Tennyson later presented to John Forster, that Richard Herne Shepherd pirated. Evidently the poem passed from Forster to Robert Browning to Thomas Powell, who sold it before leaving England in 1849. On 16 June 1870 it was sold in London by Sotheby, Wilkinson, and Hodge to Basil Montague Pickering, the bookseller and publisher. In August 1870 Shepherd borrowed the poem from Pickering, ostensibly to quote it in the second edition of a book entitled *Tennysoniana,* which he had published in 1866. Subsequently he reprinted some fifty copies of the poem, a number of which he sold.

After 1833 Tennyson apparently gave little thought to preparing "The Lover's Tale" for publication until January 1868, when his wife urged him to publish the poem, which, she felt, embodied "the very health of young love." The poet showed the poem to Kate Rawnsley and Marian Bradley, guests at Farringford in early 1868, admitting that it was "very rich and full," but adding that he could never "pick it to pieces and make it up again" (quoted by Ricks, p. 300, from Marian Bradley's manuscript Diary). Spurred by his discovery of Shepherd's piracy ten years later Tennyson changed his mind, and he had Kegan Paul and Co. publish "The Lover's Tale," including as Part IV his previously published "The Golden Supper," in May 1879.

2. Tennyson's "Prefatory Poem to My Brother's Sonnets" was first published as a preface to Charles Turner's *Collected Sonnets, Old and New* (1880).

The paucity of letters for the next several years, including the complete absence of any 1880 or 1882 letters, can most likely be attributed to a worsening of Emily's health. Early in 1880, when the Laureate and his wife went to London for their usual winter visit, Thomas Hardy came to visit and was shocked to discover his hostess lying in the drawing room, stretched out flat "as in a coffin" (*AT*, p. 449). Indeed Emily seems to have been almost as debilitated in 1880 as she had been after her collapse six years before. While in London she did little more than help entertain Frederick Locker and Edward Burne-Jones and his wife, but she returned in the early spring to Farringford and an even less demanding existence.

Meanwhile Tennyson and Hallam traveled in June to Venice, stopping on the way in Munich, Tegernsee, Innsbruck, and Cortina, and returning a month later by way of Verona, Lago di Garda, and Milan. In August the family went to Aldworth where Tennyson completed *Ballads and Other Poems.* And during December, Kegan Paul and Co. published *Ballads,* as well as the *Royal Edition* of Tennyson's poetry. By the first of the year Tennyson had also finished *The Cup,* which Henry Irving, who had previously produced *Queen Mary,* staged at the Lyceum in July 1881. Encouraged by the popular reception of his dramatic efforts, Tennyson soon set to work on *The Foresters,* a play which Irving refused because he thought it not sensational enough for his audience. The Tennysons entertained little and scarcely went out at all during the remainder of 1881, perhaps as much because of their despondency over the recent deaths of James Spedding, Drummond Rawnsley, and Arthur Stanley, as because of Emily's infirmity.

311   *To Louisa Turner*

Farringford, 19 May 1879

My own darling,
It is a lovely day. Mr. Spedding is coming. Ally wished to have
his old college friend with him. There is a very kind
sympathetic letter much of it about thee from Sophy Elmhirst[1]
from whom we have not heard for years. Of course our Charlie
is among her earliest memories. There is a telegram from
Eleanor giving good news of all. Baby nearly well, herself
better, Lionel well.

God bless thee, my own. Take care of thyself. Blessed as I
am in my Ally and our boys none can be to me exactly what
thou art.

1. Mrs. Edward Elmhirst, the former Sophy Rawnsley.

312   *To Edward Lear*

Aldworth [October 1879]

My dear Mr. Lear,
I was not aware that she was so dear to you.[1] I thought it had
been only he who is so great a friend. I grieve that you should
have so heavy a loss however fully I may indorse Ally's words
"better to have loved and lost." You have had so much of
sorrow that those who love you cannot but desire that
henceforward you should have nothing but happiness, but that
One who loves you best knows best what is good. This is the
only comfort we poor mortals can have in thinking of a sad
life, is it not? However sad yours has been few have given
more gladness to others and this thought must cheer you a
little.

I am told that your friend is a very great loss to society not
only socially but politically more especially at this time when
party spirit runs so high and is so bitter. Her house was a
centre for moderate liberals and I hear that her personal
influence sometimes subdued even the fiercest of radicals. I
will not mention names but the gist of what was said was this.

We must stay at home and take care of the little grandson

who is to come to us at Farringford in November if all be well.
. . .[2] Different hindrances have occurred to prevent Ally and
Hallam from having their usual little holiday. I am especially
sorry for this Ally being naturally in a lower state body and
mind than is his wont.

1. Lady Waldegrave, Chichester Fortescue's wife, died in early July
1879. In a letter of 9 October 1879 to Emily Tennyson (unpublished,
T.R.C.) Lear described her as "one whose place cannot be filled;—and
who could not be understood by the many, though to those who knew
her she was priceless."
2. Emily correctly predicted the birth of a grandson. Charles Bruce
Locker Tennyson (later, Sir Charles) was born at Farringford on 8
November 1879.

313   To Edward Lear

Farringford, 7 June 1881

My dear Mr. Lear,
We send our affectionate God bless you and the new house![1]
The companionship of our view is so grateful to me that,
having of late years been necessarily left very much to it, I can
sympathize more than most people, perhaps, with your loss in
that of the old villa, to say nothing of the parting from rooms
and flowers and trees and shrubs consecrated now by the
thoughts and feelings and events of so many years. You have, I
know, the one comfort that can reconcile one to the sorrows
and losses of life, the faith that they come to us from Him who
knows best what is best for us, however bad it seems to
ourselves.

I wish you could see Lionel's bairnies. I am sure you would
be as good to them as you used to be to their father and uncle.
"Anthony Gobbo"[2] is the name by which they call their
respected Uncle. . . . Eleanor is an excellent mother and
Lionel, I think, an equally good father. The bairnies have been
with us these two months and may be for some months longer
if the additional story can be added to 4 Sussex Place[3] this
summer as they hope it will. If "Enoch Arden" remains true . . .[4]

1. In May 1881 Lear moved into his new home in San Remo, which
he christened the "Villa Tennyson." It seems probable that both this
home and the earlier Villa Emily, built in 1871, were named for Emily
Tennyson.

2. Perhaps the allusion is to Launcelot Gobbo in *The Merchant of Venice.*
3. The address of the Lionel Tennysons' London home.
4. The remainder of the letter is missing.

314   To William Gladstone
British Museum

Aldworth, 15 December 1881

My dear Mr. Gladstone,
We hear that there is likely to be a vacancy among your secretaries. You know a little of all that Hallam has been to his Father and myself but it is time that he should have a career of his own and should you now or at any future time be disposed to honour him by offering him a secretaryship, we should thankfully give him up to you and take a secretary ourselves, being very sure that he would loyally and zealously serve you to the best of his ability. This of course needs no answer unless you require Hallam's services.

315   To William Gladstone
British Museum

Aldworth, 19 December 1881

My dear Mr. Gladstone,
I thank you for your most kind reply. I have been full of dread lest my letter may have seemed to you encroaching, but the intimation of the possible vacancy in your personal staff came to us unasked and I thought it would be cowardly and selfish to allow personal scruples to stand in the way of obtaining for our son the great privilege of filling the post. For whatever other possible openings to his future political work might present themselves this would be the opening which he covets, so I wrote without the loss of a day. Best Christmas wishes from us all to you all and your pardon for the trouble I have given you.

In February 1882, while the Tennysons were residing in London at 86 Eaton Square, the poet, at the request of Sir Frederic Young, reworked his 1852 "Hands All Round!" into a patriotic song for the Empire. Emily then set the recast version to music for Queen Victoria's birthday on 15 March, on which day it was sung all over Great Britain and the colonies. After their return to Farringford in the spring, the poet and his wife entertained Sir Henry Parkes, Premier of New South Wales, who was overjoyed to discover the Tennysons' great interest in the colonies, particularly, of course, in New South Wales. Tennyson devoted much of the last half of 1882 to completing his prose drama "The Promise of May," a rather improbable play which enjoyed little success when put on at the Globe in November.

Tennyson was much affected in the spring of 1883 by the Queen's grief over the death of her servant, John Brown, on whom she had grown to depend more than on anyone else since the Prince Consort's death. The Laureate wrote her several letters of sympathy, and on 7 August he visited with her alone at Osborne in Prince Albert's room. The Queen thought that Tennyson now seemed very old; his eyesight was obviously much impaired, and he was "*very shaky on his legs.*" But she also found him "very kind," just as he had always been, and a great comfort when he talked of his strong belief in immortality (Dyson and Tennyson, *Dear and Honoured Lady,* p. 102).

Soon after he returned to Farringford he wrote, at the Queen's request, a short epitaph for the pedestal of a statue of John Brown, and then on 8 September Tennyson and Hallam sailed with Gladstone on a trip to Scandinavia in the *Pembroke Castle,* which Sir Donald Currie had put at their disposal. The party, which included Sir Arthur Gordon and Sir William Harcourt as well as Currie and the Gladstone family, voyaged across the North Sea to Christiansund and thence past Elsinore to Copenhagen, where they visited with the King and Queen of Denmark and with the Princess of Wales and the Czar and Czarina, who were all staying at the Danish palace. On the way home from Copenhagen Gladstone offered Tennyson a peerage which, wrote Emily, the Queen had desired for years to bestow on him. After several days of consideration the poet informed Gladstone that he would accept the peerage, and when he reached home he wrote as follows to his Queen (Dyson and Tennyson, *Dear and Honoured Lady,* p. 109):

I have learned from Mr. Gladstone your Majesty's gracious intention toward myself, and I ask to be allowed to express to your Majesty my grateful acknowledgements.

You, Madam, who are so full of sympathy for your subjects will, I am sure, understand me when I say that the knowledge of Your Majesty's approval of what I have been enabled to do is as far as I am concerned all that I desire.

This mark of your Majesty's esteem which recognizes in my person the power of literature in this age of the world, cannot however fail to be gratifying to my nearest and dearest.

I am, Madam, always your Majesty's
faithful subject and servant

316   To Hallam Tennyson
       Yale

Farringford [May (?) 1882][1]

Mr. Woolner sent me [a copy] of the Royal Edition with this title page:

"The Works
of
Alfred Tennyson
Poet Laureate
With Photographic Illustrations
By Payne Jennings

Photo of
Alfred

London
R & A Suttaby
2 Amen Corner"

Now, what can this mean? Not a hint of Kegan Paul. The list of indexed illustrations in no one instance corresponding with the illustrations. These pushed [?] in anywhere. "The May

Queen," for instance, at the beginning of *Queen Mary*. (The portrait is the Mayall photograph.[2])

Unfortunately Sir Henry wants the book at once. Nevertheless, we have kept this back, Papa having written to tell him that he does not think he can legally inscribe his name in the volume and allow it to be given as a gift, [Kegan] Paul having at present his copyright.[3]

Please, Hallam, get a really well-bound copy of the *Royal Edition* (crimson if may be, as this is), supposing Mr. Arnold White[4] says that we cannot send this, and bring it with thee. Anyhow we ought to keep this, I think, for it must be pirated and Paul ought to see it eventually after we have ascertained, if possible, more about it.

A delightful letter came yesterday from Sir Henry Parkes. I wish that I were strong enough to copy it for you. He tells of his luncheon with the King and Queen of the Belgians, among others, and of her great admiration for Papa and how he (Sir H.P.) promised that he would get Papa to write his name for Her in a copy of his works.[5]

1. The letter survives only as an undated fragment.
2. The Tennyson photograph was taken by John Edwin Mayall (d. 1867), a popular artist and photographer who kept a shop in Regent Street from 1852 until his death.
3. Apparently the Tennysons had requested that Woolner purchase in London a copy of the *Royal Edition*, which the poet intended to send to Sir Henry Parkes (1815–96) in New South Wales. The book which Woolner sent to Farringford, however, proved to be a pirated edition, featuring illustrative photographs by Payne Jennings, whose photographic work later appeared in Constance Cotterell's *Summer Holidays in North East England* (1895) and in Annie Berlyn's *Photo Pictures in East Anglia by Payne Jennings* (1897).
4. Probably the political, legal, and military authority (1848–1925), who published *The Problems of a Great City* (1886), *The English Democracy* (1894), *When War Breaks Out* (1898), *The Modern Jew* (1899), and numerous other works.
5. After his stay at Farringford, most likely in April, Parkes traveled to Brussels and visited with the Belgian royal family. Tennyson was pleased by the Queen's appreciation for his poetry, and, as Parkes suggested he do, he sent her a copy of his collected works.

317   To Edward Lear

Aldworth, 27 August 1883

My dear Mr. Lear,
We are indeed grieved to hear that you are so weak, but there is
nothing so prostrating as a loss such as yours. It is touching to
see how the Queen's letter to Ally and yours to me agree. She
naturally dwells more on the courage of the faithful servant she
has lost, how he dared to speak to her without flattery and to
tell her when he thought she was wrong, braving her
displeasure.[1] Ally found her very depressed and one much
mixed up with the court circle told us that she is so softened
that those who used to fear her are now touched by her. I know
that from your having seen so much of her in former days you
will be interested to hear about her more than most of her
subjects. She saw Ally quite alone and made him sit down. She
herself has not sufficiently recovered from her accident to do
without a stick.[2]
    . . . Hallam is, as you know, more to us than we can say. He
has become more and more necessary to us as I have been ill
during the winter and spring and I still lose my voice and such
strength as I have with a very little talking so the care of our
numerous guests devolves on Hallam.
    Ally has been finishing one of his old world poems[3] begun
about the "Ulysses" period and discarded or what Carlyle
called "a dead dog" but Ally has come to think that the world
will receive lessons thus when it discards them in modern
garb. Our truest sympathy and love.

    1. Giorgio Kokali, the Suliot servant who was Lear's companion for
twenty-seven years, died on 8 August 1883. In a letter of 18 August
to Emily Tennyson, Lear praised Giorgio's "constant fidelity, activity,
humility, goodness of disposition,—endless cheerfulness—honesty—patience, and untold other virtues" (Noakes, *Edward Lear*, p. 300). The
Queen paid tribute to John Brown in a letter of 14 August to the poet:
"Courageous, unselfish, *totally* disinterested, discreet to the highest
degree, speaking the truth fearlessly and telling me what he thought
and considered to be 'just and right,' without flattery and without saying
what would be pleasing if he did not think it right—and *ever* at hand—he
was *part* of *my life* and quite invaluable!" (Dyson and Tennyson, *Dear
and Honoured Lady*, pp. 103–04).
    2. On 19 March 1883, Queen Victoria suffered a severe fall which
occasioned a succession of painful rheumatic attacks.
    3. "Tiresias," first published in 1885 in the volume *Tiresias and
Other Poems*.

318   *To William Gladstone*
British Museum

Aldworth, 27 September 1883

My dear Mr. Gladstone,

My Husband thinks that he had better not write to you until tomorrow after the receipt of your report of the Queen's letter; so, will you let me say, meanwhile, how grateful I am for the message you are so good as to send and how glad I am that my view of this matter does not appear to you merely a wife's conceit.

The thought that there are some objections to making the Honour (if it comes) publicly known just now had already struck me, though I had not put it in quite so flattering a form. We have not, of course, mentioned the subject even to Lionel. I hope it will not leak out at court as things are rather apt to do. That Hallam should inherit the duties belonging to this distinction is cause of deep thankfulness to me, they being among those for which I believe him most fitted as they certainly are among those in which he is most interested.[1]

My affectionate thanks to Mrs. Gladstone and yourself for having made them (my Two) sharers in all the pleasures of that most delightful voyage.

1. Emily Tennyson prized the peerage as much for her son as for her husband: "It seems to one a solemn thing," she wrote, "to enroll oneself and one's heirs, as long as the race lasts, among the legislators of England. No one could do so with more hope than Ally looking to our Hallam. Surely never parents owed more to a child than we to him, and it is a new source of thankfulness to me that he should have an honourable career marked out for him when his work for his father has ceased. Not that I am insensible to this fresh mark of respect for his father, only . . . I have been so used to homage paid to him, so, like a child, I think of my new toy—no toy but a very real thing of great importance to the child" (*AT*, p. 472).

In 1873 and again in 1874 Gladstone, in accordance with the Queen's wishes, had offered Tennyson a baronetcy. The Laureate declined the offer each time, but he inquired about the possibility of Hallam's assuming the title in his place at some future date. Gladstone indicated that a deferral of the baronetcy to the Laureate's son would be possible, but Disraeli, when he became Prime Minister, decided that such a reservation would constitute an inappropriate violation of precedent.

319   *To William Gladstone*
British Museum

Aldworth, 6 October 1883

My dear Mr. Gladstone,
My Husband is not, I grieve to tell you, very well. Will you
therefore allow me to say for him how grateful we are for all
your goodness as to the telegram and the fees and everything
else connected with the peerage, for he does not like to delay
his acknowledgements. I do hope that no "silly scribe" will get
hold of rumours and publish them between this and before
Christmas or the first of February. My Husband begs that the
Queen will fix the date which Her Majesty deems most suitable
for the announcement.

320   *To Frederick Tennyson*
Indiana University

Aldworth, 25 January 1884

My dear Frederick,
We are heartily grieved for your loss[1] and we feel how very
great, how overwhelming it is. May God comfort you! We shall
never forget her goodness to us when you received us at
Florence.[2]
    It is only the other day that someone said to Hallam, "Do
you know your Aunt? She is one of the most agreeable women
I have met, so full of vivacity." Forgive me for mentioning
such things now, but in the great losses of my own life I have
felt that there was a poor rag of comfort in knowing that my
loved ones were appreciated by others. When you feel equal to
change remember that you will have a loving welcome with us;
Hallam included.

    1. Frederick Tennyson's wife Maria died in January 1884. Since 1859,
when they left Florence, the Frederick Tennysons had been living at
St. Ewold's, Jersey, where he remained until late 1895, when he went

to London to live with his son, Captain Julius Tennyson, and Julius's wife Sophie.

2. The Laureate and his wife visited the Frederick Tennysons in Florence at the Villa Torrigiani during their 1851 tour.

Emily's health was unusually poor again during the autumn of 1883 and the winter and spring of 1884; she was too ill to travel from Aldworth to Farringford, and for the first time the Tennysons remained at Aldworth right through the winter. On 11 March the poet took his seat in the House of Lords, placing himself on the cross benches since he felt that allying himself with either party might compromise his freedom to vote always for what seemed to him the best interest of the Empire. In June Hallam was married to the Irish beauty Audrey Boyle, who had first visited the Tennysons with her aunt Mary the previous spring. Tennyson thought his wife too ill to attend the ceremony, which was performed in Henry VII's Chapel, Westminster Abbey, but at the last moment Emily determined to go. Robed in a dress of white samite, she was wheeled into the chapel in a bathchair, in which she remained throughout the wedding. Hallam and Audrey returned to Aldworth a few days later to take up residence there, and Hallam of course continued as his father's amanuensis.

321   To Julia Lady Lennard[1]
Christ Church, Oxford

Aldworth [late February 1884]

My dear Julia,

Hallam has a cold, I am sorry to say, and asks me to thank you for your very kind letter. We greatly rejoice that you agree with us as to the reviews. Certainly fresh and pleasant and thoughtful as these youthful letters are, one cannot but feel that Mr. Gaskell has done well in printing them for private circulation only, lest the public ideal of your brother should in any way be disturbed. For the same reason but on infinitely stronger grounds, we have withheld the books from my Ally and I hope that in this also you agree with us.² One has to be specially careful with so very sensitive a nature, as you know. With our kindest love and a hope that we may meet again before long.

1. Sister of Arthur Henry Hallam and wife of Sir John Farnaby.
2. In 1883 Charles Milnes Gaskell printed the correspondence of his father, James Milnes Gaskell, including many letters from his schoolmate, Arthur Hallam, in a volume entitled *Records of an Eton Schoolboy.* In January 1884, Lady Lennard wrote to Tennyson asking his opinion of a review of the book in the *Nineteenth Century* and of a proposed article about the book scheduled to appear in the *Edinburgh Review.* Hallam Tennyson objected strongly to certain letters in the volume which evidenced Arthur Hallam's love affair with Anne Wintour in Italy in 1828, and characteristically he felt that those letters and other materials he thought indelicate should have been suppressed. On 20 February he wrote to Lady Lennard, responding to her letter, which he and his mother had kept from the poet: "I have not liked to show my Father the *Records of an Eton Schoolboy,* for, as you say, there are some letters which ought never to have been inserted, and some expressions which ought to have been erased. I think that it is useless my asking my Father his opinion about a Review of the book in the *Edinburgh,* for he has set your brother on such a pinnacle before all the world, that anything now published concerning your brother can only detract from his fame. . . . As to the *XIXth Century,* I can only regret." See Christopher Ricks, " 'Hallam's Youthful Letters' and Tennyson," *English Language Notes* (December 1965), 120-22.

Emily Tennyson's letter answers Lady Lennard's reply to Hallam Tennyson's letter and reiterates their reasons for withholding Gaskell's book, the *Edinburgh* article, and her letter from the poet. The book was circulated only in a privately printed edition until 1939, when it was published under the title *An Eton Boy.*

322   To Hallam and Audrey Tennyson

Aldworth, 26 June 1884

Beloved ones,
. . . Papa is quite well. Naturally the house seemed very desolate when we returned last evening. We came together however with our Lionel who took most tender care of us, even gathering up my dress that it might not be injured by the wheels of the chair and he seemed very pleased that people in the crowd said as we went along—what a beautiful dress! . . .

I thought you all looked noble and beautiful and as if you ought to do good work for the world and by God's help you will. Lord William Seymour[1] walked by my chair and so did Constance Eliot[2] and I kissed her and Lord Selborne and Sophia. . . .[3] Papa said that Mr. Gladstone seemed troubled. He found him in a room alone at Lady Sarah's[4] looking over papers and he said something about a vote of censure which is explained in today's papers as you will see.[5]

I hope you both liked the service. We did. The servants say it was a beautiful wedding. I could not see the procession, but I wish I could thank everyone as I desire for all they did to make the day beautiful and holy. . . .

My loving thanks for the precious little bit of bridecake. I was obliged to give Lufra[6] a crumb. She raised her nostrils in the air and then insisted on having a bit. You will both excuse this rambling letter. I really feel better than I have done for a long time though of course I am too tired to write very rationally. God bless you both ever and ever. Our best love.

1. Probably Colonel William Frederick Ernest Seymour (b. 1838), promoted to general in 1902 and raised to the peerage as first Baron Seymour in 1903.
2. Unidentified.
3. Roundell Palmer, first Earl of Selborne (1812-95), attorney general, 1863-66, and lord chancellor, 1872-74, 1880-85; and his daughter, Sophia Palmer (d. 1915), later the wife of Amable Charles Franquet, Comte de Franqueville.
4. Unidentified.
5. In June 1884, the House of Commons voted to reject the French Government's proposal for joint administration of Egypt and the Suez Canal. England had moved into Egypt in 1882, after arresting the movements of Arabi Pasha.
6. Tennyson's Irish deerhound.

323   To Audrey Tennyson

Aldworth, 26 June 1884

My darling,
We shall be true Mother and Daughter through life, please God. May you be happy as I desire and happier far than I know how to desire.

324   To Lord Dufferin[1]

Aldworth, 29 September 1884

My dear Lord Dufferin,
My Husband is not able to write at once, and we are so much
afraid that you should have the trouble of calling at the India
Office now that Lionel is not there, that you will, I am sure,
forgive me if I answer your most kind letters for him. I hope
that we care too much for you to have said a word even for our
own Son, had we not known him to be capable of a true
personal devotion and a just enthusiasm for his work. . . .
    We are truly grateful for your goodness in thinking if you
can serve him. We know as little as yourself whether this is
possible. We only thought how delightful it would be if he
could be immediately under yourself, in truth we had but small
expectation that this could be.

1. Frederick Temple Hamilton-Temple Blackwood, first Marquess of
Dufferin (1826 1902), the famous diplomat who distinguished himself
in a number of important posts including those of governor general
of Canada, 1872–78, and viceroy of India, a position to which he was
appointed in 1884. Tennyson wrote to Dufferin in the early autumn
of that year asking if there were a chance of Lionel's being named
his private secretary when he assumed his new duties in India. Dufferin
replied in a letter of 13 September (unpublished, T.R.C.) that he had
already offered the position to another, but he wrote a second letter
on 27 September (unpublished, T.R.C.), suggesting that Lionel investi-
gate the possibility of having the India Office transfer him to India
"in some situation where his abilities would have a wider field than
at home, and which would give me an opportunity of pushing him
on in his career." In the autumn of 1885 Lionel decided that a first-hand
exposure to India would have a salutary influence on his work in the
India Office, and he planned a long visit to India for Eleanor and
himself and arranged to stay with Lord Dufferin. Lionel left Aldworth
and his parents on 6 October for the final time. While in India he
contracted a jungle fever from which he died en route home on 20
April 1886.

325   To Anne and Agnes Weld

Aldworth, 23 October 1885

My dearest Nanny and Agnes,
We have a post card from our Lionel today dated Venice (the

20th). He and Eleanor find it even more enchanting than they expected and he says that they are tempted to stay there rather than go on to India. He is sure that the descendants of the Lotos-Eaters must have built it!

326   To Anne Weld

Aldworth, 19 November 1885

My dearest Nanny,
You will be glad to hear that we have had a delightful letter from our Lionie describing the voyage down the Red Sea. . . . They saw a water-spout, which thing the captain had never seen in that sea, a sandstorm, a flock of flamingoes, making a little sunrise themselves when smitten by the rising sun. . . .

We have very good news of the children. Ally will be seven tomorrow if he lives. Lady Fanny[1] says that she never came in contact with such good children so well trained and obedient yet full of spirit, intelligence and individuality.

1. Lady Frances Baillie (d. 1894), widow of Evan Peter Montagu Baillie, of Dochfour, Inverness, sister of Lady Charlotte Locker, and thus Eleanor Tennyson's aunt. When Eleanor and Lionel Tennyson went to India they left their sons, Alfred and Charles, in the care of "Lady Fanny."

327   To Edward Lear

Farringford, 22 January 1886

My dear Mr. Lear,
We are indeed grieved that you should have been suffering so much.[1] In your more sunny South spring will soon be with you. May this restore you! However solitary your life has for many years been, you must not forget that to you is given the precious gift of peopling the lives of many not only of this generation but of generations to come with good and beautiful things and thoughts, to say nothing of your own life of which so many think with a loving admiration very precious to them.
. . .

Eleanor and Lionel have had varied and most interesting experiences in India ranging from prince to peasant—the latter being to them most interesting, I think. Lionel's last letter gives a very animated account of his visit to Chittagong,[2] his going for some 60 or 70 miles up the river between primeval forests, his glimpse of the Moghs[3] with whom he is much taken and several of whom came and prostrated themselves before him and his companion while they were seated in a bamboo house 8 or 10 feet from the ground.

1. Lear never fully recovered from the illness which kept him bedridden from Christmas 1885 until April 1886.
2. The English district located in what is now Bangladesh.
3. One of the Chittagong tribes.

328   To Anne and Agnes Weld

Farringford, 3 March 1886

My dearest Nanny and Agnes,
Thank God our Lionel's fever[1] had left him or had been cut but he had his usual strength to regain. The doctor did not think it wise that he should undertake a railway journey to Agra . . . for tiger shooting so this was given up and they were to return by Ceylon, the sea voyage being considered good for him.

1. Lionel first became ill while hunting in Assam in mid-January. By the end of March he appeared to have recovered sufficient strength to stand the voyage home, but he died on the Red Sea on 20 April, sixteen days after sailing from Calcutta.

329   To Anne and Agnes Weld

Farringford, 13 April 1886

My dearest Nanny and Agnes,
Our loving thanks for all words of comfort and sympathy. Nothing is impossible with God but the telegram from Colombo is, "No improvement."

330   To Anne and Agnes Weld

Farringford, 16 April 1886

My dearest Nanny and Agnes,
We are very grateful for your loving words. Of course I hope to
see you both and should be unhappy not to see you when I
can, and Uncle will hope to walk alone with Agnes. . . . All
that anyone can do for him or for us is to pray.

331   To Richard Owen

Brotherton Library, University of Leeds

Farringford, 5 April 1887

Dear Sir Richard,
It is pleasant to see your handwriting. We do not forget the
happy days when you were here and when you made the
wonderful dragon out of the bones and scales of the red cliff.[1]
It is very kind in Mr. Chadwick[2] to send my Husband his
address on a subject which has already done so much for the
world and which no doubt is destined to do so much more.
Will you offer Mr. Chadwick my Husband's best thanks and
excuse this coming through myself because of his failing eyes?

1. See above, Letter 156, n. 2.
2. Edwin Chadwick (1800–90), president of the Association of Public
Sanitary Inspectors of Great Britain, chairman of the Education Committee of the Society of Arts, and a close friend of Richard Owen's
since the two served together on the national Sanitary Commission
in the 1840s. The address Chadwick sent to Tennyson was most likely
an expansion of his defense of military drill in public schools in a
letter which appeared in *The Times* on 25 September 1885. Writing
as chairman of the Education Committee which had introduced the
military drill system into elementary schools, Chadwick censured the
Trade Union Congress for its opposition to the system, and he proclaimed
the efficacy of school drill for training children "to meet the increasing
demands for more fit labour needed for the advancement of the arts,
manufactures, and commerce." The Tennysons were of course in wholehearted agreement with both Chadwick's purposes and his means.

Emily's stalwart religious strength carried her through the hard months after Lionel's death, and, as always, her fortitude bolstered the poet. Tennyson was always comforted by sincere sympathy, and the Queen's message of her own grief "beyond measure" for the Laureate and his family also helped him to bear his loss (see Dyson and Tennyson, *Dear and Honoured Lady*, pp. 123–24). In June the poet, Emily, Hallam, and Audrey returned to Aldworth where Emily encouraged the usual stream of visitors, hoping to distract Tennyson and prevent him from lapsing into a long-term despondency. Among the new guests during July and August were Sir Andrew Clark, the renowned Scottish physician, Alfred Ainger, the popular lecturer and Temple reader, and canon of Bristol, and Lord Napier of Magdala, hero of the 1858 siege of the Lucknow garrison. Also in July Tennyson went to London where he visited the Knowleses in St. James's Park, viewed the Indian and Colonial Exhibition, and sailed on Wroxham Broad.

Despite Emily's efforts, Tennyson was restless and depressed throughout the autumn and winter; but he was never idle as he had often been during morbid periods in his youth. In December he issued a new volume which contained "Locksley Hall Sixty Years After," a sequel to the 1842 "Locksley Hall," and in February 1887 he completed his ode "On the Jubilee of Queen Victoria," celebrating the fiftieth anniversary of the Queen's coronation. The jubilee ode speaks the old romantic imperialism, but it is a rather mixed and doubtful paean, and the second "Locksley Hall" is the most pessimistic poem Tennyson ever wrote. All of his sanguine hopes for the future had paled during the long emotional decline after Lionel's death, and his morbid disappointment in the failure of his age was clearly in part the product of his own personal tragedy. During the summer of 1887 the poet found a good deal of diversion in two new friends, Bishop Boyd Carpenter and Richard Jebb, then a young fellow of Trinity College; and in July he chartered Sir Allen Young's yacht, the *Stella*, cruised with Hallam and Audrey around the coasts of Devon, Cornwall, and Wales, and thence to the Channel Islands, and returned to Aldworth a good deal refreshed and restored.

332   *To Edward Lear*

Aldworth, 19 July 1887

My dear Mr. Lear,
Ally, Hallam, and Audrey had the most perfect fortnight for
their cruise. . . . Ally had a fit of the gout and he was
recommended a little voyage so he hired Sir Allen Young's
yacht and they coasted along Dorset Down and Cornwall and
came at last to St. David's and were much delighted with its
wild shore and the fine cathedral and the noble ruins of the
Bishop's Palace.[1] You may think what great pleasure it was to
Hallamee[2] to visit with his Father those scenes of the early
vision of the Arthur *Idylls* . . .[3]

1. The most notable church in Wales, the Cathedral of St. David
is substantially a Transitional Norman building, with a foundation
ascribed to St. David, the patron saint of Wales, who is said to have
been born towards the close of the fifth century. Across the brook
Alan to the west are the extensive remains of the Episcopal Palace,
built by Bishop Gower about 1347. The palace and the cathedral are
about a mile and a half from the sea, at the extreme western tip of
the South Welsh peninsula.
2. Emily Tennyson's pet name for Hallam.
3. The remainder of the letter is missing.

333   *To Anne Weld*

Aldworth, 2 September 1887

My dearest Nanny,
Best thanks. We give our present footman £28 including beer
money. Two dress suits in a year and one working suit; but I
think it is best to ask what wages they have had (do not you?)
because of course wages ought in a measure to correspond to
capabilities. Our footman must be strong and not undersized
and able to clean plate well and get up in reasonable time in
the morning, say to be at work not later than seven, he having
boots and shoes . . . to clean and Hallamee's clothes to brush
and himself in fact to valet and to help with guests when
necessary. . . . He must be willing to do what has to be done.
    We have had a very stormy week. The boys have not been
able to go out much but they have been exceedingly good

notwithstanding, dear little fellows.[1] They delight in my telling them about the young days of their dear Father and Uncle. Eleanor may be home today if her doctor permits. Best love to you both.

1. Lionel Tennyson's sons, "Ally" and "Charlie," who had been at Farringford with their mother from the time of her return in April 1886 from the tragic trip to India.

334   To Edward Lear

Farringford, 25 December 1887

My dear Mr. Lear,
You are very often in my thoughts and often in our mouths.
. . . All is changed here since you were here. You would be startled every now and then by a railway whistle were you with us now. The cars only carry gravel at present but in March the whole way is to be open to Cairsbrook, we are told. Brick boxes multiply more and more year by year and the parish grows more and more lawless. Nevertheless this is the old beloved home to me, the dearest spot on earth.

Fortunately one's eyes look out only on the old prospect from the windows. The old prospect but a little narrowed to the north by the growth of trees. Audrey makes herself beloved by all our friends. I wish you could know her for you would love her too. . . . My Ally has been working but he is changed since you saw him though he can walk well and write wonderfully still.

We earnestly hope that you are better and that you have comfort in your surroundings. Our kindest love and all best wishes.

335   To Anne and Agnes Weld

Farringford, 31 December 1887

My dearest Nanny and Agnes,
Ally and Charlie seem to have had a very merry Christmas.

They have been to three little parties. In one they danced Irish jigs and Swedish dances. Mr. Browning has given Ally a massive silver pen and pencil case and he wrote a letter saying that Ally bore three names, one glorious, one very good, and one affectionate, as to the persons who bore them (by affectionate meaning himself).[1] Ally of his own accord wrote back, "I think your name great as well as affectionate."

Last night Hallamee read "The Single Man"[2] and "The Northern Cobbler" in the assembly room.[3] People liked both much though Hallamee could not read his best for some people would talk.

1. See above, Letter 298, n. 1. Emily called her eldest grandchild "Ally," also her nickname for Tennyson.
2. "The First Quarrel."
3. Hallam Tennyson occasionally gave public readings of his father's works in the Freshwater assembly hall. "The First Quarrel" would have been a natural choice since the dialect is that of the Isle of Wight, the scene of the action, and the doctor of the poem is the Freshwater physician G. R. Dabbs.

The new year was saddened for both Tennyson and Emily by the death of Edward Lear on 29 January at the Villa Tennyson, San Remo. Lear had devoted his last months to an enormous painting of "Enoch Arden," which he had intended to give the Tennysons on his next trip to England, and he had spent much of his time during his final years working on his series of Tennyson engravings, thirty-six of which were published a year after his death by Messrs. Boussod, Valloden and Co. In February Princess Beatrice, Prince Henry of Battenberg, and Sir Henry Ponsonby came to Farringford, and Tennyson read to them the Wellington Ode and "The Spinster's Sweet-Arts," one of his Lincolnshire dialect poems which he particularly loved to read aloud. The Charles Villiers Stanfords, Hartley Coleridge, and General Sir George Higginson, lieutenant-governor of the Tower of London, visited Farringford in the early spring, and in June Mary Anderson, the American actress, came to discuss a possible production of *The Foresters.* On the eighteenth Tennyson, along with Hallam and Audrey, took Miss Anderson on a pilgrimage to Lyndhurst to acquaint her with the ambiance of his handling of the Robin Hood legend. Drummond Rawnsley's son Willingham, master of a Park Hill school attended by Ally and Charlie Tennyson, brought the poet's grandsons to meet the party at Lyndhurst, and he drove the entire party through the New Forest. Tennyson quoted from his play and, despite his health and age, seemed as merry as a schoolboy.

In July the family moved to Aldworth where they received Boyd Carpenter, Aubrey DeVere, Franklin Lushington, the Duke of Argyll, and the Liberal statesman Lord Carnarvon, who found Tennyson "as fresh and capable as ever," but doubtful of human or social progress and "inclined to look at everything from a very narrow point of view" (quoted by Richardson, *The Pre-Eminent Victorian,* pp. 238-39). On 9 September, after a long walk through the Blackdown countryside with Sir Alfred Lyall, Tennyson noticed that his knees were slightly swollen, and within a week he was in the throes of the most serious illness of his life. Sir Andrew Clark, who diagnosed the initial attack as rheumatic gout, came from London to minister to the poet three times, and Dr. Dabbs made several visits from the Isle of Wight.

By November he was somewhat improved, and on the twenty-first Dabbs had him removed from Aldworth to the less severe climate of Farringford in a special train and ambulance carriage. A month later Tennyson had a serious relapse, and he was confined mostly to his bedroom until 9 March, when he went outside for the first time since returning to Farringford and walked for five minutes in the sunshine. By mid-May, however, Clark pronounced him fully recovered. Before the end of the month he set out with Hallam and Andrew Hichens and his wife May, a niece of Thoby Prinsep, for a cruise along the Devon and Cornwall coasts; and in July Francis Palgrave found him "in full vigour of mind and able to walk a mile" (quoted by Richardson, *The Pre-Eminent Victorian,* p. 238).

336   *To Lord Napier of Magdala*[1]

Farringford, 26 December 1888

Dear Lord Napier of Magdala,
I cannot even try to tell you how much pleasure your words give to us all.[2] Would that he himself could! But for between

three and four months he has been quite prostrate from gout and rheumatic fever and the doctors warn us that his recovery will be very slow.

Most earnestly do we hope that all is well with you and yours and that all will be most well this new year and ever. The brotherhood of those who fight for England with pen and sword is near and dear as I can testify, and my Hallam also whose testimony must be to you of better worth.

1. Robert Cornelius Napier, first Baron Napier of Magdala (1810–90), commander-in-chief of the Bombay army, 1865; governor of Gibraltar, 1876–79. For many years a soldier and engineer in India, Napier helped lead the relief of the Lucknow garrison in March 1858, a siege Tennyson immortalized in "The Defence of Lucknow," picturing the battle so exactly that Napier told the poet in 1886 he would have thought the author had been there.

2. On 24 December 1888, Napier wrote the following letter from Pas de Calais (unpublished, T.R.C.):

> Dear Lord Tennyson,
>   May this arrive in time to wish for you and all whom you love a happy Christmas. May that Pen which never fails to call upon England when she hesitates to remember Her ancient renown, Her great inheritance, and Her real power to spurn craven counsels! May that pen flourish for many years to come.
>   I remain, Yours sincerely,
>   Napier of Magdala

337   To Robert Browning
Yale

Aldworth, 22 July 1889

My dear Mr. Browning,
Forgive me if I write in spite of your prohibition. It has been cruel work and we grieve deeply for you and your son and FitzGerald's family.[1] Thank God your wife and my husband cannot suffer from the rash words of any individual. We must leave them to the ages. If I am bold enough to forestall this judgment, I must leave you to judge me.

No sister could be kinder to me than she was and I have never ceased to be grateful. More I do not presume to say. Ally bids me say with his love that Fitz never meant what you have him to mean.

1. Early in July 1889, Aldis Wright of Trinity College, Cambridge, issued a volume of the letters of Edward FitzGerald which preserved FitzGerald's remark at the time of Mrs. Browning's death expressing relief that there now would be no more "Aurora Leighs." Browning was deeply offended, and in his anger he wrote a savage attack on FitzGerald which appeared in the *Athenaeum* on 13 July. Subsequently he wrote to Emily Tennyson to defend his bitter fusillade (see *AT*, p. 512); the letter above was her reply.

338   *To Anne and Agnes Weld*

Aldworth, 10 September 1889

My dearest Nanny and Agnes,
Our poor little boys' last day of holiday here for the summer.
They are very sad at leaving. Fancy both having ridden about twenty miles yesterday to the Devil's Jumps and declaring that they were not the least tired. . . . They are very dear and good.
One of their delights is to put on an apron and work! They have made a garden too and the paths were swept two or three times yesterday to make them clean for me.

339   *To Hallam and Audrey Tennyson*

Farringford, 4 November 1889

Beloved mine,
I have told Papa that I thought you would be disappointed if the Poems[1] were not sent to you but sent direct to Mr. Craik,[2] so he lets me send them to you by this post and bids me say that he has not forgotten those points you discussed together but he has decided on leaving them as they are and he does not wish any word to be altered. . . .

I have been thinking of the new School Code.[3] Surely it will not be founded on that mockery of education, that curse of a Christian land, a Godless education. There being a God how can He be other than the foundation and source of all truth, power and goodness. A review of Lord Russell's[4] life might give thee timely opportunity of raising thy voice against such wickedness and folly. The Lord's Prayer, the Commandments, the Gospels, surely these are common ground for Christians. All distinctive sectarian views may be taught in Sunday Schools of the sects. I suppose the right to free education would be limited to a certain amount of income and I hope that such schools as ours here . . . will be allowed to remain as they are even if paid by the state.

1. *Demeter and Other Poems,* published by Macmillan in December 1889.
2. George Lillie Craik (d. 1905), husband of the celebrated author of *John Halifax.* Craik was the manager of Macmillan's and a partner in the company from 1865 until his death.
3. The National Society's proposal for the new Education Code (1889) stressed the need for effective moral teaching in the public schools, but it also implied that the Society would not emphasize the necessity for specifically Anglican religious instruction.
4. John, first Earl Russell; see above, Letter 270, n. 2.

340   To Hallam and Audrey Tennyson

Farringford, 6 November 1889

Beloved mine,

I quite agree about "Katherine"—"Mabel" robs the ballad of half its fire.[1] Papa acquiesces, I think. He only remonstrated that "Mabel is softer," but when I spoke of the loss of fire he said no more. As to the poem "The Lord Spake"[2] he does not think it clear enough and Mr. Jowett did not think it sense. I think they are right as it stands but it might easily be made clear. Father Haythornethwaite[3] is of the same mind. He is walking with Papa.

Begging letters have come every day lately, I think. One ought to give if they are real causes, ought one not? . . .

The Somersby church is a pretty sketch. I will not write if you will kindly see the artist. Papa wishes him to know that his moated grange[4] and his other things are imaginary and not Baumber's house or any other. How troublesome people are!

1. The Catherine of the ballad "Forlorn" was originally called Mabel, but Tennyson changed her name at his wife's insistence.
2. Later titled "A Voice spake out of the skies" and published in *The Death of Oenone and Other Poems* (1892). Until shortly before

publication the poem, actually written c. 1866, opened with the words "The Lord Spake."

3. Father Haythornethwaite, the Freshwater friend and chaplain of W. G. Ward.

4. The reference is to the "lonely moated grange" of "Mariana." For a discussion of Tennyson's debt to the "moated grange" of *Measure for Measure,* see Ricks, *The Poems of Tennyson,* p. 187.

5. Farmer Baumber, a neighbor of the Tennysons during the Somersby days.

341   To Hallam Tennyson

Farringford, 16 November 1889

Beloved mine,

Papa begs that he may see the book[1] again. I tell him you said that Mr. Craik would come with you and bring it. I know, belovedee, that you may not be able to come but even if not you will ask Mr. Craik to come. You must not come if you are needed—wanted of course you must be here and there too.

I think the Duke of Argyll is at Edinburgh giving his lecture. He said it was to be in the middle of this month. He is a good, true and very able man who loves Papa and you so I should like him to be Godfather to our little Lionel Hallam. . . .[2]

Papa went again yesterday to Miss Ward's[3] summerhouse and saw her again. He says that Nurse[4] will not take a chair for him, quite right she is now, so he goes to his friends' summerhouses to rest. He has begun painting and is as usual and cheerful. If you can will you call on the Dowager Lady Simeon who is in very bad spirits, her eyes being worse. . . .

Will Mr. Craik kindly bring *The Brook and Its Banks*[5] when he comes. I think this is the name of the book Papa wants.

1. The drafts for *Demeter and Other Poems.*
2. Lionel Hallam Tennyson, third Baron (1889–1951), eldest son of Hallam and Audrey Tennyson, was born on 7 November. See below, Letter 344, n. 2.
3. Unidentified.
4. A Miss Durham, who nursed Tennyson until his death.
5. That is, *The Brook by the Way* (London, 1867), a text and prayer for every day in the year.

342   *To Hallam Tennyson*

Farringford, 19 November 1889

Beloved mine,
Papa wanted his *Scraps,* but when I asked, "May I not say that
the old title may be kept," he said, "very well." Say if you can
when the book is likely to be here again. Papa says there are
two or three little things he wants to correct. Be sure to get Mr.
Craik at all events to bring it or there may be some undesirable
change.

343   *To Hallam Tennyson*

Farringford, 19 November 1889

Beloved mine,
I have told Papa that I do not think you can come until Audrey
does. You will, I trust, soon have to help to lift her to the sofa.
I am afraid it will be a bother to Mr. Craik to come, but I
dread these corrections not knowing what may happen and I
want either thyself or himself to confirm my judgment.[1]

1. Emily Tennyson always dreaded her husband's alterations in what
he had written, feeling that his initial impulses were generally his best.

344   *To Hallam Tennyson*

Farringford, 23 November 1889

I am very glad that you called on Fanny Kemble and were in
the act of calling on Mr. Woolner when Mrs. Woolner met you.
It is good to hear that Mrs. Kemble was so pleasant. She has
always been kind to me though she never praised my beauty
nor my voice! I can well understand that she and her brother
really were the first to discover that Papa was one of the
greatest English poets.[1] Shakespeare must have lent them
scales to weigh the poet and they had the wit to use them.
    But our baby will soon want some mighty scales if he begins

so soon to distinguish himself.² I shall now think I am no
dreamer when I thought that at a few days older you admired a
glorious sunset sky. . . .

Nurse thinks that a waterproof cape would be a good thing to
put over Papa in this showery weather.

1. In 1843 the Kembles supported Tennyson for the Laureateship
in succession to Robert Southey.

2. It was principally as a Test Match cricketer and international *bon
vivant* that the third Baron Tennyson distinguished himself. He played
for England against South Africa in five Test Matches, 1913–14, cap-
tained the English against Australia in four Matches, 1921, and played
against the West Indies in three Matches, 1926–27. He was also the
author of two books, *From Verse To Worse* (1933) and *Sticky Wickets*
(1955).

345   To Anne Weld

Farringford, 30 December 1889

My dearest Nanny,

I am sorry not to have written to you but indeed I have been
quite overtasked and knocked up. Of course it was useless
saying anything about it. What had to be done must be done as
long as I could do it.

Thank God, my Hallam's return has done much to restore
me. He, dearest darling, has had to trudge off again today. He
is appointed one of the pallbearers in his Father's place at
Browning's funeral tomorrow. . . .¹ Ally I am thankful to say
keeps wonderfully well in spite of the trying weather.
Hallamee says that the enthusiasm about his book among the
"big-wigs" (as he calls them) in London is wonderful. People
used to shake him by the hand expressing their admiration and
delight. . . .

18 or 20 letters in a morning as I have had some mornings to
read before I could let Ally see them are in themselves hard
work for an old and far from strong old woman, are they not?

1. Browning died in Venice on 16 December 1889, the very day
Demeter and Other Poems was published.

Although Tennyson was ill with bronchitic influenza early in 1890, he soon recovered and continued to be remarkably active, walking an hour and a half every morning and composing as usual. In February Princess Beatrice requested that he write a few appropriate words for a prayer book which the Queen's children planned to present to her on her fiftieth wedding anniversary. Within three days the Laureate responded with the following inscription:

> Remembering Him who waits thee far away,
> And with thee, Mother, taught us first to pray,
> Accept on this your golden bridal-day
>   The Book of Prayer.

At Easter, though Emily was very unwell and confined for the most part to her drawing room, she minimized her ill health to her husband and managed to receive a considerable number of guests, including the Bradleys, the Montague Butlers, the Coleridges, the Stanfords, the Brookfields, the Arthur Elliots, Annie Thackeray, and William Allingham.

346   To Anne Weld

Farringford, 13 May 1890

My dearest Nanny,
I am better than I was. My heart has been at low ebb during the present year but after all a great many people have been worse and your dear self among the rest. Once or twice I was very unwell but of course I must keep things to myself as much as possible. How glad I am that dear Edward's[1] funeral is on such a lovely day! We sent a wreath with a card in Ally's handwriting: "In loving memory, Tennyson."
    . . . I have many, many things to be thankful for. Few people more, and no one has had more delightful nearest belongings than myself, Father, Husband, Sons, Grandfather[2] . . . as men and my very, very dear Sisters besides. We should have loved our Mother I am sure and Grandmama[3] was a noble old lady. So, Nanny, looking around I may well esteem myself blessed.

1. The poet's brother, Edward Tennyson (1813-90), died in a mental institution where he had been incarcerated since his youth.
2. William Franklin (1739-1822).
3. Hannah Weeks Franklin (1751-1810).

347 To Anne Weld

Farringford, 15 May 1890

My dearest Nanny,
We were the other day much interested by having a phonograph here. What a wonderful invention it is! Mr. Stiegler,[1] who exhibited it to us, asked Ally to recite part of "The Charge of the Light Brigade" into it and when Nurse Durham who had not heard him recite it heard it through the tubes of the telephone she gave a great start it was so loud and so exactly his voice. Baby[2] shouted with delight when he heard his Grandfather reciting. . . . I could not stand the tubes. I tried for a moment and they pierced my brain. Best love to Agnes and yourself.

1. A representative from Thomas Edison who sent Tennyson the phonograph from America as a gift. On the fifteenth the Laureate recorded "The Bugle Song" from *The Princess,* in addition to "The Charge of the Light Brigade." Soon thereafter he also recorded "The Charge of the Heavy Brigade," "Ask me no more," "Northern Farmer. New Style," and portions of "Maud," "Boädicea," and the Wellington Ode. Some of the original wax cylinders still exist, have been transferred to disks, and are available for order from the Tennyson Research Centre.
2. Lionel Hallam Tennyson.

348 To Anne Weld

Aldworth, 30 June 1890

My dearest Nanny,
Mr. Church,[1] Mrs. Bentley's uncle, lunched here on Friday and was very friendly and pleasant. He is going to write notices on another set of Tennyson pictures. Rather sickening these semblances of biography which are no biography. However Mr. Church will not publish anything we do not like. It was

rather pleasant to see a picture of Harrington Hall.[2] Do you remember our being there when we were tinies and that the tapestry half frightened us. I remember too my great admiration of Arabella Cracroft[3] and her great dog. She was a lovely creature. Best love to you both.

1. Alfred Church, who in 1891 published a topographical book entitled *Laureate's Country.*
2. The Queen Anne manor house two miles from Somersby Rectory which Rosa Baring's stepfather, Arthur Eden, leased in 1825. At that time Robert and Augusta Cracroft, cousins of the Henry Sellwoods, owned Harrington Hall.
3. (1801–73), fourth daughter of John and Penelope Ann Cracroft of Hackthorn Hall, Lincoln. Miss Cracroft frequently visited her brother and sister-in-law at Harrington before her marriage to Matthew Henry Lister in 1823. (My informant is Lt. Colonel Sir Weston Cracroft-Amcotts, Hackthorn Hall.)

349   To Anne Weld

Aldworth, 7 July 1890

My dearest Nanny,
You will be glad to hear that Sir Andrew,[1] the aurist, and the oculist, etc. pronounce favourably on him.[2] I do not myself believe that he is so well as is said though wonderful considering what he has been through!

The Knowleses[3] were most kind and hospitable. The Gladstones and others dined there one night. Mr. Gladstone being very anxious to see my Ally who however did not dine downstairs but Mr. Gladstone went up and brought him down after dinner and was very delightful.[4] Everyone was very kind to him. Princess Mary came to call on him among others and it was rather odd that he should just have been driving in Hyde Park when the Queen came to town for a few hours. She recognized him. She had told Hallamee that she should like to see him again. And she has had a glimpse of him at all events.
. . . Do not overdo yourself in London. Ally felt better while there and so I trust will you, poor Nanny.

1. Sir Andrew Clark (1826–93).
2. In London from 2–5 July, Tennyson and Hallam stayed with James Knowles, who accompanied the poet on his visits to his doctors. Knowles

later recalled that although Tennyson was heartily reassured by the oculist about his eyes, as he left the office he remarked "with utter gloom, 'No man shall persuade me I'm not going blind'" (Knowles, "Aspects of Tennyson," p. 174).

3. Tennyson often stayed with Mr. and Mrs. Knowles when he was in London.

4. Hallam Tennyson noted that his father and Gladstone spent the evening talking of Homer and Browning (*Memoir*, I, 381).

While in London during the first week of July, the poet and Hallam received numerous guests at Knowles's home in Queen Anne's Gate, including Lord Acton, Lady Pembroke, Lady Brownlow, the Sydney Buxtons, and other luminaries, titled and untitled, in addition to the Gladstones and Princess Mary, the Duchess of Teck. One afternoon they went to see Burne-Jones's "Briar Rose" series at Agnew's and Edward James Poynter's "Waterloo Panorama" and his "Queen of Sheba." Inspired by the Burne-Jones depiction of Sleeping Beauty's hundred-year sleep, Tennyson subsequently read the Sleeping Beauty section of "The Day-Dream" to Lady Brownlow and Lady Pembroke, and he also read parts of "Maud" to Princess Mary.

During the late summer and autumn at Aldworth both Tennyson and Emily were more vigorous than they had been in recent years, and they received a steady stream of visitors. Dean Farrar, who came at the end of July, suggested the subject for "St. Telemachus," which Tennyson began to write within a fortnight. Ally and Charlie Tennyson came the first week of August, and they were soon followed by their mother and their stepfather, the statesman and essayist Augustine Birrell, whom Eleanor had married in May 1888. By the seventh the Bradleys and Lord Houghton (Richard Monckton Milnes's son) had also arrived, and the Duchess of Albany came to pay her respects on the sixth, Tennyson's eighty-first birthday. Still hoping to see all his dramas produced, the Laureate was from time to time in touch with Irving about *The Foresters,* and in December he learned that Lawrence Barrett, the American actor, had signed a contract to do *Becket.* In January, however, Irving informed Tennyson that he had abandoned the idea of producing *The Foresters,* and Barrett's death in March thwarted his plans for *Becket* as well.

350   To Anne Weld

Farringford, 21 February 1891

My dearest Nanny,

I hope that you will not think that I have gone rather crazy in
my old age when you hear that a volume of my music to Ally's
songs is going, I believe, to be published by Chappell.[1]
Hallamee a little time ago collected scattered sheets which he
found and then had them bound together. Mlle Janotha came
across the volume when she was with us at Aldworth and
kindly said that they ought to be published and that she would
prepare them for publication. Accordingly she has been so
good as to put modern accompaniments for which I have not as
you know science enough. Then she urged me to get
permission from the Queen to dedicate them to Her Majesty
and as Mlle Janotha had taken so much trouble I could not of
course refuse. I have received a most gracious permission and
some of the songs (there are 14 in the volume) are to be sung in
a concert under the Queen's patronage on March 13th.[2]

I confess that I feel as if I were going to take a leap into a
very cold sea, but here is the history of how it came to pass for
you. Tell it to Eleanor if she is with you but I do not want it
published further. I don't like to keep it from you or from her
so I write it.

1. The music publishing house of William Chappell (1809–88), the
musical antiquary; succeeded his father Samuel Chappell as sole manager
of Chappell and Company upon the latter's death in 1834.
    I can locate no record of the publication of Emily Tennyson's settings
of her husband's poems.
2. The songs sung under Mlle Janotha's direction at St. James's Hall
included "Lilian," "Riflemen Form!" and several others titled only
by first lines: "To sleep! to sleep! The long bright day is done," "Lady
let the rolling drums," and "Home they brought him slain with spears."
Mr. Frantzer and Mr. Maunder conducted the singing, and Mr. George
Mount conducted the Royal Amateur Orchestral Society.

351   To Anne and Agnes Weld

Farringford, 14 March 1891

My dearest Nanny and Agnes,
You are so kind as to send good wishes for the songs.
Therefore I think I had better copy Hallamee's telegram. He,
dear old boy, went up yesterday to see and hear for himself.
We hope to have him home this evening.

> Songs brilliant success, accompaniment wonderful.
> [Mlle Janotha] was presented with lyre of roses and
> ferns. I return at six.

You may think how thankful I am for it was a most brave
venture on her part to have seven of my songs sung. . . . We
have given Mlle Janotha the copyright for three years so she
can have them sung when and where she will.[1]

1. On 1 February 1893, the third number on the program of Mlle
Janotha's concert at the Royal Female School of Art was Lady Tennyson's
setting of "Lilian," sung by Mrs. Clara Wright. Doubtless Mlle Janotha
included Emily Tennyson's songs in other performances as well.

On 9 June the poet and Hallam embarked on a cruise down
the south coast in the yacht *Assegai*, lent them by their neighbor,
Colonel Richard Pearson Crozier. Some two weeks after their
return to Aldworth, they left for London, where they visited
Knowles, Aubrey DeVere, and Lord Houghton; Tennyson was
in marvelous health, and he immensely enjoyed his conversations
with his old friends. During the summer and early autumn he
continued to breakfast at eight and to walk two or more miles
each day. In late September Theodore Watts-Dunton visited the
Tennysons, and he wrote that he thought Tennyson as alert and
as active artistically as he had been forty years before: "He is
busy writing poetry as fine as anything he has ever written.
He read out to me last night three poems which of themselves
would suffice to make a poet's fame. Really he is a miracle"
(quoted by Richardson, *The Pre-Eminent Victorian*, p. 258). In
October, however, Tennyson's health waned, and when on the
thirtieth he returned to Farringford for the final time, it was
necessary to hire a special nonstop train. Early in the new year

the Laureate was shocked by the death of the Duke of Clarence, eldest son of the Prince of Wales. Immediately he wrote for the bereaved royal family a poem of consolation mourning the unfortunate duke (whom recent historians have linked with the most vicious and loathsome crimes) as a spirit "princely, tender, truthful, reverent, pure." Tennyson was not at all well when he undertook "The Death of the Duke of Clarence and Avondale," and the effort seems to have hastened the deterioration which ended in his death at Aldworth in October 1892.

352   To Agnes Weld

Farringford, 7 February 1892

We have had rather an anxious time. . . . It is difficult to do everything just as Uncle Alfred is used to have it, for we have had Colonel Collins[1] here since Wednesday and Hallamee has of course had to look after him and his Father also. . . .

Hallam could not go with [Colonel Collins] to Osborne yesterday, as he had intended but the Colonel was very pleased to see the Prince of Wales so much better than when he saw him at the funeral, and he brought a good report of all except the poor Princess of Wales who is still very much overpowered. Princess Mary is well in health though of course very sad.[2]

1. An attendant to the Queen at Osborne.
2. The Duke of Clarence died within six weeks of the announcement of his engagement to Princess Mary of Teck, afterwards Queen Mary, wife of King George V.

353   To Anne Weld

Farringford, 21 February 1892

My dearest Nanny,
The casual way in which you mention "an offer of marriage" makes me fear that it is not one Agnes will accept. The longer one lives, the more one feels how serious, nay how momentous an affair it is. Well do I remember my father's sad eyes when being himself ill he thought of me left alone in the world. It is

of course different with Agnes. She is strong and has better fortune and so more means of doing good in the world. Still for most people I think it is best to be married.

354   To Anne Weld

My dearest Nanny,

I rejoice to hear that Agnes has received so much encouragement in her literary work.[1] When you come here, will you bring her article on Mrs. Oliphant[2] with you that I may read it? I had our *Spectator* of that date looked for, but it was not to be found. I can read a little now, though I suffer a good deal even from a little.

Nanny darling, it is not easy to write much when people quite differ on any subject and you see we three are strongly impressed by St. Paul's words. The head of the woman is the man[3] and therefore we object to competition between the two though we would have both developed to the utmost, so Hallamee thought the less he said the better and I think you agree. Woman should be the complement of man not his rival, his helpmate. I don't know what Audrey thinks but the same I am sure.

1. Agnes Weld published two articles on her famous uncle, both in *The Contemporary Review.* "The Greatest Poet of the Age" appeared in the March 1893 issue, and a later article entitled simply "Tennyson" came out in the number for November 1897.

2. Margaret Oliphant (1828–97), the novelist and historical writer; a frequent contributor to *Blackwood's* in which, after 1853, many of her novels were published serially. I have found no evidence of the article by Agnes Weld.

3. I Corinthians 11:3.

The poet was slightly improved for a time in the early summer, and he and Hallam had another voyage on the *Assegai,* this time to the Channel Islands to see Frederick Tennyson. Tennyson always exulted in the sea, and he thoroughly enjoyed his last voyage in spite of his delicate condition. On 30 June he and Emily went to Aldworth together for the final time. July and August passed much as usual, with the poet working steadily at "Akbar's Dream," "Kapiolani," "The Dreamer," and other poems for his last volume, including the hauntingly beautiful "June Bracken and Heather," a dedication to Emily which he had begun the previous summer. The Tennysons entertained a host of friends, but only the Duke of Argyll spoke of the great change in the poet and sensed that the end was near. In early September Tennyson grew worse, and Emily discouraged visitors, especially during Hallam's two-week trip to Somersby, a pilgrimage designed to gratify his father's wish to know the present condition of his old home. When Hallam returned in the middle of the month, it was apparent that Tennyson had lapsed into a terminal decline.

355   To Anne Weld

Aldworth, 8 August 1892

My dearest Nanny,

I am sorry to say that my Ally is still suffering from gout in the throat and jaw which greatly depresses him. We say as little as may be about this; the newspapers, if they got hold of it, would bring endless trouble of letters, etc. Very kindly meant but very distressing to recipients.

Our lawyers and yours have sent us the particulars of the Somersby estate which is to be sold in a few days and which they want us to buy, but as £80,000 is wanted and probably 50 or 60 will be got for it some millionaire must buy it for us as we should have to sell all our belongings to purchase it ourselves. . . .[1]

1. The present owner of the old rectory at Somersby, now called Somersby House, is Lady Maitland, wife of Sir John Maitland of Harrington Hall. The present occupant is William Maitland, their eldest son.

356　To Anne and Agnes Weld

Aldworth, 18 September 1892

My dearest Nanny and Agnes,
My poor Ally has been very unwell. When Hallam came home
he telegraphed for Dr. Dabbs and I had had two doctors
before. Thank God Ally seems better now.

357　To Anne and Agnes Weld

Aldworth, 3 October 1892

My dearest Nanny and Agnes,
He became very ill the day Sir Andrew left.[1] Dr. Dabbs has
been most kind. He has been with us six nights; he stayed all
day yesterday and is coming again this evening and we have
two nurses. He has milk and brandy and such things every two
hours. . . . Thank God Dr. Dabbs is hopeful now.

If you like to show this to dear Mr. Jowett, do. You may
consider that things are going on as well as can be expected if
you hear nothing. He is, of course, in bed.

1. Sir Andrew Clark, who came from London on 29 September, thought
the poet's condition not so very serious, but the next day, after Clark
left, Tennyson was very much worse. With Emily, Hallam, and Audrey
at his side, Tennyson died at 1:35 a.m. on 6 October.

358　To Anne and Agnes Weld

Aldworth, 11 October 1892

My dearest Nanny and Agnes,
My blessing on you both. I knew nothing of arrangements
made for me. We wished you both to be present[1] as mourners.
. . . I am not able to have anyone with me except my Hallam,
at least only to look after me as far as my bodily wants. . . . He
and I feel that we live with Him still and that in this is our
best hope of a fuller life in God. I have indeed much beyond
words to be thankful for. I had been joyful in the hope of

going with Him but my Hallam tells me that I can be a help in the work to be done and nothing I can do is too much to be done either for the Father or the devoted Son of our love.

1. At the funeral in Westminster Abbey, 12 October. Neither Emily Tennyson nor Anne Weld was well enough to attend the service, but Agnes went, and she subsequently wrote her aunt a complete account of the funeral.

359   To Anne and Agnes Weld

Aldworth, 13 October 1892

My dearest Nanny and Agnes,
I know all your faithful love to Him and I bless you for it. I thank you, Agnes darling, for your most touching account of the day which will always be treasured by us. The dear Duke of Argyll writes that he has seen nothing like the scene since the funeral of the Duke of Wellington, but that yesterday it seemed that each one mourned a friend. I have not his letter but I think these were his words. . . . There is no one I would so well have had as your companion than that good and true and loving friend Franklin Lushington.

Audrey has shared in the most loving way for us. She really loved Him. The wagonette was made beautiful here with flowers and moss.[1] Our faithful William[2] led the one horse "Robin Hood" who drew it. Hallamee, Audrey and Maud and some of our people followed with other wreaths and there were school children and villagers and Hallamee says this was the most trying time for him. He felt faint in the Abbey once but got through well, thank God, and is well now I think and so is Audrey. After all Maud and Violet[3] could go because their Father and Mother could not.[4]

1. The wagonette, in which the Laureate's body was conveyed from Farringford to the ferry, was adorned with stag's horn moss and scarlet *Lobelia cardinalis*. The coffin was covered with wreaths and crosses of flowers sent from all parts of the British Empire.
2. William Knight.
3. Horatio Tennyson's daughters.
4. Only a limited number of ticket-holders were allowed to attend Tennyson's funeral.

360   To Anne Weld

Aldworth, 15 October 1892

My dearest Nanny,
My own belief is that my Ally's illness had something to do
with influenza. The doctors talked of nervous exhaustion and
this might well have been the cause. I know you will not
expect me to write much. I wish you had been well enough to
be there on the 12th, the very day on which our Lionel left this
home for the last time. We would not have had his Father live
the suffering life he has done of late. We who love him best
know that he has never been the same since his bad illness
four years ago and that from last February there was, we fear,
no enjoyment of life. But for our hope of another the void
would be unendurable. Some day we hope to tell you things
that will interest you if they are not already known, but there
are such innumerable letters to write and public letters to be
considered that we cannot now. You must tell me how you
both are.

361   To Anne and Agnes Weld

Farringford, 1 November 1892

My dearest Nanny and Agnes,
Loving thanks for the grand photographs and for the extracts
from letters which have emerged from the hundreds of letters
and poems that have come. It was most good in you to have
copied these interesting bits. You must forgive me if I do not
write much. Almost all of my strength I have to give to the
Memoir.[1] We have not yet found nearly all the journals, but
they were not cared for as they ought to have been and would
have been had a memoir been thought of in old days.

I told you about little Lionel. He has since asked about his
Baba,[2] where he was. Audrey said, "In Heaven," to which he
replied, "I was very good to him. I always showed him all my
toys."

We have a dry day here today, still and cold. Best love to you
both, you dear ones. I hope dear Agnes will resume what she
feels to be her proper work in life. We must none of us give up

that. My hope is that my Ally's life will live through my
Hallam's most of all and through that of all who have loved
him, known and unknown, will help them to do their work in
life. Yes I believe indeed that all good words are inspired, but
the words of the Gospel and epistles and of the Bible in a
higher sense inspiration than others.

   1. Emily Tennyson spent much of her last four years assisting her
son in the collection and arrangement of materials for the Tennyson
Memoir. She revised and consolidated the journals kept during most
of her married life, and she gathered together all of the family letters
she thought Hallam might use. As Hallam progressed, she criticized
his manuscripts, and she devoted her final weeks in the summer of
1896 to proofings and revisions.
   2. The grandchildren's pet name for Tennyson.

362   To Anne Weld

Farringford, 20 November 1892

My dearest Nanny,
The bairnies here are flourishing. Baby[1] has eleven teeth but
he can only say a very few words yet, though he evidently
understands a great deal of what is said. Audrey is very good in
helping Hallam to copy, but to get the journals and the letters
looked through will be a long work. The journals are my task
after Hallamee has read them at night which makes it easier for
me to condense them in the daytime.

   1. Alfred Aubrey Tennyson (1891-1918).

363   To Anne Weld

Farringford, 30 December 1892

My dearest Nanny,
Loving thanks for having copied Miss Melville Lee's[1] letter. I
fear it must have tired you writing so much. We cannot but
rejoice that one we like so much as we do her brother should
have so strong a feeling for him and that she herself should not
have been disappointed in him. Hallam and I always felt

anxious of late on this score. Our beloved one so seldom
seemed his own self and this made us unwilling that any but
old friends should see him.

Our loving best wishes for the new year for you both.
Hallamee has told you that there was no particular "Bar."[2] It is
curious how little credit people give to the imagination of a
poet. Hints from the world of course be takes, but he does not
photograph Nature or even copy Nature. The Material suggests
the Spiritual that is all. Best love to you both.

1. The sister of Arthur H. Lee of Kingston, Ontario, Canada, who
was a guest at Aldworth several times shortly before Tennyson's death.
On 12 August 1896, after Emily Tennyson's death, Lee wrote a letter
to Hallam (unpublished, T.R.C.) in which he described the indelible
impression the poet's wife had made upon him during his visits at
Aldworth four years before: "I can never forget the sweetness and ever
gracious kindness with which your dear mother always greeted me,
and it is but the simple truth to say that I, though little more than
a stranger, have honored her beyond all women I have ever known,
and that I never left her presence but with a sense of spiritual uplifting."

2. Set to music by his widow, "Crossing the Bar" and "The Silent
Voices" were sung at the poet's funeral.

364   To Agnes Weld

Farringford, 7 February 1893

My dearest Agnes,
I will copy Irving's telegrams about *Becket.*[1] It was very kind
in him sending them, also in Ellen Terry[2] writing as she did on
Sunday to say how well the Saturday's rehearsal had gone:

> 10:10 P.M., Prologue and two acts over, has gone
> beautifully and audience delighted. My truest
> congratulations.
> 11:33 P.M., Play over. A great triumph.

1. Henry Irving produced *Becket* at the Lyceum Theatre on 6 February 1893. It proved to be one of his greatest triumphs and ran for
112 nights, until 22 July. The telegram is preserved in the Usher Art
Gallery, Lincoln.

2. (1848-1928), the famous actress who first appeared with Irving
in 1878, and acted for and with him for the next twenty-four years.

Miss Terry became acquainted with the Tennysons during the summer of 1864, when she came to Freshwater as the bride of G. F. Watts. Years later in her memoirs she recalled her early visits to Farringford, and her memories of Emily Tennyson, whom she described as "a slender-stalked tea rose" who managed Farringford's myriad affairs from her crimson sofa in the drawing room (Richardson, *The Pre-Eminent Victorian*, p. 289).

365   *To Anne and Agnes Weld*

Farringford, 15 February 1893

My dearest Nanny and Agnes,

Best thanks for the letter. We don't think that it is treachery in Mr. Knowles but simply that there are such defects in his character that he is not conscious that it is treachery.[1] He is one of the cleverest men we any of us have known, with that sort of cleverness which can adapt itself to the moods of men or work upon them in differing moods—ma non. He has been hospitable and kind in his way and both Hallamee and I are glad that he shook hands with him coming out of the Lyceum the other evening, for we must forgive the grievous wrong he has done and try to repair it as best we may, must we not?

1. Emily Tennyson was offended by Knowles's "Aspects of Tennyson," which had appeared in the January issue of *Nineteenth Century* (xxxiii, 164-88). Although the article evidences respect and affection for the Tennysons, and lauds Lady Tennyson for her untiring efforts as her husband's "continual counsellor, critic, sympathiser, and friend in all his Art and Work," she evidently felt that Knowles had been indelicate in his portrayal of the Laureate "in his habit as he lived." Certainly she would have censured Knowles's sympathetic, but somewhat amused remarks about the poet's extreme sensitivity to criticism: "All the mass of eulogy Tennyson took comparatively little notice of," Knowles revealed, "but he never could forget an unfriendly word. . . . He was hurt by it as a sensitive child might be hurt by the cross look of a passing stranger; or rather as a supersensitive skin is hurt by the sting of an invisible midge."

366   *To Agnes Weld*

Farringford, 23 May 1893

My dearest Agnes,
I rejoice that you feel as you do about *Becket.* I only wish your
dear mother had been with you. Hallamee said to Irving, "You
look inspired." Irving answered, "I feel inspired." [An
unintelligible sentence is here omitted.] He wrote that actors
would be the better for acting such a play or something to this
effect.

367   *To Anne Weld*

Farringford, 24 June 1893

My dearest Nanny,
It was very kind in Mr. Barrett[1] asking Hallamee and Audrey to
go in his yacht, was it not? But as you know, it is impossible
for him to leave home at present. I fear that he has yet
thousands of letters to look through. These and all documents
must be conscientiously read of course. . . .
   Life is rather confused to me; things drift through one to
another and at last come to me. My Hallam is so overwhelmed
by people and things but thank God we are as happy as
possible in each other and he tries to do all he can to answer
the many calls of life so I have everything to be thankful for.
We are expecting Willingham and Alice[2] this afternoon.

   1. Unidentified.
   2. Willingham Franklin Rawnsley, younger son of the Drummond
Rawnsleys, and his wife. In his "Reminiscences," which appeared in
H. D. Rawnsley's *Memories of the Tennysons,* Willingham Rawnsley
wrote of visiting Lady Tennyson after the poet's death (p. 149): She
was "always interesting, always full of affectionate kindness and wonderful feeling and good sense," and a few hours with her "lifted one
out of the ruts of this world on to a higher platform altogether. One
felt that to her most fitly of all living people could Spenser's lines
be applied: 'Whose sweet aspect both God and man doth move/ In
her unspotted pleasaunce to delight.' "

368   *To Anne Weld*

Aldworth, 11 July 1893

My dearest Nanny,
You do not say how you are though I know that you must be
better being able to go to church. How I wish I could go! One
feels somewhat of an outcast not having been able to go for so
many years. Our family prayers are a comfort and the thought
that "where two or three are gathered together I am in the
midst of them."[1]

Yes, I fear indeed that our dear Edmund is going.[2] He has
been delirious three or four days. Zilly [Cecilia] is so good as
to send us a post card every day. I have not mentioned the
illness before because she begged us not to mention it and I
knew that she did write to Agnes herself.

1. A paraphrase of Matthew 18:20-21.
2. Edmund Lushington died at Park House on 13 July 1893.

369   *To Anne and Agnes Weld*

Aldworth, 4 October 1893

My dearest Nanny and Agnes,
I know that you will like to have the news of my telegram from
Hallamee. He and Audrey went to the first night of *The
Foresters.* His telegram is: "Most beautiful, brilliant success."[1]
I hope to have them home by the train arriving about four
o'clock today.

1. Despite Hallam Tennyson's telegram, Augustin Daly's production
of *The Foresters* failed miserably in London, though Daly had been
successful with the play on the New York stage the year before.

370   *To Agnes Weld*

Aldworth, 18 November 1893

My dearest Agnes,
We have heard that my Ally and Shakespeare are the only

English poets cared for in Germany. The Emperor[1] told
Hallamee so I think. It is a wonderful thing that his Father is
known and loved throughout the world, is it not? And a most
blessed one that his influence can be only for good. . . .

Isn't Mr. Palgrave wonderfully kind? He has looked over
about twenty-three thousand letters[2] for us and Hallam about
as many more, I believe. You may think what a help Mr.
Palgrave has been.

1. William II.
2. Francis Palgrave assisted Emily and Hallam in sorting the letters
of sympathy which came from all over the world after Tennyson's death.

371   To Agnes Weld

Farringford, 1 March 1894

My dearest Agnes,
We have to keep such reading as we can manage very much to
what is written about Ally. Very trying reading, though meant
to be complimentary but we have at least to glance over many
volumes, and my head is so far from strong and my eyes so far
from well that it is only now and then I can read a little myself
or I should long ago have read the Duke of Argyll's book,[1] with
which, from what I have heard of it, I should, I think, agree.
We are bound, of course, to follow as closely as we can the
politics of the day—most depressing work. . . . For the
moment the total disruption of the Empire and of society
seeming to be threatened, our grand mission in the world
forgotten or at best dimly remembered. . . .

I am indeed thankful to hear so favourable a report of your
beloved mother. I know that she has a spirit which keeps her
up when many another would succumb. With best love to you
both.

1. *The Unity of Nature* (London, 1884).

372   *To Anne and Agnes Weld*

Farringford, 19 May 1894

My dearest Nanny and Agnes,
I am very grateful for your letters but I do not wish you to
write, my Nanny, while your head is bad. Since we lost our
Father I have suffered in more ways than one from mine.
Nothing but champagne does it good even now when I have no
longer the surging and pain in the brain itself. I beg you to try
it. If the pain comes from influenza you ought to take
ammoniate of quinine. Every chemist has it, I believe. . . . I
find rubbing eau de cologne on my head often sends me to
sleep when I am restless at night from overdoing myself in any
way. Much talking I cannot stand. Let Agnes take care of you.
It is quite cold here today. Best love and best wishes to you
both.

373   *To Anne Weld*

Aldworth, 14 September 1894

My dearest Nanny,
I fear that it is much too cold for you to venture out. Here we
have rather cruel northeasters, but Agnes says that you can
sleep in the daytime and this is the next best medicine to
outdoors air, is it not? I wish I could see you, my Nanny.
   Ally and Charlie came to us on Monday and are, I hope,
happy here. Ally is very much grown and his face is
lengthening a little into the young man's and his voice
gruffening. Charlie's dear little face is sweet as ever and in his
evening dress he looks a fairy prince. He is very good to his
small cousins,[1] helping them to build their sand castles and to
play their games. Indeed the first day of the boys' arrival was a
regular Saturnalia—shouts of laughter or rather screams of
laughter almost from morning till night.

   1. Lionel Hallam and Alfred Aubrey Tennyson.

374   *To Agnes Weld*

Aldworth, 16 September 1894

God bless and comfort you. I am more thankful than I can say that she went peacefully as I prayed she might.[1] There was never a better sister to me nor a sister to all she could help.

1. Anne Weld died on 15 September 1894.

375   *To Sophie Tennyson*[1]
Indiana University

Farringford, 10 January 1895

My dear Sophie,
My correspondence is almost entirely confined to my relations now, and it is only to poor Agnes Weld since she has lost her mother that I can write more than very occasionally except the weekly letter to my Ally and Charlie and to their mother when they are not there. But it's no use bemoaning oneself. I am so much better off than most people, having two such homes, and than anyone in my devoted Hallam who is all that son can be to mother and in the past for us both.

1. The wife of Frederick Tennyson's son, Julius. She and her husband lived in Kensington.

376   *To Agnes Weld*

Farringford, 10 May 1895

My dearest Agnes,
I return the paper with many thanks. Of course universal peace would be delightful but when people talk of proportionate European disarmament and such plans they forget a few things. First and foremost that Europe by no means stands alone. Who in these days of steam is to defend Europe in case of an incursion from China or from South America or Africa if not Europe itself. The United States of America have one

central government, are one as each individual European
kingdom is one. What it may be in other countries I cannot say,
but I believe that in England the army and navy are a positive
boon to the poor, the discipline is so desirable for them and the
pension so precious. "Baba" (I shall speak of my Ally to you as
the little ones do here. "Your Uncle" sounds so formal). Baba
wished every boy in every class to be drilled. By all means let
us have no aggressive war except by way of defence and I
suppose such wars are inevitable in India. War Baba hated, war
we hate, but I fear that the time for peace has not come.

377   To Hallam and Audrey Tennyson

Aldworth, 10 August 1895

Beloved ones,
Uncle Horatio and Maud were here for a few minutes
yesterday—by here I mean with me. He declaring that he was
as deaf as a post but hearing perfectly well when I spoke to
him. He looked fairly well and Maud was very bright and said
all was going well with them at the farm. God's blessings on
the birthday[1] and on all your days!

  1. Hallam's birthday, 11 August.

378   To Frederick Tennyson
Indiana University

Farringford, 20 November 1895

My dear Frederick,
I must "take up my pen and write," as they would have said in
the old days, for I will not commit my share of thanks for the
new volume[1] even to Hallam but ask you to take it from
myself. He has just been reading me that beautiful last poem.
Many a one will be grateful to you for what so finely expresses
the thoughts and feelings of many hearts, which, but for you
might be a weight on the heart with no wings to lift it

upwards! Julius and Sophie must, I am sure, rejoice in the dedication, and I congratulate them on the rare gift. My Hallam is jubilant over the book and will . . . say so for himself.[2]

To think of your taking up your abode in England once more! Your heart is here after all, in spite of all that Greece and Italy and Jersey have done to lure it away. May you have many happy days here still and be gladdened by the welcome given to the book.

1. In 1895 Frederick Tennyson published his *Poems of the Day and Year*, dedicated to Julius and Sophie Tennyson, with whom he spent the remainder of his life.
2. At the bottom of his mother's letter Hallam wrote, "What a splendid gift to the world your book is. I am delighted with it."

379   To Agnes Weld

Farringford, 7 March 1896

My dearest Agnes,
Hallam and I most cordially commend the action of Oxford as to the B.A. certificate.[1] Let women be as educated as possible but let them remember that God has created man the head of the woman, not his rival.[2] It would be hard indeed to have to obey from the beginning to end of life were not man as a *whole* intellectually greater than woman as a *whole.* Of course individual women, and many of them, are superior in intellect to many men, but let women take care that they mate wisely with those to whom they are to be helpmates. Here is a lecture for you!!! I am sure that the order of the world gives women more power than ever so much self-assertion. Do you not think so?

1. On 3 March 1896 the proposal to permit women to compete for the Oxford B. A. degree was defeated by the university, and it was not until 1920 that Oxford granted degrees to women.
2. See above, Letter 354.

380   To Frederick Tennyson
Indiana University

Farringford, 27 April 1896

My dear Frederick,
As Patriarch of the race I am in duty bound to tell you that you had last evening another added to the number of those who owe you homage. Audrey and her baby boy[1] are, I am thankful to say, going on as well as possible.

We have from time to time splendid reports of yourself. May they long continue! Hallam's love and mine to you and to all of yours who may be with you.

Arthur and Horatio are well and both seem to enjoy Arthur's garden.[2] His wife[3] is an excellent woman and does all that a nurse could do for Horatio, who, you may have heard, was taken in by Arthur and herself when driven out by scarlet fever from his own house. The cook who was the victim is recovering and no one has taken the fever.

1. Harold Courtenay Tennyson (1896–1916) who, like his brother, Alfred Aubrey, was killed in World War I.
2. Arthur and Horatio Tennyson maintained an especially close relationship through the years, and Arthur's move in 1893 from Malvern to Freshwater was a joy to both brothers.
3. The former Emma Louisa Maynard, whom Arthur Tennyson married on 7 December 1882.

381   To Agnes Weld

Farringford, 28 April 1896

My dearest Agnes,
You are the first to whom I write the good news that another little son was born shortly before nine last evening. Dr. Hollis having scarcely to come straight here from his home. The boy sneezed out "a full God-bless-you right and left"[1] on entering the world and both he and his mother are going on well.

Hallamee says it was the most comical sight he ever saw when Leila[2] and Aubrey first looked on their brother. He said to them, "There is a great surprise for you." Aubrey guessed guinea pigs, and when they stood before the baby they both crammed fingers into their mouths and burst out into uproarious laughter asking whether it was a baby and their brother or a girl and Aubrey decided that it was better than guinea pigs and both burst again into laughter when they had touched him and kissed him. Leila met me and asked if I had heard the news and seen the boy and he was a brother and a baby.

1. "Edwin Morris," l. 80.
2. Lionel Hallam.

382   To Agnes Weld

Aldworth, 4 August 1896

My dearest Agnes,
I am sorry to have made you anxious. You are so overwhelmed with work of one kind or another that I scarcely like to write to you even when I am able. Of late I have been less and less up to letterwriting. My old attack on the membrane[1] having been almost continuous for the last two or three months and caused a good deal of pain and exhaustion.

Dr. Dabbs has changed my medicine so I hope to suffer less. He does not consider the attacks dangerous, so do not be anxious about me and you know I have the most loving and watchful guardian in my Hallamee. . . .

At present Canon Ainger and Aubrey DeVere are with us. The Canon has taken very much to the boys. When they were at home lately he had them to tea in the Temple of which, as you know, he is master. I suppose you have heard that Mr. Birrell has been appointed Professor of Law at the London University. . . .

Do you remember Mr. Wilson, one of our boys' tutors? He was here about a fortnight ago. He is now a gray-haired man with seven children, the eldest 26. He was very kind and spoke warmly of old days in the three or four minutes when I was able to see him. Best love from us.

1. For some years Emily had suffered periodically with an inflammation of the cranial membrane.

Shortly after writing her final letter Emily suffered an attack of influenza which led to a fatal congestion of the lungs. No one supposed that her death was so near, for she minimized the seriousness of her condition during her final illness as she had during the numerous periods of ill health which plagued her adult life. On Sunday, 9 August, Dr. Dabbs informed Hallam that his mother would not recover, and she died just before dawn the next morning, with her son at her bedside. On the leaf of the first volume of his *Materials for a Life of A.T.* Hallam recorded her final words: "Thank you my darling for all your great goodness to me. I hope I am not impatient. Great and small sins are the same in the sight of God in that he forgives them all." Emily then asked to see her grandsons, Lionel and Aubrey. A few moments before the end she spoke again: "I tried to be a good wife," she said, and when Hallam assured her that none could have been a better wife to his father, she answered, "I might have done more."

Intimate friends who had recently visited Aldworth were shocked by the suddenness of her death. They had grown accustomed to Emily's enduring strength, despite her longtime delicate health, and they found nothing particularly alarming in her fatigue during her final summer. In his 15 August eulogy in *The Athenaeum* Theodore Watts-Dunton recalled that Emily seemed no different from usual when he saw her during the first week of August: "For many years she, whose fragile frame seemed to be kept alive by the love and sweet movements of the soul within, had seemed as she lay upon her couch the same as she seemed when death was so near. . . ." Lord Dufferin wrote to Hallam that his mother looked so cheerful and seemed so well when he saw her in midsummer that he had looked forward to paying her another visit before returning to Ireland in the autumn. Scores of other letters came to Aldworth expressing grief and sympathy and extolling in the most lavish terms Emily's intellect, her kind, gracious charm, and the instinctive nobleness of all her thoughts and actions. Emily Ritchie wrote that since girlhood she had enshrined Emily in her heart as "the ideal of perfect womanhood. . . . Ever since she first came like a revelation of sweetness and wisdom into my life it has been the same." And Herbert Warren, president of Magdalen College, Oxford, spoke of how she had aided, encouraged, spared, and tended the poet, and of "the charm of her character, the saintliness of her spirit—the purer for suffering, the stronger out of weakness."[1]

Virtually all business in Freshwater stopped the day of the funeral, and throughout the island flags flew at half-mast. The Rev. Dr. Merriman conducted a simple service at the parish church, and Lady Tennyson was buried beside her son Lionel in the churchyard. At the graveside were Hallam and Audrey, Agnes Weld, Mrs. Arthur Tennyson, Colonel Richard Pearson Crozier, Dr. Dabbs, the Lord Bishop of London and Mrs. Temple, and Colonel Donald Browne, representing the Queen. The service included the singing of Emily's setting of Tennyson's poem "The Silent Voices."

1. Letters of 14 August 1896 (unpublished, T.R.C.).

Appendix A

The Sellwoods (sometimes spelled "Selwood" or "Selwode") were an old and landed Somersetshire family whose estates had comprehended a vast portion of the county for generations. Colonel Sellwood, who succeeded to several large tracts of Sellwood property about 1750, died without a male heir. At that time his estates passed into the hands of a Mr. John Stephens, who married Colonel Sellwood's only daughter, and subsequently into the possession of Stephens's nephew, a Mr. Tull. (My information is from Henry Sellwood's letter of 28 August 1863 to Emily Tennyson, unpublished, T.R.C.) The Henry Sellwood branch, however, still retained a very rich living when they moved to Aldworth in the late eighteenth century, but Henry Sellwood's father squandered much of the family fortune by his personal extravagance.

Henry had dreamed of a career in the army, but his mother's anxiety for his safety and the financial necessity of some sort of professional career influenced his decision to become a solicitor and his choice of Horncastle as the place to pursue his vocation. The completion of the Horncastle-Tattershall Canal around 1800 opened up communications via Lincoln and Boston with the outside world, and business in Horncastle began to boom. Accordingly there was a demand for solicitors to handle the rapidly expanding trade, the sale of land, and the building of houses and factories in the Horncastle area. Henry Sellwood took an active part in the life of the town, supporting all good causes including the Literary Club, the National School, the British School, and Watson's School. He was for many years secretary to the governors of the Grammar School, and his name appears on numerous public documents of the period. (My informant is again Mr. J. Norman Clark.)

Little is known of any member of the Sellwood family before the eighteenth century, with the exception of Abbot John de Selwode, who was elected fifty-seventh Abbot of Glastonbury on 15 November 1457. The Abbot was a native of the East Woodlands, near Frome (some forty miles from the Sellwood estates in Berkshire), where his progenitors, who were named Edmonds, had considerable possessions (*Collinson's Somersetshire*, II, 255). The Tennysons viewed the tomb of Abbot de Selwode (d. 8 July 1493) on their wedding trip, and Emily Tennyson later wrote in "For Her Sons" that it seemed "a very pleasant coincidence that this abbot should have been the only one buried in the chancel of the abbey near the real or reputed tomb of King Arthur."

374

Evidently some the of Sellwoods had established themselves in Berkshire by the mid-seventeenth century. Jonathan Hawe, mayor of the borough of Abendon, listed his borough officials on 16 March 1664, and among these was Robert Selwood, Bayliff. See *The Four Visitations of Berkshire,* ed. W. Harry Rylands (London: Harleian Society, 1907), I, 153.

Appendix B

The dress that Emily actually wore at her wedding may have a significance that has never been appreciated. H. D. Rawnsley recalled how he used to listen to his old nurse muse about the wedding and about the lovely and unusual bridal dress: "She dressed the bride for her bridal, and spoke of the beautiful eyes and hair and the sky-blue dress. . . . The bride never forgot the nurse who put upon her her wedding apparel. In a letter to my mother in 1885 she speaks of that old nurse . . . and makes mention of the sky-blue dress" (H. D. Rawnsley, *Memories of the Tennysons,* p. 72). Shortly after the wedding Emily wrote to Charles and Louisa Turner (Letter 4), "I am baby enough to be sorry I did not wear my white dress. Ally would have liked it but I took him literally about travelling dress." Her indication here that she did not wear her white dress because of Tennyson's instructions about traveling attire seems to conflict with her statement in "For Her Sons" that the white dress failed to arrive in time. In any case the poet evidently was much taken with his bride's "sky-blue dress," undoubtedly accentuating the blue of her eyes. There is a tradition in Lincolnshire that Tennyson was first attracted to Emily by her lovely blue silk dress (see "The Tennysons and Lincolnshire," an unsigned article printed in the *Lincoln, Rutland and Stamford Mercury,* 27 December 1889), and that tradition has survived despite Hallam's avowal that his mother was wearing a "simple gray dress" when she first met his father in Holywell Wood (*Memoir,* I, 148). In his *Through England with Tennyson,* Oliver Huckel avowed that Emily "was wearing that unforgettable silk pelisse, when she first met Tennyson in 1830." Perhaps oral tradition has confused the wedding dress with the Holywell dress.

In the Geraint idylls Enid's simple silk dress, which she dons at the conclusion of "The Marriage of Geraint," "Remembering how first he came on her,/ Drest in that dress, and how beloved her in it" (ll.842–43), probably owes something to Tennyson's memory of his wife's silk pelisse. And, as James Martin Gray has suggested to me, the dress of splendid silk, "Where like a shoaling sea the lovely blue/ Play'd into green," which the iniquitous earl Doorm offers to Enid in "Geraint and Enid" (l.687), may be a product of the poet's memory of Emily Tennyson's bridal dress. One might even speculate that the same silk dress inspired Tennyson's use of the term "shot-silk" to express that indefinite quality of poetry which allows one meaning to glance into another just as one color of shot-silk shades into another.

Descriptions of Emily Tennyson's physical appearance are often accompanied by some mention of her clothing. Recalling her first visit to Farringford and her first meeting with the poet's wife, Annie Fields wrote that there was "something in her bearing and trailing dress" which "gave her a medieval aspect which suited with the house" (Fields, *Authors and Friends,* p. 332). Another time she thought that "Mrs. Tennyson in her floating dress with her sweet boys upon each hand seemed more like a new creation of some new Raphael than a living woman serving in this world" (quoted by M. A. DeWolfe Howe, "The Tennysons at Farringford: A Victorian Vista," p. 452). Marian Bradley recalled her "soft white Mull Muslin dress all folds sinking into each other and no edges anywhere," and Mrs. Bradley's daughter, Margaret Woods, remembered her as always clad in dresses of the same simple early-Victorian fashion (Richardson, *The Pre-Eminent Victorian,* pp. 98–99). And Edith Nicholl Ellison described Emily as "the lady on the sofa, who must never be disturbed by raised voices or noisy steps, robed always in a trailing gown of dove-color, her auburn hair crowned with a triangular piece of old lace hanging in lappets on either side of her clear-cut, highbred face . . ." (Ellison, *A Child's Recollection of Tennyson,* p. 31).

Selected List of Works Cited

Editions

The Complete Poetical Works of Tennyson. Ed. W. J. Rolfe. Boston: Houghton Mifflin, 1898.

The Poems of Tennyson. Ed. Christopher Ricks. London and Harlow: Longmans, 1969.

The Works of Alfred Lord Tennyson. Ed. Hallam Tennyson. 6 vols. New York: Macmillan, 1908.

Books, Periodicals, and Unpublished Manuscripts

Abbott, Evelyn. *The Life and Letters of Benjamin Jowett.* 2 vols. London: John Murray, 1897.

Allingham, Helen, and Paterson, Arthur. *The Homes and Haunts of Tennyson.* London: Adam and Charles Black, 1905.

Allingham, William. *William Allingham's Diary.* Ed. Helen Allingham and D. Radford. London: Macmillan, 1908.

Basler, Roy P. *Sex, Symbolism and Psychology in Literature.* New Brunswick, N.J.: Rutgers University Press, 1948.

Browning, Elizabeth Barrett. *The Letters of Elizabeth Barrett Browning.* Ed. Frederic G. Kenyon. 2 vols. London: Macmillan, 1897.

Butler, Henry Montague. "Recollections of Tennyson." *Tennyson and His Friends.* Ed. Hallam Tennyson. London: Macmillan, 1911, pp. 206-21.

Buckley, Jerome. *Tennyson: The Growth of a Poet.* Boston: Houghton Mifflin, 1960.

Carlyle, Thomas. *Thomas Carlyle: Letters to His Wife.* Ed. Trudy Bliss. London: Victor Gollancz, 1953.

Champneys, Basil. *Memoirs and Correspondence of Coventry Patmore.* London: G. Bell and Sons, 1900.

Davidson, Angus. *Edward Lear: Landscape Painter and Nonsense Poet.* London: John Murray, 1938.

Dyson, Hope, and Tennyson, Charles. *Dear and Honoured Lady.* London: Macmillan, 1969.

Eidson, J. O. *Tennyson in America.* Athens, Ga.: University of Georgia Press, 1943.

Ellison, Edith Nicholl. *A Child's Recollection of Tennyson.* New York: J. M. Dent, 1906.

Fields, Annie. *Authors and Friends*. Boston and New York: Houghton Mifflin, 1924.

Gernsheim, Helmut. *Julia Margaret Cameron*. London: Fountain Press, 1948.

Golden, Samuel A. *Frederick Goddard Tuckerman: An American Sonneteer*. Orono, Maine: Maine University Press, 1952.

Griffin, William H., and Minchin, H. C. *The Life of Robert Browing*, New York: Methuen, 1912.

Hill, Brian. *Julia Margaret Cameron: A Victorian Family Portrait*. London: Peter Owen, 1973.

Howe, M. A. De Wolfe. "The Tennysons at Farringford: A Victorian Vista." *Cornhill Magazine* 63 (October 1927): 447-57.

Huckel, Oliver. *Through England with Tennyson*. New York: Crowell, 1913.

Joseph, Gerhard. *Tennysonian Love: The Strange Diagonal*. Minneapolis: University of Minnesota Press, 1969.

Knowles, James. "Aspects of Tennyson: A Personal Reminiscence." *Nineteenth Century* 33 (1893): 164-88.

Marshall, George O., Jr. *A Tennyson Handbook*. New York: Twayne, 1963.

Martin, A. Patchett. *Tennyson and the Isle of Wight*. London, 1898.

Masterman, C. F. G. *Tennyson as a Religious Teacher*. London: Methuen, 1900.

Merriman, Harold G. "Tennyson and Moxon." *Edward Moxon: Publisher of Poets*. New York: Columbia University Press, 1939.

Millais, John Guille. *The Life and Letters of Sir John Everett Millais*. New York: Methuen, 1899.

Morley, John. *The Life of William Ewart Gladstone*. New York: Macmillan, 1904.

Nicoll, W. Robertson, and Wise, Thomas J. *Literary Anecdotes of the Nineteenth Century*. 2 vols. London: Hodder and Stoughton, 1896.

Nicolson, Harold. *Tennyson: Aspects of His Life, Character and Poetry*. Boston and New York: Constable, 1923.

Noakes, Vivien. *Edward Lear: The Life of a Wanderer*. Boston: Houghton Mifflin, 1969.

Paden, William D. *Tennyson in Egypt: A Study of the Imagery in His Earlier Work*. Lawrence, Kans.: University of Kansas Press, 1942.

Pope-Hennessy, James. *Monckton Milnes: The Flight of Youth*. London: Constable, 1949.

Rader, Ralph Wilson. *Tennyson's Maud: The Biographical Genesis*. Berkeley and Los Angeles: University of California Press, 1963.

Rawnsley, H. Drummond. *Memories of the Tennysons*. Glasgow: J. MacLehose and Sons, 1900.

Rawnsley, Willingham F. "Personal Recollections of Tennyson." *Nineteenth Century* 97 (1925): 1-9.

———. *Tennyson, 1809-1909: A Lecture*. Ambleside: George Middleton, 1909.

Richardson, Joanna. *The Pre-Eminent Victorian*. London: Jonathan Cape, 1962.

Ritchie, Anne Thackeray. *From Friend to Friend.* London: John Murray, 1919.

———. *Records of Tennyson, Ruskin, and Browning.* London: Macmillan, 1892.

Schonfield, Hugh J., ed. *Letters to Frederick Tennyson.* London: L. and V. Woolf, 1930.

Sidgwick, Arthur. "Tennyson." *Tennyson and His Friends.* Ed. Hallam Tennyson. London: Macmillan, 1911, pp. 322-43.

Stanford, Charles Villiers. *Studies and Memories.* London: Constable, 1908.

Tennyson, Charles. *Alfred Tennyson.* New York: Macmillan, 1949.

———. *Six Tennyson Essays.* London: Cassell, 1954.

———. *Stars and Markets.* London: Chatto and Windus, 1957.

———. "The Somersby Tennysons." *Victorian Studies,* Christmas Supplement, 1963.

Tennyson, Emily. Emily Tennyson's Journal. Unpublished, T.R.C.

———. "Emily Tennyson's Narrative For Her Sons." Ed. James O. Hoge. *Texas Studies in Literature and Language* 14 (Spring 1972): 93-106.

———. "Recollections of My Early Life." *Tennyson and His Friends.* Ed. Hallam Tennyson. London: Macmillan, 1911, pp. 1-7.

Tennyson, Hallam. *Alfred Lord Tennyson: A Memoir By His Son.* 2 vols. New York: Macmillan, 1897.

———. "Draft of Materials for a Life of A.T." Unpublished, T.R.C.

———. *Materials for a Life of A.T.* 4 vols. Privately printed, T.R.C.

———, ed. *Tennyson and His Friends.* London: Macmillan, 1911.

Terhune, Alfred McKinley. *The Life of Edward FitzGerald.* London: Oxford University Press, 1947.

Tyndall, John. "A Fragment by John Tyndall." Unpublished, T.R.C.

Ward, Wilfrid. *Aubrey DeVere: A Memoir.* London: Longmans, 1904.

Weld, Agnes Grace. *Glimpses of Tennyson and Some of His Relations and Friends.* Oxford: Williams and Norgate, 1903.

———. "Tennyson." *The Contemporary Review* 72 (1897): 689-96.

Woolner, Amy. *Thomas Woolner: His Life in Letters.* New York: Chapman and Hall, 1917.

Woods, Margaret L. "Tennyson and Bradley." *Tennyson and His Friends.* Ed. Hallam Tennyson. London: Macmillan, 1911, pp. 175-85.

Index

Sources of Text

A large majority of Lady Tennyson's letters are located in the Tennyson Research Centre, Lincoln; the Lincoln letters are not included in this index.

Manuscript

Bodleian Library, Oxford, 135, 159, 186
Boston College, 57
Boston Public Library, 123, 124, 127, 129, 131, 135, 137, 145, 149, 151, 161, 162, 163, 164, 166, 173, 175, 177, 185, 201, 294
British Museum, 193, 231, 323, 328, 329
Christ Church, Oxford, 330
Harvard University, 44, 45, 67, 78, 85, 146, 169, 301
Hoge, James O., 220
Hutzler, Charles S., 60
Indiana University, 234, 329, 367, 368, 370
Leeds, University of, Brotherton Library, 48, 336
National Library of Scotland, 76
Usher Art Gallery (Lincoln), 70, 79
Virginia, University of, 165, 174
Wellesley College, 43, 112

Yale University, 198, 250, 290, 293, 304, 325, 342

Printed

Ritchie, Anne Thackeray, *From Friend to Friend*, 58, 91, 95, 126
Schonfield, Hugh J., *Letters to Frederick Tennyson*, 62
Tennyson, Hallam, Lord, *Alfred Lord Tennyson: A Memoir by His Son*, 192
Woolner, Amy, *Thomas Woolner: His Life in Letters*, 94

General Index

An asterisk indicates a letter recipient. Italic numbers locate the first page of Lady Tennyson's letters.

Abraham's Mead, 213
Acton, Lord, 351
Acworth, James, 242, 242n, 243
Acworth, Mrs. James, 242, 242n, 243, 243n
Afton, 88
Agnew's, 351
Ainger, Alfred, 337, 371
Aix-les-Bains, 284n, 285